Part Five. Editing Sentences for Grammar

Part Six. Editing Sentences for Punctuation and Mechanics

Part Seven. Editing Sentences for Word Use

Part Eight. Editing Sentences for ESL Challenges

Fifth Edition

Structuring Paragraphs and Essays

A Guide to Effective Writing

A. Franklin Parks
Frostburg State University

James A. Levernier
University of Arkansas at Little Rock

Ida Masters Hollowell
University of Arkansas at Little Rock

Bedford/St. Martin's Boston • New York

For Bedford/St. Martin's
Developmental Editors: Michelle M. Clark, Amanda Bristow
Production Editor: Deborah Baker
Production Supervisor: Catherine Hetmansky
Director of Marketing: Karen Melton
Marketing Manager: Brian Wheel
Copyeditor: Paula Woolley
Text Design: Jean Hammond
Cover Design: Hannus Design Associates
Cover Art: Bow Tie #6 by Nancy Crow
Cover Photograph: J. Kevin Fitzsimons
Composition: the dotted i
Printing and Binding: RR Donnelley & Sons Company

President: Charles H. Christensen
Editorial Director: Joan E. Feinberg
Editor in Chief: Karen S. Henry
Director of Editing, Design, and Production: Marcia Cohen
Managing Editor: Elizabeth M. Schaaf

Library of Congress Control Number: 00–103104

Manufactured in the United States of America.
9
i
For information, write: Bedford/St. Martin's, 75 Arlington Street, Boston, MA 02116 (617–399–4000)

ISBN-10: 0–312–19558–3
ISBN-13: 978–0–312–19558–8

Acknowledgments

Ali, Lorraine. "Do I Look Like Public Enemy Number One?" Originally published in *Mademoiselle,* March 1999. Copyright © 1999 The Condé Nast Publications, Inc. All rights reserved. Reprinted by permission.

Begley, Sharon, and Andrew Murr. "First Americans." *Newsweek.* April 26, 1999: 50–57.

Acknowledgments and copyrights are continued at the back of the book on page 491, which constitutes an extension of the copyright page. It is a violation of the law to reproduce these selections by any means whatsoever without the written permission of the copyright holder.

Preface for Instructors

The fifth edition of *Structuring Paragraphs* is in many ways a totally new book—one that responds to the changing needs of students in developmental and first-year writing courses. For instance, the new title *Structuring Paragraphs and Essays* grows out of our discovery that many writing teachers want more balanced instruction in a textbook. In fact, balance is the hallmark of this new edition. We have balanced our emphasis on models of effective writing—the product, in other words—with full coverage of the process of writing effective paragraphs and essays. In addition, to provide support for students who have significant sentence-level problems, we have complemented writing instruction with guidance on grammar and usage. Finally, because not all writing tasks are academic, *Structuring Paragraphs and Essays* equips students to write effectively for personal and professional purposes as well as for college courses.

Though we have made many significant changes in revising *Structuring Paragraphs,* faithful users of previous editions will find much that is familiar in the fifth edition:

- a logical, straightforward series of chapters unfolding a process for writing that builds students' skills and confidence as they move from paragraph to essay writing;
- more than fifty samples of student writing that reinforce chapter concepts and provide beginning writers with strong models to follow;
- carefully sequenced activities and writing assignments—including portfolio and collaborative activities—that reinforce our learning outcomes;
- helpful chapter summaries that highlight the main points and include cross-references to full explanations;
- a handbook that provides students with a handy, practical reference for improving their editing skills.

New to This Edition

Greater emphasis on the writing process. Our text encourages students to see effective writing as a series of manageable steps rather than an unreachable goal. Students will find

- stronger guidelines for planning, with a new chapter on assessing audience and purpose;
- extensive discussions of such prewriting techniques as brainstorming, freewriting, clustering, asking questions, and keeping a writer's journal;

- six motivational case studies and numerous works-in-progress in the writing chapters, unfolding individual students' writing processes and the challenges and rewards they encounter as they write;
- increased attention to revision throughout the writing process, with "Writer's Checklists" at the end of each writing chapter.

Stronger essay coverage. In the fifth edition, we have included additional material on essay writing to help you better prepare students to meet academic writing challenges. Five chapters in the new edition offer students the opportunity to improve their skill in writing longer works. Students will benefit from

- expanded essay coverage, including two chapters that enable students to make the transition from writing paragraphs to composing effective essays;
- a new chapter on writing persuasive essays that gives students the skills they need to succeed in a college writing course and beyond;
- a new writing-from-reading chapter that reinforces the bridge between critical reading and effective paragraph and essay writing, with six reading selections and handy, up-to-date guides to documenting sources and avoiding plagiarism;
- additional opportunities for writing paragraphs and essays in a new chapter on completing timed writing tasks.

New engaging design. *Structuring Paragraphs and Essays* is now more appealing visually and easier to navigate. Students will welcome

- a two-color design that makes important information (chapter headings, activities, cross-references, annotations) easy to find and easy to use;
- a wider margin that facilitates note-taking;
- boxes, checklists, and charts that make the text more accessible;
- new icons that indicate collaborative activities and portfolio activities .

Revised and expanded editing guide. We have kept the grammar and usage topics from the previous edition but have covered each topic more thoroughly. Plus, we have added much-requested grammar exercises. Students will discover

- four combined-skill diagnostic tests (with answers in the back of the text) that help to pinpoint areas in which students need practice;
- guidance on twenty-two grammar and usage topics, including English as a Second Language (ESL) topics;
- plenty of opportunities to practice each chapter's target skill—at the sentence level, the paragraph level, and within a student's own writing. (Answers to most practice exercises are included at the back of the book.)

New emphasis on writing as a practical skill. *Structuring Paragraphs and Essays* addresses students' need to write well both in and outside of the writing course.

We have added detailed advice for meeting the communication challenges of today's students. They will find

- strategies for completing timed writing tasks;
- coverage of online writing and basic netiquette;
- full treatment of career communication skills, including cover letter and résumé writing and plenty of models.

We are sincerely excited by the changes that have been incorporated into the fifth edition of *Structuring Paragraphs and Essays.* We think you will find that this new edition is like a carefully sewn quilt that balances creativity and control. *Structuring Paragraphs and Essays* melds these elements together by combining the best of process and product, imagination and form, rhetoric and handbook. We hope you will be pleased by what is, in many ways, a totally new book.

Ancillaries

The *Instructor's Manual to Accompany Structuring Paragraphs and Essays* is a practical resource that contains chapter overviews, teaching tips, additional writing assignments and activities, and answers to the activities and exercises in the text. We have also included advice on using Exercise Central, an extensive online collection of grammar exercises available to users of the fifth edition.

A companion Web site at <www.bedfordstmartins.com> describes the text and its features, includes links to Exercise Central and other useful resources, and offers guidance for pairing *Structuring Paragraphs and Essays* with readers published by Bedford/St. Martin's for developmental English and first-year composition.

Exercise Central at <www.bedfordstmartins.com/exercisecentral> is thorough, easy to use, and convenient for both students and instructors. Multiple exercise sets on every topic, and at a variety of levels, ensure that students have as much practice as they need at the appropriate level. Diagnostic tools can help students assess areas needing improvement, or instructors can assign specific exercises or groups of exercises. Immediate, customized feedback for all answers turns skill practice into a learning experience, and the reporting feature allows both students and instructors to monitor and assess progress.

Acknowledgments

In preparing the fifth edition, we are again in debt to those users and reviewers who helped shape previous editions of the book: Linda Bensel-Meyers, University of Tennessee at Knoxville; Constance Chapman, Georgia State University; Martha French, Fairmont State College; Patricia Hadley, Salt Lake Community College; Rosemary Hunkeler, University of Wisconsin–Parkside; J. C. B. Kinch, Edinboro University of Pennsylvania; Patricia McAlexander, University of Georgia;

Kate Mele, Roger Williams University; Paul Olubas, Southern Ohio College; Linda C. Pelzer, Wesley College; Thomas Recchio, University of Connecticut; Judith Stanford, Rivier College; and Beatrice Tignor, Prince George's Community College.

In addition, we thank the following instructors who helped us to craft the fifth edition of *Structuring Paragraphs and Essays:* Kim Baker, Roger Williams College; Jennifer Bradner, Virginia Commonwealth University; Mike Brotherton, Labette Community College; Aleta Chamberlin, Labette Community College; Marcia Dawson, Prince George's Community College; Jeannine Edwards, University of Memphis; Frank Giardina, Southwestern College; Rachel Golland, St. Thomas Aquinas College; Marland Griffith, Rockingham County Community College; Sarah Guthrie, Mississippi County Community College; Michael Hennessey, Southwest Texas State University; Donald Herzog, Longview Community College; David Himber, St. Petersburg Junior College; Janet Hubbs, Ocean County College; John Kinch, Macomb County Community College; Roy Riner, St. Philip's College; and Bryan Whitehead, Kansas City Kansas Community College. We especially thank Kim Martin Long, Shippensburg University of Pennsylvania, who wrote the grammar exercises and diagnostic tests for the text; and Carolyn Lengel, Hunter College, who wrote grammar content for Exercise Central. We also thank Alan Brown, University of West Alabama, for revising the Instructor's Manual; many users of *Structuring Paragraphs and Essays* will benefit from his experience, expertise, and good sense.

We extend special thanks to those at Bedford/St. Martin's who have made significant contributions to this revision. First, we could not have undertaken such a major revision without the help of a tireless, savvy, imaginative, and very patient editor who believed in us and in our book. We have been fortunate to have such an editor in Michelle Clark, who inspired much positive growth both in *Structuring Paragraphs and Essays* and in its writers during the process of revision. It is difficult for us to imagine a finer editor. We are also indebted to Amanda Bristow, associate editor, for her sensitive and valuable assistance, particularly in the development of the new section on "Strategies for Completing Other Writing Tasks" (Part Four) and in the development of the Instructor's Manual. We also thank Charles Christensen, president of Bedford/St. Martin's, and Joan Feinberg, editorial director, for their support of this revision; Elizabeth Schaaf, managing editor, and Deborah Baker, production editor, for their good sense and thoughtful suggestions during the production process; Paula Woolley, copyeditor, for her judicious work; Jean Hammond, text designer, for a refreshing new look for the fifth edition; and Harriet Wald, who cleared permissions at light speed.

Finally, and most importantly, we thank our students at Frostburg State University and at the University of Arkansas at Little Rock.

A. Franklin Parks
James A. Levernier
Ida Masters Hollowell

Contents

Part Two Strategies for Writing Paragraphs

Part Three Strategies for Writing Essays

Introduction for Students
Attitude Is Everything

Let's face it. Sometimes you will want to write. Other times you will have to write. In either case, having a positive attitude about a writing task will help you to write more effectively. You might also find it helpful to keep these points in mind: First, *writing is hard work.* There is nothing magical about the writing process. Even experienced writers spend lots of time and energy (and paper) on a piece of writing. Writing is never easy; it requires determination, patience, and critical thinking. Second, *writing is a skill that can be learned and developed.* As with any skill, practice leads to improvement. The more you write, the better your writing will become.

Structuring Paragraphs and Essays, Fifth Edition, will help you to build your skills and your confidence as you write paragraphs and essays both in and out of the classroom. Our nuts-and-bolts approach begins with the idea that developing a positive attitude about writing is the first step to becoming a better writer.

Here are five practical strategies that will help you to develop a positive attitude about writing.

1. **Write as often as possible.** Do not always rely on the phone or personal conversations to interact with others. Instead, write letters and e-mail messages to friends, relatives, and coworkers. Also, keep a journal of your everyday experiences, thoughts, and reactions. Write appreciation notes; write letters to the newspaper; do whatever you can to keep your writing skills in tip-top shape.

2. **Develop a writing process that is comfortable, flexible, and reliable.** Not everyone writes the same way, so find an approach that suits you. In the first chapter we examine the writing process that one student followed as he wrote a paragraph about Michael Jordan. But that process may not work for you. When you find a process that is most comfortable for you, your writing will benefit.

3. **Make writing easy on yourself.** Take steps to improve your efficiency as a writer and your experience with writing. For example, find a favorite spot to write; familiarize yourself with a powerful word-processing program; learn about sources of information that are available in the library or online; and choose a

What to Read

There is truth to the saying that a better reader makes a better writer. If you would like to read more but don't know what to read or where to look, try these suggestions:

- Check out the weekly bestseller list for both fiction and nonfiction in your local newspaper.
- While you're at it, skim the headlines in the local paper for articles that capture your interest.
- Log on to Internet sites such as Amazon.com and BarnesandNoble.com for their daily suggestions on what to read.
- Make a habit of visiting your local or college bookstore or magazine stand. Browsing for a while can be informative and fun.
- Several print magazines now exist online. Try Time.com or Newsweek.com for starters. Or check out one of the many online periodicals: Slate.com and Salon.com offer interesting articles on a daily basis.
- Take a look at monthly reading choices such as Oprah's Book Club selection, or join a monthly reading group through your library or local bookstore.
- Ask friends, family members, and coworkers what they have read lately and enjoyed.
- Choose subjects that you genuinely like to read about. Really, it matters *that* you read, not necessarily *what* you read.

reliable collaborator who will give you valuable feedback on your ideas and written work.

4. Read widely. One way to improve your writing skills (and your vocabulary) is to read the works of effective writers. Develop a list of favorite authors and study their style. Check the box above for recommendations about what to read and where to find interesting and popular material.

5. Keep a list of your most common grammar and usage errors. Keep this list close by as you write. Enjoy the experience of watching that list decrease in size as you improve your editing skills. Also, remind yourself that even experienced writers make errors in grammar and usage.

Activity

Developing a Positive Attitude toward Writing

Take a couple of minutes to examine your attitude toward writing. Have you had success in the past as a writer? What praise and criticism have you received—in the classroom, on the job, or in your personal life? If you have received criticism about your writing from your former English instructors or supervisors, what steps could you take to solve some of the problems they have identified? If you have received praise from former teachers or coworkers, how could you build on your strengths?

Part One

Using a Process for Writing

Part One presents an overview of the writing process—from determining purpose and audience and finding a topic through revising and editing. We emphasize throughout this opening section of the book that effective writing is the product of several small and manageable steps. These chapters will teach you not only how to write but also how to *pre*write and *re*write. To illustrate steps in the writing process, we present a case study of one student writer who has chosen to write a paragraph about Michael Jordan's off-court accomplishments. Finally, Part One offers helpful sets of guidelines for working with others, giving feedback to another writer, and keeping a writing portfolio.

Chapter 1

Paragraph and Process
The General-to-Specific Model

Today, we are called upon more and more to write. Ironically, the technology revolution has *added* to the writing tasks that we face on a daily basis, not decreased them. Think about the writing you do in your busy life:

e-mail messages to family and friends	résumés and cover letters
everyday notes and lists	thank-you letters
letters of complaint	travel journals

Think about the writing you do on the job:

brochures	newsletters
correspondence (letters and memos)	proposals
meeting summaries	reports

Think about the writing you do in college courses—even those that have not traditionally had a writing requirement:

case studies	proposals
essays	treatment plans
lab reports	Web sites

Whether you write for school, for work, or for yourself, this text will help you to develop your writing skills.

No matter what your writing task, however, there are several characteristics common to effective writing. Clarity—in other words, *clear* writing—is one such characteristic. To be clear, you need to structure your writing so that generalizations are always supported by specific details. One good way to acquire this basic writing skill is to start on the level of the paragraph because it is short enough to allow you to focus on improving the clarity of your writing. In particular, we will present the **general-to-specific paragraph**—the paragraph that opens with a general statement and goes on to support that statement with appropriate examples and details. Learning to write an effective paragraph of this kind means learning the skills and steps essential to good, clear writing in general. Furthermore, because this type of paragraph is good practice for longer forms of writing, mastering its form and the process behind it will help you to build a solid foundation of writing skills. (See Chapters 16–18 to learn more about writing essays.)

In this chapter, we will follow one student's experience of writing a general-to-specific paragraph about basketball superstar Michael Jordan. After examining the writer's product—the completed paragraph—we will step back and examine the writer's process—the steps he took to get there.

The General-to-Specific Model

The general-to-specific paragraph, like most paragraphs, is a group of sentences that work together to present a single, unified topic or idea. The general-to-specific paragraph, as we have said, moves from a general opening statement to the specific examples and details that support that general statement.

Understand the Importance of Specifics

A general statement requires support, or development, to be convincing. In everyday life, we make general statements that do not work on their own because our audience often needs to be convinced. The following statements, for example, need support and development to be convincing:

> I deserve a promotion.
>
> Family day care is better than group day care.
>
> There are three important things to remember when changing a flat tire.

The specific details you provide in speech help you to make your point to a listener. In the same way, the details a writer provides help readers to understand and evaluate the writer's point. Here is another sentence that makes a general statement.

> Even though former basketball superstar Michael Jordan is best known for his remarkable career with the Chicago Bulls, the "Air" has shown his versatility in other areas as well.

Unless you have particular confidence in the writer's judgment, you would need to see some evidence in support of this statement. In the following paragraph by Darnell Brooks, a first-year writing student, the writer supports and explains his point with a series of specific statements.

> Even though former basketball superstar Michael Jordan is best known for his remarkable career with the Chicago Bulls, the "Air" has shown his versatility in other areas as well. In 1993, after retiring for the first time from the NBA, Jordan

followed a childhood dream of becoming a professional baseball player. He signed a free-agent contract with the Chicago White Sox and spent one season with the Sox minor league team, the Birmingham Barons, before returning to the NBA. Baseball, it turns out, was not his strength, but for a novice he did a credible job in the field and at bat. In 1996, Jordan turned his attention to film, starring in *Space Jam,* which also featured actor Bill Murray, other NBA stars, and Looney Tunes cartoon characters such as Bugs Bunny and Daffy Duck. The movie, in which Jordan returns to the basketball court to save his Looney buddies from aliens, was a huge box-office success. It brought in millions at the ticket counter and in video sales. With the same natural charm that made him appealing to the moviegoer, Jordan has over the years also been successful as a product spokesperson for everything from men's underwear to hot dogs. His endorsements of athletic shoes and athletic apparel alone have been worth billions of dollars to the Nike corporation. Teamed up with his Looney Tunes costars from *Space Jam,* Michael Jordan is bound to be equally valuable to MCI.

The specific details you provide in speech help you to make your point to a listener. In the same way, the details a writer provides help readers to understand and evaluate the writer's point.

Darnell's paragraph provides the reader with several reasons for considering its opening statement: that Jordan's strengths go beyond basketball. By developing that general statement, the writer has taken steps to satisfy the curiosity and skepticism of his readers.

Activity

Identifying General and Specific Statements

Examine the following sentences and decide whether each sentence, if used in a general-to-specific paragraph, would serve as a general statement requiring further support or as a specific statement requiring no further support.

A. There are several stages of alcoholism.
B. Nearly twenty thousand Americans die from the flu each year.
C. Chunks of interstellar debris hit Jupiter.
D. It is difficult to be married to the president of the United States.
E. Education should do more than merely teach skills.
F. The car accident occurred on the south exit ramp of the highway.
G. Being a member of a social club has definite advantages for a college student.
H. Boston has a number of famous buildings that date back to the American Revolution.

Understand Levels of Generality

An effective general-to-specific paragraph usually has at least three levels of generality. The first and most general level is in the general statement, also called the **topic sentence.** (See Chapter 4 for more discussion of topic sentences.) The second level consists of more specific statements that directly support the topic sentence. These, in turn, may be supported by statements that are even more specific—the third level of generality—and so on.

The following outline demonstrates how Darnell's paragraph uses the general-to-specific structure:

> **Topic Sentence:** Even though former basketball superstar Michael Jordan is best known for his remarkable career with the Chicago Bulls, the "Air" has shown his versatility in other areas as well.
>
> **Specific 1:** In 1993, after retiring for the first time from the NBA, Jordan followed a childhood dream of becoming a professional baseball player.
>
> **Specific 1a:** He signed a free-agent contract with the Chicago White Sox and spent one season with the Sox minor league team, the Birmingham Barons, before returning to the NBA.
>
> **Specific 1b:** Baseball, it turns out, was not his strength, but for a novice, he did a credible job in the field and at bat.
>
> **Specific 2:** In 1996, Jordan turned his attention to film, starring in *Space Jam,* which also featured actor Bill Murray, other NBA stars, and Looney Tunes cartoon characters such as Bugs Bunny and Daffy Duck.
>
> **Specific 2a:** The movie, in which Jordan returns to the basketball court to save his Looney buddies from aliens, was a huge box-office success.
>
> **Specific 2b:** It brought in millions at the ticket counter and in video sales.
>
> **Specific 3:** With the same natural charm that made him appealing to the moviegoer, Jordan has over the years also been successful as a product spokesperson for everything from men's underwear to hot dogs.
>
> **Specific 3a:** His endorsements of athletic shoes and athletic apparel alone have been worth billions of dollars to the Nike corporation.
>
> **Specific 3b:** Teamed up with his Looney Tunes costars from *Space Jam,* Michael Jordan is bound to be equally valuable to MCI.

As the outline indicates, the most general statement in the paragraph, the topic sentence, is the first sentence. The sentences at the next level of generality are labeled Specifics 1, 2, and 3. These three sentences provide major points of

Writing a Concluding Sentence

Your instructor may require you to write a concluding sentence—a final sentence—to your paragraph. In a concluding sentence, the writer generally echoes the idea of the topic sentence without repeating it. If Darnell were required to write a concluding sentence to his paragraph, he might have written

Michael Jordan is one professional hoops player whose abilities extend beyond the court.

The words *professional hoops player* in the conclusion call to mind the words *basketball superstar* from the topic sentence. Similarly, the words *abilities . . . beyond the court* in the conclusion echo the words *versatility in other areas* from the topic sentence.

The concluding sentence adds no new information to the paragraph. Instead, it acts as a wrap-up. If you are required to write a paragraph with a concluding sentence, your paragraph will be a general-to-specific-*to-general* paragraph.

support for the topic sentence, but they become more effective when pinned down even further by the details presented in sentences 1a and 1b, 2a and 2b, and 3a and 3b.

Because the paragraph moves from general to specific, there is no place in it for a second statement as general as the first sentence. For instance, if Darnell had inserted into the paragraph the sentence

Michael Jordan has served as a positive role model for kids.

the focus of the paragraph would have shifted. The new statement has little to do with the content of the rest of the paragraph, and so it cannot function as support. Furthermore, the new statement has such a broad level of generality that it would require an entirely separate paragraph of specific explanation and support.

Activity

Determining Levels of Generality

Read the following paragraph carefully, and determine the level of generality of each sentence. Use TS (topic sentence) to indicate a sentence that is at the first level of generality and that the other sentences support. Use numbers (1, 2, 3) to indicate sentences that are at the second level of generality. Use lowercase letters (a, b, c) to indicate sentences that are at the third level of generality.

Many popular sayings are based on historical situations and customs that have been forgotten. To give someone the "cold shoulder," for example, means to ignore that person intentionally. The origin of this term is believed to go back to the ancient Scottish custom of offering guests who overstayed their welcome a "cold shoulder" of mutton instead of a warm meal for dinner. The phrase "flash in the pan" has an equally interesting origin. While today it refers to an overnight sensation whose popularity quickly fades because it fails to live up to expectations, the term originally referred to a speck of fool's gold in a miner's pan that brought immediate but false expectations of a large and valuable find. The popular phrase "knock on wood" has several possible origins. Today we "knock on wood" for good luck. One explanation for this curious custom was the reverence early Christians showed for the wood of the cross. Another tradition says that the practice of knocking on wood for luck began in medieval times, when accused criminals received sanctuary from the law as soon as they knocked on the wooden doors of a church. Still another possible origin for this custom may be the worship of trees and shrubs by the prehistoric inhabitants of Great Britain.

CASE STUDY: Overview of a Writer's Process

Examining Darnell Brooks's final draft paragraph on Michael Jordan shows us how the structure of a paragraph works. Examining his process—in other words, the steps he took to get to his final draft—will show us how one writer works. His process follows.

Determine Purpose and Audience

For the first assignment in his writing class, Darnell was asked to write a paragraph on a famous person he admired. First, he gave some thought to his purpose and his audience. The assignment didn't include any tip-off words like *summarize* or *evaluate* or *persuade* or *express,* so he set out to write a paragraph that would **inform** his readers about a major sports star. Further, the instructor did not specify an audience, so Darnell decided to write with a general audience of *non*–sports fans in mind. (See Chapter 2 for more information about determining purpose and audience.)

Find and Explore a Topic

Since Darnell was a major sports fan, he had no problem making a list of sports stars he admired. Here is a list of the topics for his paragraph:

Tiger Woods	Pedro Martínez
Venus Williams	Michael Jordan

He thought he might have enough to say about each, but his passion was basketball. He had nearly finished reading a biography on Michael Jordan, noted that Jordan had been selected as the number one sports figure of the twentieth century, and knew he could find more information if he needed it in magazines or on the Internet. (See Chapter 19, Writing from Reading, for guidelines about giving proper credit to your sources.) He decided that he would write his paragraph about Jordan.

The assignment didn't include any tip-off words like *summarize* or *evaluate* or *persuade* or *express*, so he set out to write a paragraph that would **inform** his readers about a major sports star.

When Darnell sat down in the computer lab to write, however, he discovered that *Michael Jordan* was too broad a topic to handle in a paragraph. What about him? There had already been mountains of material written on this famous athlete. Darnell's instructor had suggested focused freewriting—or writing without thinking about organization, grammar, or spelling—as a strategy for narrowing a general topic to something a writer could manage in a paragraph. Here is Darnell's freewriting (see Chapter 3 to learn more about freewriting and other prewriting strategies):

> *Michael Jordan had an awesome NBA career with the Chicago Bulls. 13 seasons, 10 scoring titles, 5 MVP awards. Plus, 6 world championships. Nickname: "Air." He is the most recognized athlete in the world. (??) He has been on TV and in the movies too. He's done tons of commercials (hot dogs, Wheaties, Gatorade, batteries, etc.) and made the movie Space Jam, which my friend Marcus and I saw three times. He was also in the news a lot when his father was killed. Not a lot of athletes are as versatile as M.J. He even quit basketball for a year to play professional baseball. For a guy who hadn't played organized baseball since he was in high school, he didn't do bad. He was a 6′6″ guard and averaged 31.5 points per game. I still remember when he scored 69 points in a single game! Marcus and I talked about that for weeks. He's pretty much a role model for us.*

Darnell took some time to look over what he had written. He discovered that he could go in one of two directions: Michael Jordan on the court or Michael Jordan off the court. Since he knew many writers had written about the superstar's career highlights and statistics, Darnell decided to write about this famous athlete's off-court success.

Write a Topic Sentence with a Controlling Idea

To begin his paragraph, Darnell knew he had to make a point in a topic sentence. An effective topic sentence for a paragraph does two things:

1. it establishes the general topic, and
2. it introduces the controlling idea.

Think of the **controlling idea** as the writer's *angle* on the topic or as the writer's specific *point* about the general topic. Darnell went back to his freewriting and underlined everything that could help him to make his point about Michael Jordan's off-court activities.

Michael Jordan had an awesome NBA career with the Chicago Bulls. 13 seasons, 10 scoring titles, 5 MVP awards. Plus, 6 world championships. Nickname: "Air." He is the most recognized athlete in the world. (??) He has been on TV and in the movies too. He's done tons of commercials (hot dogs, Wheaties, Gatorade, batteries, etc.) and made the movie Space Jam, which my friend Marcus and I saw three times. He was also in the news a lot when his father was killed. Not a lot of athletes are as versatile as M.J. He even quit basketball for a year to play professional baseball. For a guy who hadn't played organized baseball since he was in high school, he didn't do bad. He was a 6'6" guard and averaged 31.5 points per game. I still remember when he scored 69 points in a single game! Marcus and I talked about that for weeks. He's pretty much a role model for us.

Here is Darnell's topic sentence:

Topic

Even though former basketball superstar Michael Jordan is best known for his remarkable career with the Chicago Bulls, the "Air" has shown his versatility in other areas as well.

Controlling idea

(See Chapter 4 for more information about writing a topic sentence with a controlling idea.)

Develop Support for the Topic Sentence

As his next step, Darnell went about choosing points of support for his topic sentence by going back to the information he had gathered from his prewriting notes and freewriting. From that material, he obtained major areas of activity in Jordan's off-court life for possible inclusion in the paragraph. Some categories, like the fact that Jordan was the first basketball player ever to appear on a Wheaties box, seemed promising at first but could not be developed further. Darnell settled on four subcategories of information, or primary supports: Jordan's film work, his success as a spokesperson, his mourning the death of his father, and his brief baseball career. The writer then proceeded to find more information that would help him develop these subcategories even further. Here is Darnell's informal outline—in other words, his paragraph plan:

An effective topic sentence for a paragraph does two things: It establishes the general topic, and it introduces the controlling idea.

Topic sentence: Even though former basketball superstar Michael Jordan is best known for his remarkable career with the Chicago Bulls, the "Air" has shown his versatility in other areas as well.

Jordan starred in the 1996 film Space Jam.

—The movie was a huge box-office success. In the movie, Jordan returns to the basketball court to save his Looney buddies from aliens.

—The film brought in millions at the ticket counter and in video sales.

Jordan has been very successful as a product spokesperson for everything from men's underwear to hot dogs.

—Endorsements of athletic shoes and athletic apparel have been worth billions of dollars to the Nike corporation.

—He will probably be just as valuable to MCI.

Jordan showed the world his personal side as he mourned the death of his own role model: his father, James Jordan.

—The media often captures the emotion of celebrities with cameras and microphones.

—The fact that Jordan's father was murdered made the sad event even more "popular" in the eyes of the nation.

Jordan left the NBA in 1993 to follow a childhood dream of becoming a professional baseball player.

—He signed a contract with the Chicago White Sox and spent one season with the Sox minor league team before returning to the NBA. His celebrity presence increased attendance at Birmingham Barons games.

—Baseball was not Jordan's strength. For a guy who hadn't played organized baseball since he was in high school, he did a credible job in the field and at bat.

Organize Support and Write a Draft

Darnell began drafting his paragraph with his informal outline close by his side. As he drafted, he thought about the order of his major supporting points. He decided to use time order and sequenced the points so that the section about Jordan's brief baseball career and his father's death (1993) came before the part about his film debut (1996) and his many years as a product spokesperson. (See Chapter 6 for more information about time order and other ways to organize your writing.) He indented his first word and wrote his draft in complete sentences. Even though he typed his draft on a computer, he made sure to double-space so that his next step, revising, would be easier. Here is Darnell's draft paragraph:

> Even though former basketball superstar Michael Jordan is best known for his remarkable career with the Chicago Bulls, the "Air" has shown his versatility in other areas as well. Jordan showed the world his personal side as he mourned the death of his own role model: his father, James Jordan. The media often captures the emotion of celebrities with cameras and microphones. The fact that Jordan's father was murdered made

the sad event even more "popular" in the eyes of the nation. Jordan followed a childhood dream of becoming a professional baseball player. He signed a contract with the Chicago White Sox and spent one season with the Sox minor league team before returning to the NBA. His presence on the team drew sell-out crowds. Baseball was not his strength, but for a guy who hadn't played organized baseball since he was a kid, he did a credible job in the field and at bat. Jordan starred in Space Jam, which also featured actor Bill Murray, other NBA stars, and Looney Tunes cartoon characters such as Bugs Bunny and Daffy Duck. The movie was a huge box-office success. In the movie, Jordan returns to the basketball court to save his Looney buddies from aliens. It brought in millions at the ticket counter and in video sales. Jordan has over the years also been successful as a product spokesperson for everything from men's underwear to hot dogs. His endorsements of athletic shoes and athletic apparel alone have been worth billions of dollars to the Nike corporation. He is bound to be equally profitable for MCI.

Revise for Focus, Unity, Support, and Coherence

Darnell was not finished with his assignment once he completed his draft. Revision involves taking a second and even a third look at your writing to fix problems with the paragraph's controlling idea, unity, support, and coherence. Darnell put his draft aside for a day and then went to visit his school's writing lab. He and the writing tutor

- examined the topic sentence to make sure it provided a clear focus for the reader,
- checked each sentence to make sure it supported the topic sentence,
- looked for opportunities to add more specific details or rearrange existing ones, and
- considered how the sentences could flow more easily from one to another.

(See Chapter 7 for more information about revising for focus, unity, support, and coherence.)

Darnell revised by crossing out what he wanted to cut and inserting with a caret (‸) the words he wanted to add. He assured himself that he had a clearly focused topic sentence, but he made several changes to improve his paragraph.

Even though former basketball superstar Michael Jordan is best known for his remarkable career with the Chicago Bulls, the "Air" has shown his versatility in other areas as well. ~~Jordan showed the world his personal side as he mourned the death of his own role model: his father, James Jordan. The media often captures the emotion of celebrities with cameras and microphones. The fact that Jordan's father was murdered made the sad event even more "popular" in the eyes of the nation.~~ *In 1993, after retiring for the first time from the NBA,* Jordan followed a childhood dream of becoming a professional baseball player. He signed a *free-agent* contract with the Chicago White Sox and spent one season with the Sox minor league team, *the Birmingham Barons,* before returning to the NBA. ~~His presence on the team drew sell-out crowds.~~ Baseball, *it turns out,* was not his strength, but for a *novice* ~~guy who hadn't played organized baseball since he was a kid,~~ he did a credible job in the field and at bat. *In 1996, Jordan turned his attention to film, starring* ~~Jordan starred~~ in Space Jam, which also featured actor Bill Murray, other NBA stars, and Looney Tunes cartoon characters such as Bugs Bunny and Daffy Duck. The movie, *in which* ~~was a huge box-office success. In the movie,~~ Jordan returns to the basketball court to save his Looney buddies from aliens*, was a huge box-office success.* It brought in millions at the ticket counter and in video sales. *With the same natural charm that made him appealing to the moviegoer,* Jordan has over the years also been successful as a product spokesperson for everything from men's underwear to hot dogs. His endorsements of athletic shoes and athletic apparel alone have been worth billions of dollars to the Nike corporation. *Teamed up with his Looney Tunes costars from Space Jam, Michael Jordan* ~~He~~ is bound to be equally valuable to MCI.

cut unrelated details

added details

added transition

combined sentences for coherence

added transition

added transition

Why Didn't Darnell Cite Any Sources?

As Darnell collected supporting information for his paragraph on Michael Jordan from outside sources, he was careful to write down important information about those sources—for instance, the title, author, and other publication information—so that, if he needed to, he could cite them later in his paper. That way, he could avoid plagiarism—presenting someone else's words, research, or ideas as his own.

But as he read article after article and visited various Web sites, he found a great amount of repetition in the information they presented, which means that the information he wanted to include in his paragraph could be considered "common knowledge." After consulting with his instructor to be certain he was not plagiarizing, he determined he would not have to provide any source citations and documentation.

For more information on plagiarism, citing sources, and using documentation strategies, see Chapter 19, Writing from Reading.

One of the first things Darnell cut was the information about media coverage of personal events in celebrities' lives. The three sentences he cut detour the reader from the controlling idea of Michael Jordan's off-court versatility. He also cut the point about Jordan's presence drawing big crowds to the baseball fields because it, too, detours from the idea of Jordan's versatility. Darnell then took the opportunity to add additional details that help to make his point clearer and more convincing. Finally, he added transitional words and phrases and combined sentences to make his ideas flow more smoothly from one sentence to the next.

Only after he considered the larger, or more global, revision issues did Darnell edit for grammar, punctuation, spelling, word use, and so forth. Finding that his text required little editing, he ran off a final copy to submit. (You can get specific help with grammar and usage issues in Chapters 23–44 of this text.)

The process that took Darnell Brooks from a general topic to a finished paragraph on Michael Jordan is presented in this chapter as a writing guide. Let these steps help you to write a clearly focused, unified, well-supported, and coherent paragraph. The steps that are outlined in the Darnell Brooks case study are further developed in the upcoming chapters.

Summary

1. Examining the general-to-specific paragraph will help you to understand the basics of clear writing. (See p. 6.)

2. A general-to-specific paragraph is a group of sentences that presents a unified topic or idea and moves from a general opening statement to specific supporting statements. (See p. 6.)
3. The general-to-specific paragraph is usually built with three levels of generality: the general opening statement (also called the *topic sentence*), less general supporting statements, and further details that elaborate on the supporting statements. (See p. 8.)
4. A writer's process is his or her way of managing all of the steps taken to complete a writing task. These steps could include determining purpose and audience; finding, narrowing, and exploring a topic; writing a topic sentence with a controlling idea; developing support; organizing support; writing a draft; revising; and editing. (See pp. 10–16.)

Writing Activities

Other Writing Activities

1. The following paragraphs, taken from student writing, move successfully through varying levels of generality. Read the paragraphs carefully and then determine the level of generality of each sentence. Use TS (topic sentence) to indicate a sentence that is at the first level of generality and that the other sentences support. Use numbers (1, 2, 3) to indicate sentences that are at the second level of generality, and use lowercase letters (a, b, c) to indicate sentences that are at the third level of generality.

MODEL

__*TS*__ Scientists are uncovering new facts that challenge their long-held beliefs about dinosaurs. __*1*__ First of all, dinosaurs were most likely not cold blooded. __*1a*__ Unlike cold-blooded animals, they could travel quickly in cool weather. __*1b*__ Also, many lived above the Arctic Circle, where there is no sun during the winter. __*2*__ Secondly, dinosaurs may not have been a uniform dull green in color. __*2a*__ Rather, evidence points to the possibility of their being striped, spotted, and even brilliantly colored. __*3*__ Thirdly, dinosaurs were not the loners that scientists previously believed them to be. __*3a*__ For instance, the plant-eating Triceratops, often perceived as solitary, traveled in herds and went on annual migrations. __*3b*__ What is more, the predatory Tyrannosaurus Rex hunted in packs. __*4*__ Finally, and perhaps most significantly, scientists have discovered that not all dinosaurs are extinct. __*4a*__ In fact, one line exists today. __*4b*__ That line of long-lasting descendants is—surprise—*birds*.

A. Many questions linger today concerning the 1963 assassination of President John Fitzgerald Kennedy in Dallas, Texas. One major question that is often debated is the number of shots fired at the president's motorcade. Initially, investigators concluded that three shots were fired. However, subsequent evidence has pointed to four and even six. Another nagging question concerns the direction from which the shots were fired. The official investigation concluded that the three shots came from the Texas School Book Depository. But eyewitnesses have claimed that the president was fired upon from a nearby grassy knoll and from directly in front of the motorcade. Perhaps the most controversial question concerns the number of assassins involved. The investigation conducted by the Warren Commission concluded that a lone assassin, Lee Harvey Oswald, was solely responsible for the act. But since the time of the Commission report, evidence has surfaced suggesting that three or more teams of assassins were responsible.

B. Walking has recently become extremely popular among people of all ages. One important reason is the physical benefit of added strength and stamina that walking provides. In their off-seasons, professional athletes often walk or hike when they are not exercising more rigorously. Young people are now walking where they used to drive so that they can stay healthy and participate in physical activities. A second reason for the popularity of walking is that a brisk walk can burn off calories and fat. Dieters and people who have jobs that do not require a great deal of physical activity often walk because of this benefit. Lastly, walking is especially popular among older people who find other forms of exercise too strenuous. On the advice of a doctor, an older person can walk many blocks or even many miles a day without running the risk of a heart attack.

C. The inability of alcoholics to control their drinking often seriously affects the members of their families. For example, alcoholics often abuse their spouses both mentally and physically. An alcoholic may go into a rage over the smallest of irritations and argue, shout, insult, curse, or even hit a spouse. Likewise, the uncertainty of never knowing what to expect when an alcoholic comes home at the end of a day is often more than some spouses can bear. Life for the child of an alcoholic is often full of fear, tension, and insecurity. Yesterday's permitted behavior incurs severe punishments today. The child of an alcoholic never knows what to expect because rules for bedtime, curfews, and television hours are always changing. Evidence of psychological and emotional damage may not appear in the child until years later. Younger children living in families with an alcoholic parent frequently think that they deserve to be punished for something that they haven't really done and in later life continue wanting to punish themselves, sometimes by becoming alcoholics. Similarly, adolescents who must endure the trauma of living with an alcoholic parent often feel embarrassed and ashamed to bring friends or dates to their homes, and this embarrassment in turn generates guilt for them in later life.

2. Write a general statement on a topic of your choice. Then exchange statements with another student in your class. Think about possible specifics that could be used to develop your classmate's general statement into an expository paragraph. Are there many possibilities for development? Or does the sentence require no further support? After you have had time to think about the general statement, share your reactions with your classmate. (For help with working with a classmate, see the "Guidelines for Working with Others," on page 26.)
3. Write a paragraph comparing and contrasting your writing process with the one described in this chapter. Think about whether your process includes all of the stages that Darnell Brooks, the writer of the Jordan paragraph, experienced in his. Maybe you could add a few stages. Maybe your ordering is different. How could the writer's process be more effective? How could yours?

Chapter 2

How to Determine Your Purpose and Audience

While no step-by-step guide to the writing process can capture the many substeps that you will take when you write, it helps to sort out each major step and to learn more about it so that you can carry it out with greater confidence. This chapter will help you to understand one part of the planning stage of the writing process: It will help you discover how to determine your purpose and audience.

You may be asked to write on a particular topic with the purpose and audience already established in the instructor's guidelines:

audience — purpose

> Write a convincing letter to the college president in which you support or oppose paying higher student activity fees.

However, in other situations, like the one Darnell faces in Chapter 1, you may be left to come up with your own topic. As you hunt around for an appropriate topic, you may find yourself determining purpose (your reason for writing) and audience (the reader for your writing) before you write. You might ask yourself, as Darnell does, Why am I writing about this topic? What's my goal? Who is my reader? What does my reader need to know about my topic?

Determine Your Purpose

Your **purpose** is your reason for writing. Writers write for a variety of reasons, both private and public. As you prepare to write, spend some time determining a clear purpose. Does your writing task require you to express feelings? To summarize? To explain? To persuade? Or to fulfill some other general purpose? When writers explore their personal experiences, feelings, and reactions, often they are trying to understand the experience and gain some control over it. When they write for other people, generally their goal in communicating their understanding is either to inform their audience or to persuade them to think a certain way.

Writing to Understand

Your **purpose** is your reason for writing. Writers write for a variety of reasons, both private and public. As you prepare to write, spend some time determining a clear purpose.

The following is an excerpt from a student's journal. The writer's purpose is to express frustration about a problem she is facing in her personal life. Writing about a situation sometimes helps a writer to understand the situation more thoroughly.

> *Being a working parent is difficult. I often feel as if I'm doing neither job to my full potential because I am always having to divide my time and energy in half. My plan before I had a child was to become a manager in the human resources field. With a daughter in preschool, though, I find that it's hard to stay at work late, arrive early, and attend various last-minute meetings—all of which I see the managers at my company doing. I need to be available if my daughter is sick during the day, and I also need to have the energy to care for a busy three-year-old at the end of the day. I would consider quitting my job as a benefits coordinator altogether, but our family needs my salary. Plus, I like the job a lot.*

Writing to Communicate Understanding

To let others know what we know, we use our speaking and writing skills. When we speak, most of what we say is often lost or subject to memory. When we write, however, we present information to others in a permanent form, a form that allows them to examine it more closely and to think about it over a long period of time. When we use writing to communicate our understanding and knowledge to others, we do so either simply to present information that we think they can use or to persuade them to think a certain way about that information.

Read the two passages that follow, both on the subject of attention deficit hyperactivity disorder. How do the two differ?

Writing to Inform

> Attention deficit hyperactivity disorder (ADHD) is a condition in children that is often difficult to diagnose because of the variety of symptoms that its sufferers may display. One characteristic that can signal ADHD is hyperactivity. Children with ADHD may talk constantly. They may also be incapable of sitting still, constantly fidgeting and squirming in their chairs or even running around the room. A second notable characteristic in many ADHD patients is an inability to concentrate. Children with ADHD cannot focus on one activity at a time. They listen poorly and are easily distracted. Further, they have problems with details, often making careless mistakes, misplacing items, or forgetting important things that they have to do. Finally, these children may exhibit disruptive behavior. Sometimes

that behavior takes the form of calling out in class or not taking turns. At other times, the disruption can take the form of touching or bothering others, throwing tantrums, or even hitting classmates.

Writing to Persuade

Ritalin, the drug that is prescribed for children with attention deficit hyperactivity disorder (ADHD), can cause as many problems as solutions. Ritalin does enable school children who are taking it to perform better in class and to interact more positively with classmates and teachers, thereby improving their overall self-image. But the question is at what cost does this modified behavior come? Often Ritalin has the negative side-effect of making the hyperactive student go to the opposite extreme of becoming passive and unresponsive. Also, the drug has been known to create negative short-term effects such as decreased appetite, insomnia, and nervous tics. Further, medical professionals are not certain about the long-term medical risks. Perhaps the most important issue, however, is psychological. As children who are taking Ritalin mature, they are sometimes confused by the two sides of their personality. They do not know if they are the person they are when they are under the influence of Ritalin or that other person who surfaces when they are off the drug.

The purpose of the first paragraph is chiefly to inform the audience about the symptoms of ADHD. Another term for this type of writing whose main goal is to inform is *expository writing.* The second paragraph, on the other hand, makes an argument. The writer is trying to convince the reader that Ritalin is not always the answer to ADHD.

If your assignment or writing task does not specify a purpose, be sure to clarify your purpose as part of the planning that you do before you write.

Consider Your Audience

Your **audience** is the reader or readers you most want to reach with your writing. Taking the time to think about your audience as you prepare to write can help you make decisions about which details to include and how formal or informal to be at a later stage in your writing process.

Writing for Ourselves

There are times when what we write is intended to be private, not meant for others to read. Sometimes teachers ask their students to keep journals to store ideas and reflections as well as to mull over concepts that are being discussed in class. In the passage that follows, one student explores her reactions to an idea that has been presented in her class:

In class we have been talking about evolution, and I have to admit that our discussions have left me with a lot of questions—particularly where evolution knocks up against what I learned in church. As a child I felt that the story of Genesis was a beautiful one with ideas that made sense. I really liked the image of someone in charge. A God with a purpose and a set of rights and wrongs. When we discuss evolution in class, however, I am convinced that the Earth isn't as young as the church people would have us believe and that some of the events in the Bible are more symbolic than real. How can you disagree with fossils and other "proof"? But despite the scientific evidence supporting a long evolution of humanity, I still wonder how such life as we know it could have stemmed from such a coincidence, and I am frightened at the idea that there's no one guiding the process and that there is nothing at the end of our existence.

The interesting thing about writing for ourselves is that it often leads to writing for others. What a writer stores in a journal, for example, might become the basis for a class discussion or even a paragraph or essay. If so, the benefit is that the writer has already spent some time pondering the issue.

Writing for Others

In our personal and professional lives, we often write for specially defined audiences. Regardless of the form or situation, an awareness of the reader has to be there—in the voice we assume when we communicate with the other person and in the information we provide.

When we write letters or e-mail messages to our friends, most of the time we try to be ourselves and to sound casual. Therefore, the language we use is conversational, filled with contractions and slang. Also, much of the information shared in the correspondence is often understandable only to the two people involved in the exchange, as shown in the following personal e-mail message:

Your **audience** is the reader or readers you most want to reach with your writing. Taking the time to consider your audience as you prepare to write can help you make decisions about which details to include and how formal or informal to be at a later stage in your writing process.

Hi there.

Surprise, surprise, huh? You know, I never really associated you with biking. But hey, I'm happy for you and impressed that you're out there exercising. I'm lucky these days to go walking, but I still try to keep as active as I can.

Your short little get-away sounded wonderful and I'm sure you and Frank needed to escape the cold. And you sure know how to eat! All that great seafood . . . yummy.

We're trying to organize a family vacation next year to celebrate lots of stuff: Tom's mother's 60th birthday, Mom and Dad's 40th anniversary, etc. You're invited to join us. Don't you have a BIG birthday coming soon???

Well, it's time for lunch, so gotta go. Remember, you and Frank are always welcome here. We have Napa Valley, San Francisco, Lake Tahoe, etc., so don't ever be shy about visiting.

Love ya kiddo,

Barbara

Contrast the casual words and phrases, the informal punctuation, and content of this personal note to the following excerpt from a business memo. The next writer's goal is to demonstrate competence and good judgment—not to entertain or to connect with the reader informally. The writer's audience is his company's executive committee.

To: Executive Committee
From: Raymond Dufresne
Re: Corporate Greening Research
Date: September 18, 2000

As you know, construction of a new production facility is scheduled to begin in January. The purpose of our committee was to research and report on current developments in corporate greening—that is, the conducting of business in an environmentally conscious manner. We will want to consider this research as we build our new plant.

Our corporation was founded on the idea of being a consumer-oriented enterprise, and as surveys have shown, many of our consumers are environmentally concerned and aware. Recent evidence of this fact comes from a survey conducted in 1999 by the Michael Peterson Group and is shown in Figure 1. . . .

In this example, the writer does not use casual language and makes no assumptions about the reader's understanding of terms like "corporate greening." Also, he backs up the conclusions he draws and recommendations he makes with survey evidence. Within a business setting, a writer still needs to identify a very specific audience. After all, writing intended to be read by a client or consumer differs from writing that will be read by a supervisor or group of coworkers.

In academic writing, the audience may not be easy to define. Students may think that the audience for an academic assignment can only be the instructor. Sometimes your instructor may specify a real or hypothetical audience as part of the assignment. If you can't determine a specific audience, however, assume it is your instructor. In this case, your writing, even if it is a brief response to a quiz question, should use formal language and should provide enough background information and supporting detail to demonstrate your understanding of the subject or to convince your reader of your point. When your audience is your instructor, do not assume that he or she has expert knowledge of your subject. The following response to a quiz question demonstrates an understanding of audience:

Quiz Question

How is relationship selling different from traditional selling?

Student Answer

Relationship selling differs from traditional selling in a number of ways. First, relationship selling rests on the idea that building long-lasting relationships with customers and potential customers is the way to achieve success. The emphasis in relationship selling is on service to the customer—before, during, and, most importantly, after the sale. Traditional selling, on the other hand, involves no such customer-centered philosophy. In traditional selling, the "relationship" ends as the salesperson closes the sale. Once the transaction is complete, there is no more relationship. Second, in a relationship-based business model, salespeople provide a service, acting as consultants and problem solvers, not merely a product, as in traditional selling. Successful relationship sellers help customers to identify needs and then do what they can to tailor a product to those needs. Third, in relationship selling, time spent with the customer is considered a valuable investment. In traditional selling, time spent with the customer is considered a necessary sacrifice.

Even though the writer of the quiz answer has to be brief in order to finish the entire quiz in a limited amount of time, she is demonstrating her understanding of the question and providing sufficient detail in her answer to make and support her point.

In these examples, the language, the voice, and the supporting evidence are tailored to the expectations of the audience.

Activity

Determining Audience and Purpose

Read the following passage carefully. With a partner, determine what you think are the purpose and audience for this piece of writing. Be prepared to say how you reached your determination. (For help with working with a classmate, see the "Guidelines for Working with Others" on page 26.)

What is all this furor about homework? Parents and students are complaining that two hours of homework in middle school is too much. They say it results in the loss of unstructured family time, stress for the student, tension in the house, and even serious illness. What they are overlooking is the fact that homework is not the only thing causing these negative effects. The mania for structured after-school activities is also driving families apart. Think about all of the tension and frustration that a heavy schedule of soccer matches, piano practices, and karate lessons causes. And these activities cannot boast the kind of value that a purposeful session of homework provides. A reasonable amount of homework each evening, researchers have shown, improves academic performance, encourages

Guidelines for Working with Others

Use these guidelines to help you work more effectively with others, whether collaborating on a writing assignment or on a reading activity.

- **Understand the task.** Make sure each member of the team or group knows what it is the team is supposed to do or accomplish.
- **Keep an eye on the clock (or calendar).** Whether you have a few minutes or an entire week to complete an activity or assignment, use your time wisely.
- **Take notes.** One member of the team should be responsible for writing notes for the group. Notes provide an important reference if the team has to report back to the class after a brief activity or if team members need to check the decisions or progress made at a previous meeting about a longer assignment.
- **Respect others.** Be open to new ideas and different points of view of other team members. In the case of a disagreement, try to reach a compromise—some middle ground that is acceptable to both sides.
- **Speak up.** A team benefits most from the *active* participation of its members. If you are usually the more active member of a group, encourage others to share their ideas. If you are usually less active, try to contribute at least two or three ideas per session.
- **Show up.** If your team meets outside of class for a long-term assignment, be sure to attend all meetings and complete all assigned tasks.
- **Stay focused.** If the discussion is going off track, pull the members of the team back to the task by focusing on what the team is supposed to accomplish and the progress the team has already made toward the group goal.
- **Summarize.** As a self-check, take some time at the end of a team meeting to go over what it is you considered, decided, or accomplished.

For help in giving feedback to another writer, see the "Guidelines for Giving Feedback" on page 49.

good study skills, and helps students become self-starters. Plus, it elevates the performance of students on standardized tests, which increases their chances of getting in a good college later on. Let's see a karate lesson do that.

☑ Writer's Checklist: Purpose and Audience

_____ Is your purpose for writing clearly defined in your assignment?

_____ If not, ask yourself what your *reason* for writing is. Are you writing to

  _____ express feelings?

  _____ explain something?

  _____ provide information?

_____ understand a personal experience?
_____ convince someone?
_____ or to accomplish some other purpose?

_____ Is the audience for your writing clearly defined in your assignment?

_____ If not, ask yourself whom you are writing for. In other words, who will read what you write?
_____ yourself?
_____ others? (Describe.)

_____ How much do your readers know about your topic? Are they
_____ informed?
_____ uninformed?

_____ What would be more appropriate for your audience?
_____ casual language?
_____ formal language?

Summary

1. Determining your purpose and your audience is part of the planning stage of the writing process. (See p. 20.)
2. Your **purpose** for writing is your reason for writing. The many purposes for writing can be broadly classified into two categories: writing to understand and writing to communicate understanding. (See p. 20.)
3. Your **audience** is the reader or readers for which your writing is intended. Considering your audience early in the process can help you make key decisions later in the process. (See p. 22.)

Writing Activities

Other Writing Activities

1. Make a list of the various writing activities that you perform on a regular basis. Next to each listing, record your audience and purpose. Then reflect on how your writings change as you move from activity to activity. Do you always worry about careful editing? Which ones require that you write to impress?
2. Write a letter to a friend giving first impressions of one of your instructors. Now revise the letter as if you were sending it to the head of that instructor's department. What changes would you make?
3. Write a letter to the editor of a local newspaper, voicing your opinion on a current issue. What steps will you need to take to ensure that your letter is taken seriously by the editor and the people who eventually read it in the newspaper?

4. Read the following passages. Then determine each writer's audience and purpose. How do you know?

   A. After reviewing the applications of twenty candidates for the accounting position at our company, I recommend that we interview Sharon K. Holbrook. Ms. Holbrook impressed me with her outstanding preparation and experience. Her work experience includes serving as a part-time bookkeeper in two reputable businesses while she was earning her B.S. in accounting at Broadfield University. While at Broadfield, she has distinguished herself as a student, achieving an overall grade point average of 3.96 on a 4.0 scale. Ms. Holbrook has also been active as a member of the Accounting Association and the business honors club.

   B. Last night I got home at 6:30 after working for six hours, attending class, researching in the library, and picking up our son Josh from soccer practice. When we walked in the door, tired and hungry, I couldn't believe it. The house was in shambles. My husband Ron, who had been home since 5:00, was watching reruns on TV, and when I came in the TV room, he had the gall to turn to me and ask what's for dinner. Well, I told him to figure it out. Then I stormed up to our bedroom and shut the door. A few minutes later, there was a small tap at the door. When I wouldn't answer, Ron cracked the door a bit and apologized for not having done his share, that he had just ordered pizza. I thought that's just great! Pizza for the third time this week!

   C. Every day our privacy is invaded in a number of ways. First of all, the secrets of employees may not be so secret after all. When workers use their company insurance plan or prescription card, their employers can gain access to information about those employees' illnesses. Also, employee ID scanners can tell employers the whereabouts of their workers on a regular basis. A second way that our privacy is compromised is through the use of electronic devices. When individuals surf the Web or make purchases, records of their activities are often recorded by sites that they visit. Every time bank customers use an ATM, full records of their transactions are stored for later consultation. And when people use their credit cards, records of their purchases are similarly stored in a database for any number of people and organizations to examine. Finally, an even more sinister form of privacy invasion is becoming popular with people who want to know other people's business: surveillance. Surveillance cameras, which in the past have been chiefly used for security purposes in retail, banking, and residential environments, are now being used on the streets to monitor everyday activities of citizens in some cities. Not content with what the cameras reveal, some snoopers have resorted to high-power satellites that can focus on individuals and their activities from a perch two hundred miles above the earth.

D. Photosynthesis is the process that plants use to convert water and carbon dioxide into food, specifically carbohydrates. The carbohydrates that plants make are actually types of sugar. Along with the carbohydrates, the plants also make oxygen as a by-product. This oxygen is very valuable because without it animal life on earth would be impossible.

Chapter 3

How to Find and Explore a Topic

Early in the writing process, experienced writers and beginning writers alike find themselves asking this question: *What am I writing about?* In other words, *What is my topic?* Some writers answer this question quickly because they have been assigned a topic or have been asked to choose from among several topics. Others need some time to discover their topic. This chapter will help you to discover a promising general topic, narrow that general topic down to something more specific and manageable, and explore that narrowed topic to see if it's worth writing about.

Discovering a Topic

Finding a suitable topic is easy once you know what makes a good topic. In most cases, you can discover lots of ideas from your experiences and reading. If after consulting your experiences and reading you still have trouble thinking of a general topic to write about, you may find the list on page 33 helpful.

What Makes a Good Topic?

How do you tell if your topic is a good one for a paragraph? Ask yourself these questions about a topic you are considering:

TopicCheck

1. Is it a topic that interests me or that I care about?
2. Is it something I have experience with, know about, or can find out about through research?
3. Is it specific enough to fit my assignment?

If your answer to any of these questions is *no,* you run the risk of writing a paper that doesn't work because it is underdeveloped or it is too broad or dull to be convincing. If your answer to question 3 is *no,* see page 34 for hints about how to narrow your topic from something broad (such as *music*) to something specific (such as *the origins of hip-hop music*).

Where Do Writers Discover Good Topics?

Writers generally have two sources for effective paper topics: experience and reading.

Topics from Experience

Do not underestimate your interests, activities, and daily experiences and interactions as sources of topics for your writing or assume that others would find them boring to read about. For instance, if you work part-time in a supermarket, you may be able to write a more interesting paragraph on how to pack a grocery bag than on a complex subject like assisted suicide or human cloning.

The following paragraph is on a topic with which the student writer had little familiarity, but which he chose because he thought it would be "interesting to the reader":

> Mexico is a land of extremes. A friend told me that during the day temperatures get very high, but at night you have to wear a coat. The streets of cities like Acapulco are crowded with square stone haciendas, green trees, and gorgeous flowers; but these cities contrast sharply with Mexico's deserts, which are populated only by lizards and cactus plants. A television commercial once showed someone diving from one of the high cliffs near Acapulco. These cliffs are spectacular. The Aztecs who used to dive from these cliffs had developed an advanced civilization. They knew a great deal about building and about astronomy. In fact, they had cities and temples and art long before the United States was ever thought of.

Obviously the writer had never been to Mexico and had not gathered enough information about the topic to provide support for the opening sentence. What the writer knows about Mexico as a "land of extremes" is exhausted after a few sentences, so he fills out the paragraph with sketchy bits of information, drifting from a discussion of a modern diver to Aztec divers to Aztec civilization. None of this information provides specific support points for his description of Mexico.

The next paragraph is very clearly focused and much more engaging. It is clear that the student writer chose a topic with which she had firsthand experience.

Do not underestimate your interests, activities, and daily experiences and interactions as sources of topics for your writing or assume that others would find them boring to read about.

> Taking a test is a nerve-racking experience for me. Even if I have done well in homework assignments and have studied hard, when the test questions are handed out, my hands become sweaty, my heart begins to pound, and my hands shake so much I can hardly hold my pencil. All during the test, I am afraid that I am failing it. Even the simplest questions become very difficult for me. If anyone coughs, my attention is instantly diverted. The time seems to pass too quickly. Each time

> the instructor announces the time remaining for completion of the test, I become more nervous. When the instructor says that we have only a few minutes to finish, I panic even if I have already finished and am going back to check my answers.

This writer is able to support her point effectively because she has chosen her topic with care. She has chosen to write about something she is interested in—not merely something she feels will interest a reader—and something she knows about.

Topics from Reading

We are not saying that you should choose *only* those topics with which you already have knowledge or experience for a writing assignment. After all, writing is, in part, a process of discovery. Even if you don't have firsthand knowledge of a subject, you may choose a topic based on a desire to know more about it. The following is a successful paragraph that contains some information gathered from reading outside sources. (Note: If you use the words or ideas of other writers, you must **cite,** or give credit to, the other writer or writers. Chapter 19, Writing from Reading, shows you how to do this.) After being assigned to "write an informative paragraph on any topic," this student writer satisfied her curiosity about Mexico by taking some time to browse the Internet. From her brief research, she was able to narrow her topic to "Mexican foods" and then more specifically to "Aztec influences on Mexican food."

> Some of the principal foods of Mexico have come down from the days of the Aztecs. For example, the Aztecs used corn as the foundation for their cooking, and corn remains the basic item of Mexican cooking today. Tortillas made from corn flour, for instance, form a staple of the Mexican diet, and tamales, steamed in cornhusks according to the same process once used in ancient Mexico, regularly appear on the tables of modern Mexico (Atanasoff-Frisk). Also served with modern Mexican dinners is a corn soup called pozole, an item that has retained its popularity among the people of Mexico for centuries. Other popular Mexican dishes whose origins date back to Aztec times are largely made from frijoles, or beans. Most commonly eaten boiled, beans are also served fried, refried, and occasionally even refried again. Similarly, the same kinds of fowl that graced Aztec tables hundreds of years ago please Mexican palates today. Chicken is, of course, quite popular, and the fact that Mexicans value turkey as a delicacy probably derives from the ancient Aztec religious ritual of sacrificing turkey meat to the gods. In addition, many of the fruits harvested and eaten by the Aztecs can still be found in Mexican markets today. Just as the Aztecs did in ancient times, Mexican shoppers walk through open markets where they purchase avocados, mangoes, and papayas (Koeller). Finally, beverages the Aztecs liked still continue in favor. Hot chocolate is eagerly enjoyed, and mescal and tequila buoy up the spirits of the Mexicans of today just as they did those of the Aztecs of more than a thousand years ago (Atanasoff-Frisk).

Why Did the Writer Cite Her Sources?

You may notice that the writer of the "Aztec Influences on Mexican Foods" paragraph (page 32) has cited, or given credit to, two outside sources within the text of her paper. As she conducted her research, she discovered that some of the information she wanted to include in her paragraph was unique to particular sources. In other words, she would have been plagiarizing someone else's writing if she had chosen to use the information without acknowledging her sources. Even though the student writer does not use direct quotations from her sources, she still must cite them because she is using borrowed information. Her list of works cited, submitted along with her paragraph, would include the following citations:

Atanasoff-Frisk, Marisa. Rediscovering the Aztec Indians. New Haven: Yale Teachers Institute. 1998. 29 Jan. 2000. <http://yale.edu/ynhti/curriculum/units/1992/2/92.02.05.x.html>

Koeller, David W. The Aztec (Mexica) Empire. 1998. North Park University. 11 Feb. 2000. <http://campus.northpark.edu/history/WebChron/Americas/AztecEmp.html>.

Not only did reading suggest a topic to the writer of the paragraph on Aztec influences on Mexican food, it helped her to fill the paragraph with interesting and detailed examples.

If you have been assigned to write a paper using ideas and information from something you have read, see Chapter 19, Writing from Reading, for critical reading and writing strategies and for information about how to give credit to your sources.

Topic Sampler

If you have trouble discovering a general topic from your experience and reading, this list may provide you with a starting point.

advertisements	day care	hobbies	politics
aging	depression	holidays	poverty
books	diets	hunting	prejudice
campus life	diseases	lifestyles	sports
careers	enemies	mistakes	status symbols
cars	exercise	money	study habits
clothes	fears	movies	success
computers	gambling	music	technology
dancing	gardening	obsessions	travel
dating	heroes	pets	TV

Activity

Discovering Something to Write About

After examining the list of general topics in the "Topic Sampler" (see page 33), select two or three that you think may provide a starting point for an effective paragraph. (Or, if you have already been assigned a topic, write that topic down on a piece of paper.) Of each potential topic, ask the TopicCheck questions on page 30. If your answer to question 3 is *no,* can you narrow the general topic?

Prewriting to Narrow and Explore Your Topic

Many writers use **prewriting strategies** to help them in the planning stages of the writing process. These strategies, sometimes called "invention strategies," can help you do two things:

- First, they can help you **narrow** a general topic, such as *money,* to a more specific topic, such as *financing a college education.* (Whether you have been assigned a general topic or you are free to choose your own, you will have to decide what *aspect* of your topic—in other words, what manageable part of your topic—to focus on in your writing.)
- Second, once you have a narrowed topic, these strategies can help you **explore** that topic to determine whether it can be developed appropriately for the assignment.

This section presents six prewriting strategies. You may find some more helpful than others, depending upon your assignment and your topic. Remember that none of these strategies commits you to a single idea; instead, prewriting allows you to explore possibilities. Also keep in mind that the only audience for your prewriting is you.

(See Chapters 4 and 5 to learn more about using these strategies at later stages in your writing process.)

Brainstorming

When you **brainstorm,** you list everything that comes to mind about your topic—facts, personal impressions, emotions, quotations, and questions. The process of brainstorming creates a "storm" of information and ideas in your mind. In a storm, things get tossed about in a way that is anything but orderly. Worry about order later. Here are some things to keep in mind as you brainstorm:

- Don't worry about grammar, spelling, or punctuation mistakes.
- Use words and phrases rather than complete sentences.
- Keep writing until you exhaust everything that crosses your mind about a topic.
- You'll have more than you need when you are through. That's a good thing.

One student used brainstorming to narrow her general topic:

General topic: Gambling
horse racing
famous race horses and jockeys
off-track betting
the most important horse race: the Kentucky derby
casino gambling—why is it so popular?
slot machines
most popular slots
video poker
are casinos good for local economies or bad?
lots in the news about legalizing casinos
why are lots of casinos run by Native Americans?
types of gamblers
compulsive gambling
twelve-step programs
my first experience with gambling
everyday people in everyday clothes
spending more than I planned to
winning $400 and then losing it all
my Aunt Sarah goes to the casino across the state line several times a month
increase in gambling by young people (18–25)
state lotteries
lotteries as a way to raise money for education and other things
new $10 lottery ticket in Massachusetts
media attention on gambling
Powerball
big winners: did their lives change?

Interested in the popularity of gambling among her friends and fellow college students, the writer decided to brainstorm in order to narrow the general topic to something she could manage in a short paper. She now has several possible directions. If, for example, she chooses to write about *types of gamblers,* she can brainstorm further to explore that narrowed topic. The writer now needs to know if there is enough to say about the narrowed topic.

Narrowed topic: Types of gamblers
Recreational gamblers
—See gambling as a once-in-a-while pastime
—Often gamble with friends
—Often stick with only the few games they are familiar with
One-time gamblers
—Maybe gambled on a bet

—Once bitten, twice shy motto
First-time gamblers
—Why they gamble
—What they gamble
Compulsive gamblers
—What's the thrill?
—When gambling interferes with work or relationships
—Stealing money to gamble with
—Treatment for compulsive gamblers

Freewriting

When writers **freewrite,** they write without thinking about topic, organization, grammar, or spelling. Using this prewriting strategy, a writer jumps immediately into the writing process with a loosened mind and pen (or keys!). The writer writes for a specific period of time—usually ten minutes or so—on whatever comes to mind. In **focused freewriting,** the writer writes without regard to grammar, spelling, or organization but *does* have a topic in mind. Some things to consider as you freewrite:

- Don't worry about grammar, spelling, or punctuation mistakes.
- Use words, phrases, or complete sentences to record your ideas.
- Keep writing until your time is up. (Set the timer on your watch, your oven, or your computer to ten minutes.)
- Write nonstop, even if you occasionally have to write "I don't know what to write."
- You'll have more than you need when you are through. That's a good thing.

Here is one student's focused freewriting on the subject of *campus life*:

I've never done anything like freewriting before, and I have ten minutes to do it in and no idea what I'm supposed to be doing. The instructor told us to write on the subject of campus life. What does that mean? Is there life on campus? I guess I think about campus life in terms of the people I know, my schedule (which is hell this semester), where I eat lunch when I get a chance to eat lunch, finding a place to park. There's something. I spent twenty minutes this morning driving around and around and was late for my Algebra class this morning because I couldn't find a place to park anywhere. We all pay over a hundred bucks a year at this place for the chance to hunt for a parking space that never seems to be there. I'm sure the administration sells about fifty times more permits than there are spaces to park and what does it matter to them? They get the money and we get marked absent when we're not in class on time. Four missed classes and it's all over for me. I wish this school would build another lot or come up with some better system for parking so that I wouldn't have to worry about being late. Just about every day.

This example of freewriting does the job it is supposed to do. It allows the writer to explore his ideas about a general topic *(campus life)* and then to begin to focus on an aspect of the general topic *(parking problems on campus)*. At the end of the prewriting exercise, the writer wishes his school administration would develop "some better system for parking." That idea would make an excellent topic for a paragraph or essay because it is a specific subject that the writer is interested in and knows something about.

Once the writer has arrived at a possible narrowed topic, he can do another ten minutes of freewriting to explore the more specific idea of a better parking system.

Activity

Using Brainstorming and Freewriting

A. Using brainstorming, narrow one of these topics: *stressful situations, office politics, clothes.*

B. Freewrite for ten minutes on one of these topics: *Monday mornings, annoying people, obsessions.*

After you do each prewriting activity, ask yourself if you've discovered a more specific aspect of the larger, more general topic. If you have, then ask yourself if the narrowed topic is (1) something you are interested in and (2) something you know about or can find out about. You may, in fact, have discovered a topic for your next writing assignment.

Clustering

A "cluster" is a bunch or a group of something. In a **clustering** exercise, a writer bunches or groups ideas together on paper, linking the ideas visually. In fact, clustering is a prewriting strategy that may appeal more to you if you tend to learn better with visual information—that is, if you'd rather find your way to a new place with a road map than with written directions, or if you'd rather assemble a new product using a diagram than following step-by-step instructions.

Here's how clustering works:

- Write your general topic in the middle of a blank sheet of paper. Then circle it.
- Begin "branching" off of your topic. Write down words, phrases, and ideas that relate to your topic. Draw a circle around each and connect it to the general topic with a line.
- Continue branching out as ideas cross your mind. Draw lines from one circle to another to show connections and relationships between ideas. You should find that you're developing several clusters of information. Ideally, each cluster of information might be a narrowed topic.

Let's take a look at the following sample cluster by a student who is comparing family day care (where someone provides care for one or more children

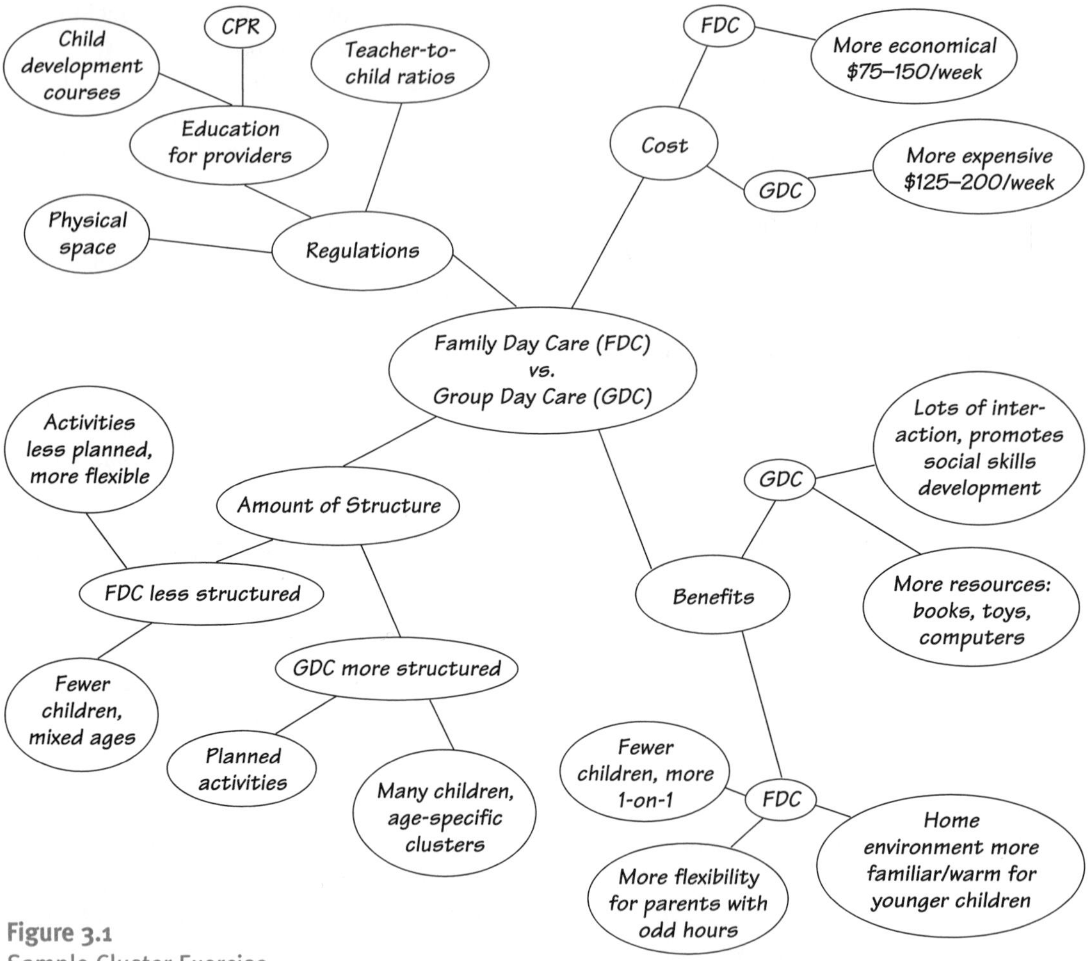

Figure 3.1
Sample Cluster Exercise

in his or her home) with group day care (where children are cared for in a day care center).

This writer has already narrowed her topic from *day care* to *comparing family day care to group day care.* In this example, the writer uses the clustering strategy to explore her narrowed topic. After she finishes her clustering diagram, she can review it to decide which point she wants to make about her narrowed topic and whether she has enough details to support that point.

Asking Questions

In trying to narrow a broad topic, some writers find it useful to ask questions. Think about a reporter covering a news story. News writing involves finding answers to six common questions about people, events, or ideas: *Who? What? Where? When? Why?* and *How?* You may find that asking similar questions about your general topic will help you to find a narrowed topic and perhaps to explore that narrowed topic for supporting details. Keep the following tips in mind as you ask questions about your general topic:

- Don't worry about grammar, spelling, or punctuation mistakes.
- Write only questions—do not attempt to find answers at this stage.
- You'll have more than you need when you are through. That's a good thing.

This "picking apart" of a broad subject area is what leads to a focused topic—one you can manage in a short writing assignment. The writer who explored the subject of *fears and phobias* knew that there was no way to write about that subject in a paragraph without narrowing.

One writer used this strategy to help him narrow the general topic of *fears and phobias.*

Topic: Fears and phobias

Who? Who has fears? Does everyone fear something? Who is most likely to develop a phobia? Who are people most afraid of? Who am I most afraid of? Who do people go to for help solving problems with fears?

What? What makes a "phobia"? What am I afraid of? What are the emotional signs of fear? What are the physical signs of fear? What can people do about a phobia? What is agoraphobia? What is technophobia? What is it that adults most fear? What do children most fear?

When? When are people most likely to be afraid? During childhood? Adolescence? Adulthood? During relationships? During a test or examination? When they're alone? When do people overcome common childhood fears? When should a person seek treatment or therapy for a phobia?

Where? Where are people most likely to be afraid? In an airplane? On a cliff? In the water? On the Internet? In an unfamiliar place? Where can one go for help with fears or phobias? Where is research being done about this subject?

Why? Why do people become afraid? Why does the body react the way it does in a scary situation? Why does the mind act a certain way? Why do people learn to live with fear? Why is fear seen as a motivational force?

How? How does a fear differ from a phobia? How do fears and phobias affect the way people live their lives? How do different people cope with fear?

Several potential topics emerge when the general topic is picked apart in a questioning activity. This "picking apart" of a broad subject area is what leads to a focused topic—one you can manage in a short writing assignment. The writer who explored the subject of *fears and phobias* knew that there was no way to write about that subject in a paragraph without narrowing it. If you're an inquisitive, analytical person outside of the classroom, you might find that the questioning strategy works well for you as you narrow or explore a topic.

Activity

Asking Questions to Narrow a Topic

Choose a general topic from the list on page 33, or use one that you already have in mind. Use the questioning strategy to narrow the general topic. Ask *Who? What? When? Where? Why?* and *How?* and then make a list of three or four potential narrowed topics.

Keeping a Writer's Journal

You may keep a journal already. If you do, you may find that keeping a journal is a useful way to find or explore topics for your writing assignments—even if your journal entries are about your personal life and seem to have little to do with your writing class.

If you don't currently keep a journal, start now. A **journal** can be your place to

respond to something you recently saw, read, or heard;
reflect on a decision you made or something you experienced;
comment on some personal, professional, or political situation; or
figure out something you don't understand.

If you make a habit of writing a brief entry in a journal several times a week, you'll have a tremendous source of potential writing topics and—here's the bonus—you will be used to writing on a regular basis. To keep a journal:

- Obtain a notebook whose sole purpose is for journal writing. If you prefer to write on the computer, create a folder on a disk or on your hard drive that you label "journal."
- Write in your journal for at least ten minutes three times a week. Include the date as part of each entry.
- Keep your writing informal and casual.
- Experiment with different kinds of writing. Your journal could include freewriting, brainstorming, questioning, clustering, or other kinds of writing activities. Also, journal writing shouldn't feel like an assignment, so choose subjects that are important to you.

When the time comes to select a topic for a paragraph or essay, reviewing your journal is likely to suggest all kinds of interesting topics that you might otherwise have forgotten or overlooked.

The following journal entry was written by a student who had lost his checkbook. The writer was upset by the new experience and chose to record his feelings about it—as well as what he learned from it—in his journal:

9/28/2000

Today I lost my checkbook. I've only had a checking account for about six months. I don't have a ton of money in my account, but I like to keep an emergency balance of about $50.00. That way I know if I absolutely need extra cash, getting it is no big deal. Of course the ATM card that comes with the account is handy. My worst fear about the checking account was losing the checkbook. Panic immediately set in when I reached for it at the bookstore checkout and it wasn't there. Did I lose it or was it stolen? I calmed myself down and figured I had just misplaced it, but after searching my apartment for an hour, I gave up. So I called the bank and asked what I should do. The people at the bank were cool. No, I wasn't an irresponsible idiot. No, I wasn't responsible for any forged checks. All I had to do was make "stop payments" on the missing checks and the bank would take care of the rest. I learned some valuable things today. Even though it's probably natural to do so, I shouldn't freak out as much as I do when something goes wrong. I also learned something practical about personal finance: how to stop payment on a check.

When later reviewing his journal, this student writer found the kernel idea for a how-to paragraph.

Considering Audience

One more strategy that writers use to explore a topic is to consider the needs of the audience. The information that a certain circumstance or reader requires may help to determine the focus of the writing. For instance, you may be asked by your supervisor to write a summary of your department's achievements over the course of the year. If you know you are writing something intended for the chief accounting officer, you'll likely focus on the revenues earned by your department over the year. If the audience is the president of the company, you may focus on product development or how the department fulfilled the company mission statement. If you are writing for the customer, perhaps you'll focus on your department's gains in the area of customer service and support. Because audience determines the appropriateness of a topic, you can benefit from exploring your general topic by first asking yourself what your readers expect.

Writer's Checklist: Topic

_____ Have you thought carefully about the general topic you have chosen or have been assigned?

_____ Is your topic something that interests you or that you care about? Is it something you have experience with, know about, or can find out about through reading and research? If your answer to either question is *no,* use a prewriting strategy to find a new topic.

_____ Is your topic specific enough to fit your assignment? If not, can your general topic be divided into several more specific aspects of the topic? If so, can you use a prewriting strategy to identify an aspect of the topic that you think would make a good paper?

_____ Once you have a narrowed topic, why not use a prewriting strategy to decide if you have enough information to write a paragraph or essay on that topic?

Summary

1. Early in the writing process, a writer should answer the question *what am I writing about?* or, in other words, *what is my topic?* (See p. 30.)
2. A writer should be familiar enough with the topic, either through experience or reading, to develop it effectively in a paragraph. (See pp. 31–33.)
3. An effective paragraph considers one specific aspect or angle of a broader or more general topic. (See p. 34.)
4. Sometimes called "invention strategies," some basic prewriting techniques for narrowing and exploring a topic include brainstorming (page 34), freewriting (page 36), clustering (page 37), asking questions (page 38), keeping a writer's journal (page 40), and considering audience (page 41).

Writing Activities

Other Writing Activities

1. Write a journal entry on something that you have either heard or read about in the media (on television, on the radio, on the Internet) during the past week. Begin by summarizing what you heard or read, and then record your own thoughts, feelings, or observations about the situation. After completing your entry, circle any ideas that you might consider writing about in a paragraph.
2. Choose a general topic on your own or from the list on page 33. Discuss with a classmate the possible audiences that might require you to write about that topic. From your discussion, identify five different approaches you might take to the general topic based on the expectations and needs of different readers.

3. Brainstorming is an invention device that lends itself naturally to group activities. With a small group of three or four other people, brainstorm about the general topic of "responsibility." Decide on one person to take notes for your brainstorming session. After about ten minutes or so, take a short break, and then have someone read the notes to the group. Have each member of the group write down a potential narrowed topic. Then use the Topic-Check questions (page 30) to test each topic. (For help with working with a classmate, see the "Guidelines for Working with Others" on page 26.)

Chapter 4

How to Write a Topic Sentence

Once you have discovered your narrowed topic, you are ready to begin writing your general-to-specific paragraph. In a general-to-specific paragraph, as you may recall from Chapter 1, the first sentence announces your topic and makes a general statement about it that the rest of the paragraph will show, explain, or prove. This sentence is the **topic sentence.** The remaining sentences in the paragraph provide specific information to support the topic sentence, which is the most important sentence in the paragraph.

What Is a Topic Sentence?

Quite simply, writers write to make a main point. The topic sentence, usually the first sentence in a paragraph, announces the narrowed topic and states the main point of your paragraph. Think of your main point as the controlling idea behind all of the support that you will gather for your paragraph.

Narrowed topic	+	controlling idea (main point)	=	Topic Sentence

The Topic Sentence as a Contract

You may also find it helpful to think of the topic sentence as a contract. In business, a contract is a formal agreement between two or more people or groups. People generally use contracts to set forth clearly any terms, guidelines, and expectations *at the beginning* of a project. A contract states the responsibilities of each party and the terms of the agreement. For example, if you live in an apartment, you may have signed a lease agreement, which is a contract between you and your landlord. You agree to pay a certain amount in rent each week or month and to remain a tenant for a specific period of time; you may also agree to follow certain guidelines like not having a pet or not parking more than two cars in the driveway. In return, the landlord's part of the agreement usually involves general upkeep of your apartment and the building, creation of a safe environment (by installing appropriate door locks and smoke detectors), and a freeze on your rent amount for the term of the agreement.

Writing a topic sentence that includes a narrowed topic and a controlling idea is like signing a contract with your reader. A topic sentence makes a promise and binds the writer to a responsibility. A writer who writes "Improving American schools involves taking three important risks" is promising not only to say something about improving American schools (the topic) but also to explain the three risks involved (the controlling idea) in achieving the task. It is your responsibility as the writer to fulfill the terms of the contract as set forth in your topic sentence. The degree to which you succeed in doing so determines how effective your paragraph will be.

A topic sentence makes a promise and binds the writer to a responsibility. A writer who writes "Improving American schools involves taking three important risks" is promising not only to say something about improving American schools (the topic) but also to explain the three risks involved (the controlling idea) in achieving the task.

What Is a Controlling Idea?

The **controlling idea** is the part of your topic sentence in which you signal to your reader the main point you will make about your narrowed topic. To understand this concept, read the first sentence of the paragraph on Mexican foods from Chapter 3 (see page 32):

> Some of the principal foods of Mexico have come down from the days of the Aztecs.

This opening sentence indicates that the topic of the paragraph is *foods of Mexico,* but besides identifying this topic, the topic sentence also makes a point about Mexican foods. Here we learn that the author will show that many modern Mexican foods *have come down from the days of the Aztecs.* This idea—the aspect of the topic that will be focused on in the paragraph—is the controlling idea.

The Difference between a Topic and a Controlling Idea

Understanding the difference between a topic and a controlling idea, both of which are essential to the topic sentence, is an important step toward writing successful paragraphs. A topic alone cannot give your paragraph the focus and direction that you need to develop the paragraph. For example, look at the following items:

1. The Vietnam War
2. The Vietnam War altered the lives of a generation of Americans.

3. There are several important lessons to be learned from the Vietnam War.
4. The Vietnam War is responsible for many changes in American foreign policy.

Item 1 is simply a topic. By itself, it does not suggest any one aspect of the Vietnam War for a writer to focus on. Items 2, 3, and 4, however, suggest three possibilities. Each of these items can be used as a topic sentence because each goes beyond the topic to convey a controlling idea or main point that can be shown, explained, or proven. The topic in each of these items remains the same—the Vietnam War—but these topic sentences would lead to three very different paragraphs because of their controlling ideas. The controlling idea in sentence 2 is signaled by the words *altered the lives of a generation of Americans.* In sentence 3, the writer will focus on *several important lessons* learned from the war. Finally, topic sentence 4 indicates the controlling idea of *many changes in American foreign policy.* Unlike item 1, sentences 2, 3, and 4 can be used as topic sentences because they announce the topic of the paragraph *and* convey a controlling idea.

Activity

Identifying Topic and Controlling Idea

In each of the following topic sentences, identify (1) the topic and (2) the words or phrases that state the point about the topic (the controlling idea) that the writer will show, explain, or prove.

EXAMPLE First-year college English is a time-consuming course.

First-year college English — Topic; is a time-consuming course. — Controlling idea

A. A student who works full-time and runs a household has busy evenings.
B. Drop/add policies at this school are too strict.
C. E-commerce has saved many suffering businesses.
D. The protective ozone layer surrounding the earth has shown signs of deterioration in the past two decades.
E. There are four key steps to running the office copy machine.

Deciding on a Controlling Idea

Because the controlling idea is crucial to the success of the paragraph, try to write at least a rough topic sentence—one that includes the narrowed topic and the controlling idea—before you move on to the body of your paragraph. If you simply start writing about a topic with no controlling idea in mind, your paragraph will lack focus and wander off in different directions. At this stage in the writing process, your goal should be to find a controlling idea for your topic and then to write a topic sentence that clearly states both your narrowed topic and your controlling idea. Think about the *main point* you want to make about your topic. If you find you aren't making a point, your readers will ask, "So what?"

Effective controlling ideas are neither too focused for further development nor too general for adequate development in a single paragraph. They tend to hit a happy medium, giving the writer a clear head start for developing the rest of the paragraph.

Think about the *main point* you want to make about your topic. If you find you aren't making a point, your readers will ask, "So what?"

What if my controlling idea is too focused?

After being assigned to write about a family member he admired, this student writer decided to write his paragraph on his Uncle John. Here is the writer's first attempt at a topic sentence:

> My uncle, John Harter, was born and raised in Chicago.

This sentence would not make a good topic sentence for a general-to-specific paragraph because it is too narrowly focused and would be nearly impossible to develop. Its controlling idea—*born and raised in Chicago*—is a statement of fact that doesn't need to be shown, explained, or proven. This topic sentence leaves the reader asking "So what?"

The writer revised his topic sentence after reviewing some earlier freewriting about his uncle. How is this sentence—with the same topic but a slightly different controlling idea—more effective?

> The fact that John Harter was born and raised in Chicago had an important effect on his life.

The writer will have better luck with this topic sentence because it expresses an idea that can be developed in the paragraph. The writer will go on to show *how* being born and raised in Chicago affected his uncle's life. One mark of a workable controlling idea is that it raises a question or a series of questions that you, as the writer, are expected to answer in your paragraph. In this case, the questions raised might be the following:

Were his family life and education influenced by where he was born and raised? If so, how?

Was John Harter's career influenced by the place where he was born and raised? How so?

Might he have chosen a different career if he had been raised in a rural environment?

How did living in Chicago shape his character?

In what ways is John Harter a typical Chicagoan?

Did his life in Chicago affect his health?

Did he meet someone in Chicago who changed his life? Was this change for the better or for the worse?

What if my controlling idea is too vague?

At the same time, you should avoid using a topic sentence with a controlling idea that is too vague for effective discussion. For example:

> Colorado is a great place.

This sentence is just as difficult to develop as the topic sentence "My uncle, John Harter, was born and raised in Chicago," but for a different reason. The sentence about Uncle John is far too narrow to develop into a general-to-specific paragraph. On the other hand, the "Colorado" sentence, because its idea is not narrow enough, fails to indicate a direction for development. A sentence such as the following, however, calls for expansion:

> Colorado is a vacationer's paradise twelve months of the year.

This sentence is an effective topic sentence because it needs development *and* provides a clear road map for the writer: He or she must show how Colorado offers a "paradise" to vacationers throughout the year.

Activity

Expressing a Controlling Idea

For each of the following topics, write a topic sentence that expresses a clear controlling idea. Label each controlling idea.

EXAMPLE Shopping online

Shopping online relieves many holiday shopping headaches.

Controlling idea: relieves many holiday shopping headaches.

A. Television talk shows
B. Jump-starting a car
C. Designing a living room
D. Single-sex colleges
E. Creating a personal budget

Exploring Topics for Controlling Ideas

Through the entire writing process, from the earliest planning stages to the last details of editing, good writers return again and again to using the prewriting strategies that we discussed in Chapter 3: brainstorming, freewriting, clustering, asking questions, keeping a writer's journal, and considering audience. Just as you used these strategies to narrow general topics, so too can you use these same techniques to explore your narrowed topic for clear controlling ideas.

A quick session of brainstorming on the topic of *a good summer job for a college student,* for example, suggested to one student the controlling idea *easier to*

Guidelines for Giving Feedback

Use these guidelines as you review another writer's paragraph or essay. These guidelines will help you to become a more effective peer editor.

- **Understand the writer's goals.** Ask the writer to describe the purpose and audience for the paragraph or essay *before* you read it.
- **Read carefully.** Instead of just skimming the paragraph or essay, give it your full attention and read thoroughly from beginning to end. Take notes—either on the writer's paper or on your own. If you need to, read through the paragraph or essay a second time.
- **Identify the main point.** Tell the writer what you think the main point of the writing is. If the main point is not clear, say so.
- **Begin on a positive note.** Tell the writer what works for you. Writers need to be aware of strengths as well as weaknesses. Begin with "I like how you . . ." or "The strongest part of your paragraph/essay is . . ."
- **Say what needs improvement.** Is the topic/thesis sentence unclear or unfocused? Does the writer get off track? Does the paragraph or essay lack enough supporting detail? Is the writing confusing or hard to follow? By the end, has the writer failed to show/explain/prove his or her main point? If your answer to any of these questions is yes, tell the writer so, and then make suggestions for how to improve the paper.
- **Be specific.** Feedback like "It's good" or "I didn't like it" is not particularly helpful.
- **Offer help, not judgment.** Peer review should be comfortable rather than confrontational. Instead of saying, "This is totally disorganized. What were you thinking?" you might try something like, "Your paragraph would be stronger if you used time order to organize your main points."

For help in working with others on an activity or assignment, see the "Guidelines for Working with Others" on page 26.

find this summer than last summer. This combination produced the following workable topic sentence:

> A good summer job for a college student will be easier to find this summer than last summer.

Similarly, freewriting about *a hiking trip through the Adirondacks,* another student focused on her experience of *learning the history of the region* as she and her friends talked to local residents along their way. She wrote the following clearly focused topic sentence:

> Taking a hiking trip through the Adirondack Mountains is an excellent way to learn the history of the region.

Asking the questions *Who? What? When? Where? Why?* and *How?* about your topic is also a good way to come up with a workable controlling idea. Also, by keeping a journal, you may very well find yourself in the enviable position of not having to scramble for a topic or for a clear controlling idea when you have a writing assignment. If you did a clustering exercise earlier in your writing process, go back to it. Follow one of the main clusters until your writing suggests a clear direction or point to be made about the topic you placed in the center of the page.

Writer's Checklist: Topic Sentence

_____ Does your topic sentence contain a narrowed topic and a controlling idea (the main point you want to make about your topic)?

_____ Have you checked your controlling idea to make sure that it is neither too focused nor too general for effective development in the rest of your paragraph?

_____ If your controlling idea seems difficult to show, explain, or prove in a paragraph, can you do some additional prewriting to focus your topic differently?

_____ Have you made sure that your topic sentence is as clear and sharp as you can make it at this point?

Summary

1. The topic sentence, usually the first sentence in a paragraph, announces your narrowed topic and conveys the controlling idea (main point) of your paragraph. The topic sentence can be thought of as a contract between you and your reader. (See p. 44.)
2. The controlling idea limits the topic by focusing on a single specific aspect of the topic. The controlling idea "controls" the direction that the rest of the paragraph will take. (See p. 45.)
3. Just as the prewriting strategies discussed in Chapter 3 (brainstorming, freewriting, clustering, asking questions, keeping a writer's journal, considering audience) provide excellent strategies for narrowing topics, these strategies can also be used to explore topics for controlling ideas. (See p. 48.)

Writing Activities

Other Writing Activities

1. Supply topic sentences for the following paragraphs. Be certain that each topic sentence conveys a clear controlling idea.

MODEL *Successfully transplanting a tree requires careful attention to details.*

^ Before planting, check to see if the tree's roots are moist; if they are not, soak them in water for two or more hours until they appear soggy. While the roots are soaking, find a sunny spot in which to plant the tree. The soil should be a dark brown color—indicating that it is rich in nutrients. If the soil is in poor condition, mix in peat moss or potting soil. Next, dig a hole big enough to allow the tree's roots room to spread out. Place the tree in the hole and, while holding the tree straight, fill in the hole with dirt; pack the dirt lightly. Water the tree every day for a week so that the roots can take hold in the ground.

A. Home computers can perform tedious bookkeeping tasks that most families never seem to have time to do properly. They can balance checkbooks in seconds, a practical boost to those of us who are always overdrawing our accounts. They can keep track of family budgets and can make filling out income tax forms easier. In addition, home computers can provide entertainment for the whole family. There are, of course, many computer games on the market—both for children and adults. And with a little study of programming techniques, buyers can learn to program their own games. There are many other applications for home computers as well. Computers can be programmed to control heating systems, to function as security systems, or to act as efficient memo pads for important messages and dates.

B. One telltale sign of depression is a feeling of sadness or helplessness that lasts for more than a few weeks. Depressed individuals tend to feel that their problems are hopeless and that no solutions exist for the difficulties in their lives. Another sign of depression is a constant feeling of fatigue, especially if accompanied by difficulties in getting to sleep. People who suffer from serious depression usually complain of being tired, and yet they tend to lie awake at night and often experience extended bouts of insomnia. In addition, depressed individuals tend to lose interest in sex, and they have problems in concentrating. Perhaps the most significant sign of depression, however, is recurring thoughts of suicide. Because depressed people feel overwhelmed by a sense of hopelessness, they often think that suicide is the only answer to their suffering.

2. Working with a partner, consider each of the following sentences as a possible topic sentence. Determine which sentences would make effective topic sentences and why. Rewrite any sentences that you find too specific or too vague. (For help with working with a classmate, see the "Guidelines for Working with Others" on page 26.)

   A. Raleigh is the capital of North Carolina.
   B. The World Series of [year of your choice] offered baseball fans some real surprises.
   C. General George Washington was president of the United States for two terms.

D. NASA has several exciting space projects planned for the next few decades.
E. Bread frequently costs two dollars or more a loaf today.
F. Many people love ice skating.
G. Jewelry serves more purposes than just ornamentation.
H. Open communication is a crucial part of every parent-child relationship.

3. Write a paragraph for one of the following topic sentences. Feel free to alter the topic sentence according to your preferences, opinions, and experiences. For example, if you have never thought of buying a home but are a car enthusiast, you might alter sentence C to read, "An antique car is a worthwhile investment."

   A. Commuting to school has its advantages and its disadvantages.
   B. An habitually slow driver is as dangerous as a speedster.
   C. A home is a worthwhile investment.
   D. Final exams are an outdated custom.
   E. Quiet people make better friends than do talkative people.
   F. Instructors who grade leniently are not always the best teachers.
   G. American women are currently obtaining positions of leadership in career fields once dominated by males.

4. Exchange rough drafts of the paragraphs you and a classmate are writing for Writing Activity 3 (above). Read the paragraphs, focusing on the role of the topic sentence as well as the quality of the information that is being used to support the topic sentence. After you have read and thought about each other's paragraphs, share reactions and constructive suggestions with your classmate. (For help with responding to writing, see the "Guidelines for Giving Feedback" on page 49.)

5. Start a portfolio (a collection of the paragraphs and essays that you write during the semester). Accumulating your work in a portfolio will enable you to have a record of your development. Your portfolio will also provide you and your instructor with specifics to discuss when you meet to talk about your writing. Throughout this text, you will be asked to draw from your portfolio and to reflect on your progress. You can begin your collection of writings with the paragraph you wrote in response to Writing Activity 3 above. (For help with maintaining a writing portfolio see the "Guidelines for Keeping a Portfolio" on page 61.)

Chapter 5

How to Develop Support for Your Topic Sentence

Now that you've stated your point in a topic sentence, you have to *make* your point in the rest of your paragraph. You will do this with the details, facts, and evidence you use to support your topic sentence.

What Is Support?

To understand the function of support in your writing, think of yourself as an architect. As an architect, you are responsible for the design of a structure such as a house or some other building. The architect is the one with the knowledge to make certain every beam, column, footing, and joist is in place to provide support for walls, floors, ceilings, entryways, and staircases. Without proper support, the building could not remain standing and would crumble to the ground. It is the job of the architect to lay the plans for a sound, well-supported structure. As a writer, you are an architect in a way. Without support, the point you want to make will "crumble to the ground." In other words, your readers will remain unconvinced. Support is any specific detail, fact, or bit of evidence that you can use to illustrate, explain, or prove your point.

As a writer, you are an architect in a way. Without support, the point you want to make will "crumble to the ground." In other words, your readers will remain unconvinced.

Strategies for Discovering Details, Facts, and Evidence

If you find yourself wondering how to develop support for the point you want to make, try these strategies.

Return to your prewriting.

If you did some freewriting, brainstorming, clustering, or other type of prewriting to narrow and explore your topic, return to it with fresh eyes and a highlighter. Highlight (or circle or underline) any information that may help you to show, explain, or prove your main point. Look for details that are specific, directly related to your controlling idea, and targeted to your particular audience.

One student was assigned to write a restaurant review for her school's newspaper. She did some prewriting in a small notebook throughout her meal. Later, she arrived at her topic sentence:

An afternoon at the Monago Bay Café is full of pleasant surprises.

Next, she went back to her notes to identify specific details that would help her to make her point.

The driving directions to get here—awful

Less than impressive exterior, small sign

Wonderful smell of home cooking inside

Small inside, but neat decorating—paintings and prints by local artists, original seashell sculptures on every table, huge tropical fishtank in the center of the dining area.

3 minutes to be seated; 10 minutes before someone came to take my order! And it wasn't even busy!

Couple fighting in the next booth

Creamy clam chowder, lots of clams, very tasty

Terrific homemade lemonade

Salad is plain—just iceberg lettuce and a few tomato slices.

Waitress is very friendly. Chats about next week's waterfront festival. Tells me the restaurant will be giving out free fish 'n chip lunches.

Acoustic guitar music—nice atmosphere.

Fettuccine is overdone.

Fettuccine is overpriced! $7.50

Dessert menu contains lots of fresh fruit options

Bathroom is clean

Every diner gets a coupon for $3.00 off their next meal as they leave. Good way to keep business.

Do some more prewriting.

Unlike prewriting for a topic or a controlling idea, prewriting for supporting information requires that you *focus* on your controlling idea as you brainstorm. Now you are searching specifically for information that will help you to show, explain, or prove the point that you state in your topic sentence. One writer considers his topic sentence:

> Washington, D.C., has many exciting places for tourists to visit.

The controlling idea, signaled by the words *many exciting places for tourists to visit,* indicates that the writer now needs the support of several exciting tourist attractions. His preliminary list looks like this:

Watergate complex	Capitol
White House	U.S. Holocaust Memorial Museum
Washington Monument	Ford's Theater
Arlington National Cemetery	Smithsonian Institution
National Gallery of Art	Lincoln Memorial
Botanical Gardens	Jefferson Memorial

If you take a similar route and continue to brainstorm or freewrite for information to support your controlling idea, you'll probably end up with more information than you need to draft your paragraph. This is a good sign. Crossing items off of a list is always easier than coming up with new ones.

Do some research.

You may find that you have good ideas about how to support your topic sentence but that gathering the details, facts, and evidence you need requires a trip to the library or a couple of hours online. You may, for example, know something about herbal remedies for common illnesses—enough to state in a topic sentence that "Herbal medicine offers a safer and less expensive alternative to traditional medicine"—but you may benefit from information available in outside sources. Use the keywords in your topic sentence to begin your search. If you were doing research to support the sentence above, you might try searching print and electronic databases for "herbal medicine," "herbal remedies," and "alternative medicine"—as well as the names of any specific herbs you think you might discuss in your paper. (See Chapter 19, Writing from Reading, for guidelines about using and citing sources in your writing.)

Activity

Discovering Details, Facts, and Evidence

Choose one of the following topic sentences. Identify the word or phrase that conveys the controlling idea. Then work with another student to brainstorm details, facts, and evidence that you could use to support the controlling idea.

A. Professional wrestling should be taken off of the air.
B. A student's life is stressful.
C. There are three important things to remember when giving an oral presentation.

Building a Support Structure

It's time to think like an architect again and begin to build your support structure. Once you have a topic sentence with a controlling idea and a scattered collection of supporting information, you can begin to put into place the statements that will provide primary support and secondary support for your topic sentence.

Primary Supports

Begin by reviewing the supporting information you currently have and identifying those items that might best support your controlling idea. Once you have identified those items, put the ideas in sentence form. These sentences will be the major support sentences—the **primary support**—in your paragraph. These sentences are primary supports because they function as the strongest and most important details, facts, and evidence that you will use to support the controlling idea in your topic sentences.

Effective primary supports

- relate directly to the controlling idea,
- are more specific than the topic sentence,
- can be developed further.

Each primary support should be less general than your topic sentence (the first level of generality) and should provide details that directly support the topic sentence. Primary supports should not be so specific that they cut off further development, however. You will further develop your paragraph with secondary supports—but we will discuss those a little later.

Effective primary supports relate directly to the controlling idea and are more specific than the topic sentence, but they can be developed further.

Let's return to the student who has chosen to write about "many exciting places for tourists to visit" in Washington, D.C. Because his brainstorming list (see page 55) contains more information than he could possibly use in a paragraph, he takes the time to choose the items that he thinks will provide the most effective support for his controlling idea. He decides to use a questioning strategy *(Who? What? When? Where? Why? How?)* to evaluate the usefulness of his support information.

Where in Washington should all tourists make it a point to visit?

What is it about these places that makes them so important and exciting?

Why are these places more significant than the other places on the list?

The writer annotates his list:

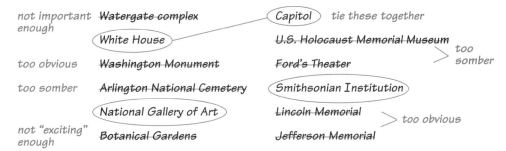

not important enough	~~Watergate complex~~	Capitol	tie these together
	White House	~~U.S. Holocaust Memorial Museum~~	too somber
too obvious	~~Washington Monument~~	~~Ford's Theater~~	
too somber	~~Arlington National Cemetery~~	Smithsonian Institution	
	National Gallery of Art	~~Lincoln Memorial~~	too obvious
not "exciting" enough	~~Botanical Gardens~~	~~Jefferson Memorial~~	

He decides that the three presidential memorials, for example, are indeed interesting and important places to visit in Washington, D.C., but they are obvious stopping places and can be appreciated quickly, even from a distance. Other places such as Ford's Theater (where Lincoln was assassinated), the Holocaust Memorial, and the Arlington National Cemetery are also important stops for a visitor to make, but rather than "exciting" places to visit, these are more somber, reflective stops. The Capitol building and the White House, however, are more appropriate as support for the controlling idea of *exciting places to visit,* especially for first-time visitors.

After a careful process of review and selection, several items will stand out as the strongest primary supports for your controlling idea. The student writer of the Washington, D.C., paragraph decides he will focus on the Smithsonian, the National Gallery of Art, and the two major landmarks of American government: the White House and the Capitol. (Note that instead of planning separate primary supports for the White House and Capitol, the writer thinks about how these sites are similar and then groups them together as important government landmarks.)

The writer now drafts sentences of primary support. As you draft your sentences of primary support under your topic sentence, you should see your paragraph begin to take shape.

Topic Sentence:	Washington, D.C., has many exciting places for tourists to visit.
Primary Support 1:	One of the most fascinating places to see in Washington, D.C., is the Smithsonian Institution.
Primary Support 2:	Another spot that every visitor will want to see is the National Gallery of Art.
Primary Support 3:	Finally, no trip to Washington, D.C., would be complete without stops at America's two most important government landmarks: the White House and the Capitol.

Each of the primary support sentences does two important things:

1. It directly and effectively supports the controlling idea (by answering the promise of "many exciting places").
2. It leaves open the possibility for further development and discussion.

As you will see in the next section, "Secondary Supports," the writer can easily continue to develop this paragraph by providing specific details that show *why* he has singled out each place as a must-see for visitors. But for now, the topic sentence and the primary supports provide a solid structure for the finished paragraph. When you find yourself at this stage, take a breath. But don't throw away any of your prewriting yet. As you begin to develop your paragraph more fully, you may wish to delete one of your primary supports in favor of another potential support item, or you may wish to add still more primary supports to your paragraph.

Activity

Choosing Primary Supports

Read each of the sentences below, and determine which ones might serve as primary support for the topic sentence listed. Remember that primary support relates directly to the controlling idea and promises further development.

Topic Sentence: Women who drink alcohol during pregnancy risk harming their unborn children.

Babies born of alcoholic mothers are frequently retarded.
Pregnant women who drink often don't exercise as much as they should.
Doctors have compiled detailed studies on pregnant women who are heavy drinkers.
Studies have indicated that if a pregnant woman consumes an average of one or two ounces of alcohol per day, there is one chance in five that her baby will develop a serious disease called fetal alcohol syndrome.
Alcohol makes pregnant women feel sluggish.
Pregnancy often involves some degree of risk.
Pregnant women who are alcoholics frequently neglect their health and rarely maintain a proper diet.
Alcoholic women who are expecting a baby can easily forget important appointments with their physicians.

Activity

Writing Primary Support Sentences

For each of the following topic sentences, identify the controlling idea and then write three sentences of primary support for that controlling idea.

Controlling idea

EXAMPLE

Topic Sentence: Working students have unique problems.

Primary Support: Their time in the library is limited.

Primary Support: Fewer courses are offered in the evenings.

Primary Support: Work often causes them to miss class.

A. Topic Sentence: Tragedies bring people together.
B. Topic Sentence: Hollywood has given us different kinds of classic movie monsters.
C. Topic Sentence: Early detection is important in treating illness and disease.
D. Topic Sentence: Students who pay their own way through college value their education more than students who do not have to pay their own way.

Secondary Supports

Instead of reinforcing the controlling idea directly, as primary supports do, **secondary supports** reinforce primary supports by adding details that help to explain a primary support. They offer a writer's answer to the reader's challenge: *Tell me more.* For example, let's say you are planning your first trip to Washington, D.C. You may trust the writer who said earlier in this chapter that the most exciting places to visit are the Smithsonian Institution, the National Gallery of Art, the Capitol, and the White House—but you may not. You may find yourself asking, "Well, what's so great about the Smithsonian?" or saying, "Convince me." In other words, you may want the writer to tell you exactly why he is characterizing these four places as "exciting places for tourists to visit."

Take a look at the following informal outline, in which the writer has included two secondary support statements for every primary support. TS stands for topic sentence, PS is primary support, and SS is secondary support.

TS: Washington, D.C., has many exciting places for tourists to visit.

PS 1: One of the most fascinating places to see in Washington, D.C., is the Smithsonian Institution.

SS 1a: This world-famous museum displays thousands of items of great interest to anyone studying American culture and history.

SS 1b: Among the many permanent exhibits in the Smithsonian are the plane that Charles Lindbergh flew across the Atlantic and stones that the Apollo astronauts brought back from the moon.

PS 2: Another spot that every visitor will want to see is the National Gallery of Art.

SS 2a: The National Gallery holds one of the world's most outstanding collections of priceless original paintings.

SS 2b: The National Gallery houses a collection of sculpture that represents the finest achievements of both ancient and modern artists.

PS 3: Finally, no trip to Washington, D.C., would be complete without stops at America's two most important government landmarks: the White House and the Capitol.

SS 3a: The White House has been home to every American president since John Adams and is open to the public for daily tours.

SS 3b: The Capitol houses the Congress of the United States and has become the world's greatest symbol of democracy and freedom.

The secondary supports strengthen the paragraph by providing specific details that make the primary supports clearer and more convincing. For example, supports 1a and 1b offer specific reasons and examples to show *why* the Smithsonian is a place that visitors to Washington, D.C., will definitely want to visit. As you develop support for your topic sentence, keep this rule of thumb in mind: Primary supports reinforce the controlling idea directly. Secondary supports reinforce the primary supports and, indirectly, the controlling idea.

Secondary supports reinforce primary supports by adding details that help to explain a primary support. They offer a writer's answer to the reader's challenge: *Tell me more.*

(Turn to page 203 for information about writing a traditional formal outline.)

Activity

Writing Secondary Support Sentences

Write two sentences of secondary support for each primary support.

Topic Sentence: Job applicants should always look their best for an interview.

Primary Support 1: Job candidates should wear clothes that are pleasant and tasteful.

Primary Support 2: In addition, job candidates should make sure they look clean and well-groomed.

Primary Support 3: Above all, job candidates should appear cheerful and relaxed.

Guidelines for Keeping a Portfolio

Use these guidelines to make the most of your writing portfolio.

- **Understand what a portfolio is.** Basically, a portfolio is a collection. If you have been asked to keep a portfolio for your writing course, you need to maintain a collection of all of the paragraphs and essays that you write as part of your coursework. A writing portfolio can help you to see your progress as a writer over the course of a semester.
- **Know your instructor's expectations.** Your instructor may have specific requirements for the size and contents of your portfolio. Some instructors allow students to choose what type of folder to use for the portfolio; others have a specific preference. If your instructor has a preference (for example, a manila file folder, a case with a velcro or string closure, or an e-folder on a floppy disk), follow his or her instructions. Also, know what your instructor expects you to place *into* the portfolio. For example, does he or she require that all writing (prewriting, drafts, finished work) be included? Or perhaps just graded papers? Or maybe a specific number of papers (your best five paragraphs or essays out of the eight you wrote in the semester)? Again, know what is expected of you.
- **Keep a running table of contents.** It is often helpful to include a cover sheet that lists the papers in your portfolio. You can list them by title ("Chronic Fatigue Syndrome: Legitimate Medical Condition or Major Cop-Out?") or by description (Definition Essay #2). It may also be helpful to list goals for each assignment and the grade received, if graded.
- **Don't lose your work.** Keep a copy, either a photocopy or a computer file, of all of the work in your portfolio. Since much of the work in your portfolio likely includes comments from your instructor or from peer editors, make every effort to keep the original contents of your portfolio for the entire semester.
- **Stay organized.** Arrange the papers in your portfolio in reverse chronological order. This means the most recent paper you wrote will be up front, and the first paper you wrote will be in the back.
- **Build your skills.** As you write a new paragraph or essay, look back through your portfolio of previous papers for advice from your instructor (or other readers) about organization, support, focus, or other areas. Reviewing your portfolio each time you write can help you to avoid problems and build on your strengths.
- **Keep a writer's log.** You may be required to keep a log of what you have learned about writing or your own writing process as the semester continues. If you aren't required to do so, consider keeping one anyway.
- **Review your portfolio.** Some instructors require students to write a review of the portfolio at the end of the semester. (This review is sometimes called a *cover letter* or *reflective essay* or *portfolio introduction*.) This review gives a writer the opportunity to discuss briefly each piece of writing, to chart progress made through revisions, to demonstrate what he or she has learned about writing/the writing process, to recognize the challenges that remain, and to prepare the reader to evaluate the student's work.

☑ Writer's Checklist: Support

_____ Does your topic sentence have a clear and specific controlling idea?

_____ Have you developed support for your topic sentence by gathering any details, facts, and evidence that may show, explain, or prove your main point? In this process, have you:

- _____ returned to your prewriting to find details, facts, and evidence?
- _____ prewritten some more to find details, facts, and evidence?
- _____ conducted whatever research is necessary to find details, facts, and evidence?
- _____ asked yourself how else you can make your point clearer and more convincing?

_____ Have you chosen the best and strongest support points to be the primary supports for your controlling idea?

_____ Have you selected additional details that explain or further clarify the primary supports as your secondary supports?

Summary

1. Support is any specific detail, fact, or bit of evidence that you can use to show, explain, or prove your main point. Without support for your topic sentence, your reader is likely to remain unconvinced. (See p. 53.)
2. Using prewriting techniques such as brainstorming, freewriting, and questioning helps a writer to find possible support for a topic sentence and controlling idea. Looking back at prewriting that was done to narrow or explore a topic can also help you to develop support. (See pp. 53–55.)
3. Sometimes, the best supporting information for your controlling idea comes from outside sources. Don't overlook the opportunity to do some research. (See p. 55.)
4. Primary supports reinforce the controlling idea of the topic sentence. They function as the strongest and most important support statements that a writer uses to show, explain, or prove the main point of the paragraph. (See pp. 56–58.)
5. Secondary supports strengthen a paragraph by providing specific details that make the primary supports clearer and more convincing. (See pp. 59–60.)

Writing Activities

Other Writing Activities

1. For each of the following paragraphs, work with a partner to identify the topic and the controlling idea expressed in the topic sentence. Then decide whether the remaining sentences offer primary support or secondary sup-

port. If any sentence fails to support the controlling idea either directly (as primary support) or indirectly (as secondary support), delete it.

A. (1) Pet owners who wish to keep their dogs fit and trim need to understand the reasons overweight dogs tend to become obese. (2) The most common reason dogs become overweight has to do with lack of exercise. (3) If a dog consumes more calories than it burns, it gains weight. (4) Similarly, dogs that lead idle lives also tend to become bored, and bored dogs tend to become overweight. (5) Like humans, dogs often eat when they are bored as a way of indulging themselves. (6) Another factor contributing to canine obesity is neutering. (7) The exact reasons neutered pets gain weight are uncertain, but neutered animals definitely have a greater tendency toward obesity than do their unneutered counterparts. (8) Some diseases can also contribute to a dog's gaining weight. (9) Glandular diseases, for example, tend to increase a dog's appetite. (10) Finally, puppies that are overfed tend to become overweight as adults. (11) By feeding a puppy too much food, dog fanciers inadvertently increase the number of fat cells in their pet, thus predisposing it to obesity and illness.

B. (1) If a wooden pool cue is to remain an accurate piece of equipment, it must be properly cared for. (2) The tip, or crown, of the cue should be kept rough and well chalked. (3) Keeping the tip of the cue in good condition helps prevent it from slipping when it strikes the ball. (4) The first eight inches of the cue's shaft should be rubbed with steel wool and kept covered with a layer of baby powder. (5) This procedure keeps oil and residue from collecting at the end of the stick and producing unnecessary friction. (6) Excess friction can severely impair the speed and accuracy of a pool shot. (7) In addition, the cue stick should be kept away from extreme heat and dampness. (8) Heat and moisture cause the stick to warp, making shooting a ball on center difficult. (9) For this reason, wooden pool cues should be kept in a case when not in use. (10) Cue cases reduce exposure to heat and moisture.

C. (1) There are three popular fallacies concerning Egyptian pyramids. (2) First, they were not built by slaves but by farmers. (3) During the spring, when the Nile overflowed its banks and flooded adjacent farms, farmers who could not till their fields were hired by the pharaoh to work on the construction of the pyramids. (4) These workers were paid in food and were free to quit whenever they wished. (5) Second, the pyramids weren't, as some people think, built by ancient astronauts as landmarks for flying saucers. (6) They were built as memorials to the pharaohs who were buried within them. (7) Third, pyramids were not built as sturdily as most people imagine. (8) The reason that they have survived for so long is the lack of humidity and rainfall in the Egyptian climate. (9) If the pyramids had been built in a climate like Michigan's, they would have been a heap of decayed and scattered stones by now.

2. Consider the topic sentence that was used for the Washington, D.C., model discussed in this chapter: "Washington, D.C., has many exciting places for tourists to visit." Substitute for Washington, D.C., the name of a city where you grew up or where you once visited. Then develop support for that topic sentence by writing three primary supports and at least three secondary supports that support the controlling idea of *exciting places for tourists to visit.*
3. Write a paragraph using one of the following topic sentences. In your paragraph, use three primary supports and follow each primary support with two secondary supports.

   A. Preparing a Thanksgiving dinner involves more than just roasting a turkey.
   B. Not all students want the same thing from a college education.
   C. Several rock stars (or you could use *film stars*) have made significant contributions to society.
   D. Different kinds of vehicles suit the needs of different kinds of people.

4. Write a paragraph on one of the following general topics. First, you will have to narrow your topic (see Chapter 3) and write a topic sentence that conveys a controlling idea (see Chapter 4). Develop your paragraph using primary and secondary supports. Underline each primary support and make sure it relates directly to the controlling idea. Then make certain your secondary support statements give additional details and explanations that clarify and strengthen the primary supports.

   A. Dancing
   B. My favorite movie
   C. Taxes
   D. Sex symbols
   E. Slang
   F. Product slogans
   G. Computer games
   H. A pastime I absolutely cannot appreciate

5. Don't forget your portfolio! When your instructor (or peer-review partner) returns the paragraphs you wrote for this chapter, place them in your portfolio. Look through the paragraphs in the folder. Are you improving? Are there areas where you need work? (See page 61 for advice about making the most of your portfolio.)

Chapter 6

How to Organize Support and Write a Draft

By this point in the writing process, you have a strong foundation for a successful paper. You have

- *determined your purpose* (your reason for writing) *and your audience* (your reader or readers;
- *narrowed your topic* to one that is specific, that interests you, and that grows out of your knowledge, experience, or research;
- *written a topic sentence* that includes your narrowed topic and conveys a controlling idea (main point);
- *considered the best ways to show, explain, or prove your main point* by gathering details, evidence, and facts to use as primary supports and secondary supports.

In addition to being clearly focused and well supported, effective writing is well organized. A paragraph is well organized if the ideas and events within it are presented in the order that best shows the relationships between them. This chapter will help you to determine the best way to organize your supporting statements.

Three Ways to Organize Your Support

The following are the most common ways to arrange support for a topic sentence:

time order
space order
order of importance

Depending upon your topic, your purpose, and your audience, you may find that one way works better than the others for your paragraph.

Time Order

Time order, also called *chronological order,* simply means that events in a paragraph are arranged in the order in which they occurred or in which the reader would expect them to occur. If a paragraph focusing on a series of events does not discuss the events in chronological order, readers will feel that it is disordered. Time order is most useful when you are telling a story or describing a process.

The following paragraph, which presents directions for preparing and eating burritos, is organized according to time order:

> Burritos are as easy to make as they are fun to eat. First, take a package of frozen tortillas out of the freezer, remove the tortillas, and spread them out on a cookie sheet. Preheat the oven to 400°, place the tortillas in the oven, and bake them for approximately eight minutes. After baking, cover them to keep them moist. Then brown one pound of hamburger meat mixed with onion and chili seasoning. While the hamburger is browning, empty an eight-ounce can of pinto beans into a bowl and heat them in the microwave. While the beans are warming, grate four ounces of cheddar cheese, shred one quarter of a head of lettuce, and chop two tomatoes into small pieces. When all the ingredients—the tortillas, the browned hamburger meat, the pinto beans, the cheese, the lettuce, and the tomatoes—are ready, it is time to put the burrito together. Lay each tortilla out flat. Now put some of the warm beans onto the tortilla, and spread a small amount of hamburger on top of the beans. Sprinkle the cheese over the hamburger, and top it with the lettuce and tomatoes. To enjoy a burrito, you must learn the trick of folding the tortilla so that the mixture inside will not fall out. First fold the bottom flap up, then the right side over, and finally the left side over. Now it's time to eat and enjoy!

Organization is the key to understanding the process being described in this paragraph. Imagine the confusion if the writer had told the reader to insert the hamburger before it was browned or if the writer had left out a step completely—say, preheating the oven.

> Time order is most useful when you are telling a story or describing a process.

The following paragraph about mistakes that job applicants make during interviews is also effectively organized through time order:

> Job applicants who are well qualified for the position they are seeking sometimes fail to be hired because of a slip they make before or during the interview. For example, some candidates do not dress properly. One applicant may appear for an interview in clothes that are much too casual to convey a sense of respect for the job to a prospective employer. Another may make a bad impression by overdressing for an interview. Some applicants, although dressed tastefully, arrive five or ten minutes late for an interview, only to find that the interviewer has moved on to the next candidate. Other applicants talk too much during an interview. In their eagerness to please, they are entirely too chatty and end up annoy-

ing the interviewer. And, finally, when the interview turns to the question of salary, some applicants appear more interested in this aspect of the job than in the duties they will have to perform. Such applicants may impress the potential employer as being self-seeking rather than committed to hard work.

In providing examples of reasons that qualified job applicants are sometimes not hired, the writer *first* points to failure to dress properly, *then* to arriving late for the interview, *then* to being too talkative, and *finally* to showing too much interest in money. Because these mistakes are presented in the order in which they are likely to be made, the paragraph's organization seems logical and natural to the reader.

Activity

Placing Events in Time Order

The following topic sentence is followed by a series of supporting sentences. Number the supporting sentences according to the time sequence in which they are likely to occur.

Topic Sentence: Learning to go up and down stairs on crutches takes time, but it is not as difficult as most people think.

The patient quickly brings the crutches up to the next step and braces herself.

While going down the stairs, the patient places the crutches on the first step beneath her.

She repeats this process of leg first, then crutch until reaching the top of the stairs.

The physical therapist slowly explains and demonstrates both procedures.

Going up the stairs, the patient steps on the first step with the unbroken leg.

The patient repeats this procedure of crutch first, then leg until reaching the bottom of the stairway.

The patient steps down with the unbroken leg, making sure to keep the broken leg slightly in front of the other in order to prevent stumbling on the stairs.

After the patient has experimented on the practice stairs, she realizes that it really isn't that difficult, even though there is a little time involved.

After the therapist demonstrates the process, the patient must practice until it has been learned properly.

Space Order

Another way to organize the support in a paragraph is according to **space order**—that is, according to a visual arrangement or pattern. Space order is most useful in describing a physical place or object. For example, while one student was planning her paragraph about how the recent renovations to her campus health center have improved access for physically disabled students, she chose to order the paragraph according to the physical layout of the building. She began by discussing the new ramps and automated doors that provided easy access to the ground floor of the building. She then went on to discuss the benefits of the large addition to the ground floor and the two new elevators. She finished by describing specific features of individual rooms: wider doorways, lower examination tables, and support bars in restrooms. When she finished her draft, one of her classmates told her he could "travel" through the building with her paragraph as a guide. The writer then knew she had chosen the best organization for her topic.

Space order is most useful in describing a physical place or object.

Because space order enables your reader to visualize what you are describing, it can be a particularly effective way to organize your writing. In the following paragraph, the supporting sentences are effectively arranged according to a spatial pattern:

> Each major section of Wisconsin is noted for the food that it provides the nation. Bordered on the north by Lake Superior and on the east by Lake Michigan, the northeastern section of the state supports a thriving fishing industry. Every year thousands of tons of trout, salmon, perch, and bass from the region are harvested for sale to the public. Indeed, few other areas in the country produce as much fish as northeastern Wisconsin. While the southeastern portion of Wisconsin also boasts a fishing industry, it is primarily noted for the fruit grown in its orchards. Because it has milder winters and warmer summers than the northern part of the state, southeastern Wisconsin has a climate ideally suited to raising peaches, apples, cherries, and other fruits. The southwestern section of Wisconsin, on the other hand, is one of the most famous grain-producing areas in the world. Its rich soil is perfect for growing wheat, barley, and especially corn, the region's most important product. More rocky than the southwestern part of the state, the northwestern section of Wisconsin earns the state the title "America's Dairyland." Every day the thousands of cows that graze on the rolling hills of northwestern Wisconsin produce millions of gallons of milk, much of which is processed into butter, cream, or cheese. Like the other regions of Wisconsin, this area has an identity all its own, created at least in part by the food it produces.

The writer of this paragraph could simply have listed the many foods produced in Wisconsin. Instead, he divided the state into four sections and discussed each region in terms of the food produced there. As a result, readers are able to "follow" the writer as he "moves" clockwise from region to region. In doing so, they also learn that the state's food production and its geography are closely linked. The paragraph is more logical than it would have been if the writer had merely listed food products one after another.

Activity

Making a Floor Plan

Imagine that you've been assigned to write a paragraph using one of these topic sentences:

> Most supermarkets have a familiar layout.
>
> Most libraries have a familiar layout.
>
> Most laundromats have a familiar layout.

Draw a map of the supermarket, library, or laundromat you know best, and then write three to five sentences of primary support for the topic sentence. Then ask yourself why you arranged your primary support sentences the way you did.

Order of Importance

Still another way you can organize the supporting material in your paragraphs is to arrange your ideas according to their **order of importance**—that is, according to how strongly you wish to emphasize each one. (This organizing method is also called *emphatic order.*) With this method, you present the least important idea first, then the next important, and so on until you end the paragraph with the most important idea. Importance order, a save-the-best-for-last method of ordering supporting sentences, is useful for persuading readers or for making an argument.

In the following paragraph, for instance, the student writer organizes the ideas in her paragraph from least important to most important:

> Most students dislike spur-of-the-moment, in-class writing assignments. In the first place, they may not have with them the kind of paper or pen that they like to use, and they will probably find themselves without a dictionary. Second, students often find that if the choice of topic is left to them, they are unable, on such short notice, to think of anything worthwhile to write about. If, on the other hand, they are given a number of topics to choose from, they may not be able to think of enough to say about any of them. A still greater source of discomfort for many students is the classroom environment itself. Nervous students may be whispering and coughing, asking the teacher questions, or otherwise distracting those who are trying to concentrate. The most difficult problem with unannounced, in-class writing assignments, however, is the pressure involved. Students know that they have only forty-five or fifty minutes in which to produce a finished paragraph or essay, and every glance at the clock causes a rise on the pressure gauge. Being compelled to produce a well-written paragraph or essay on demand creates so much pressure, in fact, that some students are unable to write anything and therefore turn in a blank sheet of paper. Other students, feeling the pressure almost as much, submit a few incoherent sentences. And most students would admit

that whatever writing they turn in is bound to be the worst they have produced during the semester.

In this paragraph, the writer discusses causes for students' dislike of in-class writing assignments in this order: lack of writing materials, difficulty in choosing a topic, classroom distractions, and the pressure to perform. By moving from a valid but mild cause, to more important factors, and finally to the most important cause—pressure—the writer achieves a well-developed, well-organized paragraph.

When you decide to arrange the supporting evidence in a paragraph according to order of importance, you may find it helpful to do the following. After you have selected the primary supports for your controlling idea, list them according to their importance to you, with the most important point first, the next most important point second, and so on. When you begin to draft your paragraph, reverse your list and discuss the least important point first; then move on up through your list so that you conclude your paragraph with the most significant point.

Importance order, a save-the-best-for-last method of ordering supporting sentences, is useful for persuading readers or for making an argument.

Activity

Determining Importance

The first sentence in each group below is a topic sentence. The rest of the sentences in the group are the primary supports for a paragraph that develops the topic sentence. Rearrange the supports according to what you believe to be their order of importance, placing the most important first, the second most important second, and so on. Then reverse the order of your supports according to the way they would appear in the finished paragraph.

A. Topic Sentence: Instituting a fall semester break at colleges results in many advantages for the student.

1. Students have the opportunity to take a break from the constant pressure of classes and exams.
2. Students catch up on work for classes that they are behind in.
3. Students have the opportunity to spend a few days at home visiting with family and friends.

B. Topic Sentence: Regular exercise is beneficial in four important ways.

1. Regular exercise has been proven to prolong life.
2. Exercise can be a fun pair or group activity.
3. Regular exercise helps achieve weight loss goals.
4. People who are physically fit have more energy than those who are not.

C. Topic Sentence: The American jury system is in jeopardy for several reasons.

1. Court testimony and evidence are becoming far too complex for the everyday juror to understand and interpret.
2. Most people view jury duty as a needless hassle that distracts from their work and their family responsibilities.
3. Lawyers often prevent potentially competent jurors from participation by excusing them without valid reason.
4. Jurors who are involved in certain types of trials run the risk of being sought out afterwards for retribution.
5. Today's trials and subsequent deliberations can be lengthy, inconveniencing jurors for long periods of time.

Tips for Writing a Draft

Writing a draft means writing the first whole version of your paper. We say *the first* whole version because it's likely that you will rewrite some parts of your paper after you get feedback from others and spend some time evaluating how you can improve the draft. There is no magic number of drafts that you should write before you submit the final version of your paragraph, but you should write at least one. Why?

- It provides a built-in opportunity for improvement.
- It allows you to concentrate on stating a clear point and supporting that point without worrying about grammar and mechanics.
- It gives you, your instructor, and reviewers something to respond to.
- It means you are more than halfway through your writing project.

☑ Writer's Checklist: Organizing and Drafting

_____ Have you reminded yourself of your topic, your purpose, and your audience?

_____ Have you reread your topic sentence and your support statements?

_____ Did you choose what you feel is the best way to organize the support for your topic sentence?

  _____ Time order: Support points arranged in the order in which they occurred or in which the reader would expect them to occur.

  _____ Space order: Support points organized so that your reader can visualize what you are describing.

  _____ Importance order: Primary supports listed with your most important or strongest support first, then the next most important or strongest, and so on to the least important or least powerful. If you have employed importance order, did you reverse the list so that you "save the best (support) for last"?

Tips for Writing a Successful First Draft

1. Have all of your planning materials handy: your prewriting; your topic sentence; and any supporting details, facts, and evidence you have pulled together to help you make your point.
2. Begin your paragraph with your topic sentence, indenting the first word. (If you are drafting on a computer, press the tab key once to indent.)
3. Write the remainder of your draft in complete sentences.
4. If you are required to write a concluding sentence for your paragraph, check the guidelines on page 9 of this text.
5. If you are writing on a computer, double-space your draft so that you, your instructor, and your peer reviewers will have room to make revision suggestions.
6. If you are writing your draft by hand, use white lined paper, and write on every other line (skipping a line in between the lines that you write).
7. If you are required to submit a paper copy of your draft, make sure to keep a copy for yourself so that you can begin to revise when you are ready.

_____ Did you write a draft that begins with your topic sentence and includes complete sentences of primary and secondary support in the order you have determined is best for your paragraph?

_____ Did you submit a double-spaced draft, keeping a copy for yourself?

Summary

1. A paragraph is well organized if its supporting sentences are presented in an order that shows a clear relationship between them. (See p. 65.)
2. The basic organizational patterns for ordering supporting sentences are time order, space order, and order of importance. (See p. 65.)
3. Time order (also called *chronological order*) means that the supporting elements in a paragraph are arranged in the order in which they occurred or in which the reader might expect them to occur. Time order works well for telling a story or describing a process. (See pp. 65–67.)
4. Space order enables a reader to visualize what is being described. Supporting sentences are arranged according to a logical visual "map" of the place or object that the writer is writing about. Space order is often best for describing a place or object. (See pp. 67–69.)
5. Importance order (also called *emphatic order*) means that the supporting details, facts, and evidence in a paragraph are arranged according to how

strongly a writer wants to emphasize each one. Generally, writers using this pattern begin with their least important point and end with their most important point. Importance order is helpful for persuading readers. (See pp. 69–70.)

6. There are several benefits to writing a first draft. A draft is a version of your paragraph in which the first sentence is indented, the topic sentence appears first, your supporting ideas are expressed in complete sentences, and your primary supports and secondary supports are arranged in the most effective order for your topic, purpose, and audience. (See pp. 71–72.)

Writing Activities

Other Writing Activities

1. Think of a process that you experience on a regular basis—for example, a morning ritual or a job-related activity. Then communicate that process to a partner in the order in which you perform it, being certain not to leave out any steps. After you have detailed that process, ask your partner to tell you what he or she can remember of your process. Has your partner forgotten any steps? If so, why? Did he or she order any of the steps incorrectly? Would the process have suffered greatly with those steps out of order? Share your results with the class. (For help with working with a classmate, see the "Guidelines for Working with Others" on page 26.)
2. Using time order to organize your supporting sentences, write a paragraph on one of the following topic sentences. Be sure that your supporting points consistently follow a chronological sequence and that no important point is left out.

   A. From start to finish, moving from one apartment (or house) to another can be a demanding chore.
   B. Teaching someone to drive a car can tax the patience of even the best of friends.
   C. A handful of important inventions have changed the course of the world.
   D. Each of the pets I have owned has had its own unique personality.

3. Write a paragraph using one of the following topic sentences. Order your support according to space order. Remember to try to describe your supporting details so that your readers can visualize their spatial relationships.

   A. From bumper to bumper, a minivan (or other vehicle) is a better buy than a sport utility vehicle (or other vehicle).
   B. Children's playgrounds can be dangerous places.
   C. Students sit in different parts of the classroom for a variety of reasons.
   D. An old house frequently has a number of hidden problems.

4. Develop a set of primary supports for one of the following topic sentences. Then rank each primary support according to its importance, beginning with the most important support and working down to the support of least importance. Finally, reverse the order of your supports according to the way they would appear in the finished paragraph.

   A. Attending a distance-education class is different from attending a class taught by a site instructor.
   B. A student should consider several important factors when choosing a college.
   C. Owning a car (house, computer, business) has definite advantages.
   D. Children can learn a lot about money when they are still very young.

5. Do Activity 4 with a partner. After you've finished creating primary supports for A, B, C, or D, focus your discussion on how you might arrive at what is the most important primary support for the topic sentence. How would varying the *audience* of the paragraph affect which support is most or least important? Write down two potential audiences for a paragraph that uses the topic sentence and primary supports that you have chosen. Would you organize the paragraph one way for one audience and a different way for another audience? Rank the primary supports from most important to least important for each audience. (For help with working with a classmate, see the "Guidelines for Working with Others" on page 26.)

6. Look through your portfolio of paragraphs you have written so far. How have you organized each of them: By time order? Space order? Or order of importance? Choose one that you feel needs reorganizing. Write a note to yourself explaining which pattern of organization you should use and why. (For help with maintaining a writing portfolio, see the "Guidelines for Keeping a Portfolio" on page 61.)

Chapter 7

How to Revise for Stronger Writing

Experienced writers recognize the importance of revising their work. Revising gives writers the opportunity to think critically about the purpose of their writing, the audience for their writing, and the ways in which they can strengthen and clarify their point and their meaning. In the prewriting, organization, and drafting stages, writers figure out what they want to say; in revision, they figure out how they can say it best. When you revise, you may add or delete words, rewrite sentences, change the order of support points, or—gulp!—scrap much of your first draft and begin all over again.

What Is Revision?

Editing is like wiping down the kitchen counters to remove crumbs and spills. Revising, on the other hand, is more like replacing the counter tops after carefully considering your personal taste, your budget for the project, and the function of your kitchen.

Revision is the act of re*seeing*. When you revise a piece of writing, you take another look at your draft with the aim of improving it. Don't confuse revising with editing, the final step in the writing process (see Chapter 8). When you edit, you inspect your writing for problems with grammar, punctuation, spelling, and word choice. Editing is like wiping down the kitchen counters to remove crumbs and spills. Revising, on the other hand, is more like replacing the counter tops after carefully considering your personal taste, your budget for the project, and the function of your kitchen. When you revise, you ask yourself how you can make your point clearer, stronger, and more convincing by working on the paragraph's focus, unity, support, and coherence.

Revise for Focus

If you've ever listened to someone tell a story or make an argument and then found yourself asking the speaker, "What's your point?" you have recognized the

Preparing to Revise: Four Tips

1. **Give yourself time.** Spend at least a day away from your draft. Doing so allows you to come back to the draft with fresh energy and a clear head. Also, give yourself enough time to revise.
2. **Ask for feedback.** Whether they belong to a friend, coworker, classmate, instructor, or writing tutor, another pair of eyes and ears always helps to improve a draft. A reviewer can point out when you're getting off track or where an example isn't clear. (See the "Guidelines for Giving Feedback" on page 49 for more specific help.)
3. **Read your draft out loud.** Sometimes you'll notice gaps and inconsistencies when you "listen" to your paper.
4. **Use a checklist.** It helps to approach revision in a systematic way. Use the checklist on page 90 to help you identify problems with focus, unity, support, and coherence in your writing.

importance of focus in communicating an idea. Listeners often become impatient when a speaker lacks **focus**—a central idea or message—in his or her communication. Many readers feel the same way about unfocused writing, writing that doesn't make a clear point.

Your first step in revising your writing is to determine if your work is focused. Ask yourself:

- Does my paragraph have a clearly stated topic sentence?
- Does the topic sentence include my narrowed topic and a controlling idea (main point)?
- Is my controlling idea neither too general nor too specific for adequate development?
- Does my topic sentence state something that I can show, explain, or prove in a paragraph?

If you answer *no* to one or more of these questions, try to rework your topic sentence so that you begin your paragraph with a clear focus.

Revise for Unity

Once your paragraph has a clear and focused topic sentence, make certain that everything in your paragraph relates to it. A piece of writing is **unified** when every sentence supports the controlling idea expressed in the topic sentence. However, remember that not all sentences that relate to the topic of a paragraph necessarily help to unify the paragraph. If a sentence provides information about the topic that is accurate and interesting but doesn't develop or support the controlling idea, it will destroy the paragraph's unity.

To understand the importance of unity, examine the following paragraph, which is not unified:

> (1) Pilots' poor judgment is the primary cause of many aircraft accidents. (2) Ignoring their responsibilities, many pilots fail to perform their duties efficiently, and tragedy has all too often been the ultimate result. (3) National Transportation Safety Board records indicate that many fatal accidents have occurred, for example, because pilots failed to heed air traffic controllers' warnings about potential disasters. (4) To become an air traffic controller, one must be extremely intelligent. (5) Sometimes pilots are overtired, and they neglect to take the precautions necessary to avoid accidents. (6) They may even be taking certain drugs that slow down their physical reactions. (7) As we all know, statistics indicate that many college students abuse drugs, and these students should realize that if they continue to use drugs they will never enter careers such as aviation. (8) Sometimes accidents occur through a malfunction in the plane's equipment. (9) A door may open during flight, or a tire may blow out as the plane takes off. (10) Pilots, of course, aren't responsible for these kinds of accidents. (11) Perhaps most startling is the fact that every year one or two air traffic accidents are caused by student pilots who attempt journeys beyond their capabilities and end up causing catastrophes that destroy life and property. (12) Because they don't employ student pilots, commercial airlines are the safest form of air transportation. (13) The next time you take a commercial flight, you should be sure to ask yourself the following questions: Does the pilot look happy and healthy? What are the weather conditions outside? Do there seem to be any cracks in the wings or tail of the plane?

You might have had difficulty following the writer's reasoning in this paragraph. While all of the sentences in the paragraph relate at least in some way to the topic, *aircraft accidents,* the paragraph lacks unity because not every sentence supports the controlling idea that "pilots' poor judgment is the primary cause" of these types of accidents. In addition to supporting the controlling idea, this writer takes several detours to discuss qualifications for air traffic controllers (sentence 4), drug abuse among students who might wish to become pilots (7), mechanical malfunctions (8–10), and commercial airline safety (12). She even provides a list of precautionary questions for the commercial airline passenger (13). But since none of these sentences supports the controlling idea directly, they detract from the unity of her paragraph. With each sentence, we wonder what the writer is saying and why; we may even stop reading as we lose track of the idea we thought we were following.

A piece of writing is unified when every sentence supports the controlling idea expressed in the topic sentence.

The other sentences in the paragraph do support the controlling idea. If the writer had included only those sentences, the result would have been a more compact and unified paragraph:

Pilots' poor judgment is the primary cause of many aircraft accidents. Ignoring their responsibilities, many pilots fail to perform their duties efficiently, and tragedy has all too often been the ultimate result. National Transportation Safety Board records indicate that many fatal accidents have occurred, for example, because pilots failed to heed air traffic controllers' warnings about potential disasters. Sometimes pilots are overtired, and they neglect to take the precautions necessary to avoid accidents. They may even be taking certain drugs that slow down their physical reactions. Perhaps most startling is the fact that every year one or two air traffic accidents are caused by student pilots who attempt journeys beyond their capabilities and end up causing catastrophes that destroy life and property.

When you revise, think about ways to improve the unity of your paragraph. Ask yourself these questions:

- Does every sentence in my paragraph support my controlling idea?
- Are there places where I detour from my main point?
- How can I revise so that my writing is unified?

Activity

Sharpening Unity

Read the following paragraph carefully. Collaborate with a partner to identify the controlling idea expressed in the topic sentence. Underline the controlling idea. Then, examine the paragraph for unity. Cross out any sentence or detail that does not develop the paragraph's controlling idea. (For help with responding to writing, see the "Guidelines for Working with Others" on page 26.)

A successful yard sale requires advance preparation. Approximately two weeks before the sale, a location and date should be determined. The location should be easy for people to find and large enough to hold a crowd of a few dozen people with plenty of room for the items on sale. Saturday mornings are an excellent time to hold a yard sale because more people are available to attend yard sales on Saturdays than on any other day of the week. For the yard sale to be a success, moreover, advance advertising is essential. Local newspapers should carry notices about the sale. In addition, well in advance of the yard sale date, signs directing buyers to the sale should be posted. Posters announcing the sale can be displayed in front of the home and at nearby intersections. During the week before the sale, the merchandise to be sold should be collected, categorized, and priced. Computer equipment and electronic items, for example, should be separated from clothing and tools. Most clothing purchased at yard sales is a good buy. Many people come just to get a bargain on clothing, especially baby clothes. Because most purchases range from two or three to ten dollars, a plentiful supply of one-dollar bills, five-dollar bills, and quarters is a necessity at every successful yard sale.

Revise for Support

While you read through your draft, try to imagine your audience's reaction. Do you think they will be convinced?

When you revise, you should make certain that you have made your point convincingly with enough supporting details, facts, and evidence. While you read through your draft, try to imagine your audience's reaction. Do you think they will be convinced? If you find that parts of your paragraph need strengthening to convince a reader, you may need to add or revise your primary and secondary supports.

How Much Support Is Enough?

Your primary supports and secondary supports should work together to develop and support your controlling idea effectively and logically. Sometimes the topic sentence provides a clue to the number of **primary supports,** as in the following examples:

This topic sentence	needs at least this many primary support sentences:
Having one's wisdom teeth removed can be a *frightening* and *painful* experience.	2
Regular exercise *relieves stress,* s*trengthens muscles,* and *reduces the risk of heart disease.*	3
Benjamin Franklin will long be remembered for his achievements as a *diplomat, inventor, printer,* and *writer.*	4
When planting new shrubs, one should follow *five basic steps.*	5

In each of the sentences, the italicized words suggest to the reader that a certain number of primary supports will follow. If your topic sentence and controlling idea make a similar promise, check whether your primary supports follow logically from your opening.

Not every paragraph you write, however, will have a topic sentence that commits you to a definite number of primary supports. For those that don't, you will have to decide how many primary supports—sentences that show, explain, or prove your main point—to include. A general rule of thumb (*not* a hard-and-fast rule) is to provide at least three primary supports.

Knowing how many **secondary supports** to use is more difficult than deciding on the number of primary supports. Keep this in mind: Secondary supports are necessary to back up any primary supports that you feel your readers are unlikely to understand or accept without additional explanation.

If your primary support is a straightforward and specific statement of fact, you probably don't need to develop it with secondary supports. Use secondary supports when your primary support is an assumption based on facts or ideas unfamiliar to your reader,

your primary support is a statement of fact that requires additional information before it can be fully understood, or

your primary support is a fairly general statement that needs the clarity of an additional detail or example.

Take a look at the following draft in which Rohan Singh, a student writer, describes an online shopping process. The topic sentence is the first sentence of the paragraph. Each primary support sentence is underlined and marked with a number. Each secondary support is marked with a number and a letter: Secondary support 1a, for example, supports primary support 1. Rohan has made notes in the margin of his draft to show where he could add additional primary and secondary supports.

Mention Amazon.com and BarnesandNoble.com.

other

Can a shopper "browse" by title, author, subject?

Oops! What about paying for the purchase?

(TS) Buying a book online is far simpler than the first-time Internet shopper might think. (1) First, select a book-selling Web site. (1a) Buyers can find shopping sites using an Internet search engine. (2) After contacting the Web site of your choice, select the book or books that you want to buy. (2a) If you already know which book or books you want to purchase, simply enter the title or author information on the appropriate line of the online order form. (3) Once you have decided to purchase, add your selections to your "shopping basket." (3a) If you decide later that you do not wish to make a purchase, you can remove unwanted titles from your basket or cancel the entire order. (4) When you have finished making your selections, proceed to the cyber checkout counter. (4a) First-time buyers may be prompted to set up an account on the site. (4b) Menu instructions will guide you on how to provide information necessary for establishing an account. (5) Finally, verify the order, and wait for delivery of your purchase. (5a) Most Web sites guarantee delivery within forty-eight hours of payment.

In examining his primary supports, Rohan realizes that he has missed an important part of the online shopping process: paying for the purchase. Since he knows this is the part of online shopping that consumers are most nervous about, he decides to add a primary support between 4 and 5. He also decides to add several secondary supports. For example, he'll include the names of some popular Internet booksellers to support primary support 1. He will also include information about browsing an online bookstore. The following paragraph shows Rohan

Secondary supports are necessary to back up any primary supports that you feel your readers are unlikely to understand or accept without additional explanation.

Singh's revised paragraph, in which the support for the topic sentence and the controlling idea is stronger and more convincing. Revisions are shown in color.

> *(TS) Buying a book online is far simpler than the first-time Internet shopper might think. (1) First, select a book-selling Web site. (1a)Amazon.com and BarnesandNoble.com are among the most popular major bookselling sites. (2a) Buyers can find other shopping sites using an Internet search engine. (2) After contacting the Web site of your choice, select the book or books that you want to buy. (2a) If you already know which book or books you want to purchase, simply enter the title or author information on the appropriate line of the online order form. (2b) If you don't know exactly what you want to buy, you can generally "browse"—by subject matter or author—the online shelves. (3) Once you have decided to purchase, add your selections to your "shopping basket." (3a) If you decide later that you do not wish to make a purchase, you can remove unwanted titles from your basket or cancel the entire order. (4) When you have finished making your selections, proceed to the cyber checkout counter. (4a) First-time buyers may be prompted to set up an account on the site. (4b) Menu instructions will guide you on how to provide information necessary for establishing an account. (5) Next, choose a method of payment. (5a) Most Web sites offer consumers the choice to pay with a credit card or by sending a check or money order. (5b) If you choose to pay by credit card, most sites now guarantee the security of your credit card information. (6) Finally, verify the order, and wait for delivery of your purchase. (6a) Most Web sites guarantee delivery within forty-eight hours of payment.*

When you revise your paper for support, ask yourself the following questions:

- Do I have enough details, facts, and evidence to show, explain, or prove my main point?
- Does my paragraph include enough primary support to convince my reader of my controlling idea?
- Does each primary support have enough secondary support when additional explanation or examples are needed?
- Is my support organized in the most logical manner for my purpose and audience?

Activity

Providing More Details

Read the following paragraph. As you read, pay close attention to the details, facts, and evidence provided to develop and support the controlling idea. Where does the writer need additional detail? Is the writer missing any obvious primary supports? Are there primary supports that need the help of secondary supports?

Anyone can resolve an argument with a friend or loved one by taking four important steps. First, each person involved needs to respect the other, even when they are in total disagreement about an issue. Second, the people involved should make it a point to find a comfortable and neutral location and rid the situation of distractions. A meaningful discussion can't happen when one person is, let's say, also trying to wait on customers at the video store or when the two are in a group with other people. Finally, each person needs to be open and honest about the issues involved. It is impossible, after all, to resolve an argument if the people involved don't really know—or admit—what they are arguing about. If the argument begins with a squabble about the laundry, for example, but is really about one person taking the other for granted, the two should say what the issues are—out loud.

Revise for Coherence

Coherence means "sticking together." When a paragraph is **coherent,** the reader moves smoothly from sentence to sentence without becoming confused or losing the writer's train of thought. Writers achieve coherence by providing signals that help the reader understand the relationships between sentences and ideas in a paragraph. If there are no guideposts along the way to indicate how one sentence or idea flows from another, the writing will seem choppy, awkward, and ineffective—even if the paragraph is unified and well-supported.

If there are no guideposts along the way to indicate how one sentence or idea flows from another, the writing will seem choppy, awkward, and ineffective—even if the paragraph is unified and well-supported.

Here are four ways in which you can strengthen coherence as you revise your paragraph:

- Use transitional words and phrases.
- Repeat key words and phrases.
- Combine sentences.
- Maintain grammatical consistency.

Use Transitional Words and Phrases

Transitional words and phrases—such as *therefore, in addition, for example,* and *on the other hand*—add coherence to your paragraphs by linking the ideas in one sentence with those in the next and showing their relationships. Transitions act as reminders of what you have already said and as signals indicating where you are going. When used effectively, they can make the difference between an easy-to-understand paragraph and one that is difficult to follow.

Transitions act as reminders of what you have already said and as signals indicating where you are going.

In this student's paragraph on the responsibilities of drivers involved in car accidents, the sentences are arranged in a logical order, but the paragraph lacks signals that could help readers see the relationship between the ideas. In revising his paragraph, the writer added transitions to improve the coherence of his paragraph.

> Owners or drivers of automobiles in this state should know the traffic laws concerning accidents. *For example, anyone* ~~Anyone~~ involved in an accident must remain at the scene until the police arrive. *In addition, the* ~~The~~ drivers should exchange names, addresses, and registration information. If the police are not present, someone should phone them as soon as possible. *But if* ~~If~~ an officer is present, the drivers can supply the necessary information at the scene of the accident. *Frequently, accidents* ~~Accidents~~ result in a great deal of damage and/or personal injury. If there is damage to one of the cars in excess of $250 but no injury, the driver of that car must file a written report with the Department of Motor Vehicles within thirty days. If there is *also* personal injury, both drivers have to file a report within five days. Sometimes people forget to file reports in the required time, and the result may be a severe fine. *Therefore, it* ~~It~~ is important to know state laws concerning the responsibilities of drivers involved in accidents.

Activity

Using Transitional Words and Phrases

From the list of transitional words and phrases on page 84, select the word or phrase that best fits in the indicated spaces in the following paragraph.

> Once you have set foot on Ireland's soil, you will never want to leave it. A land of many outstanding characteristics, Ireland has as its most striking quality a beautiful countryside. It contains, (1) _____ , a magnificent, flat-topped mountain, called Ben Bella, that hovers over the landscape. (2) _____ the mountains there are rock-ribbed hills where for centuries flocks of sheep have grazed. (3) _____ lining these hills are rock fences, originally constructed as boundaries by farmers who cleared the rocks from their croplands. (4) _____ , the traveler who wants natural beauty cannot visit a lovelier country than Ireland.

Common Transitions

To signal an example

especially	for example	for one thing	specifically
first of all	for instance	in particular	such as

To signal an addition

also	as well as	in addition	in the first (second, third) place
and	further	moreover	
another	furthermore		

To signal a contrast

although (even though, though)	in contrast	on the other hand	whereas
but	however	rather	yet
instead	on the one hand	still	

To signal a comparison

at the same time	in the same way	likewise, like	similarly
as			

To signal cause and effect

as a result	consequently	so	therefore, thus
because	finally	then	

To signal a concession

certainly	I admit	naturally	no doubt
granted (that)	I concede		

To signal time

after	eventually	meanwhile	soon
as	finally	next	then
at last	first (second, third)	now	when
before	last	since	while
during	later		

To signal space

above	below	inside (outside)	to the left (right, side)
across	beside	near, next to	under
at the bottom (top)	beyond	opposite	where
behind	farther (further)	over	

To signal importance

above all	in fact	most	worst
best	more (less) important	most (least) important	

Repeat Key Words and Phrases

Repetition of key words and phrases is another strategy you can use to achieve coherence in your paragraphs. Of course, words and phrases should not be repeated so often that they begin to distract the reader. Rather, to maintain focus on your controlling idea, you can repeat particular words and phrases that emphasize this idea. In the following paragraph, the writer maintains the focus on her controlling idea—the importance of the multivitamin in a child's diet—by either repeating certain key words or using closely related phrases:

> The *multivitamin* plays an important role in a child's diet. Laboratory tests show that most children do not obtain the recommended daily allowances *of vitamins and minerals* from the food they eat. To maintain and build healthy bodies, therefore, most children need a *dietary supplement.* One *multivitamin* each day provides the *vitamins* A, B-6, B-12, C, D, and E, as well as folic acid, thiamine, riboflavin, niacin, and even iron. For children who do not eat a well-balanced diet or who are unable to absorb essential *vitamins and minerals* from their regular meals, a single *supplementary tablet* may ensure good health.

In this example, repetition of the words *multivitamin* and *vitamins* keeps the focus of the paragraph clear. To avoid too much repetition, though, the writer also uses two closely related phrases: *dietary supplement* and *supplementary tablet.* These phrases add variety to the paragraph. They also add coherence because they echo the key words around which the paragraph is structured. When you revise your paragraph, check to see where you can help focus your reader's attention on your controlling idea by repeating a key word or phrase.

Activity

Identifying Key Words and Phrases

With a partner, identify all key words and phrases that are repeated in the following paragraphs. Also identify variations of key terms. (For help with working with a classmate, see the "Guidelines for Working with Others" on page 26.)

> Even with the popularity of the Internet, television provides one of the most effective means of advertising. One of the reasons for its effectiveness is simply that millions of Americans view television every day. It is estimated that the average American family watches "the tube" four hours a day. Second, television is more effective than, say, radio because TV can appeal to the prospective buyer through both ear and eye. Viewers who can see the product that is being sold are more likely to buy it. And, finally, television advertising in the last twenty years has become so sophisticated that television advertisers have been able to determine what kinds of audiences watch at specific times of the day. They can now air commercials that appeal specifically to the audience watching at any given time, and the result is, of course, that their pitches are more successful than when they promote their products randomly.

Combine Sentences

Still another way to achieve coherence in your paragraphs is to combine two or more short, single-idea sentences into a longer sentence that relates the same ideas clearly and more effectively. There is nothing wrong with short, single-idea sentences; however, too many of them in succession creates a choppy, monotonous rhythm and forces your readers to figure out the connections between your ideas. Combining sentences—and choosing which ideas to emphasize—often helps to improve continuity and cut down on monotony.

The following partial paragraph has a clear controlling idea and follows a logical order. The writer has begun to revise by combining sentences.

> El Castillo, is a marvel of the Western Hemisphere. ~~El Castillo is~~, an ancient pyramid, *built by the* ~~The~~ Maya Indians ~~built El Castillo~~ between 300 and 900 c.e., *which* The pyramid, is located in the ruins of the Mayan city of Chichen Itza, ~~Chichen Itza is located~~ on the Yucatan Peninsula *of Mexico,* ~~The portion of the Yucatan Peninsula that contains Chichen Itza is in Mexico. The pyramid~~ was used for religious ceremonies. El Castillo was dedicated to Kulkulcan, *who* ~~Kulkulcan~~ was a powerful god of creation and transformation. ~~The pyramid has four sides.~~ On each of the *pyramid's four* sides is a staircase. At the base of the staircases are serpents' heads *that* ~~The serpents' heads~~ point to natural wells *where human* ~~Human~~ bones and jewelry have been found. ~~in these wells. Human bones and jewelry are~~, evidence of human sacrifices ~~The sacrifices were made~~ to Kulkulcan.

Activity

Combining Sentences

Combine these sentences into a brief paragraph of three to five sentences. Your new sentences should better express the relationships between the ideas in the original sentences.

A. Tornadoes are found in severe thunderstorms.
B. Tornadoes are intense low-pressure areas.
C. Tornadoes are only a few hundred feet in diameter.

D. Measuring devices are broken when tornadoes hit them.
E. The measuring devices cannot measure the speed of the winds in tornadoes.
F. The tornado first touches down on a mountaintop.
G. In such a situation, the tornado may skip along the mountain peaks.
H. And the tornado will leave the valleys in between untouched.
I. A tornado leaves behind a trail of destruction.
J. The trail is also of devastation.
K. Houses are leveled.
L. Buildings are torn to shreds.
M. Some trees are uprooted.
N. Other trees are blown down.
O. People are killed and injured.

Maintain Grammatical Consistency

Writing that shifts from one point of view to another or from one verb tense to another is difficult to understand. As you revise, check your draft for grammatical consistency—or, more specifically, consistent pronoun person and consistent verb tense.

Consistent Pronoun Person

One of the choices writers make about their writing is its point of view. Paragraphs can be written from a first-person *(I, we)*, second-person *(you)*, or third-person *(he, she, it, they, one)* point of view. Whether you use first-person pronouns or third-person pronouns depends on the type of writing you are doing and on the kind of feeling you wish to generate in your writing.

Use:	**if you are:**
First person *(I, we)*	writing from personal experience
Second person *(you)*	writing instructions, giving advice, explaining a process
Third person *(he, she, it, they, one)*	writing about a subject in an objective (distanced) way (The third-person point of view is most appropriate for formal academic and business writing.)

The main point to remember about the use of pronouns, however, is that you should remain consistent in the person of your pronouns throughout each paragraph. Unless there is a clear-cut reason for doing so, mixing the persons of the pronouns in a paragraph usually results in awkward shifts in viewpoint that can destroy coherence.

This student writer bounces around from third-person (italics) to second-person (underlined) point of view as he begins his paragraph on the importance of cancer screening:

> Because early detection is still the first and best step to curing cancer, *every male* over the age of fifty should schedule regular prostate cancer screening tests with *his* primary care physician. During the first visit, *the patient* learns about two ways to screen for prostate cancer: digital rectal examination (DRE) and a prostate specific antigen (PSA) test. Of the two, the PSA test is the more controversial. A PSA test measures the amount of prostate specific antigen in your blood. If a man is in good health, *his* PSA reading is generally lower than 4.0 nanograms per milliliters of blood (ng/ml). Prostate cancer is just one of many reasons your PSA level may be higher than 4.0 ng/ml.

As you revise, think about your audience. The writer of the paragraph above, for example, should probably stick with third-person point of view—especially if he is not writing for the very specific, very clearly defined audience of "males over fifty." Third person is *generally* more appropriate for formal academic and business writing, though using the first person *I* is sometimes acceptable and more effective. However, never use the pronoun *you* in your writing unless you have a definite audience in mind. Once you choose the point of view most appropriate to your writing task, be consistent throughout your paragraph.

Consistent Verb Tense

Another choice writers make is whether to write in past, present, or future tense. Briefly stated, *tense* means "time." When you select a verb tense for a single sentence, you consider when the action or state of being that is expressed in the sentence occurs—in the past, in the present, or in the future. Similarly, when you select a predominant verb tense for a paragraph, you consider at what point in time a series of events or ideas exists.

There are three major tenses in English:

Present I look

Past I looked

Future I will look

If you begin a paragraph in one tense, you should stick to that tense throughout the paragraph. You can make exceptions, though, when a given sentence logically requires the use of another tense. For instance, when you recount a past experience as support for a topic sentence, shifting from the present tense into past tense is natural and not disturbing to your reader.

The writer of the following partial paragraph shifts back and forth unnecessarily between present, past, and future in her draft. Her annotations

Writing that shifts from one point of view to another or from one verb tense to another is difficult to understand.

show how she revised her verbs throughout to be in the present tense. When she maintains a consistent tense, her writing is smoother and more coherent, and thus much more effective.

> Starting college sometimes results in a quick weight gain for beginning students. One explanation for this rapid gain in weight is the pressure new students have to deal with. College students feel pressure mainly because so much more ~~will be~~ is expected of them as far as studies and grades are concerned. Such pressure makes students nervous, and, as a result, they eat more food. Social pressure also ~~played~~ plays an important role in weight gain, since going to parties to make friends increases their consumption of beer, soda, and snack foods.

Activity

Eliminating Shifts in Pronoun Person and Verb Tense

In the first paragraph, revise to eliminate shifts in pronoun person. In the second, revise to eliminate any shifts in verb tense.

A. I enjoy using my creative abilities when I teach elementary school. I prefer making my own teaching materials, such as educational games, learning centers, drill cards, and exercises. So when funds for professionally made textbooks and workbooks are low and materials are difficult to obtain, my students never suffer. And you find that your materials are better anyway. I also enjoy creating my own bulletin-board materials. Why should you go out and buy snowflakes or Thanksgiving scenes or letters made by a machine when you can make them yourself? My students appreciate the items on the bulletin board more when they realize the effort that I have put into them. And I find that my creative efforts help students to discover the rewards of using their own creative abilities. Can you imagine the satisfaction they feel when they see something they made—a map or a picture—up on the bulletin board? No professionally made materials can instill that sense of accomplishment and pride.

B. Driving erratically is a characteristic of some drivers. They weave all over the road as if unaware of their actions. On a four-lane road, these drivers will usually drive in two lanes because they are unable to stay in one. On a two-lane road, on the other hand, they drive down the center of the road, not only because they are unable to stay in one lane, but also because they were afraid of hitting the curb at the side of the road. When a car approaches from the opposite direction, they moved into their own lane slowly, scaring the other driver half to death. Therefore, careful drivers should be on the alert for erratic drivers who will not always stay in the proper lane.

As you revise, think about how you can make your draft more coherent. Ask yourself these questions:

- Are the ideas in my paragraph smoothly connected? Is the relationship between ideas and sentences clear?
- Have I chosen transitional words and phrases appropriate to the ideas in my paragraph?
- Can I revise or combine sentences to make them less choppy or awkward?
- Have I maintained a consistent point of view throughout my writing?
- Have I maintained consistent verb tense throughout my writing?

☑ Writer's Checklist: Revising

_____ Before revising, did you give yourself a break or ask for feedback from reviewers?

_____ In your effort to improve your draft, have you sharpened your focus?

    _____ Did you make certain your paragraph has a clearly stated topic sentence that includes your narrowed topic plus a controlling idea? Your topic sentence should state something that you can show, explain, or prove in a paragraph.

    _____ Have you reviewed your draft to ensure that it is unified?

    _____ Did you read your draft carefully, noting places where you detour from your main point?

    _____ Have you revised so that every sentence in your paragraph supports your controlling idea?

_____ Is the support for your topic sentence strong?

    _____ Read your draft from the point of view of your audience. Have you included enough support (details, facts, and evidence) to convince your audience of your main point? Is your support organized in the most logical manner for your purpose and audience?

    _____ Did you add (or reorganize) primary support statements where necessary to reinforce your controlling idea?

    _____ Did you add (or reorganize) secondary support statements where additional examples or explanation is needed?

_____ Are your support statements arranged coherently?

    _____ Are ideas linked smoothly and clearly by using transitional words and phrases and by repeating key words and phrases?

    _____ Did you combine some short, single-idea sentences into longer sentences that express related ideas clearly and more effectively?

    _____ Did you choose a point of view and primary verb tense and stick with them?

Summary

1. Revising means *reseeing* your writing and making changes to improve it.
2. Writers can prepare to revise a draft by giving themselves a break from the draft, asking for feedback from reviewers, reading the draft out loud, and using a revision checklist. (See p. 90.)
3. A paragraph is focused when it communicates a clear central point or message. Writers can improve their focus by making certain that the topic sentence is stated clearly. (See pp. 75–76.)
4. A paragraph is unified when every sentence supports the topic sentence and controlling idea. Revising often means looking for detours from the main point and dropping unrelated ideas. (See pp. 76–78.)
5. A paragraph is well supported when primary and secondary supports work together to provide enough evidence to show, explain, or prove the writer's main point. Revising means determining whether a topic sentence needs further support or a different arrangement of supporting statements. (See pp. 79–82.)
6. A paragraph is coherent when the ideas and sentences within it "stick together." Reading a coherent paragraph, the reader moves smoothly from one sentence to the next without being confused or losing the writer's train of thought. Writers strengthen coherence by using transitional words and phrases, repeating key words and phrases, combining sentences, and maintaining grammatical consistency. (See pp. 82–89.)

Writing Activities

Other Revising Activities

1. Read each of the following paragraphs carefully. Working on your own, specify the controlling idea expressed in the topic sentence and then examine the paragraph for unity. Identify by number any sentence that does not develop or support the paragraph's controlling idea.

   A. (1) The real cowboys of the American West had little resemblance to the myth created by films and television shows of the 1940s and 1950s. (2) First of all, not all cowboys were white. (3) Indeed, a substantial number of them were black. (4) Several thousand African Americans worked as cowboys during the era of the open range, and at times as many as one in four cowboys was black. (5) Secondly, not all cowboys were heroic. (6) Many became rustlers, bank robbers, and outlaws. (7) Even working cowboys were known for breaking the law. (8) In fact, such Western celebrities as Wyatt Earp and Bat Masterson built their reputations by protecting towns from the trouble that cowboys frequently caused at the end of cattle drives. (9) Finally, not all those who qualified to be called "cowboys" were boys at all. (10) On the contrary, many women rode the range, carried six-guns, and dressed in chaps, high boots, and the signature "cowboy hat." (11) At least two of these women, Annie Oakley and Calamity Jane, achieved celebrity status that equaled that of the most famous cowboy figures. (12) Calamity Jane became the focus of numerous popular novels and magazine stories, and Annie Oakley earned widespread fame as one of the best sharpshooters of the Old West.

B. (1) Soap operas deal with true-to-life problems. (2) Frequently depicted on soap operas, criminal acts such as murder and rape are problems that we all fear and may face, directly or indirectly, at some time in our lives. (3) Hundreds of murders occur weekly in the United States. (4) Rape, too, is an all too frequent crime that police and citizens in every major city try to combat and prevent. (5) Soap operas also show characters suffering from serious diseases, such as breast cancer and AIDS, which many people must face in real life. (6) One out of every four Americans will eventually suffer from cancer. (7) Many forms of cancer are curable if discovered during their early stages. (8) Fortunately, medical science has devised several effective tests for diagnosing cancer at an early stage. (9) Unfortunately, however, most people don't take the time to receive these important tests when they should. (10) If you know people who have symptoms that may indicate cancer, be sure that they receive the proper medical attention. (11) Otherwise they may suffer the unhappy fate of some of the characters on television soap operas.

2. Read the following paragraph carefully. Working with a partner, identify areas where additional details, facts, or evidence would make the controlling idea clearer or more convincing. Revise the paragraph to reflect your revision suggestions. (For help with working with a classmate, see the "Guidelines for Working with Others" on page 26.)

Despite its portrayal of brutality and bullying—real or manufactured—professional wrestling has become one of the most popular forms of sports entertainment in America. First, millions of viewers, primarily boys and men between the ages of twelve and thirty-four, tune in each week to matches hosted by the World Wrestling Federation (WWF) and World Championship Wrestling (WCW). The sport is so popular that the WWF's cable show *Raw Is War* was rated number one in cable programming for over a year. In addition, sales and rentals of pro-wrestling home videos routinely top others in the sports category. Second, professional wrestling's popularity is evident on the Internet. Finally, WWF and WCW merchandise sales have skyrocketed in recent years. Sales of consumer products related to pro-wrestling brought in $400 million last year. WWF action figures outsell even Pokémon merchandise.

3. From the list of transitional words and phrases (see page 84), select the word or phrase that best fits in the blank spaces in each of the following paragraphs.

   A. Genetic screening in business—testing the genes of employees to see if they are susceptible to workplace-related diseases—may present problems for the tested. (1) _____ , the genetic screening tests and technology in general are in their infancy stages. (2) _____ , many physicians and health professionals doubt their reliability. (3) _____ , once genetic information is recorded on employees, it cannot always be kept secret. Even though employees are assured that their medical files are confidential, clerical staff have access to them. (4) _____ , if they are entered into a computer database, they are available to anyone with access. (5) _____ , some argue that such screening procedures are violations of personal rights. (6) _____ , many cite similarities between genetic screening and drug testing, noting that both involve a process of obtaining information from unwilling individuals that might affect them adversely. Opponents of genetic screening point out that some employees with the potential for workplace diseases would rather run the risk than lose their jobs.

   B. One of the most useful techniques in the sport of body building is called *supersetting.* To understand supersetting, one must understand that in weightlifting a "set" is the completion of a specified number of repetitions of an exercise. Supersetting, (1) _____ , is the practice of combining sets of exercises for muscles located on opposite sides of the body. (2) _____ , one would do a set of an exercise for the muscle on the front of the arm, the bicep, and (3) _____ proceed immediately to a set of exercises for the muscle located on the back of the arm, the tricep. Supersetting is valuable because it saves time. One can work two body parts in the time it would normally take to work one. (4) _____ , supersetting promotes cardiovascular fitness by placing a greater demand on the heart and lungs. A (5) _____ advantage of supersetting is the sense of both stimulation and relaxation experienced when a part of the body is fully exercised.

4. Select a paragraph from your portfolio. Underline the transitional words and phrases that you used in that paragraph. Do you tend to use a variety of transitional words and phrases? Or do you rely on the same ones each time you write? Are there places where you might have used a transition and did not? Do you tend to use too many transitions? After answering these questions, revise your paragraph either by inserting appropriate transitional words and phrases to make it more coherent or by deleting or changing unnecessary or inappropriate transitions. (For help with maintaining a writing portfolio, see the "Guidelines for Keeping a Portfolio" on page 61.)

5. Underline all key words and phrases that are repeated in the following paragraph. Also underline variations of key terms.

    Owning a dog creates several responsibilities for the owner. First of all, feeding the new pet regularly is necessary to its well-being. A puppy needs to be fed twice a day as opposed to an adult dog, who needs feeding only once a day. Second, a healthy dog requires regular exercise. Taking it for daily walks or allowing it to run for lengthy periods of time increases its chances for good health and a sound muscular structure. Exercise also helps the dog to release the tension that builds up while it is confined. Finally, the dog must be protected from disease and health problems and therefore requires occasional trips to the veterinarian's office. It should be inoculated against distemper and rabies as well as tested for worms and skin ailments.

6. In this paragraph, too many of the sentences are of similar length and structure. Revise the paragraph for coherence, combining sentences where you can.

    Blood pressure is a force. This force is the flow of blood against the walls of the arteries. The pumping action of the heart creates this force. The pressure of the blood rises with each contraction of the heart. The pressure of the blood then falls as the heart relaxes. The blood goes throughout the body. The blood goes by way of a system. This system is a system of vessels. These vessels eventually return the blood to the heart. The movement of blood is rapid. A drop of blood usually requires less than one minute to complete a trip. This trip is from and to the heart.

7. Read the following paragraph carefully, and identify areas where the writing could be more coherent. Take notes on where the writer should add particular transitions, repeat key words, combine sentences, or be consistent in point of view and verb tense. Then rewrite the paragraph to reflect your revision suggestions.

    Of all the possessions successful bass anglers must have, four are highly important. Successful bass anglers must have a solid rod, a reliable reel, the proper bait, and a large quantity of patience. The rod should be approximately five and one-half feet in length and should have the proper degree of rigidity. The eyelets should be lined up and smoothly sanded to ensure the proper flow of the line when it is cast. The reel must provide a smooth cast. Its "drag" system will not function efficiently. Successful bass anglers need the right bait. Some anglers preferred plastic worms and others "top water" and shallow diving lures. Successful anglers know that the right kind of bait catches the most fish. They must have vast amounts of patience. Bass anglers may cast their baits for hours on end without so much as a strike. Anglers who had patience may be rewarded with a fine day's catch. Anglers who refused to give up may be rewarded with a fine day's catch.

Chapter 8

How to Edit for Clearer Writing

After you have revised your paragraph and have a draft that is focused, unified, well supported, and coherent, edit it one last time before handing it in. Of course, editing occurs throughout the writing process, but setting aside time at the end of your process to focus on problems of grammar, punctuation and mechanics, and word use as well as any English as a second language (ESL) challenges can increase your chances of success.

Successful writers know the benefits of careful editing:

- individual sentences that are easy to read and easy to understand
- a clear overall message that isn't lost among a bunch of errors

Use the Writer's Checklist presented in this chapter to help you edit your writing. The individual items in the checklist will refer you to the sections on editing in this text (Chapters 23–44).

The student who wrote the following paragraph feels satisfied with its content and is now ready to edit. His edits are shown here as handwritten annotations. You may prefer to do your editing completely on-screen at your computer. This writer, however, chose to print out his revised draft, mark the changes on his hard copy, and then make the changes to his computer file before submitting his final paper. Whichever way you choose to edit, be sure to proofread your paper after you enter the changes.

> *Pittsburgh*
> Roberto Clemente, the famous ~~Pittsburg~~ ^ Pirates out-
> fielder, was deserving of his nickname, "The Great One."
> *major leagues*
> In his eighteen-year career in the ~~Major Leagues~~, he
> *won*
> ~~nailed down~~ four batting championships. He was also the
> eleventh man in the ~~past~~ history of baseball to get
> *At his position in right field, he*
> three thousand hits. ~~He~~ was equally remarkable. ~~at his~~

~~position in right field.~~ He would make ~~unbeleivable~~ *unbelievable* catches of pop-flies in shallow center field, just behind second base, and he would ~~stole~~ *steal* home runs from batters by jumping above the right field fence and retrieving potential home runs from the stands. With his powerful arm, he would also intimidate hitters and runners*, throwing* ~~Throwing~~ them out at the ~~basis~~ *bases* or at home. What perhaps made Roberto Clemente truly "The Great One,"~~,~~ however, was his ~~humanitarianisms~~ *humanitarianism*. In fact, his death indirectly ~~resulting~~ *resulted* from his concern for ~~his fellow man~~ *other people*. Heading ~~a~~ *an* effort~~,~~ in 1972~~,~~ to bring relief to earthquake victims in Nicaragua, ~~It was necessary for~~ Clemente *had* to fly to Managua to ensure that food, clothing, and medical aid ~~was~~ *were* reaching the victims. On the way, the plane crashed*, killing* ~~The crash killed~~ the passengers and ~~was a shock and a sad event to~~ *shocking and saddening* Clemente's countless fans.

☑ Writer's Checklist: Editing

Grammar

_____ Is every sentence in your paragraph a complete sentence? (See pages 340–45.)
_____ Have you corrected run-on sentences? (See pages 346–50.)
_____ Do your subjects and verbs agree in number? (See pages 351–56.)
_____ Have you used the correct forms of your verbs? (See pages 357–63.)
_____ Do your pronouns agree with their antecedents in number and gender? (See pages 364–66.)
_____ Do your pronouns clearly refer to their antecedents? (See page 366.)
_____ Are the pronouns in your paragraphs in the proper case? (See pages 367–69.)
_____ Have you used adjectives and adverbs properly (for example, *good* vs. *well*)? (See pages 372–76.)
_____ Have you corrected misplaced and dangling modifiers? (See pages 377–81.)
_____ If your sentences have lists or paired items, are they parallel? (See pages 382–86.)

Punctuation and Mechanics

_____ Have you used commas correctly? (See pages 391–96.)
_____ Have you used apostrophes only where appropriate? (See pages 397–401.)

_____ Have you used semicolons correctly? (See pages 402–05.)
_____ If your paper contains quotation marks, have you used them according to the guidelines? (See pages 406–10.)
_____ Have you checked other punctuation that you have used for correctness? (See pages 411–16.)
_____ Have you used capital letters and lowercase letters appropriately? (See pages 417–22.)

Word Use

_____ Have you avoided slang, clichés, wordiness, and vague terms? (See pages 427–32.)
_____ Are your sentences varied in structure? (See pages 433–37.)
_____ Have you consulted a dictionary for the spelling of unfamiliar words or for words you tend to misspell? (See pages 438–44.)
_____ Have you chosen the appropriate spelling of commonly confused words (such as *affect* and *effect; to, too,* and *two*)? (See pages 445–50.)
_____ Have you avoided sexist language? (See pages 451–55.)

ESL Challenges (These questions will be most helpful for writers whose native language is not English.)

_____ Have you pluralized count and noncount nouns properly? (See pages 461–62.)
_____ Have you used articles correctly? (See pages 462–63.)
_____ Have you reviewed your verb forms to make sure that your use of verbs + infinitives, verbs + gerunds, progressive tense verbs, and phrasals are correct? (See pages 466–71.)
_____ Have you used prepositions correctly? (See pages 472–75.)

Summary

1. Successful writers know the benefits of careful editing: individual sentences that are easy to read and easy to understand, and a clear overall message that isn't lost among a bunch of errors.
2. When writers finish structuring their paragraphs and reviewing their work for focus, unity, support, and coherence, they edit for grammar, punctuation and mechanics, word use, and ESL challenges.

Writing Activities

Editing Activities

1. Using the Writer's Checklist on pages 96–97, edit the following paragraph:

There are many ways to reduce ones' chances of having a heart attack. One of the most important of these are to reduce the amount of saturated fat and Cholesterol in one's diet. For example, cooking should be done with water, polyunsaturated margarine, or you can use cholesterol-free cooking spray. Also, the amount of eggs and whole-milk dairy products can be strictly limited. Or replaced with an egg substitute and fat-free milk. Another way to avoid trouble is to keep trim life expectancy is longer for men and women who maintain a reasonable weight. Dieting may be necessary to be sure that they do not put on extra pounds. Another important safeguard against heart attack is regular exercise. People, who have sedentary jobs, and who do not make an effort to exercise are much more susceptible to heart attacks than those who's jobs involve physical activity or who engage in sports to stay fit. Finally, since smokers are known to be at greater risk for heart attacks than non-smokers, one should avoid smoking all together. Even long-time smokers who quit can improve there chances for survival. By and large, people can reduce their risk to heart attack by following these simple rules for maintaining a strong heart and the healthy cardiovascular system.

2. Using the Writer's Checklists on pages 90 and 96–97, edit a graded paragraph from your portfolio. (For help with maintaining a writing portfolio, see the "Guidelines for Keeping a Portfolio" on page 61.)
3. Practice being an editor. Exchange editorial suggestions with a partner. As you examine your partner's paragraph, use the Writer's Checklist on pages 96–97 as your guide. (For help with responding to writing, see the "Guidelines for Giving Feedback" on page 49.)

Part Two

Strategies for Writing Paragraphs

In Part One you learned about the process of writing effective paragraphs from the first stage of determining audience and purpose to the final stages of revising for strength and editing for clarity.

Part Two presents the various strategies that writers use to develop their writing. These strategies, also known as *methods of development,* provide not only a way to organize information within a paragraph but also a way to approach a topic from the beginning. A narrowed topic such as *narcolepsy* could suggest, for instance, a cause and effect paragraph (beginning with the topic sentence "Narcolepsy is a disease that affects a person's personal, professional, and academic life"), an example paragraph ("Today, narcolepsy can be treated in many ways"), a classification paragraph ("Of the several types of sleep disorders, narcolepsy is the least understood"), or even a narrative ("Laura Shea's life changed significantly when she developed narcolepsy, a neurological sleep disorder"). This section of the book will help you to determine which paragraph strategy best fits your assignment, your purpose, and your main point.

Chapter 9

Narration

What Is *Narration*?

To *narrate* means to tell a story. Narration is the most basic and familiar paragraph strategy because telling stories is something you do in everyday conversations. Usually you tell a story to illustrate a point. Narrative writing uses stories about events, experiences, and situations to communicate an idea to a reader. The challenge in writing a narrative paragraph is to make sure your story illustrates a point. For example, the writer who begins with this topic sentence

Topic: being a good parent — Controlling idea: doesn't always mean being your child's friend

> Some learn the hard way that being a good parent doesn't always mean being your child's friend.

will have to support the controlling idea by telling the story behind the lesson learned. The events in the narrative should make the point that good parenting and parent-child friendship do not always go hand-in-hand.

Guidelines for Writing a Narration Paragraph

1. **Make a point in your narrative.** Never tell a story just for the sake of telling a story. Decide what is important about the story, and communicate that idea in your topic sentence.
2. **Include the events of the story that are most useful for making your point.** Include only those events that most directly support your controlling idea.
3. **Include enough details to make the story vivid and real.**

Make a Point

Everything in your narrative paragraph should point to a conclusion that you want the reader to draw from the story. Many writers state that idea in the topic

Using Narration in Real Life

You already have experience telling and listening to stories that make a point.

- You tell a friend, "My first day of high school was the worst day of my life." Your friend asks, "Why? What happened?"
- You tell your boss that today's sales presentation to a potential client didn't go so well. He scowls and says, "Tell me everything."
- Your best friend calls to tell you that she just got engaged. You say, "Okay, start from the beginning. How did he ask you?"

sentence of the paragraph. The narrative that follows in the rest of the paragraph then illustrates—or tells the story behind—that point.

Read a narration paragraph.

Eva Karnaukh-Gordy, a student in a gender studies course, opens her paragraph with the following topic sentence:

Topic: Deborah Sampson | Controlling idea: was born in Plympton, Massachusetts, during the winter of 1760.

Her controlling idea, *was born in Plympton, Massachusetts, during the winter of 1760,* promises a story about Deborah Sampson's life. Here is Eva's draft paragraph:

> Deborah Sampson was born in Plympton, Massachusetts, during the winter of 1760. When the American colonies went to war with Great Britain for their independence, Sampson was filled with patriotic enthusiasm. She saw no reason why she couldn't fight as well as any man, so she disguised herself in a soldier's outfit and in 1782 enlisted in the army. She identified herself as a man named Robert Shirtlief. During the nearly two years after her enlistment, Sampson distinguished herself for her bravery and her heroism. Remarkably, no one seems to have discovered her secret. After she was shot in the leg, she took a knife and removed the bullet herself rather than seek medical treatment and risk discovery. At the end of the war, Sampson received an honorable discharge. She returned to Massachusetts, married, and raised three children. In later life, she asked for and was given a pension from the United States government for her services to her country. When she died in 1827, her husband received the first pension granted by the United States to the spouse of a female war veteran.

What's wrong with this narration paragraph?

Eva is effective in telling the life story of Deborah Sampson, but she gives her reader no sense of the point she is making in telling this story. What conclusion are we supposed to draw from the narrative? That patriotism will make a person do anything? That war veterans deserve benefits no matter who they are? Eva needs to revise her paragraph to include a topic sentence that says what is important or significant about this story.

Read a revised narration paragraph.

In her revised paragraph, Eva establishes a clearer focus by beginning with an effective topic sentence. In her topic sentence she stresses that the point of her story of Deborah Sampson is that "not all veterans of the war were men."

> Although only men were allowed to serve their country as soldiers during the American Revolution, not all veterans of the war were men. Deborah Sampson was born in Plympton, Massachusetts, during the winter of 1760. When the American colonies went to war with Great Britain for their independence, Sampson was filled with patriotic enthusiasm. She saw no reason why she couldn't fight as well as any man, so she disguised herself in a soldier's outfit and in 1782 enlisted in the army. She identified herself as a man named Robert Shirtlief. During the nearly two years after her enlistment, Sampson distinguished herself for her bravery and her heroism. Remarkably, no one seems to have discovered her secret. After she was shot in the leg, she took a knife and removed the bullet herself rather than seek medical treatment and risk discovery. At the end of the war, Sampson received an honorable discharge. She returned to Massachusetts, married, and raised three children. In later life, she asked for and was given a pension from the United States government for her services to her country. When she died in 1827, her husband received the first pension granted by the United States to the spouse of a female war veteran.

Activity

Identifying the Point of a Narrative

Think about a story that you heard within the last few days—from a friend, family member, classmate, or on the radio or television. Think about the events in the story. What was the point of the story?

____

Include the Events of the Story Most Useful for Making Your Point

After you have determined which story you want to tell and identified the point you want to make in your narrative, you have to choose which events of the story you will use to make your point. It isn't necessary to include all of the events of

Organizing a Narration Paragraph

In Chapter 6 you learned that in addition to being clearly focused and well supported, effective writing is well organized. A paragraph is well organized if the ideas and events within it are presented in the order that best shows the relationships between them. In a narration paragraph, a writer generally uses time order to tell the story.

the story—only those that will best reinforce your controlling idea. Also, keep in mind that your reader will be least confused if you present your events chronologically—that is, in the order in which they occurred.

It isn't necessary to include all of the events of the story—only those that will best reinforce your controlling idea.

Read a narration paragraph.

Tina Pierce, a student writer, begins her narration paragraph with the following topic sentence:

Controlling idea — Topic

The emotional cost of missing a family obligation is far greater than the financial cost of making it.

Her controlling idea, *the emotional cost is far greater than the financial cost,* promises a story about the emotional consequences of missing an important family event. Here is Tina's draft:

> The emotional cost of missing a family obligation is far greater than the financial cost of making it. It was dinnertime on a Thursday night in March when I got the phone call from my father. My Nana, who had been battling bone cancer for almost a year, had passed away earlier in the day. My best friend's grandmother had just passed away the previous week. I experienced a range of emotions. First, I was filled with grief. My Nana had been a tender companion, a great friend, and a wise teacher. I would miss her powdery smell and the way she would always draw out the "ee" sound in my name, making "Tina" sound like *Teeeeeeeeena.* I was also relieved that she would no longer have to suffer so much pain. Finally, I am embarrassed to admit that I was also stung by the panic of a nearly empty bank account. How would I make it to the funeral in Smyrna, Georgia, all the way from Minneapolis? After I decided not to go to the funeral, I was haunted by remorse. My Dad must have sensed the panic in my voice. He told me that it didn't matter if I made the trip or not and left the decision up to me. I could have gone, I thought; but then it was too late.

What's wrong with this narration paragraph?

Tina has a compelling story to tell and a point to make. However, she needs to rethink the events she has chosen to include in her story and the way in which she has arranged them. For example, she can probably cut the sentence about her best friend's grandmother. Though it's an interesting detail, it doesn't support the controlling idea of her paragraph. Also, it is unclear whether Tina's father told her that she didn't have to attend the funeral *before* she made her decision or *after.* Finally, in a conference with a writing tutor, Tina discovered that including two more important events—the day of the funeral and her visit to the cemetery long after the funeral—would make her narrative much more effective.

Read a revised narration paragraph.

The following revision is stronger because the events included are the most useful ones needed in telling the writer's story, and they are arranged in the most logical order:

> The emotional cost of missing a family obligation is far greater than the financial cost of making it. It was dinnertime on a Thursday night in March when I got the phone call from my father. My Nana, who had been battling bone cancer for almost a year, had passed away earlier in the day. I experienced a range of emotions. First, I was filled with grief. My Nana had been a tender companion, a great friend, and a wise teacher. I would miss her powdery smell and the way she would always draw out the "ee" sound in my name, making "Tina" sound like *Teeeeeeeeena.* I was also relieved that she would no longer have to suffer so much pain. Finally, I am embarrassed to admit that I was also stung by the panic of a nearly empty bank account. How would I make it to the funeral in Smyrna, Georgia, all the way from Minneapolis? My Dad must have sensed the panic in my voice. He told me that it didn't matter if I made the trip or not and left the decision up to me. After I decided not to go to the funeral, I was haunted by remorse. On the day of the funeral, I cried over a photo album and an afghan that Nana made for me when I left home for college. I could have gone, I thought; but then it was too late. Just last week, ten months after Nana's death, I made it back home and visited the cemetery where she was buried. I remembered her powdery smell and her sandy voice *("Teeeeeeeeena . . ."),* and I cried all over again.

Activity

Choosing Events to Support a Main Point

Use one of the following sentences as your topic sentence. First, circle the topic and underline the controlling idea. Next, think of a story from your own life experience that you could tell to illustrate that topic sentence. Write down a list of events, in time order, that you would use to tell that story.

A. Tragedy often brings people closer together.
B. Stress can be a powerful motivator.

C. Technology is helpful, but it has its limits.
D. Creating a strong relationship is hard work, but worth the effort.
E. Holidays are overrated.

Include Details That Make the Story Vivid and Real

Successful storytellers use details at each stage of a story to make what they are saying come to life for the listener or reader. Details will strengthen a narrative and make it seem more real to a reader if they paint vivid pictures and create striking mental images for the reader.

Read a narration paragraph.

This first-year writing student begins his narrative with the topic sentence

Topic: bears — Controlling idea: can be extremely dangerous and destructive.

> Although they may appear friendly, bears can be extremely dangerous and destructive.

His controlling idea, *can be extremely dangerous and destructive,* promises a story about an encounter with dangerous and destructive bears. Here is the student's draft paragraph:

> Although they may appear friendly, bears can be extremely dangerous and destructive. I learned this lesson on a camping trip last summer. A friend of mine and I were setting up camp when our attention was directed toward two large bears. We continued our work. Afterward, we built a fire and cooked supper. Being inexperienced campers, we left food scraps around the campsite when we went to sleep. We awoke to a frightening sound. Bears were eating the abandoned scraps of food and going for our backpacks. Seeking safety, we climbed a tree and watched helplessly as the bears demolished our camp. After destroying just about everything in the camp, the bears, to our surprise, walked into the forest. As we later learned, however, they might have attacked us had we threatened or antagonized them.

What's wrong with this narration paragraph?

Although the writer tells his story to make a point and includes the events in the story most useful for making that point, the narrative lacks the realism that additional details can provide. A reader is left wondering about a number of specifics. For example, where were the campers camping? What was their initial reaction to the bears? What were they cooking that was so attractive to the bears? What sound did they awaken to? As written, the story is rather straightforward. Adding more detail to fill in the picture, however, would help to engage the reader more.

Choosing Transitions for a Narration Paragraph

In Chapter 7, you learned that transitions add coherence to your paragraphs by linking the ideas in one sentence with those in the next and showing their relationships. Transitions act as reminders of what you have already said and as signals indicating where you are going. These transitions are particularly effective in writing that is developed by narration:

after	eventually	meanwhile	soon
as	finally	next	then
at last	first (second, third)	now	when
before	last	since	while
during	later		

Read a revised narration paragraph.

The writer revised his paragraph to include more specific details. This version is much more effective because it creates a more vivid picture in the reader's mind:

Although they may appear friendly, the bears in Yellowstone National Park can be extremely dangerous and destructive. I learned this lesson on a camping trip last summer. My friend Robert and I were setting up camp close to a dry riverbed in one of Yellowstone's canyons when we noticed two large bears walking peacefully down a narrow path. Unafraid, we continued our work. Afterward, we built a fire and cooked bacon and eggs for supper. Being inexperienced campers, we left food scraps and bacon drippings—an obvious attraction for wild animals—around the campsite when we went to sleep. Thirty minutes later we awoke to the sound of growls and crunches. Two bears were eating the abandoned scraps of food and tearing at our partially filled backpacks. Seeking safety, we climbed a nearby pine tree and watched helplessly as the bears demolished our camp in an apparent search for more food. After destroying just about everything in the camp, the bears, to our surprise, walked into the forest, completely unaware of—or unconcerned about—our presence. As we later learned, however, they might have attacked us had we threatened or antagonized them.

☑ Writer's Checklist: Narration

_____ Does your topic sentence include your topic and your controlling idea—the main point you are making by telling your story?

_____ Do you support your controlling idea with a narrative that illustrates your main point?

  _____ Have you checked to make sure your narrative makes a point and that you have communicated that point in your topic sentence?

    _____ Did you check to see that the events you have included in your narrative are the most useful ones? Did you drop any unrelated or insignificant events, and add events that will help tell the story you want to tell?
    _____ Have you checked to be sure you have included enough specific details to make your story vivid and real?

_____ Did you make certain your paragraph is organized appropriately by time order?
_____ When writing your draft, did you seek feedback from a friend, classmate, instructor, or tutor?
_____ Have you revised your draft for focus, unity, support, and coherence? (See Chapter 7.)
_____ Did you edit your work (see Chapter 8), and are you ready to submit a clean copy of your paragraph?

Summary

1. To narrate means to tell a story. The challenge in writing a narration paragraph is to make sure that your story illustrates a point. (See p. 101.)
2. The topic sentence in a narration paragraph generally states the conclusion that the writer wants the reader to draw from the story. The narrative that follows the topic sentence then illustrates—or tells the story behind—that conclusion. (See p. 101.)
3. In effective narratives, events are arranged in time order. (See p. 104.)
4. Successful storytellers use vivid details to bring a story to life for their readers. (See p. 106.)

Writing Activities

Other Writing Activities

1. Working with a partner or in a small group, read each of the following narrative paragraphs, and then talk about how effective each is. Answer the following questions for each paragraph. (For help with working with a classmate, see the "Guidelines for Working with Others" on page 26.)

    - Does the writer use the narrative to make a point? What is the point?
    - What events does the writer choose to tell the story? Are they arranged in a logical order? Are all the events relevant to the point of the story?
    - Does the paragraph lack detail? Does it have too much detail? What would you improve?

    A. The unsightly plastic drain pipe sat on the lawn for two months after I finished installing the plumbing for our new kitchen. Where do you put a large, ten-foot pipe full of holes about the size of a dime? The pipe was long and hard to lift, but with a small riding lawnmower, I was able to put it onto a trailer and bring the pipe to my garage. The rafters in the garage seemed like the perfect place to store the pipe. By standing on the trailer, I could just reach the rafters. A ladder was near, but using the trailer seemed the best way to lift the pipe onto the rafters. As I picked up the pipe by its middle, one of my fingers poked through one of the holes in the pipe. As I tossed it onto the trailer, I felt what seemed to be mud in the middle of the pipe. I positioned the trailer next to the barn, and, by standing on my toes, I started to move the pipe into its new resting place. I guided about half of the pipe into place and then gave a quick push to finish the job. That push prompted a long, thick, poisonous snake to emerge from the pipe. Standing awkwardly on my toes, I felt the snake land across my shoulders. It entangled itself in my overalls and began thrashing about in terror. The smell given off by the snake was almost unbearable. At that moment, both the snake and I tumbled to the ground. The snake jerked into strike position and was about to deliver a bite, but in preparing itself to strike, it managed to get loose from my clothing. I felt instant relief when it chose freedom rather than retaliation. The snake's odor still hung in the air as it slithered into the woods behind the garage.

B. Few people know that Hollywood's most famous vampire was inspired by a real European prince named Vlad Dracula. This Dracula inherited his name from his father, whose ferocity in leading armies against foreign invaders led to his induction into the order of the dragon, or "Dracul." The son carried on the tradition of brutality. When the father died, the son became ruler of Wallachia, a province in what is now Romania. Prince Vlad quickly revealed his violent nature. One of his first acts involved the murder of hundreds of nobles who opposed his rule. His method of execution earned him another nickname: Vlad the Impaler. During his rule, Vlad tortured and killed thousands of his own people by impaling them (to *impale* someone is to run a spear through his or her body) on huge wooden stakes. On one occasion, he learned that an army of invaders had entered his country, and he ordered the deaths of nearly ten thousand enemy prisoners. Their bodies were left on stakes. When the enemy general saw this forest of the dead, he was so horrified that he bypassed Wallachia rather than face the ruthless Dracula. As a result, some Romanians still consider Vlad a patriot and a hero. However, he is also remembered as a tyrant whose violence and cruelty inspired a vampire legend.

C. I have learned that it is better not to walk away from a stressful situation. Doing so only makes the situation worse. Our house was chaos one morning earlier in the week. Our kids, Katie and Tom, were throwing their waffles at one another rather than eating them. My wife, who was anxious about a presentation she was due to make at work that day, growled at the kids when she saw syrup on the wall. Our hot-water heater was broken, and so showers were out of the question. As a result, we all tried our best to look tidy with a little soap and cold water, a hairbrush, and a toothbrush. I was trying to settle the kids down and get them into their jackets, but I had my eye on the clock, too. I knew if I didn't catch the train in ten minutes, I would be late for class for the third time this semester. Walking the kids to the babysitter's house would probably mean missing the train. Katie, our four-year-old, finally had her coat on and was waiting at the door with her lunchbox, but Tom, our two-year-old, had other plans. He had a tantrum and threw himself on the floor at just about the same time Carol, my wife, discovered a syrup stain on her blouse. A good deal of frustration and complaint were in the air, but I decided that I was going to make that train. "Well, I have to run," I said quickly as I grabbed my own coat and breezed out the kitchen door. That was three days ago. Carol hasn't talked to me since.

D. My grandmother's journey from Europe to the United States is a story of determination and courage. Born in Italy in 1900, my grandmother, Carlotta Ferraro, was fourteen when World War I began. Just a few months before the war, her own mother had left Italy for Chicago, where she planned to bring her family as soon as she found a job and a place to live. With the outbreak of the war, however, all travel between Italy and the United States was halted. Since the two countries were on opposite sides of the conflict, even the delivery of mail became impossible. My grandmother was left to care for her three younger brothers and sisters and her eighty-year-old grandmother. When the war ended, arrangements were made for the family to come to America. Since money was scarce, however, the only way the family could finance the trip was to arrange a "mail order" marriage for my grandmother, then eighteen years old. Life during wartime was hard, and there wasn't always enough food. For more than a year, the family lived in a basement of a bombed-out house, without heat or running water. The family survived a dangerous ocean voyage, and the day after they arrived in Chicago, my grandmother married a man she had known for only a day. Nevertheless, their marriage was a success. They now have descendants living all over the United States.

2. Write a narration paragraph using one of the following topics as the focus of your paragraph. Be sure to write a topic sentence that includes the topic and your controlling idea—the point that you will make in your narrative. Follow the three guidelines presented in this chapter as you write (see p. 101).

   A. A time when my life was in danger
   B. My first romantic experience

C. Putting an old or ill pet to sleep
D. An obstacle I (or someone else) overcame
E. A time when I went with the crowd against my better judgment
F. An incident that I deeply regret

3. By this point, your portfolio should be growing in size. Add to your portfolio any paragraphs that you have developed through narration. Look through the other paragraphs in your portfolio, and see whether any of their topic sentences might also have been developed by narration. Finally, ask yourself, *What story does my portfolio tell about my work in this course?* (For help with maintaining a writing portfolio, see the "Guidelines for Keeping a Portfolio" on page 61.)

Chapter 10

Example

What Is *Example*?

Example is a paragraph strategy that you probably use often in conversation. Whenever you make a statement in writing and then use a specific instance or sample to show what you mean, you are using example. The challenge in writing an example paragraph is selecting enough appropriate and specific examples to support the controlling idea (main point) expressed in the topic sentence. For example, the writer who begins with this topic sentence

Topic — Controlling idea

Smoking is hazardous to one's health.

will have to support the controlling idea by providing examples of the various types of health hazards associated with smoking.

Guidelines for Writing an Example Paragraph

1. **Choose appropriate examples** that show or explain the point expressed in your topic sentence.
2. **Choose specific examples** rather than general ones. Your writing will be more effective if you are concrete and clear.
3. **Provide enough examples** to convince your reader.

Choose Appropriate Examples

Every example you use in your paragraph should illustrate (in other words, show or explain) your controlling idea directly and clearly.

Read an example paragraph.

Marlene Doyon, a first-year writing student, begins with the topic sentence:

Using Example in Real Life

You probably already have experience making a point and providing examples to support it.

- You tell a friend that there are lots of ways to make extra money while going to school. She says, "Okay, name some."
- You complain to a salesperson that your new stereo system is not user-friendly. He asks, "What do you mean?"
- You tell your sweetheart that he is so irresponsible. He asks, "What have I done?"

Topic — Controlling idea

The World Wide Web offers many search engines that help users find the information they want.

Her controlling idea, *offers many search engines that help users find the information they want,* promises a discussion of several helpful search engines. Here is Marlene's draft paragraph:

> The World Wide Web offers many search engines that help users find the information they want. For example, Yahoo! (at www.yahoo.com) is one of the most frequently used search engines. It offers the user a giant table of contents for just about every site on the Web. To assist users in their search for information, Yahoo! places Web sites into categories such as "Health," "News and Media," and "Entertainment." By exploring these categories, users can locate Web sites with information on whatever subject interests them. AltaVista (at www.altavista.com) is another popular engine for searching the Web. Users of AltaVista type in words related to the information they seek, and the engine scans its databases for sites that mention or have something to do with those words. AltaVista might find Web sites that Yahoo! misses, but it might also find sites unrelated to what the user wants to find. Amazon (at www.amazon.com) is another popular site for users searching the Internet. Through Amazon, users can search for books on a variety of subjects. Amazon lists virtually every book in print and even some that are out of print. Users of Amazon can look for books simply by typing in the title, the author's name, or the subject.

What's wrong with this example paragraph?

Marlene has some revising to do. Her first two examples—Yahoo! and AltaVista—are appropriate examples to support her controlling idea. Both are search engines that Internet users can access to help them locate Web sites containing the information they want. The third example, however, is not appropriate because Amazon is not a search engine but a specific Web site. While it offers tools for searching for something very specific within its gigantic site, Amazon cannot enable users to search the entire World Wide Web.

Read a revised example paragraph.

Marlene revised her example paragraph to include three appropriate examples. Her paragraph is more consistent now because each of the examples she uses illustrates her point that there are *many helpful search engines* on the Web.

> The World Wide Web offers many search engines that help users find the information they want. For example, Yahoo! (at www.yahoo.com) is one of the most frequently used search engines. It offers the user a giant table of contents for just about every site on the Web. To assist users in their search for information, Yahoo! places Web sites into categories such as "Health," "News and Media," and "Entertainment." By exploring these categories, users can locate Web sites with information on whatever subject interests them. AltaVista (at www.altavista.com) is another popular engine for searching the Web. Users of AltaVista type in words related to the information they seek, and the engine scans its databases for sites that mention or have something to do with those words. AltaVista might find Web sites that Yahoo! misses, but it might also find sites unrelated to what the user wants to find. A third example is Lycos (at www.lycos.com), which also offers Web users a useful means for searching the Internet. Among other tools, Lycos maintains separate search pages for users who wish to search for only certain kinds of information. For instance, Lycos has search pages for locating music and for finding people. When someone searches in one of these areas, the system automatically weeds out sites that are unrelated to the user's subject.

Choose Specific Examples

All of your examples should be made concrete and clear by the use of specifics. Not only is the following paragraph too brief to be effective, but the examples the writer chooses are much too vague.

Read an example paragraph.

This student writer begins with the topic sentence:

Topic: The Bible — Controlling idea: presents a great variety of literary genres.

The Bible presents a great variety of literary genres.

Her controlling idea, *presents a great variety of literary genres,* promises that she will give the reader examples of the variety of genres (types of writing) found in the Bible. Here is her draft paragraph:

> The Bible presents a great variety of literary genres. It includes books that deal with history. It offers dramas as interesting as many dramas today. In the Bible,

Organizing an Example Paragraph

In Chapter 6 you learned that a well-organized paragraph presents ideas and events in the order that best shows the relationships between them. In an example paragraph, a writer could use time order, space order, or importance order, depending upon his or her topic sentence.

Topic sentence	Best way to organize
This week of training has been the most demanding one yet.	Time order
The Sarah Orne Jewett house reflects the writer's simple lifestyle.	Space order
Four important American generals were involved in the Persian Gulf War.	Importance order

one can read numerous biographies. The Bible also offers poetry in many of its books.

What's wrong with this example paragraph?

The writer does offer some appropriate examples: She lists as literary genres what she calls "history," "drama," "biography," and "poetry." But the examples are not specific enough. The average reader may not be aware that the Bible does in fact contain many kinds of literature. To illustrate her point, the writer should name specific books of the Bible that contain the literary genres she has listed and supply other explanatory details.

The trick is to choose—wisely—enough examples to be clear and convincing. A good rule of thumb is to use three or more examples.

Read a revised example paragraph.

The writer revised her paragraph, giving specific examples of the various types of writing that exist in the Bible. Her revised paragraph is more effective than her draft:

> The Bible contains a great variety of literary genres that provide us with some very interesting reading. It gives us history in Kings, Judges, Samuel, and other books. It gives us drama in Exodus and in the Book of Job. In fact, the story in Exodus of how the Israelites escaped from Egyptian slavery became the plot for a popular movie starring Charleton Heston as Moses, and the Book of Job has been turned into a well-known modern play. Indeed, Job has become one of the best-known characters in all literature. The Bible also contains several biographies. The Book of Ruth, for example, contains one of the few existing biographies of a woman from ancient times. The best known biography is, of course, that of Jesus. The first four books of the New Testament contain four versions of the life of Jesus, recounting the events of his life from his birth and childhood to his cruci-

fixion. The Bible also offers poetry in many of its books, but the psalms are the most famous of its poems. They have been recited and sung in churches and synagogues and make up perhaps the most celebrated and recognized of all poetry.

Activity

Identify Examples That Are Appropriate and Specific

Read each of the following paragraphs carefully. Underline each sentence that begins a new example; then list the number of examples contained in each paragraph. State whether each example is *appropriate* and *specific.*

A. There are many ways to cut the costs of grocery bills. Purchasing store brands instead of the popular brands advertised on television and in magazines saves money, since the cost of advertising does not have to be included in the cost of store-brand items. Peanut butter and canned vegetables with store-brand labels usually are of the same quality as widely advertised national brands. Another way to make pennies count is to clip money-saving coupons from newspapers and to watch for weekly specials. Buying in quantity can also cut per-item expenses. And shopping for fresh fruits and vegetables when they are in season can result in considerable savings for the shopper. Finally, shoppers who bring grocery lists and stick to them avoid the temptation of buying on impulse and thus avoid spending money that they otherwise would not spend.

B. Researchers have found in case after case that even when identical twins have been raised in completely different environments they still show an amazing number of similarities. In one such case, two female twins, Rosalie and Corinna, accidentally encountered each other when both were attending a teachers' convention in New York. They immediately recognized that they must be related and soon concluded that they were twin sisters. They had been separated when less than a year old, and they had been raised in different states. Nevertheless, the two shared a remarkable number of similarities. Not only were both women high school teachers, but both taught biology. Each had given birth to two children, and each had authored two illustrated children's books. Moreover, they liked the same foods, they had the same favorite movie, and both had a passion for collecting and restoring antique furniture. In another extraordinary case, two male twins, both named Bill, found each other forty-two years after having been separated when they were five days old. The two were astounded by the things they shared in common. Both men had married women named Martha, divorced them, and then remarried women named Ann. One had named his son William Arthur, and the other had named his Arthur William. Both men drove blue Jeep Cherokees, and both had worked as game wardens. They each enjoyed fly fishing, and both played the guitar.

Provide Enough Examples

In writing an example paragraph, the writer does not have to use every appropriate example that comes to mind. The trick is to choose—wisely—enough examples to be clear and convincing. A good rule of thumb is to use three or more examples, each of which will serve as a primary support. (To review primary supports, see pages 56–59.)

Read an example paragraph.
This student writer begins with the topic sentence:

Topic — Controlling idea

College students who need financial assistance with their education [Topic] often have more options available to them than they realize. [Controlling idea]

His controlling idea, *often have more options available to them than they realize,* promises that he will present several options for financial assistance to college students. Here is his draft paragraph, which includes only two options:

> College students who need financial assistance with their education often have more options available to them than they realize. For example, loan programs, such as the Federal Perkins Loan and the Federal Stafford Loan, are available at relatively low interest rates to students who qualify for them. Both undergraduate and graduate students may be eligible for a Perkins Loan, which can pay as much as $3,000 a year toward an undergraduate student's educational expenses and $5,000 a year for a graduate student's expenses. Similarly, a Stafford Loan can range from $2,625 per year for a first-year, dependent undergraduate to $8,500 per year for a graduate student.

What's wrong with this example paragraph?
The two examples of financial assistance programs for college students are not enough to explain in adequate detail the controlling idea that college students in need of financial assistance "have more options available to them than they realize." The writer must present more examples to develop the controlling idea effectively.

Read a revised example paragraph.
The writer's revised paragraph, which includes specific information about the Federal Work Study program, the Pell Grant, and the Federal Supplemental Education Opportunity Grants program, is stronger than his draft because it truly presents the college student with "options":

> College students who need financial assistance with their education often have more options available to them than they realize. For example, loan programs, such as the Federal Perkins Loan and the Federal Stafford Loan, are available at

relatively low interest rates to students who qualify for them. Both undergraduate and graduate students may be eligible for a Perkins Loan, which can pay as much as $3,000 a year toward an undergraduate student's educational expenses and $5,000 a year for a graduate student's expenses. Similarly, a Stafford Loan can range from $2,625 per year for a first-year, dependent undergraduate to $8,500 per year for a graduate student. Students also may qualify for aid programs that do not require that the amount received be paid back. One such program is Federal Work Study. This popular program provides a part-time job, usually on campus, for students willing to work up to twenty hours a week. Another possibility that involves an award and not a loan is the Federal Pell Grant, a program that provides a maximum of $3,000 to qualifying undergraduates. A final program granting awards to college students is the Federal Supplemental Educational Opportunity Grants program, which provides as much as $4,000 to students who qualify.

Activity

Generating Enough Examples for a Controlling Idea

Read the following topic sentences; then think of three or more examples that you can use to support each one. Be sure that your examples are appropriate and specific.

A. The widespread use of computers has given the English language many new words.
B. Late-night talk shows feature outrageous people doing and saying outrageous things.
C. People who report sighting a UFO risk being ridiculed.
D. Racism comes in many forms.
E. History is full of stories of a single individual changing the world.
F. _____ is a reliable friend. (Fill in the blank with the name of one of your friends.)

☑ Writer's Checklist: Example

_____ Have you written a topic sentence that includes your topic and your controlling idea—the main point you are making about your topic?

_____ Did you support your controlling idea with examples that show or explain your main point?

- _____ Have you checked to see that each example you include in your paragraph is appropriate? Did you drop any examples that do not directly help to illustrate your main point?
- _____ Did you check to see that each example you include is specific? You may have to add supporting details to make your examples more specific.
- _____ Have you checked to see that you have enough examples (at least three) to support your point? You may need to add more examples.

Choosing Transitions for an Example Paragraph

In Chapter 7, you learned that transitions add coherence to your paragraphs by linking the ideas in one sentence with those in the next and showing their relationships. Transitions act as reminders of what you have already said and as signals indicating where you are going. These transitions are particularly effective in writing that is developed by example:

especially	for example	for one thing	specifically
first of all	for instance	in particular	such as

_____ Did you choose an appropriate organizational pattern for your paragraph: time order, space order, or importance order?

_____ When writing your draft, did you seek feedback from a friend, classmate, instructor, or tutor?

_____ Have you revised your draft for focus, unity, support, and coherence? (See Chapter 7.)

_____ Did you edit your work (see Chapter 8), and are you ready to submit a clean copy of your paragraph?

Summary

1. You are using example whenever you make a statement in writing and then present a specific instance or sample to show what you mean. In writing an example paragraph, you must select enough appropriate and specific examples to support the controlling idea. (See p. 112.)
2. Every example in the paragraph should illustrate (in other words, show or explain) the controlling idea directly and clearly. (See p. 112.)
3. All examples should be made concrete and clear by the use of specifics. (See p. 114.)
4. An example paragraph should include enough examples—usually three—to be clear and convincing. (See p. 117.)

Writing Activities

Other Writing Activities

1. Read each of the following paragraphs carefully. Underline each sentence that begins a new example; then list the number of examples contained in each paragraph. State whether each example is *appropriate* and *specific.* Revise any examples that are not appropriate and specific.

A. Would you believe that something as small as the peanut could have hundreds of uses? Every year millions of peanuts are turned into peanut butter, one of America's favorite foods. Roasted peanuts are salted and eaten as snacks or used in candies and bakery products. Salad oils and margarines are made from peanuts. Farmers use peanut vines, hulls, and skins as feed for their animals. Other products made from the peanut are cosmetics, soap, packing oil, medicines, and even explosives. In fact, there are more than three hundred uses for the peanut plant and its fruit.

B. According to ancient superstitions, moles on the body reveal a person's character and foretell the future. Some moles reveal strengths and weaknesses of character. A mole on the back of the neck indicates that the bearer is a spendthrift. Moles on both sides of the neck reveal extreme stubbornness. A mole on the left knee is a sure indication that the bearer is unwise in business matters. In fact, a mole on any part of the leg indicates that one is both indolent and wasteful. A mole over the left eyebrow hints of laziness as well as selfishness. Anyone who meets a person with a mole on any finger should hold on to their wallet: According to superstition, the person is sure to be a crook. But a friend with a mole on their nose is strong of character and will always remain a true friend. In addition to revealing character, moles are said to foretell the future. For example, an old saying claims, "A mole on the neck, money by the peck." If the mole is on the front of the neck, good luck may come from any source. A mole on the ear also brings good luck in the form of money. A mole over the right eyebrow means success in love, money, and career. A mole on the hand, however, is the most to be desired: It forecasts the good news that one will be talented, healthy, rich, and happy.

C. Representatives in Congress really enjoy the "gravy" provided by the American tax dollar. To start with, the salary itself is impressive. In 2000, our representatives' salaries were $141,300. The leaders in the House and Senate earned $151,800, and the Speaker of the House received $175,400. In addition to their salaries, representatives receive fringe benefits galore. Available to them is a base allowance to cover expenses incurred in carrying out their duties. These expenses can range from the costs of stationery and postage to those incurred for grooming and recreation. Further advantages include numerous free round trips per year between their homes and Washington, subsidized international travel, a free furnished office in Washington, and a hefty allowance for staffing. Moreover, Congressional representatives are covered for life by generous life and health insurance programs. Finally, when they retire they do so on a substantial pension that would be the envy of most of the voters that elected them.

D. In many ways the staff at this university has given me a hard time with my education. When I first arrived here three years ago from my native

China, Mr. "N," in the Office of International Students, lost my visa. Since then the staff and computers have given me innumerable occasions for worry and frustration. For three years in a row, the people in the registrar's office have sent me notices saying that I was not carrying a full-time load when, in fact, I was carrying a fourteen-hour load, two more hours than is required of full-time students. The office lists my birth date as August 1, 1974, but they insist that I am forty-eight years old. They say that I am a first-year student, but I am really a junior. They have made many other mistakes, but the one that takes the cake is their informing me, just last week, that I am an American Eskimo from Tunisia.

2. From the list of topic sentences that you developed in the activity "Generating Enough Examples for a Controlling Idea" on page 118, choose one sentence for discussion with a classmate. Take turns describing the examples you would use to develop that topic sentence, explaining your choices according to the guidelines in this chapter (see page 112).
3. Write a paragraph on one of the following topics. Develop your topic sentence through the use of examples. Before you submit your paragraph to your instructor, share it with a classmate. Ask your partner to comment on the appropriateness and specificity of the examples as well as on whether the paragraph is engaging and convincing. (For help with giving feedback to another writer, see the "Guidelines for Giving Feedback" on page 26.)

   A. Body language
   B. Celebrities
   C. Balancing college and a job
   D. Sexist language
   E. Phobias
   F. Eating disorders
   G. E-mail etiquette
   H. Computer games
   I. Unusual pets

4. Using example as your method of development, write a paragraph on a topic of your choosing. Be certain that your examples are appropriate and specific. And be certain that you use enough examples to support your controlling idea adequately.
5. Collect the paragraphs you have written thus far in your portfolio. As you look back over your work, your classmates' feedback, and your instructor's evaluations, identify your strengths as a writer. Where could your writing improve? (For help with maintaining a writing portfolio, see the "Guidelines for Keeping a Portfolio" on page 61.)

Chapter 11

Cause and Effect

What Is *Cause and Effect*?

Exploring causes or examining effects is a useful paragraph strategy that naturally fits the human needs to know and to understand. Discussions of causes and effects are used to communicate relationships between an event and other events that precede or follow it. When you examine causes of an event, you answer the question *Why did it happen?* When you examine effects of an event, you answer *What's the result?*

The writer who begins with the topic sentence

Topic — Controlling idea

The reasons our school hired security guards are easy to identify.

will have to support her main point by providing and explaining the causes behind the school administration's decision. On the other hand, the writer who begins with

Topic — Controlling idea

The presence of security guards in the school has had profound effects on students' morale.

will have to support his main point by presenting and explaining the effects of the decision on students.

Guidelines for Writing a Cause and Effect Paragraph

1. **Cite the most important and convincing causes or effects.** This means looking for causes or effects that are clearly and directly related to the event you are writing about.

Using Cause and Effect in Real Life

You probably already have experience explaining or examining causes and effects.

- You say to a friend, "You want to know how my parents' divorce affected me? I'll tell you."
- Your mother asks why you're quitting your job. You tell her your reasons.
- You and your neighbors learn that your community's drinking water supply has tested positive for toxic chemicals. You want to know the cause of the pollution and, more importantly, its effects on your health.

2. **Do not mistake conditions for active causes and effects.** By *conditions,* we mean some related circumstances, events, or background information.

Cite the Most Important and Convincing Causes or Effects

In developing a paragraph by cause, you must be sure that each detail you label as a "cause" clearly and directly produced the effect introduced in the topic sentence. Further, your specifics must be accurate and convincing when you say that A was the cause or effect of B.

Read a cause paragraph.

Trinh Ngo, a student studying economics, begins the following paragraph with the topic sentence:

Topic — Controlling idea

The reasons for increased interest and participation in the stock market are not hard to pinpoint.

His controlling idea, *the reasons are not hard to pinpoint,* promises an examination of the causes of the stock market's recent popularity boom. Here is Trinh's draft paragraph:

> The reasons for increased interest and participation in the stock market are not hard to pinpoint. In the first place, the current generation of investors, most of whom are now in their twenties and thirties, have more faith in business than their parents and grandparents do. Previous generations grew up experiencing and remembering the effects of the stock market crash of 1929 and the depression that followed, but the present generation has no such memories. Therefore, the younger generation is more willing to invest their cash in the market. Furthermore, the spectacular earnings that the stock market has posted during the

> past two decades have led many new investors to feel that they can't afford to pass up the opportunity for equally high future earnings. To their thinking, *not* investing in the stock market is a stupid decision. Finally, people today just seem to be greedier than people from previous generations. They want more and more, and they don't want to work hard for what they get. As a result, the stock market seems to offer the free ride through life that new investors have come to expect.

What's wrong with this cause paragraph?

Trinh tried to bring together some of the important causes for the recent popularity of stock market investing. His first cause is valid: The newest generation of investors probably *is* more comfortable with the idea of investing than their parents were because they haven't experienced the consequences of a severe market crash. His second cause is probably equally valid: Recent high profits probably *have* boosted investor confidence. But there is no reason—by any stretch of the imagination—to think that the newest generation of investors is any more or less greedy than its parents. In fact, greed might just as well explain why a potential investor would wish to stay out of the stock market, which some consider the riskiest form of gambling.

Read a revised cause paragraph.

In the following revision, Trinh deletes his reference to greed and adds a more valid cause to his paragraph:

> The reasons for increased interest and participation in the stock market are not hard to pinpoint. In the first place, the current generation of investors, most of whom are now in their twenties and thirties, have more faith in business than their parents and grandparents do. Previous generations grew up experiencing and remembering the effects of the stock market crash of 1929 and the depression that followed, but the present generation has no such memories. Therefore, the younger generation is more willing to invest their cash in the market. Furthermore, the spectacular earnings that the stock market has posted during the past two decades have led many new investors to feel that they can't afford to pass up the opportunity for equally high future earnings. To their thinking, *not* investing in the stock market is a bad decision. Finally, the attention the media has given to both the success of the stock market and the insecurity of social security has led people to feel that they need to be invested in the market. Feeling that they can't depend on their social security benefits to finance their retirement, young investors view the stock market as their best hope for a brighter future.

Read an effect paragraph.

In a paragraph exploring effects, the writer must include details that have a direct relationship to the event being discussed. The writer of the following paragraph, which describes the effects of cocaine use, does this well:

Organizing a Cause and Effect Paragraph

In Chapter 6 you learned that a well-organized paragraph presents ideas and events in the order that best shows the relationships between them. In a paragraph developed by cause or effect, a writer could use time order or importance order, depending upon his or her topic sentence:

Topic sentence	Best way to organize
Several events led up to my mother's recent promotion.	Time order
An eating disorder has very serious long-term effects on one's health.	Importance order

Cocaine use has very serious consequences—both for addicts and occasional users. Cocaine is one of the most highly addictive of all narcotics. Laboratory animals addicted to cocaine prefer cocaine over food even if they are at the point of starving to death. Research has shown that using cocaine on only one or two occasions can result in a serious addiction. Cocaine also affects the heart. Under certain circumstances, even a small dose of cocaine is capable of producing a fatal heart attack in an otherwise healthy individual. Habitual cocaine users are likely to experience serious cardiac problems such as palpitations of the heart, angina, and various other heart-related complications. In addition, cocaine alters the neurological centers of the brain and can permanently damage the nervous system. Habitual users are likely to experience a variety of psychological disorders ranging from total sexual dysfunction to loss of memory and even lasting states of psychosis and neurosis.

Activity

Which Is More Useful: Explaining Causes or Presenting Effects?

The following topic sentences can be developed by cause or effect. Read each and determine whether it would be developed more effectively in a paragraph of cause or a paragraph of effect. Then choose one of the topic sentences, and list four causes or four effects that could support the controlling idea.

A. People lie for a variety of reasons.
B. Too much stress can lead to poor health.
C. Many parents are turning to home schooling as an alternative to public education.
D. Drinking and then driving is extremely dangerous.
E. More employers are offering their employees flexible work schedules.

Do Not Mistake Conditions for Active Causes and Effects

Sometimes, through faulty reasoning, writers assume that conditions or circumstances surrounding an event have caused the event, when in fact the so-called cause is not directly responsible at all. These writers mistake circumstances for actual causes.

Read an effect paragraph.

One student began her paragraph with the following topic sentence:

> When the tomb of King Tut was opened by archaeologists in Egypt in 1922, a curse [Topic] was released that claimed the lives of several people. [Controlling idea]

Her controlling idea, *that claimed the lives of several people,* promises to show the effects of a supposed curse on the discoverers of the tomb. Here is her draft paragraph:

> When the tomb of King Tut was opened by archaeologists in Egypt in 1922, a curse was released that claimed the lives of several people. The first to die was Lord Carnarvon, the British aristocrat who had financed the expedition. While shaving, Carnarvon opened a mosquito bite, and he died a few weeks later from an infection, with the work of excavating the tomb just underway. Shortly thereafter, an official with the Department of Egyptian Antiquities died of a stroke after exhausting himself from too much work in the desert sun. The deadly effects of the curse continued to claim victims for decades to follow. Others who entered the tomb of Tut died of various illnesses—some suddenly. As late as the 1970s, the curse was still working. When objects from the tomb were being prepared for a world tour, one of the first people to see them dropped dead on the spot.

What's wrong with this effect paragraph?

Because the controlling idea is flawed, the remainder of the paragraph is weak and unconvincing. Despite rumors and newspaper reports to the contrary, a curse did not *cause* the deaths of anyone who entered King Tut's tomb or handled his possessions. Every death attributed to the curse is explainable according to natural, not supernatural, causes. Lord Carnarvon died of an infection, and his associate suffered heat stroke. The vast majority of the people who worked on excavating the tomb lived long and productive lives. In fact, Howard Carter—the explorer who found the tomb, handled every object it contained, and supervised the unwrap-

> Sometimes, through faulty reasoning, writers assume that conditions or circumstances surrounding an event have caused the event, when in fact the so-called cause is not directly responsible at all.

Choosing Transitions for a Cause and Effect Paragraph

In Chapter 7, you learned that transitions add coherence to your paragraphs by linking the ideas in one sentence with those in the next and showing their relationships. Transitions act as reminders of what you have already said and as signals indicating where you are going. These transitions are particularly effective in writing that is developed by cause or effect:

as a result	finally	then
because	furthermore	therefore
consequently	so	thus

ping and autopsy of the king's mummy—lived another seventeen years and died a peaceful death. There is no scientific evidence that any sort of magical curse was placed on Tut's tomb or that such a curse would have the power to cause illness or death. This writer needs to rewrite her topic sentence with a different controlling idea—one that expresses clear and reasonable causes or effects. As an alternative to her original topic sentence, the writer might have developed the following in a paragraph:

> Though legend has it that the discoverers of King Tut's tomb were cursed and subsequently met untimely deaths, the truth of the situation is far different.

Of course, this paragraph would be developed with examples and not effects.

☑ Writer's Checklist: Cause and Effect

_____ Have you examined causes or effects in your paragraph?

_____ Did you write a topic sentence that includes your topic and your controlling idea—the main point you are making about your topic?

_____ Have you supported your controlling idea with the most important causes or effects related to the event you are discussing?

- _____ Did you check to see that each cause or effect is clearly and directly related to the event you are writing about?
- _____ Did you check to see that you are not mistaking mere circumstances or conditions for active and logical causes or effects?

_____ Have you chosen an appropriate organizational pattern for your paragraph: time order or importance order?

_____ When writing your draft, did you seek feedback from a friend, classmate, instructor, or tutor?

_____ Have you revised your draft for focus, unity, support, and coherence? (See Chapter 7.)

_____ Did you edit your work (see Chapter 8), and are you prepared to submit a clean copy of your paragraph?

Summary

1. When you examine an event in relation to other events that *precede* it (why did it happen?) and *follow* it (what's the result?), you are exploring causes and effects. In writing a paragraph developed by cause or effect, you must make sure that the specifics you include are important and convincing. (See p. 122.)
2. Sometimes, through faulty reasoning, writers assume that conditions or circumstances surrounding an event have caused the event, when in fact the so-called cause is not directly responsible at all and the cited effect does not follow from the cause. These writers mistake circumstances for actual causes or effects. (See p. 126.)

Writing Activities

Other Writing Activities

1. With a classmate, choose one topic sentence from the list in the "Which Is More Useful: Explaining Causes or Presenting Effects?" activity on page 125. Take turns describing the causes or effects that you would use to develop that topic sentence, explaining your choices according to the guidelines in this chapter (see p. 122). (For help with working with a classmate, see the "Guidelines for Working with Others" on page 26.)
2. Carefully read the following paragraphs. Each shows a student's attempt to develop a paragraph by cause or effect. Some paragraphs use the method well; others are not so effective. After considering each paragraph, answer the following questions:

   - Has the writer of the paragraph attempted to develop it by cause or by effect?
   - Is the attempt successful or not? Give specific reasons for your answer.
   - Which paragraphs, if any, merely show *circumstances* related to a result rather than actual *causes* of the result?

   A. Many situations can cause pressure and tension to build up inside of us. Performing in front of an audience commonly produces pressure. We suffer from fear of making an embarrassing mistake during the performance. Many of us also experience tension when among new people. In such situations, we become quiet out of fear that other people may label us as "loud mouths." Coaches and athletes often feel tension before big games because they do not want to commit errors that might cause their teams to lose. I feel tension right now as I write this paragraph. I want it to be the best paragraph I've written this semester because this is my last chance to better my grade in this course. Pressure and tension are common in our environment. No matter how hard we try to avoid them, there will inevitably be times when breathing becomes hard and fear gets a grip that is difficult to loosen.

B. In the past few years, higher education has become increasingly important to young people everywhere. Higher education is essential for those who wish to enter the fields of medicine, engineering, and communications. These fields are essential for the survival of the human race. In the future, successful people will undoubtedly be those who have received technical instruction in fields such as these. Without this education, humans cannot survive. The very existence of the human race depends on the ability to progress in highly technical fields.

C. Entering a hospital isn't always in one's best interest. Many doctors give a standard battery of tests to every incoming patient. Such a procedure means that some patients receive more tests than they actually need. Sometimes these tests can even be dangerous. X-rays, for example, involve radiation, and exposure to radiation can sometimes result in birth deformities or in cancer. Before many medical tests, the patient must undergo enemas, which involve the use of harsh laxatives that sometimes dehydrate the body. Most doctors feel that individually these tests do little harm to a patient; however, doctors don't seem to consider the fact that the average hospital patient receives as many as four or five tests in a single day. This many tests can weaken even a healthy person. In addition, statistics indicate that 9 percent of all hospital patients develop an illness or infection while in the hospital. So sometimes the cure is worse than the disease.

D. Transferring from a two-year college to a four-year university has been very difficult for me. First of all, I lost a number of course credits during the transfer. At the community college, I took courses to fulfill the general education program there. However, those courses do not count for general education credit at the school I now attend. In fact, some of them do not even apply toward graduation. As a result, I will have to spend an additional semester making up the difference. Secondly, at the university I cannot always get the courses I need to fulfill my major requirements. The competition for courses is greater here than at the community college because of the size of the student body. Seniors get first choice, and what is left is often not enough for the rest of us. Finally, sometimes I feel that I am a number and not a person in this environment. Lecture classes are often very large, and the discussion sessions are taught by graduate assistants and not the professor. So it is difficult to determine where to go when I need help. On these occasions, I feel abandoned and look back with some relish to my time at the community college.

3. Using cause or effect, develop a paragraph on one of the following topics. Before you write a draft of the paragraph, share your plan with a classmate. Discuss whether the topic can be better developed by dealing with causes or by dealing with effects, and then get your partner's feedback on your topic sentence to make sure that the purpose of your paragraph is clear. (For help with responding to writing, see the "Guidelines for Giving Feedback" on page 49.)

   A. A decision that changed my life
   B. Spending too much time in the sun
   C. Domestic violence
   D. Age discrimination
   E. Computer crashes
   F. Handguns
   G. Obesity
   H. Adult education
   I. A natural disaster (hurricane, earthquake, storm, etc.)
   J. Sports injuries

4. Using cause or effect as your method of development, write a paragraph on a topic of your own choosing. Be sure that you cite causes and effects that are important and directly related and that you do not mistake circumstances for active causes or effects.

5. Collect the paragraphs you have written thus far in your portfolio. Compare the cause and effect paragraphs you have just written with other paragraphs in your portfolio. How are they different? How are they alike? Are you improving? If you are, write a cause paragraph examining the reasons for your improvement. (For help with maintaining a writing portfolio, see the "Guidelines for Keeping a Portfolio" on page 61.)

Chapter 12

Process Analysis

What Is *Process Analysis*?

So much of what we do in our daily life involves following a process—a series of steps followed through in a definite, logical order. We follow processes when changing a baby's diaper, applying for a job, or downloading information from the Internet. Throughout this book, we have been talking about the writing process, the steps you follow when you write a paragraph or essay. Process analysis is a paragraph strategy that you use whenever you give instructions or describe how something works. The challenge in writing process analysis is getting the steps down right. For example, the writer who begins with this topic sentence

Topic: Breast reduction surgery | Controlling idea: now a safe and uncomplicated procedure.

Breast reduction surgery is now a safe and uncomplicated procedure.

will have to support the controlling idea by detailing the steps in the procedure.

Guidelines for Writing a Process Analysis Paragraph

1. **Present all of the steps** involved in completing the task you are writing about.
2. **Present the steps in a logical order**—usually time order.

Present All of the Steps

Your process analysis paragraph should present the essential steps in the process you are describing. Be sure to present the steps in enough detail so that your readers can do the task themselves or can understand the process.

Read a process analysis paragraph.

This first-year writing student begins with the topic sentence

Using Process Analysis in Real Life

You probably already have experience explaining or following a process.

- You confidently tell a friend that doing a 180-degree turn while in-line skating is simple. She asks, "Okay, how do I do it?"
- You open a checking account but have no idea how to balance a checkbook. You sit down with a bank representative and ask him to describe the process. He begins, "Well, the first thing to do . . ."
- Your child asks you, "Can I plant a flower garden?" You begin by saying that growing flowers is easy if you follow all of the right steps.

Topic — Controlling idea

Building a good campfire involves a routine that serious campers learn very early.

His controlling idea, *involves a routine that serious campers learn very early,* promises a detailed explanation of the routine. Here is the writer's draft paragraph:

> Building a good campfire involves a routine that serious campers learn very early. In laying the fire, the campers first make a small pile of grass in the center of the firesite. Next, they stack twigs in a pyramidal or teepee shape around the grass. As the fire progresses, they add small sticks of dry wood and then larger pieces as the fire spreads out and becomes hotter. When the fire is very hot and is fully established, the campers add the largest pieces of wood available. By following these steps, almost anyone can build a roaring campfire.

What's wrong with this process analysis paragraph?

The writer's draft gives a beginning camper some helpful information about starting a campfire, but he must fill in certain gaps for the reader to have a complete, step-by-step picture of the process. Does building a fire, for example, require any special preparation? Can a camper use any kind of twigs? Should a camper add all of the large pieces of wood at once? The writer has left out some important steps and some necessary details.

Process analysis is a paragraph strategy that you use whenever you give instructions or describe how something works.

Read a revised process analysis paragraph.

This student revised his process analysis paragraph to include additional details and all of the important steps a reader might follow to complete the task of building a roaring campfire. His paragraph is stronger now because the routine he describes is easier to follow.

Organizing a Process Analysis Paragraph

In Chapter 6 you learned that a well-organized paragraph presents ideas and events in the order that best shows the relationships between them. In a process analysis paragraph, a writer generally uses time order.

Building a good campfire involves a routine that serious campers learn very early. Before trying to start a fire, the campers prepare a site. They clear an area with a radius of about ten feet to ensure that the fire will not spread. They must then gather the following materials: dry grass, dry twigs, and some dry logs of pine or spruce wood. In laying the fire, the campers first make a small pile of grass in the center of the firesite. Next, they stack twigs in a pyramidal or teepee shape around the grass. They usually start the fire with matches, though experienced campers can also start a fire by rubbing two sticks together. As the fire progresses, they add small sticks of dry wood and then larger pieces as the fire spreads out and becomes hotter. When the fire is very hot and is fully established, the campers add the largest pieces of wood available. Veteran campers know, however, that too many pieces added at one time may put the fire out or cause a lot of smoke, so they add the largest pieces one at a time. By following these steps, almost anyone can build a roaring campfire.

Present the Steps in a Logical Order

For your process analysis paragraph to be effective, you must present the steps in the order in which they occur or should be taken. Doing so will help your readers better understand—or actually complete for themselves—the process you are describing.

Read a process analysis paragraph.
Julia Merida, a student writer, begins with the topic sentence

Topic	Controlling idea
Installing new software on a computer	is a fairly simple procedure.

Her controlling idea, *is a fairly simple procedure,* promises a clear explanation of the process of installing software on a computer. Here is her draft paragraph:

Installing new software on a computer is a fairly simple procedure. Insert the software CD into the CD-ROM drive. A dialog box will appear asking you if you want to install the software. Click "Yes" to install. After you have passed the Welcome screen, the "Select Destination Directory" dialog box will appear. Read the information in the "Welcome" dialog box, and click "Next." The "Select Destina-

> tion Directory" dialog box allows you to choose where on your hard drive you want the program to live, so to speak. Verify that the default directory—the one that appears automatically in the dialog box—is the one you want to use. If it is, click "Next." If it is not, click "Browse" to locate a new directory. When you arrive at the directory you want, click "OK." To complete the installation, follow the final on-screen instructions. Before you install any new software, you should close any open programs. To close a program, go to the "File" menu and select "Exit."

What's wrong with this process analysis paragraph?

Julia has presented the essential steps in the process she is describing—installing new computer software—but she jumps around too much for her reader to be able to follow the process. For example, she advises her reader to close any open programs before beginning the installation procedure, but she leaves that important information for the end of the paragraph. She also reverses the instructions related to the "Welcome" dialog box and the "Select Destination Directory" dialog box. In a how-to paragraph, it is important that the writer put the steps in a logical order. In doing so, she helps the reader understand or complete the process that she is describing.

> In a how-to paragraph, it is important that the writer put the steps in a logical order. In doing so, she helps the reader understand or complete the process that she is describing.

Read a revised process analysis paragraph.

The writer revised her paragraph, placing the steps of the process in the most logical order and using directional transitions such as "first," "next," and "then." Julia's revised paragraph is more effective than her draft:

> Installing new software on a computer is a fairly simple procedure. First, you should close any open programs. To close a program, go to the "File" menu and select "Exit." Next, insert the software CD into the CD-ROM drive. A dialog box will appear asking you if you want to install the software. Click "Yes" to install. Read the information in the "Welcome" dialog box, and then click "Next." After you have passed the Welcome screen, the "Select Destination Directory" dialog box will appear. This box allows you to choose where on your hard drive you want the program to live, so to speak. Verify that the default directory—the one that appears automatically in the dialog box—is the one you want to use. If it is, click "Next." If it is not, click "Browse" to locate a new directory. When you arrive at the directory you want, click "OK." To complete the installation, follow the final on-screen instructions.

Activity

Listing the Steps in a Process

Each of the following topic sentences can be developed by process analysis. Choose three sentences. For each, list the steps involved in the process described

Choosing Transitions for a Process Analysis Paragraph

In Chapter 7, you learned that transitions add coherence to your paragraphs by linking the ideas in one sentence with those in the next and showing their relationships. Transitions act as reminders of what you have already said and as signals indicating where you are going. These transitions are particularly effective in writing that is developed by process analysis:

after	finally	now
as	first (second, third)	since
at last	last	soon
before	later	then
during	meanwhile	when
eventually	next	while

in the topic sentence. List the steps in the most logical order so that a reader could understand or follow the process.

A. Painting a room requires a good deal of planning.
B. Drivers should know what to do if a police officer stops them for speeding.
C. Studying for an exam requires following an effective routine.
D. Quitting smoking is a gradual process.
E. Online shopping is easier today than it was even a year ago.
F. Though it looks simple enough, __________ is tougher than most people imagine. [Fill in the blank with your own topic.]

☑ Writer's Checklist: Process Analysis

_____ Have you written a topic sentence that includes your topic and your controlling idea—the main point you are making about the process?

_____ Did you support your controlling idea with the essential steps that show or explain your main point?

  _____ Did you check to see that you have included all of the steps that are necessary for a reader to understand or to perform the process you are describing? If not, add the missing steps.

  _____ Did you check to see that the steps you have included are in the most logical order?

  _____ Have you provided specific details to make each step easier to follow?

_____ Have you used appropriate time order transitions to clarify connections between steps (see the list above)?

_____ When writing your draft, did you seek feedback from a friend, classmate, instructor, or tutor?

_____ Have you revised your draft for focus, unity, support, and coherence? (See Chapter 7.)

_____ Did you edit your work (see Chapter 8), and are you ready to submit a clean copy of your paragraph?

Summary

1. Process analysis is a paragraph strategy that you use whenever you describe how something works or give instructions. The challenge in writing process analysis is getting the steps down right. (See p. 131.)
2. Your process analysis paragraph should present the essential steps in the process you are describing. Be sure to present the steps in enough detail so that your readers can do the task themselves or can understand the process. (See p. 131.)
3. For your process analysis paragraph to be effective, you must present the steps in the order in which they occur or should be taken. Doing so will help your readers better understand—or actually complete for themselves—the process you are describing. (See p. 133.)

Writing Activities

Other Writing Activities

1. From the list of topic sentences that you developed in the activity "Listing the Steps in a Process" on page 134, choose one for discussion with a classmate. Take turns describing the steps you would use to develop that topic sentence, explaining your choices according to the guidelines in this chapter (see p. 131). (For help with working with a classmate, see the "Guidelines for Working with Others" on page 26.)
2. Read the following paragraphs carefully, and answer these questions for each paragraph:

   - Is the writer analyzing a process, or is the paragraph simply an account of an event or series of events?
   - If a process is being presented, has the author included all of the steps in the process, or have some important steps been overlooked?
   - Are the steps presented in the most logical order? If not, how would you rearrange them?

   A. Creating a personal Web site is a relatively simple procedure. Before creating your own site, visit a few others and note the features you like and dislike within each. If you don't own a computer, you can get access to the Internet at most local public libraries or at your campus library. Begin by visiting a simple, informative site. Then try visiting a more advanced site, such as one that sells merchandise or services. Typically, Internet Service Providers (ISPs), such as AOL, AT&T, and Prodigy, make Web site space a part of your account. Plenty of free Web site space also exists for people without established Internet accounts. Free sites require the user to carry advertising, usually on the first page of the site. Until recently, establishing a personal site required knowing complicated computer language. Now the necessary language exists within most word processing programs. Using a word processing program or Web site authoring tool, create the pages that you want the world to read on the Internet. A transfer program copies your Web site files to an Internet computer. There are several free or inexpensive programs available for transferring files. ISPs usually give step-by-step guidance to assist users in making their personal sites fully operational.

B. Have you ever wondered why leaves turn color in the autumn? In late summer and early fall, a ring of corky cells grows across the base of the leaf, slowly blocking the routes that carry food and water to and from the blade. By early October, the vein system of the leaf is totally cut off from its former source of nourishment. Without water, the leaf stops making food. Green chlorophyll disappears, and a bright yellow pigment called xanthophyll, which during the summer had been masked by the green of the chlorophyll, gradually becomes visible. Leaves that contain a substance called carotene start to turn red or orange. Deep reds and purples show up in leaves that contain a chemical compound called anthocyanin. At last the transformation from summer to fall colors is complete. With its nourishment cut off, the leaf loses all its green and yellow coloring and bursts forth into a brilliant and dazzling display of beauty.

C. About a year and a half ago, when I was in one of my annual "It's time for a change" moods, I stopped eating meat. I have felt healthier and happier ever since. I had been reading with great interest about the pros and cons of low-protein diets when I began to entertain the possibility of becoming a vegetarian. At the time meat prices were soaring, as they still are, and the fact that I was living in a college dormitory and eating cafeteria food of unknown origin forced me to consider the possibility all the more seriously. To test my curiosity and willpower, I eliminated all forms of beef from my diet and gradually cut back my consumption of poultry and pork. Realizing that I was losing weight and feeling better than I had in several years, I stopped eating meat altogether. Vegetables, fruits, and dairy products began to taste better, and I knew that I had successfully replaced an old habit with a new, healthier one.

D. To make good lasagna, follow these simple instructions. First, slowly brown one pound of Italian sausage and spoon off the excess grease. Stir in the following ingredients: one clove of minced garlic, one tablespoon chopped fresh basil, one-and-a-half teaspoons salt, one one-pound can of tomatoes, and two six-ounce cans of tomato paste. Simmer the ingredients for thirty minutes, stirring occasionally. In the meantime, cook ten ounces of lasagna noodles in boiling salted water until tender, drain the water, and rinse the noodles. Next, beat two eggs and add three cups cream-style cottage cheese. Add to the egg mixture the following ingredients: one-half cup grated Parmesan cheese, two tablespoons parsley flakes, one teaspoon salt, and one-half teaspoon pepper. Next, assemble the four items to be layered: the noodles, the cottage cheese–egg mixture, one pound of mozzarella cheese, and the meat sauce. To layer, first place one-third of the noodles in a 13×9×2-inch baking dish. Cover the noodles with some cottage cheese filling, add a layer of mozzarella cheese, and cover with meat sauce. Repeat this procedure twice until all the ingredients are used up. Bake the lasagna at 350° for about thirty minutes. When the lasagna is done, let it stand for about ten minutes before serving.

E. Out-of-shape people who want to take up jogging need to prepare themselves by following a fifteen-week program that gradually builds muscles and strengthens the heart. No one should ever begin serious exercise without first consulting a physician. Only after a thorough physical examination and the full approval of a physician should anyone attempt exercise. Once a physician's approval has been given, a potential jogger should purchase a good pair of jogging shoes and should learn stretching exercises. These exercises prepare the muscles for stress and strain and should be performed before each attempt at jogging. For the first five weeks, would-be joggers need to practice walking. During the first week, they should walk approximately twenty consecutive minutes every other day. A day of rest between walks allows the muscles to relax. For each of the next four weeks, potential joggers should add ten minutes to the time they walk until by the end of the fifth week they find themselves able to walk one full hour every other day. At this point, they should alternate ten minutes of walking with five minutes of jogging for approximately thirty minutes of exercise. Again, a day of rest should be taken between each attempt to exercise. During the weeks to follow, joggers should gradually increase the length of time that they spend jogging while gradually decreasing the intervals of walking. Even after reaching the point where it is possible to jog for thirty consecutive minutes, joggers should still walk at least two or three minutes after each half-hour of jogging. And jogging should never be done on a daily basis.

Even the strongest of runners needs a day between episodes of strenuous exercise for the muscles to recover from the strain that jogging inevitably entails.

3. Write a paragraph on one of the following topics. Before you write a draft of the paragraph, share your plan for using process analysis to develop your controlling idea with a classmate. Explain to your partner each step in the process in the correct time sequence. Ask him or her to point out where your process lacks clarity. Then reverse roles and listen to his or her plan. (For help with working with a classmate, see the "Guidelines for Working with Others" on page 26.)

    A. Obtaining a credit card
    B. Sending a fax
    C. Balancing a checkbook
    D. Conducting a successful interview
    E. Bathing a cat, dog, bird, or other pet
    F. Frying an egg (making fudge, etc.)
    G. Parking a car
    H. Applying for a job (or loan or financial aid)

4. Using process analysis as your method of development, write a paragraph on a topic of your own choosing. Make sure that you include all the steps involved in the process being discussed and that you present the steps in the order in which they occur.
5. As you place your process analysis paragraphs in your portfolio, think about the methods of paragraph development that you have tried so far (narration, example, cause and effect, process analysis). Which method did you like the best? Which method do you think you will use the most? Are there some general challenges that writers confront no matter which method they use? If so, what are they? Place your responses to these questions in your portfolio. (For help with maintaining a writing portfolio, see the "Guidelines for Keeping a Portfolio" on page 61.)

Chapter 13

Definition

What Is *Definition*?

Definition is a writing strategy used to explain the meaning of a word or phrase for a reader. Whether you are writing in an academic, personal, or professional setting, clearly defining a word or phrase helps you to avoid confusion and misinterpretation. The challenge in writing a definition paragraph is to define a word or phrase clearly and precisely enough so that your reader understands exactly what you mean. For example, the writer who begins with this topic sentence

Topic — Controlling idea

Friendship means offering support to someone even when you don't agree with his or her choices.

will have to support the controlling idea by presenting additional details and specific information to explain her definition of friendship.

Guidelines for Writing a Definition Paragraph

1. **Decide between formal and informal definition** for the term you are defining.
2. **Place the term** you are defining **in a meaningful class and distinguish it from other items in the class.** This guideline is especially important in formal definition of a concrete term.
3. **Develop the definition** with additional details, an extended analogy or story, or by contrasting facts.

Decide between Formal and Informal Definition

Some terms can be very clearly and concretely defined in a formal sense—as they are in the dictionary. *Graffiti,* for example, is writing that is done on a wall,

Using Definition in Real Life

You probably already have experience providing a clear definition for a word or phrase.

- You tell your father that your new sweetheart comes from a good family. He asks you to define *good family.*
- In your job as a personnel assistant, you must explain to a new part-time employee the meaning of nonexempt status.
- You complain to a store manager that *customer service* does not mean being put on hold for ten minutes and then having to deal with an unfriendly employee. She asks you to explain your version of "customer service."

door, fence, or other public place. However, more abstract terms—like *patriotism, loyalty,* and *common sense*—do not always lend themselves to a formal definition. Instead, their meanings depend upon a person's point of view. An informal definition of such terms is often more appropriate and meaningful.

If your assignment calls for you to define a term with a concrete, formal definition, you can probably provide one by consulting a dictionary. For example:

> Freedom is the state of being free of limitations.
>
> A book is a collection of pages fastened on one side and bound between two covers.
>
> AIDS, or Acquired Immuno-deficiency Syndrome, is a viral disease that weakens the body's ability to fight off infection.

Notice how the following topic sentences differ from the ones just given:

> Freedom is owning one's own car.
>
> A book is an inexpensive way to travel.
>
> AIDS is, in some ways, a lifelong prison term.

Each of the topic sentences in the second group will need the support of examples and details. Why? Each is based upon an informal comparison that needs further explanation to be clear. After all, if a writer is defining a book by placing it into the class "ways to travel" and identifying its special characteristic as "inexpensive," he or she will need to explain the comparison with specific details.

Place the Term in a Meaningful Class and Distinguish It from Other Items in the Class

Providing a clear, precise definition often involves breaking a word or phrase down into two elements: class and distinguishing characteristics. *Class* is the broader group or category to which a word belongs. *Distinguishing characteristics* are the special or unique features that set the term apart from all other terms in the same class. The class and distinguishing features become a writer's controlling idea.

Read a formal definition paragraph.
Will Odeti, a first-year writing student, begins with the topic sentence

Topic: Kwanzaa — Controlling idea: is a worldwide holiday.

Kwanzaa is a worldwide holiday.

His controlling idea, *is a worldwide holiday,* promises a discussion of this relatively new holiday. Here is Will's draft paragraph:

> Kwanzaa is a worldwide holiday. The idea for Kwanzaa goes back to the 1960s. Today, Kwanzaa begins on December 26 and extends to January 1 and is celebrated by an estimated fifteen million people. The holiday is named for the Swahili term *kwanzaa,* which means "first fruits of the harvest." On the last day of Kwanzaa, families and friends join together for a special celebratory dinner.

What's wrong with this definition paragraph?
Will has placed the term *Kwanzaa* into a class (holidays), but he hasn't included the important characteristics of Kwanzaa that set it apart from other holidays. Lots of holidays are celebrated by millions of people worldwide, and lots of holidays are celebrated by enjoying food in the company of family and friends. Though the writer has included the origin of the holiday's name, this information doesn't help to define what Kwanzaa, the holiday, is. Will needs to rewrite his topic sentence to include the distinguishing characteristics of the term as a part of his controlling idea.

> *Class* is the broader group or category to which a word belongs. *Distinguishing characteristics* are the special or unique features that set the term apart from all other terms in the same class.

Read a revised definition paragraph.
Will revised his definition paragraph to include the special features, or distinguishing characteristics, of Kwanzaa that set it apart from other holiday traditions. His paragraph is stronger now because he has offered a clearer, more precise, more meaningful definition of the term.

Organizing a Definition Paragraph

In Chapter 6 you learned that a well-organized paragraph presents ideas and events in the order that best shows the relationships between them. In a definition paragraph, a writer could use time order or importance order, depending upon his or her topic sentence:

Topic sentence	Best way to organize
Acute lymphocytic leukemia is a type of cancer that spreads very quickly.	Time or space order
Success means more to me than earning a high income.	Importance order

Kwanzaa is a worldwide holiday that celebrates African culture and traditions. The idea for Kwanzaa goes back to the 1960s, when Dr. Maulana Ron Karenga, a college professor in California, envisioned a special holiday for people of African background living around the world. Today, an estimated fifteen million people celebrate Kwanzaa, which begins on December 26 and extends to January 1. The holiday is named for the Swahili term *kwanzaa,* which means "first fruits of the harvest." During the Kwanzaa festival, the family gathers to discuss and share the meaning of such values as creativity, unity, responsibility, and self-determination. On each of the seven days, the family also lights a candle. On the last day of Kwanzaa, families and friends join together for a special celebratory dinner.

Activity

Identifying Class and Distinguishing Characteristics

For each of the following topic sentences, identify both the class in which the term belongs and the characteristic that separates the term from others in its class.

A. A chameleon is a lizard that has the ability to change the color of its skin.
B. Weeds are worthless plants.
C. A pessimist is a person who sees only the negative side of life.
D. Yom Kippur is the Jewish holiday on which one asks for forgiveness of one's sins.
E. Hip-hop is a type of music that includes breaks, beats, and scratches.

Develop the Definition

After you have presented a basic definition in your topic sentence—either by identifying a class and special characteristic or by making an informal comparison—you need to provide information to explain the meaning of the term you are defining. This added information may be in the form of

- *details* that further define the term,
- *an extended analogy* or *story* that supports the controlling idea,
- *contrasting facts* that show what something is by explaining what it is *not.*

At all times, a writer should be asking, *What else should I include so that my reader will grasp my meaning?*

Read an informal definition paragraph.

This student writer begins with the following topic sentence:

Topic — Controlling idea

Snow is a wolf in sheep's clothing.

Her controlling idea, *a wolf in sheep's clothing,* promises an explanation through an extended analogy that explains one thing in terms of another. A reader will want to know exactly how snow, a weather phenomenon, is anything like the proverbial disguised wolf. Here is her draft paragraph:

> Snow is a wolf in sheep's clothing. Snow is a type of precipitation formed within clouds as water vapor in the air freezes. Snow falls to earth when this combination occurs: an ample supply of moisture in the air and cloud temperatures that reach or fall below freezing point. Snow often produces dangerous driving conditions.

What's wrong with this definition paragraph?

The writer provides no information to support her controlling idea. Since she is defining *snow* by drawing an analogy, the reader expects the paragraph to include details that show how snow is like something harmful dressed up as something harmless. However, the writer ends up describing snow formation—which might have been suitable if she had had a more formal, technical topic sentence. To revise, she needs to find details that will clarify her informal definition of *snow.*

At all times, a writer should be asking, *What else should I include so that my reader will grasp my meaning?*

Read a revised definition paragraph.

The following revised paragraph is much stronger than its draft. The writer chose to keep her controlling idea and built her definition paragraph on examples and details that show her reader exactly what she means when she defines *snow* as "a wolf in sheep's clothing."

> Snow is a wolf in sheep's clothing. Snowflakes fall from the clouds with silent grace and innocence. On the ground they form an elegant blanket that covers many of the earth's imperfections. As beautiful as it is, however, snow can also

Choosing Transitions for a Definition Paragraph

In Chapter 7, you learned that transitions add coherence to your paragraphs by linking the ideas in one sentence with those in the next and showing their relationships. Transitions act as reminders of what you have already said and as signals indicating where you are going. These transitions are particularly effective in writing that is developed by definition:

also	but	in addition
although (though)	for example	in particular
another	furthermore	
as well as	however	

cause severe trouble. Though a single featherlike flake of snow cannot do much damage, several million (a day's worth of steady snow) can combine to knock down power lines, bury cars, and cave in roofs. Snow also produces dangerous driving conditions, and it can leave cities and towns isolated and immobilized for days. Though it seems harmless—especially to skiers and Christmas carolers—heavy snow can be harmful and even fatal.

☑ Writer's Checklist: Definition

_____ Have you written a topic sentence that includes your topic and your controlling idea—the main point you are making about your topic?

_____ Did you support your controlling idea with information that helps to explain clearly and precisely the meaning of the term you are defining?

- _____ Have you checked whether you have chosen the best route for your paragraph: formal or informal definition?
- _____ If you have chosen formal definition, did you check to see that you have placed your term within a meaningful class and have used details to distinguish it from other items in the same class?
- _____ Have you checked to make certain you have developed your definition in a way that leaves no doubt about your meaning in your reader's mind?
- _____ Did you use one or more of these strategies to develop your definition: additional details, an extended analogy or story, or contrasting facts?

_____ Have you chosen an appropriate organizational pattern for your paragraph: time order or importance order?

_____ When writing your draft, did you seek feedback from a friend, classmate, instructor, or tutor?

_____ Have you revised your draft for focus, unity, support, and coherence? (See Chapter 7.)

_____ Did you edit your work (see Chapter 8), and are you ready to submit a clean copy of your paragraph?

Summary

1. Definition is a writing strategy used to explain the meaning of a word or phrase for a reader. Writing a definition paragraph presents the challenge of defining a word or phrase clearly and precisely enough so that your reader understands exactly what you mean. (See p. 140.)
2. Some terms can be very clearly and concretely defined in a formal sense—as they are in the dictionary. Other terms have meanings that depend upon a person's point of view; informal definition is often a more appropriate strategy for these terms. A writer must decide whether to define a term formally or informally. (See p. 140.)
3. Providing a clear, precise definition often involves breaking a word or phrase down into two elements: *class* and *distinguishing characteristics. Class* is the broader group or category to which a word belongs. *Distinguishing characteristics* are the unique features that set the term apart from other terms in the same class. (See p. 142.)
4. A writer must develop his or her definition in a way that leaves no doubt about a term's meaning in the reader's mind. A definition can be developed with additional details, with an extended analogy or story, or with contrasting facts. (See p. 143.)

Writing Activities

Other Writing Activities

1. In each of the following examples, a student writer has attempted to develop a paragraph by definition. Work with a partner to answer the following questions about each paragraph. (For help with working with a classmate, see the "Guidelines for Working with Others" on page 26.)

   - What term is being defined?
   - Does the writer use formal definition? If so, identify the class and distinguishing characteristics.
   - Does the writer use informal definition? If so, how does the writer make sure that the reader grasps the special significance of the term being defined?

   A. An enabler is a significant person in an addict's life who helps to maintain the addiction. For instance, in a marriage between an alcoholic and a nonalcoholic spouse, the nonalcoholic enabler might enable the other's drinking in a variety of ways, including covering up or excusing excessive drinking. Curiously, though, the enabler might appear to be working against the addictive behavior while in reality enabling it: Continuous nagging to "stop drinking so much" might cause the alcoholic to perceive the nagging as an irritant that can be stopped only by drinking even more. An enabler, then, enables by focusing on the behavior of the other, the addict, instead of focusing on the self. In order to stop enabling, enablers must learn to stop attempting to control the addict and to start looking after themselves. As the saying made famous by Alcoholics Anonymous states, enablers need to seek the courage to change what they can change—not others, but themselves.

B. Sickle-cell anemia is a disease in which red blood cells become sickle-shaped because of the malformation of the large oxygen-carrying molecule, hemoglobin. Although the malformation involves only a tiny part of the molecule, it causes a great reduction in the ability of the entire cell to carry oxygen. In addition, the distorted cells cannot pass through the capillaries. Instead, the sickle cells form clumps that can grow and collect, sometimes blocking important larger vessels and preventing whole sections of tissue from getting necessary oxygen. This causes cell death and can be excruciatingly painful for the victim. Another problem is that the blocked vessels do not allow free passage of substances necessary for protection from diseases and repair of damaged tissue. Perhaps the greatest problem, though, concerns treatment: Sickle-cell anemia has neither a cure nor a preventive. The disease is inherited, occurring most often in African Americans, although members of other groups may suffer from it. Because it is possible to carry the trait for the disease without being harmed by it, all couples who are planning to have children should be tested for the trait. Those people who do carry the gene for sickle-cell anemia should think carefully about the chances their children might have for a healthy life.

C. A black hole is not a hole at all. Rather, it is the remains of a star that in dying collapses on itself. As this happens, the star becomes dense enough to develop a very strong gravitational field, pulling in all matter surrounding it, including its former planets. As time goes on, the black hole becomes increasingly strong and dense as it "eats" more and more galactic matter. Eventually, it begins to migrate from one galaxy to another, its own gravity pulling it toward other bodies. When scientists first noticed these wandering phenomena, the black holes seemed to them to be areas containing a strong force but no matter—mysterious moving vacuums. Later, however, astronomers discovered that a black hole's center indeed does have a tremendous amount of matter, although its volume might be no larger than the head of a pin.

D. Confidence is the key to getting a job. First, a person who appears confident and speaks confidently is impressive, regardless of his or her qualifications. Since many employers offer their own job-specific training programs, they often have better luck seeking out job candidates who are positive people convinced of their own abilities and worth than trying to match their open position with a candidate's previous work experience. Second, since many employers view their employees as company representatives—no matter what job the employee does—employers look for candidates who can offer a positive image of the company in a variety of business settings. Finally, since confident people are in general more motivated and self-reliant on the job, employers can feel (you guessed it) *confident* that the new employee will do whatever it takes to learn the job well.

2. Using either formal or informal definition, develop a paragraph on one of the following topics. Decide whether the paragraph can be developed better by formal or by informal definition. If you choose formal definition, first jot down the class to which the term belongs and the characteristics that make the item different from other members of the class. If you use informal definition, jot down the special qualities you wish to communicate to your reader. Then write your paragraph.

   A. Road rage
   B. Cult
   C. Chat room
   D. Parenthood
   E. Education
   F. Cyberspace
   G. Museum
   H. Responsibility
   I. Sexual harassment

3. Write two paragraphs on a topic or topics of your own choice. Develop one by formal definition and the other by informal definition. You can use the same topic for both paragraphs or two different topics. Be sure that the terms you define lend themselves to the method of definition you have chosen.
4. Examine other paragraphs that you have placed in your portfolio. For any of them, have you used formal or informal definition as a development strategy? If so, can they be improved? If not, could any of their topic sentences have been developed by means of formal or informal definition? While you are thumbing through your folder, ask yourself if you could write a formal or informal definition paragraph on the word *portfolio.* (For help with maintaining a writing portfolio, see the "Guidelines for Keeping a Portfolio" on page 61.)

Chapter 14

Comparison and Contrast

What Are *Comparison* and *Contrast*?

When you examine the ways in which two or more items are alike, you are *comparing* them. When you concentrate on the differences between or among two or more items, you are *contrasting* them. Comparison/contrast writing is often used to help readers make a decision or judgment about something. When you write a comparison or contrast paragraph, it is usually best to focus on either comparing or contrasting rather than to try to do both. However, you may find that for your subject the similarities and differences are equally important. In a comparison or contrast paragraph, you must present a clear and balanced understanding of each item being examined. For example, the writer who begins with this topic sentence

Visiting a tanning booth and applying self-tanning cream are very different ways [Controlling idea] of achieving a tan. [Topic]

will have to support her controlling idea by offering clear points of contrast between these two tanning methods.

Guidelines for Writing a Comparison or Contrast Paragraph

1. **Compare or contrast items in the same class.**
2. **Make sure the class is meaningful** by choosing a class that is narrow enough for an effective comparison.
3. **Choose clear points of comparison or contrast.**

Using Comparison and Contrast in Real Life

You probably already have experience comparing or contrasting two items.

- You tell a friend that Papa Gino's pizza and Pizzeria Uno pizza just aren't the same. He responds, "They're both pizza. What's the difference?"
- You are selling athletic footwear for the summer, and a customer asks you to explain why one pair of running sneakers costs $55 and another pair of running sneakers costs $80. You explain, "Although they look similar, they have very different features."
- After you return home to Atlanta from a visit to San Francisco, your friend asks you to describe San Francisco. You begin by saying, "Well, it's like Atlanta in a lot of ways."

Compare or Contrast Items in the Same Class

To effectively compare or contrast two or more items, you must choose items in the same class. In other words, the items must be in the same related group or category. It makes no sense to compare an alligator and a guitar, or for that matter, to contrast the two because these items could not be put in the same class. On the other hand, comparing (or contrasting) an alligator and a crocodile—or perhaps a guitar and a banjo—would make sense. A workable paragraph would explain similarities or differences between the items in detail.

It makes no sense to compare an alligator and a guitar, or for that matter, to contrast the two because these items could not be put in the same class. On the other hand, comparing (or contrasting) an alligator and a crocodile—or perhaps a guitar and a banjo—would make sense.

Make Sure the Class Is Meaningful

After you have made certain that the items you are comparing or contrasting are in the same class, check to see that the class is narrow enough for the contrast to be meaningful.

Read a contrast paragraph.
Ted Alfano, a first-year writing student, begins with this topic sentence:

Controlling idea: many differences — Topic: Volkswagen Beetle GL and a Buick Park Avenue Ultra

There are many differences between a Volkswagen Beetle GL and a Buick Park Avenue Ultra.

His controlling idea, *many differences,* promises a discussion of the many ways in which these two automobiles differ. Here is Ted's draft paragraph:

> There are many differences between a Volkswagen Beetle GL and a Buick Park Avenue Ultra. On the one hand, the Beetle GL is an economy car. It averages at least 35 miles to a gallon of gas. The Buick Park Avenue Ultra, on the other hand, is a luxury car. It averages approximately 20 miles to a gallon. Second, the Beetle has less leg-room and is not nearly as comfortable on longer trips as the more spacious Park Avenue. Third, the Park Avenue offers far more cargo space for groceries or luggage than the Beetle, which has no trunk. Finally, the list price of a new Beetle GL is approximately $16,000, while the list price of a new Park Avenue is just under $40,000.

What's wrong with this contrast paragraph?

In Ted's paragraph, which he develops with a point-by-point contrast, the topic sentence emphasizes the differences between the two cars. However, while the paragraph is technically a proper contrast between items in the same class (automobiles), the controlling idea of the paragraph is not very significant. Why? The two cars are so far apart in price that few people would ever seriously group them together. A prospective buyer of a Volkswagen Beetle GL might more meaningfully compare or contrast this car with another economy car.

Read a revised contrast paragraph.

Ted revised his paragraph by narrowing the class from "automobiles" to "economy automobiles" and choosing to contrast the Beetle GL with another car within that narrower class. Here is his revised paragraph:

> Despite being in the same price class, the Volkswagen Beetle GL and the Chevrolet Cavalier are very different cars. First, the cars have a very different image from each other and, therefore, appeal to different segments of the economy car market. The Beetle, viewed as the more "hip" of the two, is more popular with the under-thirty driver. The Cavalier is the more family-oriented of the two and appeals to the over-thirty driver. Second, the Beetle has less leg-room and is not nearly as comfortable on longer trips as the more spacious Cavalier, which has 22 percent more interior space. Third, the Cavalier offers far more cargo space for groceries or luggage than the Beetle, which has no trunk. Finally, insurance costs for the Beetle GL run higher by about $110 per year since the insurance industry has rated it as having a higher risk of theft than the Cavalier.

Activity

Identifying Class for a Comparison or Contrast Paragraph

Read each of the following topic sentences. Identify the items being compared or contrasted. Then, determine whether the items are in the same class. Finally, say whether the class is narrow enough to produce a meaningful comparison or contrast paragraph.

A. American football shares many similarities with European rugby.
B. Going through childbirth classes is nothing like I thought it would be.
C. Buying a five-bedroom house is a better decision than renting a studio apartment.
D. Of all the ways I could commute to school, taking the subway is the most economical.
E. Eating five servings of fruits and vegetables each day is a greater health benefit than taking a stress management class.
F. Parents of infants must choose between cloth diapers and disposable diapers.

Choose Clear Points of Comparison or Contrast

When planning a comparison or contrast paragraph, you must choose clear and specific points of comparison or contrast. In the previous paragraph, the writer contrasts two vehicles on four distinct points: market, interior space, cargo space, and insurance costs. If, instead of selecting clear bases for direct comparison or contrast, you randomly give facts about one item and then the other, your paragraph will seem scattered.

Read a comparison paragraph.

Michele Rocha Barra, a student writer, begins her paragraph with the following topic sentence:

Topic

Although cable and satellite television providers like to stress their differences,

Controlling idea

their services are actually very much alike.

Her controlling idea, *are actually very much alike,* promises a discussion of the many ways in which these two types of media service are similar. Here is Michele's draft paragraph:

> Although cable and satellite television providers like to stress their differences, their services are actually very much alike. Satellite television usually provides outstanding reception. Neither variable terrain nor high buildings affect the quality of satellite transmissions. Since all the channels on a satellite system originate in the same place, the reception is equally good for every channel. Cable television offers popular entertainment channels such as SciFi, A&E, Discovery, and MTV. It also provides several news and information channels like CNN, the Weather Channel, and ESPN. Both cable and satellite television usually have numerous "premium" movie channels like HBO and Showtime, and both offer a number of optional packages that customers can tailor to their own specific viewing prefer-

ences. Satellite television provides several pay-per-view channels that let users buy special movies or programs on a one-time basis. The prices for services range from $3 to $5 per month on top of the monthly charge. The basic cost of cable television is approximately $30 per month.

What's wrong with this comparison paragraph?

In her draft, Michele presents only a sketchy view of the similarities between cable and satellite television instead of offering the reader a paragraph organized around direct points of comparison. Most likely, the writer has specific bases of comparison in mind. She does, for example, discuss reception, variety of programming, and price. However, she hasn't used these aspects to draw a clear and direct comparison. Although she tells her readers that satellite television offers excellent reception, she doesn't include any information about the reception from cable television. Similarly, readers learn that cable television offers several popular channels, but we are not told anything specific about the range of channels provided by satellite television.

If, instead of selecting clear bases for direct comparison or contrast, you randomly give facts about one item and then the other, your paragraph will seem scattered.

Read a revised comparison paragraph.

Michele's revised paragraph is stronger because she has chosen four clear and specific points of comparison. This paragraph leaves the reader with a more distinct impression of the writer's main idea—that cable television and satellite television share many similarities. Here is Michele's revised paragraph:

> Although cable and satellite television providers like to stress their differences, their services are actually very much alike. For example, both cable and satellite television usually have outstanding reception. Neither variable terrain nor high buildings affects the quality of their transmissions. Also, since all the channels on a cable or satellite system originate in the same place, the reception is equally good for every channel. In addition, both systems offer a great number of channels, and they tend to provide the same channels. Both have several news and information channels like CNN, the Weather Channel, and ESPN, and both feature special entertainment channels like A&E, SciFi, Discovery, and MTV. They also present many of the same "premium" movie channels like HBO and Showtime. Furthermore, both cable and satellite providers offer users the opportunity to choose from similar viewing "packages." Both systems have a basic package for the most popular channels and then several optional packages that customers can choose to fit their own specific viewing preferences. Finally, the prices for most cable and satellite services are about the same. In most cases, users can purchase basic services from either cable or satellite for approximately $30 per

Choosing Transitions for a Comparison or Contrast Paragraph

In Chapter 7, you learned that transitions add coherence to your paragraphs by linking the ideas in one sentence with those in the next and showing their relationships. Transitions act as reminders of what you have already said and as signals indicating where you are going. These transitions are effective in writing that is developed by comparison:

as	both	likewise, like
at the same time	in the same way	similarly

In writing that is developed by contrast, the following transitions are most successful:

although (even though, though)	in contrast	still
but	on the one hand	whereas
however	on the other hand	yet
instead	rather	

month, with additional charges of $5 per month for premium channels and $3 per month for pay-per-view movies and special events such as concerts or prizefights.

Two Ways to Organize a Comparison/Contrast Paragraph

Writers generally have two options for organizing a comparison or contrast paragraph. As you write, you can present specific details in either a **point-to-point** arrangement or a **whole-to-whole** arrangement.

Point-to-Point

Here is an outline for a comparison paper with a point-to-point organization:

Topic Sentence: As I age, I am becoming more and more like my mother.

Point 1: First, we share a similar attitude toward health and fitness.

1a. Mom, worried about her failing health, began walking daily at the age of forty.

1b. I work out three or four times a week to stay fit and fight off disease.

Point 2: Second, we share a similar attitude toward money.

2a. Mom was always very practical with her money; she never spent impulsively.

2b. I now keep myself on a strict financial budget—something I never did five years ago.

Point 3: Finally, we share a similar attitude toward education.
  3a. Mom was determined to finish her education, even though it meant taking classes at night while we were still young.
  3b. I have recently cut back my hours at work because for me, right now, school is first priority.

The writer chooses three clear and specific bases of comparison for her paragraph and presents them point-by-point. In this method of organization, the reader gains a better understanding of the items being compared by going back and forth from one to the other on two or more points.

Whole-to-Whole

Here is an outline for the same paper with a whole-to-whole organization:

Topic Sentence: As I age, I am becoming more and more like my mother.
  Item 1: My Mother
    1a. Mom, worried about her failing health, began walking daily at the age of forty.
    1b. Mom was always very practical with her money; she never spent impulsively.
    1c. Mom was determined to finish her education, even though it meant taking classes at night while we were still young.
  Item 2: Me
    2a. I work out three or four times a week to stay fit and fight off disease.
    2b. I now keep myself on a strict financial budget—something I never did five years ago.
    2c. I have recently cut back my hours at work because for me, right now, school is first priority.

In this type of organization, one item is explained in full detail before the writer moves to the second item being compared.

Before you draft your comparison or contrast paper, decide which method of organization will work best for you. For a short assignment like a paragraph, either arrangement can be effective. Sometimes, however, writers who choose whole-to-whole run the risk of writing at length on the first item and skimping on the second. On the other hand, writers who take up each point of comparison or contrast in turn may find that their writing is sharper and more effective. Whichever organizational pattern you choose, making an outline and sticking to it as you draft is a successful strategy.

Writers generally have two options for organizing a comparison or contrast paragraph: point-to-point arrangement or whole-to-whole arrangement.

Activity

Point-to-Point or Whole-to-Whole?

Read the following paragraph. Determine whether the writer uses a point-to-point organization or a whole-to-whole organization. Then, ask yourself: Is this the best arrangement of ideas for this paragraph?

Kung fu, the Chinese form of self-defense fighting, differs in several ways from the modern Japanese version, known as karate. "Karate is straight-line action," say some kung fu instructors, "while kung fu involves circular motions." Kung fu uses punches and kicks similar to those in karate, but kung fu movements are more flowing. A karate session looks like an army drill; a kung fu practice resembles a ballet. Karate fighters generally stand in one position and step forward or backward, while kung fu fighters move sideways and back and forth continually. Karate is easier to learn because the fighter remains relatively stationary, moving only the arms and legs. The kung fu fighter, on the other hand, is always moving and therefore needs to develop a high degree of coordination.

☑ Writer's Checklist: Comparison and Contrast

_____ Does your topic sentence include your topic and your controlling idea—the main point you are making about your topic?

_____ Did you support your controlling idea with clear and balanced points of comparison or points of contrast?

  _____ Are the items you are comparing in the same class—in other words, the same related group?

  _____ Is the class narrow enough for an effective comparison?

  _____ Have you chosen several clear, direct points of comparison or contrast?

_____ Have you chosen an appropriate organizational pattern for your paragraph: point-to-point arrangement of points or whole-to-whole arrangement of points?

_____ When writing your draft, did you seek feedback from a friend, classmate, instructor, or tutor?

_____ Have you revised your draft for focus, unity, support, and coherence? (See Chapter 7.)

_____ Did you edit your work (see Chapter 8) and are you ready to submit a clean copy of your paragraph?

Summary

1. *Comparing* means considering the ways in which two or more items are alike. *Contrasting* means examining the ways in which two or more items are different. The challenge in writing a comparison or contrast paragraph is to

present a clear and balanced understanding of each of the items being examined. (See p. 149.)

2. To effectively compare or contrast two or more items, you must choose items in the same class. In other words, the items must be in the same related group or category. (See p. 150.)
3. The class of items being examined should be narrow enough so that the comparison or contrast is meaningful and realistic. (See p. 150.)
4. When you write a comparison or contrast paragraph, you must choose clear and specific points of comparison or contrast. If you randomly give facts about one item and then the other, your paragraph will seem scattered. (See p. 152.)
5. Writers have two options for organizing a comparison or contrast paragraph. As you write, you can present specific details in either a point-to-point arrangement or a whole-to-whole arrangement. (See p. 154.)

Writing Activities

Other Writing Activities

1. Read each of the following topic sentences. For each sentence, identify the class for the items being compared. Next, write down three points of comparison or contrast for each sentence.

MODEL

Grocery shopping online is not so very different from good-old-fashioned "offline" grocery shopping.

Class: Ways to buy groceries

1. Still have to go "up and down the aisles" and select items for your "basket"
2. Still room for human error
3. Still have to make the time to put the groceries away once they are in your house

A. Taking public transportation is often more convenient than driving.
B. For a busy student, a cat is a better pet to own than a dog (or vice-versa).
C. Field hockey is similar to lacrosse in many ways.
D. [Talk show 1, your choice] and [talk show 2, your choice] are similar in many ways.

2. Read each of the following paragraphs. Select two paragraphs, and answer the following questions about each:

- Is the paragraph developed by comparison or contrast or by some other method?
- Identify the points of comparison or contrast. Are the points clear?
- Identify the class for the items being compared.
- Does the writer use (or attempt to use) a point-by-point arrangement or whole-to-whole arrangement?

A. Peacetime flying is different for navy carrier pilots than for their air force cousins. Air force pilots usually live on air bases with their families. Navy pilots make frequent trips to sea away from their loved ones. Flying off ships is also dangerous for navy pilots. When they take off, they have very little space to get up enough speed to stay in the air, so a special device blasts them from a standstill to 150 mph in just three seconds. If something goes wrong, the pilots have only a split second to eject. Landing presents problems for navy pilots too. They land on unstable carrier decks, often at night with only lights to guide them. Air force pilots are also sent to isolated foreign bases, but they have the advantage of flying over land and can use landmarks like rivers and mountains to help them navigate. Even if they have trouble landing, they can usually find help somewhere nearby.

B. The Ibos and the Yorubas, prominent African tribes living in the Republic of Nigeria, are similar in many respects, but one striking difference between them has impressed itself on the minds of visitors more than the similarities between the two cultures. The Ibos have been much influenced by their contacts with Europeans. They have acquired a deep consciousness of the value of education. Many of them have also become Christians. The Yorubas, likewise, have acquired many Western ways and values. They devote themselves seriously to education, and some, like many of the Ibos, have adopted Christianity. The Ibos, except for the Christians among them, practice polygamy. Christian Ibos, of course, respect the Christian taboo on the practice. The Yorubas who have not been converted to Christianity also practice polygamy. The Christians among them do not. What separates the two tribes decisively in the minds of outsiders, however, is a wide difference in the attitude of the two peoples toward the supernatural. Belief in supernatural powers does not play an important part in the life of the Ibos. On the other hand, the Yorubas find life governed to a large extent by a real belief in the existence of spirits and supernatural powers that are very close and that must be considered in daily life. Belief in such spirits is obvious in their stories, art, and customs.

C. Several recent movies have made progress in correcting the negative view of Native Americans that Hollywood has historically presented. For example, Hollywood movies have traditionally portrayed Europeans coming to America as benevolent emissaries of a superior culture. However, the Canadian-Australian film *Black Robe* correctly challenges this view. *Black Robe,* based on the novel by Brian Moore, points out the narrow-minded and intolerant attitudes that Europeans have often displayed toward other groups of people. Moreover, it accurately depicts a Native American culture as moral, tolerant, and extremely complex. Hollywood, in movies like John Ford's *The Searchers,* has also shown European Americans as the victims of Native American aggression. Nevertheless, Kevin Costner's *Dances with Wolves* provides a more accurate picture by reversing the roles. Costner's film, which won an Academy Award for Best Picture, represents European Americans as aggressive opportunists who will go to any lengths to acquire tribal lands. In this film, as was often the actual case, the rapacious greed of European Americans forces Native Americans to respond to violent attacks on their land, heritage, and culture. Finally, Hollywood movies have repeatedly implied that Native Americans would benefit by abandoning their traditional values and adopting European ones. Conversely, the movie *Thunderheart* rightly questions this assumption. In this movie, which is based on an actual incident, an FBI agent of Native American extraction travels to an Oglala Sioux reservation in order to investigate a murder. Until the visit, the agent has disavowed his own Native American background. However, his experiences at the reservation reawaken his inner being, and he grows to recognize the spirituality and beauty that characterize the Native American cultures.

D. For most Americans, breakfast is radically different from lunch and dinner: Whereas most foods eaten at lunch can be served at dinner as well, breakfast foods are often reserved exclusively for the morning meal. Cereals, for example, are rarely served except at breakfast. The same is true for toast, which often appears on the breakfast table but seldom on the lunch or dinner table. In fact, part of the breakfast ritual in America involves browning bread to the desired shade and then buttering it. Bacon and eggs are a breakfast staple across the United States, but they are rarely served as a main dish at other meals. Jam and jelly appear most often at breakfast and only as an occasional extra at lunch and dinner. Unless one eats at an establishment that specializes in waffles and pancakes, these foods are usually consumed only for breakfast. On the other hand, most items found on lunch and dinner tables never show up at breakfast. Roasted meats and fowls, for example, are hardly ever eaten for breakfast. Salads and vegetables are likewise reserved almost exclusively for other meals. And those all-important dishes—soup and dessert—that frequently begin and end lunch and dinner just aren't to be found on American tables before noon.

3. Write a paragraph on one of the following topics. Develop your controlling idea by either comparison or contrast. Then, exchange drafts with a classmate. Each of you should read the other's draft and suggest ways in which the controlling idea, points of comparison or contrast, or the organization could be made sharper. Then revise your paragraph. (If you need help with

commenting on the work of another writer, see the "Guidelines for Giving Feedback" on page 49.)

A. Attending a two-year college and attending a four-year college
B. Desktop computers and laptop computers
C. Traditional medications and herbal remedies
D. Buying a previously owned vehicle and buying a new vehicle
E. Two United States Presidents
F. College sports and professional sports (choose one sport in particular to discuss)

4. Examine two paragraphs from your portfolio: one from earlier in the term and one you have written recently. Do you see similarities and differences between the two paragraphs? Write a paragraph of comparison or contrast in which you support your answer to the previous question. (For help with maintaining your writing portfolio, see the "Guidelines for Keeping a Portfolio" on page 61.)

Chapter 15

Classification

What Is *Classification*?

In a paragraph developed by classification, a writer makes a statement about a subject or class of objects by sorting and analyzing its parts. Writers use this paragraph strategy to break a larger subject such as *holidays* into smaller parts such as *religious holidays, patriotic holidays,* and *cultural holidays.* The challenge in writing a classification paragraph is to divide your subject according to a single principle. For example, the writer who begins with this topic sentence

Topic	Controlling idea
The guests attending our wedding	fell into three distinct groups.

will have to support her controlling idea by clearly dividing the broader class of *wedding guests* into three groups according to some specific principle, such as "relationship to the couple."

Guidelines for Writing a Classification Paragraph

1. **Select a single basis for classifying your subject** when planning your draft, and stick to it as you write.
2. **Select categories that do not overlap.** When you are classifying, your subcategories should be mutually exclusive. This means that each of the parts of your subject should not fit into more than one category.
3. **Choose useful details** that fit into each category.

Select a Single Basis for Classifying Your Subject

In a paragraph developed by classification, the writer must categorize the subject according to a single, specific basis or principle. In other words, the writer must decide how he or she will divide the subject. For example, let's say the writer of the "wedding guests" topic sentence from the example above has chosen

Using Classification in Real Life

You probably already have experience dividing and classifying parts of a larger whole.

- Your three-year-old son wants to help you by putting away the silverware after you've washed it. When he is finished, you discover that the silverware tray is a mess. You say, "Honey, let me help you to organize this a little better."
- As a supervisor, you have to read through a stack of job applications and determine whom to call in for an interview. Your assistant asks, "How do you decide which applicants to call?"
- While on a hunting trip, you tell your friend (a beginner), "There are three things you should never do while following an animal."

relationship to the couple as her basis for sorting the wedding guests into groups. On this basis, she comes up with three groups: family members, friends, and coworkers. If she had chosen as a fourth group *guests over the age of fifty,* her classification would be faulty. Why? There might be guests over fifty years old in one or more of the other groups. She could, however, decide that she wants to sort by age. If so, her three groups might be guests under thirty, guests between thirty and fifty years old, and guests over fifty years old. A classification paragraph is only as effective as its organizing principle.

In a paragraph developed by classification, the writer must categorize the subject according to a single, specific basis or principle. In other words, the writer must decide how he or she will divide the subject.

Read a classification paragraph.

Student writer Sury Pranav begins his classification paragraph with the following topic sentence:

People in the market for a bicycle [Topic] can choose from several basic types [Controlling idea].

His controlling idea, *several basic types,* promises a clear breakdown of the broad topic *bicycles* into several subcategories. Here is Sury's draft paragraph:

> People in the market for a bicycle can choose from several basic types. Those bikers who prefer to ride on paved surfaces such as roads and sidewalks will be happiest with a road bike. Road bikes have thin tires with a light tread, providing the biker a smooth ride on hard surfaces. Also, their frame is more open, with a higher top bar than those of other types of bikes and a lower positioning of the chain rings, resulting in potential for greater speed. There is also the recumbent bike. On this bike, riders are in a reclining position. If, however, the biker prefers

> wooded trails and rutted paths, he or she can choose a mountain bike. The mountain bike has thick knobby tires that help to plow through mud puddles and cushion the blow against rocks and fallen branches. Raleigh and Trek also make wonderful bikes, and a bicycle enthusiast might want to test one of their models. Some companies even make tandem bikes that can be driven by two people at the same time.

What's wrong with this classification paragraph?
In this paragraph, the writer fails to classify the topic (bicycles) using a single basis or organizing principle. He begins by sorting bicycles according to *construction and use* and then moves on to describe a specific type of bicycle, the recumbent bike. Then, with his discussion of the mountain bike, Sury returns to classification according to construction and use. However, the paragraph ends with yet another basis for classification: *bicycle manufacturers.*

Select Categories That Do Not Overlap

When classifying, always choose categories that are mutually exclusive and do not overlap. In the preceding example, the writer breaks this rule. He classifies bicycles primarily by construction and use, but he also sorts them according to specific type of bicycle and then by manufacturer. The problem exists in the overlap between categories. For example, *manufacturers* as a category certainly overlaps with *specific types.* Even *specific types* and *construction and use* have some overlap. Effective writers of classification paragraphs separate their subject into several useful, meaningful categories.

Effective writers of classification paragraphs separate their subject into several useful, meaningful categories.

Read a revised classification paragraph.
In his revision, Sury Pranav makes the divisions in his paragraph much clearer by organizing his ideas around a single basis for classification: *construction and use.* Here is his revised paragraph:

> People in the market for a bicycle can choose from several basic types. Those bikers who prefer to ride on paved surfaces such as roads and sidewalks will be happiest with a road bike. Road bikes have thin tires with a light tread, providing the biker a smooth ride on hard surfaces. Also, their frame is more open, with a higher top bar than those of other types of bikes and a lower positioning of the chain rings, resulting in potential for greater speed. If, however, the biker prefers wooded trails and rutted paths, he or she can choose a mountain bike. The mountain bike has thick knobby tires that help to plow through mud puddles and cushion the blow against rocks and fallen branches. In addition, its tighter, often thicker frame enables the mountain bike to withstand the sudden jolts and stress that characterize off-road cycling. Finally, people who anticipate riding on both paved

and unpaved surfaces can purchase the hybrid bike, which is a blend between the road bike and the mountain bike. The hybrid's tires are thick and enduring enough for a backwoods trail but not so thick as to slow a rider down significantly on a hard surface. Furthermore, its body structure is neither as open as a road bike's nor as tight as a mountain bike's, allowing it both speed and strength.

Activity

Identifying a Basis for Classification

Each of the following topic sentences is followed by several subcategories. Identify the basis for classification—in other words, the single organizing principle—for each group of categories.

MODEL

Topic Sentence:	My refrigerator is separated into three distinct "zones."
Category 1:	Fruits and vegetables
Category 2:	Leftovers
Category 3:	Beer and soda
Basis for Classification:	Things to eat and drink

A. Topic Sentence: The rentals at my local video store are arranged into four groups.

Category 1: Comedy
Category 2: Horror
Category 3: Drama
Category 4: Action/Adventure

B. Topic Sentence: At my job, an employee has three routes to a promotion.

Category 1: Above average sales
Category 2: Outstanding customer relations
Category 3: Positive interactions with coworkers

C. Topic Sentence: Interior paints come in three different types.

Category 1: High gloss
Category 2: Semigloss
Category 3: Flat

Choose Useful Details

Once you determine your basis for classification and select appropriate subcategories, you must then build support for your paragraph by choosing specific facts and details that fit into each category.

Organizing a Classification Paragraph

In Chapter 6 you learned that a well-organized paragraph presents ideas and events in the order that best shows the relationships between them. In a classification paragraph, a writer could use time order, space order, or importance order, depending upon his or her topic sentence:

Topic sentence	Best way to organize
Children exhibit various types of behavior before, during, and after their parents divorce.	Time order
The icons on my computer desktop are arranged in four distinct sections.	Space order
Our study shows three types of risk associated with binge drinking.	Importance order

Read the following outline for a classification paragraph:

Topic Sentence: Eastern Shore Community College offers courses designed to help me advance in my career.

1. English courses will help me to be a better communicator.
   - 1a. Writing for Business
   - 1b. Public Speaking
2. Technology courses will give me necessary computer and Internet skills.
   - 2a. Introduction to Local-Area Networking
   - 2b. Principles of Web Site Design
3. Marketing courses will sharpen what I already know about my field and introduce me to new ideas.
   - 3a. Marketing Communications Management
   - 3b. Business Solutions for E-Commerce Advertising

The writer of this paragraph is planning to classify the courses at her college. Her organizing principle, or basis for classification, is *courses that will advance my career.* She has chosen three useful categories: *English courses, technology courses,* and *marketing courses.* In addition, she is planning to include specific English, technology, and marketing courses that she feels will be helpful to her in her profession. In this way, she is using details from each category to support her controlling idea that the courses at her school are designed to help the career-minded student. Doing so will strengthen her paragraph.

Activity

Choosing Useful Details

For each numbered category listed, give at least two specific details that support the overall basis for classification and fit into that category.

A. Topic: Things needed for a home office

1. Computer/printer
2. Fax machine
3. Copier

B. Topic: Types of international foods that I enjoy

1. Chinese
2. Thai
3. Mexican

C. Topic: Types of country music

1. Bluegrass
2. Texas swing
3. Nashville sound

A Word of Caution: Avoid Oversimplification

In writing a paragraph developed by classification, avoid simplistic statements that a given item has three categories: the one extreme, the opposite extreme, and the in-between. For example, a paragraph that classifies students into three categories—those who study hard and never go to parties, those who don't study at all and spend all of their time socializing, and those who balance the time they spend studying and socializing—may not be very effective. Such a classification is too simplistic. It overlooks many other kinds of students. There is nothing wrong, of course, with writing a three-class paragraph, provided that the three categories you include—and the details you use from each category—reflect your subject accurately.

There is nothing wrong, of course, with writing a three-class paragraph, provided that the three categories you include—and the details you use in each category—reflect your subject accurately.

Writer's Checklist: Classification

_____ Does your topic sentence include your topic and your controlling idea—the main point you are making about your topic?

_____ Did you support your controlling idea by dividing and classifying your subject in a sensible way?

- _____ Do you have a single organizing principle, or basis, for sorting your subject?
- _____ Have you selected useful categories that do not overlap?
- _____ Have you included specific details that fit into each category?

_____ Have you chosen an appropriate organizational pattern for your paragraph: time order, space order, or importance order?

Choosing Transitions for a Classification Paragraph

In Chapter 7, you learned that transitions add coherence to your paragraphs by linking the ideas in one sentence with those in the next and showing their relationships. Transitions act as reminders of what you have already said and as signals indicating where you are going. These transitions are effective in writing that is developed by classification:

additionally (in addition)	and	first (second, third)	next
also	another	finally	

_____ When writing your draft, did you seek feedback from a friend, classmate, instructor, or tutor?

_____ Have you revised your draft for focus, unity, support, and coherence? (See Chapter 7.)

_____ Did you edit your work (see Chapter 8), and are you ready to submit a clean copy of your paragraph?

Summary

1. In a classification paragraph, a writer makes a statement about a subject or class of objects by sorting and analyzing its parts. Your challenge in writing a classification paragraph is to divide and classify your subject according to a single principle. (See p. 161.)
2. In a paragraph developed by classification, the writer must divide the subject according to a single, specific basis or principle. In other words, the writer must decide how he or she will sort out the subject. (See p. 161.)
3. Effective writers of classification separate their subject into several useful, meaningful categories. When classifying, choose categories that are mutually exclusive and do not overlap. (See p. 163.)
4. Each category within the classification should include specific items and details that fit in that category. (See p. 164.)

Writing Activities

Other Writing Activities

1. For each of the following topics, write a topic sentence that could be used to develop a classification paragraph. Then identify the basis for classification for each—in other words, tell *how* you will sort the subject.

   A. Boyfriends/girlfriends
   B. Bosses

C. Childhood illnesses
D. Sports
E. Pets

2. Read each of the following sentences. If you were to use each as a topic sentence for a classification paragraph, which subcategories would you choose?

   A. Television talk shows tend to focus on the same types of topics.
   B. Many types of family vehicles are on the market today.
   C. Blue-jeans customers now have several different "fits" to choose from when they shop.
   D. Dogs can be classified in several ways.
   E. Any checker at a supermarket can tell you that shoppers fall into one of three categories.
   F. Karaoke performers come in three basic types.

3. In each of the following paragraphs, a student writer has tried to develop a topic by classification. Read each paragraph carefully, and answer the following questions:

   - What is the basis for classification?
   - Is there any overlap in categorizing the items?
   - What details does the writer provide within each category?
   - Is the paragraph successful? Why, or why not?

   A. Despite the prosperity of recent years, not all aging baby-boomers face a rosy economic future during their "golden years." Approximately one-third of all baby-boomers will live out the American dream well into their retirement. Well supported by generous 401k programs, private pension funds, and a lifetime of investing in a thriving economy, these seniors will most likely spend the last years of their lives in greater luxury than they ever imagined. Because many of their parents also saved large sums, this group of baby-boomers is likely to inherit even more money. In fact, they will be so well-off financially that social security checks will be nothing more than extra spending money. Another one-third of the baby-boomers will also find themselves financially stable, but this group won't be as well-off as some of their peers. Seniors from this group are likely to own their own homes and have some savings and perhaps a small pension. They most likely will not inherit any additional wealth. While they may not be able to afford the retirement of their dreams, they will most likely never do without necessities. A final third of all baby-boomers face the grim reality of growing old without the resources they will need to maintain even a modest lifestyle. The total net worth of seniors from this category of baby-boomers will be less than $1,000 per person. Having lived in rented housing for most of their lives, they won't own any real estate. Without private pensions to enhance their incomes, they will be forced to rely on skimpy social security checks for all their needs.

B. Carnivorous plants, which are distinguished from other plants by their ability to entrap and digest unwary insects, can be divided into two groups according to the way they catch their prey: active trappers and passive trappers. The familiar Venus's-flytrap belongs in the class of the active trappers. The leaf structure of the flytrap contains trigger hairs that protrude from a hinged surface. When an insect touches one or more of these hairs, the leaf closes, and the insect is trapped inside. Once the leaf is closed, glands on the surface of the leaf secrete enzymes that digest the entrapped victim and thereby supply nutrients to the plant. The equally well-known pitcher plant fits into the category of the passive trappers. This plant exudes an enticing nectar that lures insects into a slippery funnel containing a reservoir of digestive fluid. The fluid then digests the trapped insect, turning it into food for the plant. Carnivorous plants like the Venus's-flytrap and the pitcher plant possess unique and subtle skills, and they must be considered some of nature's more exotic experiments.

C. The origin of English words—their "etymology"—divides them into three distinct groups: Germanic words, Latinate words, and words borrowed from just about everywhere else. Most basic English words come from the Germanic language. For example, almost all of our everyday names of people and objects—like *mother, father, daughter, home, door,* and *bed*—originate in German. Moreover, such common verbs as *walk, talk, sit,* and *sleep* also come from the Germanic tongue. On the other hand, English has also added words from Latinate languages. For example, many English words that relate to law, literature, and religion have Latin roots. Words like *jury, contract,* and *legal* stem from Latin as do *crucifix, cathedral, author,* and *manuscript.* Finally, many English words come from places where English-speaking explorers found things that did not exist in Europe. For instance, from Native American languages they derived the labels for *tobacco* and *hickory* as well as names for places such as *Mississippi* and *Massachusetts.* From the languages of India, English speakers obtained words such as *jungle, bandanna,* and *calico.* While in Australia, they learned words such as *boomerang,* and in Africa, it is believed, they acquired *cocktail.*

D. Although the reasons for failing to vote are as numerous as the people who don't vote, these reasons tend to fall into several categories. Unnecessarily strict voting laws sometimes keep many people from voting. Poll tax laws and "grandfather" clauses are among the types of legislation that discriminate against voters by making it difficult for them to vote. Many college students who attend out-of-state schools cannot vote in the state where their schools are located. Other people fail to vote because they lack interest in either of the major political parties. Many of today's voters feel less and less committed to a specific party, and thus have little motivation to vote. Probably the largest group of stay-at-home eligible voters, however, consists of people who simply have a feeling that they, as individual citizens, have little effect on the outcome of elections. These voters feel powerless and alienated. Apathy toward voting is the outcome, and recent scandals involving high-ranking public officials have contributed greatly to this apathy. In conclusion, it is safe to say that most people who don't vote are either prevented by law from voting, are apathetic to both political parties, or just feel that their votes don't count.

E. Car owners have several ways to prevent burglaries and to help ensure the return of their cars if a theft does take place. First, car owners can take precautions that make theft difficult. The most obvious is locking a car, even one left for a short time in a safe parking lot. At night drivers should park in well-lighted areas only. They should be sure never to leave the keys in the car, even for a few moments. The owner who parks overnight in a driveway can prevent theft by parking with the front of the car facing the street, so that a prospective car thief will run the risk of being seen tampering with the engine. Second, when buying a new car, a driver should insist on having the new devices that have been developed to discourage theft, such as tapered door locks and an alarm system. Third, the car owner can take measures that ensure against the theft of items from the car. Here, again, locking the car helps. Packages, clothing, luggage, and sports equipment should be locked in the trunk, not left on the seat in plain view. Finally, car owners can take precautions that will help the police to identify a car if it is stolen. They can remove license and registration cards from the car when it is not in use, thus making it difficult for thieves to sell the car. All car owners should know the identification numbers on their cars, and they can even mark the car somewhere out of sight with a mark known to no one else. They can also place a small card with a name on it somewhere inside a seat. Identification numbers and hidden markings facilitate the location and return of stolen motor vehicles.

4. Write a classification paragraph on one of the listed topics. Then, exchange drafts with a classmate. Each of you should read the other's draft and answer these questions:

   - Has the writer established a clear organizing principle for the classification?

- Do items fall into more than one category?
- Has the writer included enough details that fit into each category?

Then revise your paragraph. (For help with commenting on another writer's work, see the "Guidelines for Giving Feedback" on page 49.)

A. Drivers
B. Music videos
C. Public transportation
D. Infomercials
E. Parents
F. Football (or hockey, baseball, etc.) fans
G. Movie ratings
H. Science fiction movies

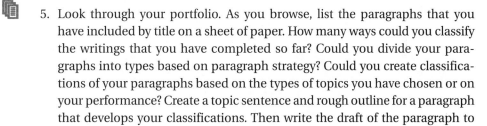

5. Look through your portfolio. As you browse, list the paragraphs that you have included by title on a sheet of paper. How many ways could you classify the writings that you have completed so far? Could you divide your paragraphs into types based on paragraph strategy? Could you create classifications of your paragraphs based on the types of topics you have chosen or on your performance? Create a topic sentence and rough outline for a paragraph that develops your classifications. Then write the draft of the paragraph to include in your portfolio. (For help with maintaining a writing portfolio, see the "Guidelines for Keeping a Portfolio" on page 61.)

Part Three

Strategies for Writing Essays

In Part Two you learned about strategies that writers use to develop paragraphs. Part Three presents strategies for developing essays. Whether your assignment is to write an expository essay (one that explains something) or a persuasive essay (one that makes an argument), these chapters offer guidance in planning your own essay and plenty of models to follow as you write. Specifically, you will learn how an essay differs from a paragraph and how to structure an effective "1-3-1" essay.

Chapter 16

Writing an Essay by Expanding a Paragraph

Up to this point, you have learned how to plan, unify, develop, organize, and revise paragraphs. Though some writing assignments call for a brief response such as one paragraph, others require multiparagraph writing. Because paragraphs serve as building blocks for longer forms of writing, learning how to structure paragraphs effectively is an important step in mastering longer forms of writing, like the essay. This chapter will teach you how to write an essay by expanding a paragraph. (For an explanation of writing an essay from scratch, see Chapter 17. For specific information about writing a persuasive essay, see Chapter 18.)

How Is an Essay Different from a Paragraph?

Both a paragraph and an essay express a single main point about a topic. In a paragraph, the writer discusses the topic briefly in a topic sentence and in several statements of support. In an essay, which is simply a multiparagraph paper, the writer has the opportunity to explore the topic in greater detail. If the paragraph is the two-minute version of the "big story" on the morning news, the essay is the ten-minute in-depth account of the same story that evening.

If the paragraph is the two-minute version of the "big story" on the morning news, the essay is the ten-minute in-depth account of the same story that evening.

Understanding the 1-3-1 Essay

One of the most commonly assigned forms of the essay consists of five paragraphs: an *introduction,* three *body paragraphs,* and a *conclusion.* Because of its five-paragraph structure, this type of essay is often called the 1-3-1 essay. The following diagram shows you the form and the function of the 1-3-1 essay.

Introductory Paragraph

Introduction
Thesis sentence
Divisions

The *introduction* catches the reader's attention, states the writer's main point (thesis) in a *thesis sentence,* and indicates how the writer will go about developing this thesis. The thesis sentence is the most important sentence in an essay. Like the topic sentence of a paragraph, it expresses the controlling idea that the divisions of the essay develop and support.

Body Paragraphs

First Paragraph of Support

Topic sentence: Primary support 1
Details, facts, evidence

The *topic sentence* introduces the first primary support for the thesis. The writer develops the point with specific *details, facts,* and *evidence.*

Second Paragraph of Support

Topic sentence: Primary support 2
Details, facts, evidence

The *topic sentence* introduces the second primary support for the thesis. The writer develops the point with specific *details, facts,* and *evidence.*

Third Paragraph of Support

Topic sentence: Primary support 3
Details, facts, evidence

The *topic sentence* introduces the third primary support for the thesis. The writer develops the point with specific *details, facts,* and *evidence.*

Concluding Paragraph

Summary of main point or restatement of thesis
Final thoughts

In the *conclusion,* the writer brings the essay to a close by *summarizing* the main point or *restating* the thesis. Often the writer will end with a general insight, recommendation, or prediction.

The following essay illustrates the 1-3-1 form:

Introduction

The controversy over human cloning was fueled by the cloning of a sheep in 1997 by Scottish embryologist Ian Wilmut. Wilmut, who set out to improve the productivity of farm animals, got a cell from an adult mammal to behave like a developing embryonic cell. Despite his success, Wilmut opposes the cloning of humans. However, others such as physicist Richard Seed and certain Korean researchers, have publicly announced that they intend to clone humans. This process, Seed claims, will benefit infertile couples and replace lost loved ones. Despite the assertions of such advocates, the question remains whether researchers should try to clone humans.

Thesis sentence

Many scientists, including Ian Wilmut, the famous cloner of the sheep Dolly, believe human cloning should not be done.

Divisions

They cite reasons such as the process, the motives, and the results.

Topic sentence (1st support point)

First of all, scientists have concerns about the cloning process itself.

Details, facts, evidence

Currently, the incidence of death is much higher in cloning than in natural reproduction. In fact, it is ten times greater than normal before birth and three times greater than normal after birth. Also, scientists are uncertain about the effect of using cells from an older person. Will the cells take over where they left off in the original, cutting short the life of the clone? Or will the aging clock be reset in the cloned person? Furthermore, they question the quality of the cells and genes used in the process. Genetic errors accumulate in our cells as we age. We have systems that correct these errors during normal reproduction, but scientists do not know if this correction occurs during cloning.

Topic sentence (2nd support point)

Secondly, many researchers find cloning advocates' motives for copying people very questionable.

Details, facts, evidence

The advocates state that their efforts will enable people to replace lost loved ones, such as older relatives or victims of tragic accidents. However, the opponents argue that this motive is selfish. It is, after all, not the lost loved one who is served in this case but those who survive. The advocates also forecast that the cloning process will enable infertile couples to have children. In this case, a cell would be chosen from one parent, but, critics ask, which parent would they choose? And would a parent want to have a cloned child who is a carbon copy of his or her partner? Finally, the process promises that parents could have the child of their dreams by purchasing a cell from a great scientist or athlete. Researchers point out that for many, the usual motivation for having a child is to give life to someone that you can care for and through whom you can pass on your genes. However, in the case of buying cells to clone, the motivation is very likely wealth and fame.

Topic sentence (3rd support point)

Even when scientists can ignore the arguments against cloning in the first place, it is hard for them not to be against the questionable results. A clone is a genetic duplicate, but not an exact copy. Because the cloned person would be affected by the environment in which he or she was raised, the clone might have personality traits that are distinctly different from the original. The negative effects on the cloned person also must be considered. Scientists and behaviorists point to the problems that could emerge if the cloned human has trouble filling the shoes of the original. In that instance, the clone might develop a negative self-image as a result. The problem would only be worse if the individual was a clone of an intellectually gifted or talented person. What if the clone did not repeat the famous person's accomplishments? Would he or she be abandoned by the disappointed parents?

Details, facts, evidence

Closing generalization

Restatement of thesis

These and other questions about human cloning continue to challenge and split the scientific community. For now, however, the majority of scientists seem to resist the urge to consider human cloning as a miraculous breakthrough in scientific discovery. In fact, these scientists are more concerned about the inefficiency of the cloning process, the suspicious motives for human cloning, and its potentially disastrous results.

Adapting the 1-3-1 Essay

You may feel, at first, that the 1-3-1 essay is a confining form. But keep in mind that no hard-and-fast rule requires you to follow the 1-3-1 formula when you write an essay. In fact, two well-developed paragraphs can often support a thesis

Why Didn't the Writer Cite Any Sources?

Why didn't the writer of the essay on cloning cite sources for the information contained in the piece? Writers have the responsibility to give credit to those sources that provide unique information, ideas, and quotations about a topic. Writers who do not give proper credit are guilty of plagiarizing someone else's work. As the writer of the cloning essay read through her sources, she found that there was a good amount of repetition of information, so she did not cite any specific source.

As a rule of thumb, check to see if the information and ideas included in one source have also been included in two other sources you encounter. If so, the information can be considered "general knowledge" and doesn't need to be cited. For more information on citing sources and avoiding plagiarism, see Chapter 19, Writing from Reading.

sentence. And, of course, you may often find that you need more than three body paragraphs to back up your thesis sentence. But the 1-3-1 formula, while it may seem mechanical, provides you with a structure for building your essay.

Writing the Essay

One way to write a 1-3-1 essay is to expand an existing paragraph into an essay. (If you have been keeping a portfolio for this course, you probably have several paragraphs to choose from.) A paragraph that follows one of the patterns suggested in this text often provides a useful starting point for writing an essay on the same topic. Each of the paragraphs in the body of an essay supports the thesis sentence in the same way that each of the primary supports in a paragraph backs up the topic sentence.

Each of the paragraphs in the body of an essay supports the thesis sentence in the same way that each of the primary supports in a paragraph backs up the topic sentence.

Five Basic Steps

To reshape a paragraph into an essay, follow these five basic steps:

1. Make the topic sentence of the paragraph the thesis sentence of the essay. (The thesis sentence will appear in the introductory paragraph.)
2. Make each of the primary supports in the paragraph the topic sentence of a body paragraph in the essay.
3. Develop each body paragraph of the essay by supporting the topic sentence with details, facts, and evidence.

4. Write an introductory paragraph that catches the reader's attention, states the main point, and presents a preview of the divisions of the essay.
5. Write a concluding paragraph that restates the main point and offers a closing idea.

Figure 16.1 shows the relationship between the parts of a paragraph and the parts of an essay on the same topic.

The following paragraph, for example, has potential material for a 1-3-1 essay:

> The name Nelson Mandela has come to symbolize for people around the world the struggle for justice and freedom in South Africa. From his youth, Mandela dedicated himself to opposing apartheid, the government policy of racial segregation, by studying and practicing law under unfavorable conditions. Mandela's early interest in law was inspired by the cases that appeared before his father, Chief Henry Mandela of the Tembu tribe. With this knowledge, he became determined to pursue a degree in law and to make a difference. When Mandela finished his education, he opened a law practice in Johannesburg, where his work put him in daily contact with blacks who were being displaced by new laws. Due to the oppression that Mandela observed as a young black growing up in South Africa and experienced as a lawyer, he became in 1944 an active member of the African National Congress (ANC), the country's major civil rights group. His first role in the ANC was that of organizer of the Youth League. When the ANC launched its Campaign for the Defiance of Unjust Laws in 1952, Mandela assumed his sec-

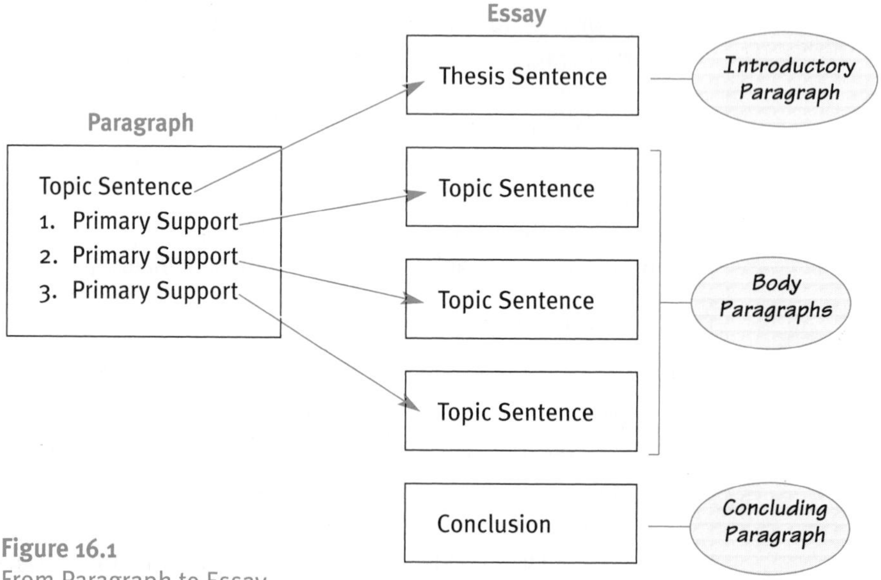

Figure 16.1
From Paragraph to Essay

ond major post, that of National Volunteer-in-Chief. In the late 1950s, however, Mandela determined that his peaceful efforts at overcoming the oppression of apartheid were not working, so he assumed a third major role in the ANC: commander-in-chief of the armed branch of the ANC, the Umkhonto we Sizwe. Holding this position ultimately landed him in jail for twenty-nine years. However, in the early 1990s, when South Africa went through major political and social changes, Nelson Mandela emerged from prison to become the nation's first black leader. Facing growing unrest at home and increased pressure from other countries, President F.W. de Klerk released Mandela and lifted the ban on the ANC in 1990. At the national convention of the ANC held in South Africa in 1991, Mandela was named its president. Then in 1994, after the country's first multiracial elections, Mandela became the first black president of South Africa.

Following the Five Basic Steps

The writer of the Nelson Mandela paragraph now follows the steps for building an essay from an existing paragraph.

Step 1: Make the topic sentence of the paragraph the thesis sentence of the essay.

With slight modification, most topic sentences can function as thesis sentences because the topic sentence and the thesis both serve as contracts that the writer establishes with the reader. That is, both topic sentences and thesis sentences introduce a topic, both convey a controlling idea (main point) about the topic, and both become the central focus of the writer's attention. In constructing an essay from the paragraph on the famous South African leader, the writer would begin by simply taking the topic sentence, *The name Nelson Mandela has come to symbolize for people around the world the struggle for justice and freedom in South Africa,* and using it in the introductory paragraph of the essay as the thesis sentence.

Step 2: Make each of the primary supports in the paragraph the topic sentence of a body paragraph in the essay.

In the paragraph on Nelson Mandela, there are three points of primary support, each introducing a different role Mandela has played in South Africa.

Primary Support 1: From his youth, Mandela dedicated himself to opposing apartheid, the government policy of racial segregation, by studying and practicing law under unfavorable conditions.

Primary Support 2: Due to the oppression that Mandela observed as a young black growing up in South Africa and experienced as a lawyer, he became in 1944 an active member of the African National Congress (ANC), the country's major civil rights group.

Primary Support 3: However, in the early 1990s, when South Africa went through major political and social changes, Nelson Mandela emerged from prison to become the nation's first black leader.

In an essay on Nelson Mandela's accomplishments, these points of primary support will serve as the topic sentences for the body paragraphs.

Step 3: Write a paragraph developing each point of primary support.
To carry out this step, follow the process you learned for writing paragraphs:

- select primary supports that can be developed further with secondary supports,
- choose a suitable method of development, and
- organize your material in the most logical way for your purpose.

In constructing the *primary* supports for the topic sentence of each body paragraph, you may find that you can use facts and ideas that served as *secondary* supports in the original paragraph. Then you will have to add new secondary support to develop those new primary supports, as the writer does in the paragraphs on Mandela on pages 182–84 (see the material underlined in color). For the sake of overall coherence, you may need to add transitional material at the beginning of a body paragraph to smooth your reader's way between paragraphs. This is like using transitional devices to enable your reader to move easily from one idea to the next or from one sentence to the next in a paragraph.

The author of the paragraph on Nelson Mandela did not need to provide additional transitions for her topic sentences when she wrote the following three body paragraphs for her essay because she had already smoothed out the connections between her points in the original paragraph. Note her topic sentences (underlined in black) as well as the transitional devices in the second and third body paragraphs.

Body Paragraph 1

From his youth, Mandela dedicated himself to opposing apartheid, the government policy of racial segregation, by studying and practicing law under unfavorable conditions. Mandela's early interest in law was inspired by the cases that appeared before his father, Chief Henry Mandela of the Tembu tribe. In his father's court, he observed the legal processes that operated in Tembuland at the time. He also encountered firsthand the history and tribulations of his people. With this knowledge, he became determined to pursue a degree in law and to make a difference. Mandela started his higher education by attending the University College of Fort Hare, where he was suspended for joining a protest boycott. After his suspension, he moved to Johannesburg, completed his bachelor of arts degree by mail, and began to study for his law degree. In 1952, while he was confined to Johannesburg because of his political activities, Mandela took his attorney admission exam and was admitted to the profession. After finishing his education, Mandela opened a practice in Johannesburg, where his work put him in daily contact with blacks who were being displaced by new segregationist laws. These people were being removed from their land by the government even though their families had lived there for generations. In fact, Mandela and his law partner were also forced to move their practice from the city to a location where the bulk of their clients could not reach them.

Body Paragraph 2

Due to the oppression that Mandela observed as a young black growing up in South Africa and experienced as a lawyer, he became in 1944 an active member of the ANC, the country's major civil rights group. His first role in the ANC was that of organizer of the Youth League. In this role, Mandela led nonviolent protests against the Afrikaner government, despite persistent arrests. In response to an apartheid victory at the polls in 1948, Mandela and other Youth League leaders drew up the Programme for Action, which advocated boycott, strike, civil disobedience, and noncooperation, along with major reforms. When the ANC launched its Campaign for the Defiance of Unjust Laws in 1952, Mandela assumed his second major post, that of National Volunteer-in-Chief. In this position, he traveled South Africa organizing resistance to discriminatory legislation. Because of his role in the campaign, Mandela was brought to trial but was given a suspended prison sentence due to his advocating nonviolence. In the late 1950s, however, Mandela determined that his peaceful efforts at overcoming the oppression of apartheid were not working, so he assumed a third major post in the ANC: commander-in-chief of the armed branch of the ANC, the Umkhonto we Sizwe. Holding this position ultimately landed him in jail for twenty-nine years. After illegally leaving South Africa in 1961 to address a conference in Ethiopia and to arrange guerilla training for his Umkhonto we Sizwe members, he was arrested, tried, and sentenced to five years in prison. Then, while serving this sentence, he was tried again for sabotage, found guilty, and sentenced to life.

Body Paragraph 3

However, in the early 1990s, when South Africa went through major political and social changes, Nelson Mandela emerged from prison to become the nation's first black leader. Facing growing unrest at home and increased pressure from other countries, President F.W. de Klerk released Mandela and lifted the ban on the ANC in 1990. When he was released, Mandela took up where he had left off and plunged back into his work with the ANC. At the national convention of the ANC held in South Africa in 1991, Mandela was named its president. As ANC president, Mandela worked with de Klerk to end apartheid. For their efforts, Mandela and de Klerk shared the 1993 Nobel Peace Prize. Then in 1994, after the country's first multiracial elections, Mandela became the first black president of South Africa. His most notable achievement as president was to negotiate and finally sign in 1996 a new constitution for South Africa. This constitution, made possible by the efforts of one man to find justice for his people, ensures human rights and guarantees nondiscrimination.

Activity

Analyzing Secondary Supports

Reread the three body paragraphs of the Nelson Mandela essay on pages 182–84. Describe how the underscored material strengthens the body paragraphs.

Step 4: Write an introductory paragraph for the essay.

Once you have completed the body paragraphs, you are ready to write an introductory paragraph to the essay. The introduction to an essay should accomplish three things:

1. Capture the reader's interest.
2. State the thesis.
3. Introduce the major divisions of the essay.

Most introductions begin by attracting the reader's interest and *then* go on to state the thesis and introduce the divisions to be discussed in the body paragraphs.

How does a writer capture the attention of a reader? Or put another way, how does a writer convince a reader that the essay to come will be informative, interesting, entertaining, or otherwise worth reading? In the following introductory paragraph, for example, the writer attracts the reader's attention by making a generalization about Mandela's importance as a leader and a visionary.

How does a writer capture the attention of a reader?

> [Interest] During the past half-century, one man has led the fight against the oppression of South African apartheid, or *apartness*. [Thesis] The name Nelson Mandela has come to symbolize for people around the world the struggle for justice and freedom. [Divisions] As a lawyer, member of the African National Congress (ANC), and national leader, Mandela has worked tirelessly to gain equality for black South Africans.

Other strategies for drawing your reader into your essay follow on pages 186–87.

Activity

Capturing an Audience

Most likely you have seen many television commercials, which in a way are visual essays. Each television commercial has a main point (you should buy X) and at least a few divisions of "support" (the reasons X is a superior product). Each television commercial also uses specific strategies to capture the attention of its audience. Think about a commercial you saw recently on television. Describe the strategy used to draw the audience in. Was it effective? Explain why or why not.

Step 5: Write a concluding paragraph for the essay.

Once you have completed the introduction, you should carefully reread the four paragraphs you have written and prepare a concluding paragraph that will accomplish the following:

1. Restate the thesis and divisions of the essay (in different words).
2. Bring the essay to an appropriate end, without raising major new issues.

In its most basic form, the concluding paragraph may consist of a brief summary of what has been said in the essay. At first you may find this approach the easiest. Such a conclusion should simply restate the thesis and the divisions of the essay in words that differ from those used in the introductory paragraph. The thesis and divisions usually appear after a closing generalization.

In addition to bringing your essay to a close, you should make your ending meaningful and appropriate. Try asking yourself questions—"What do we learn by knowing this information?" or "How should this information change our way of thinking about the subject?"

How to Capture a Reader's Interest

When you write an essay, one of the challenges you face is capturing a reader's attention and interest in your opening paragraph. You could begin your essay with your thesis sentence, but that strategy is often too abrupt. Better yet, you can draw your reader into your thesis in one of several ways. Here are several approaches that the writer of the human cloning essay (see pages 177–78) might have taken to introduce the thesis sentence:

> Many scientists, including Ian Wilmut, the famous cloner of the sheep Dolly, believe human cloning should not be done.

A Simple, Well-Focused Generalization

The debate over cloning humans has erupted in the scientific community. *Many scientists, including Ian Wilmut, the famous cloner of the sheep Dolly, believe human cloning should not be done.* They cite reasons such as the process, the motives, and the results.

Personal Insight

When I first heard about the successful cloning of a sheep in Scotland, I was astonished and appalled. I envisioned the next step to be the creation of a race of bizarre humans straight out of the *Mad Max* movies. Then I started to believe that human cloning was not such a bad idea after all. It seemed to me that we as a species could eliminate genetic defects in our offspring by choosing which humans to clone. Still, I was not surprised when I learned that many in the scientific community oppose my view. *In fact, many scientists, including Ian Wilmut, the famous sheep cloner, believe human cloning should not be done.* They cite reasons such as the process, the motives, and the results.

Anecdote (brief story or incident)

Since a sheep in Scotland skyrocketed to fame in 1997 as the first clone of an adult mammal, the world has been infected with Dollymania. Her wool has been knitted into a valued museum display. And, like a rock superstar, her love life has been the subject of the scandal sheets. When she subsequently gave birth to baby Bonnie, the muckrakers took turns trying to identify the father. To share the glow of the spotlight, a controversy has emerged regarding the implications of her cloning. Some scientist see Dolly as an important step toward the cloning of humans. *Other scientists, including Dolly's cloner, Ian Wilmut, believe that human cloning should not be the next step.* The scientists who oppose human cloning cite reasons such as the cloning process, the motives for human cloning, and its results.

Facts and Data

The first successful cloning of a sheep was accomplished by Ian Wilmut and his colleagues at the Roslin Institute in Edinburgh, Scotland. They succeeded in their cloning process, where others had not, by transferring a cell nucleus from a mammary cell of an adult sheep to an unfertilized sheep egg whose nuclei had been removed by microsurgery. This step gave to the egg a complete set of genes, just as if it had been fertilized by sperm. The researchers then cultured the egg before planting it into a mother sheep. This sheep, in turn, carried the egg and the developing fetus full-term to a successful birth. The resulting lamb turned out to be an exact genetic copy of the adult sheep that had provided the nucleus for the egg. When this result was published in the February 27, 1997, issue of *Nature,* the scientific world was stunned and divided. Some researchers hailed the experiment as a step toward human cloning. *Others, including Wilmut, believed human cloning should not be the next step.* They cite reasons such as the process, the motives, and the results.

Quotation

Harvard-trained scientist Richard Seed has described human cloning as "the first serious step toward becoming one with God." However, most of his colleagues in the scientific community seem unimpressed. *In fact, many scientists, including Ian Wilmut, the famous sheep cloner, believe human cloning should not be done at all.* They cite reasons such as the process, the motives, and the results.

Question(s)

Is it right to clone another human being—to make a genetic copy of yourself, your best friend, your spouse, or your grandma? What use could we as a society possibly have for technology so promising, yet so frightening? And what would life be like for a clone? For those whose motives are pure, cloning could offer a miracle, but what of those individuals who would clone for personal gain or other less pure motives? Further, is human cloning safe? There are no easy answers to these questions, even among the scientific community. *In fact, many scientists, including Ian Wilmut, the famous cloner of the sheep Dolly, believe human cloning should not be done.* They cite reasons such as the process, the motives, and the results.

As a conclusion to the essay on Nelson Mandela, the following paragraph is effective because it restates, in different words, the thesis and divisions presented in the introduction (p. 185) as well as brings the essay to a close:

> When Nelson Mandela stepped down from the presidency of South Africa in 1999, certainly not all of that country's problems had been solved. Nonetheless, Mandela paved the way for a brighter future for his country, leaving behind a legacy of hard work, devotion, determination, and integrity. Perhaps there will be others who come after him who will transform his dream of true equality and harmony into a reality, but in the meantime we can remember the sacrifices he made as a crusading lawyer, as an ANC revolutionary, and as the first black president of his nation.

As you become more comfortable writing essays, you can vary the form of your concluding paragraphs. A concluding paragraph should always summarize your main ideas by restating the essay's thesis and divisions in different words. But in addition, you can use other techniques (see the box on page 189) to give your essay a smooth and significant ending.

How to Make a Smooth Exit

Another challenge you face when you write an essay is composing an effective, memorable conclusion. You should summarize your point for your reader by restating your thesis sentence (in fresh language), but you can go beyond that as well. Look for a way to echo your main point and tie your essay together in some interesting way. Here are several approaches that the writer of the human cloning essay (see pages 177–78) might have taken to conclude her essay.

The Generalization

These and other questions about human cloning continue to challenge and split the scientific community. *For now, however, the majority of scientists seem to resist the urge to consider human cloning as a miraculous breakthrough in scientific discovery.* In fact, these scientists seem more concerned about the inefficiency of the cloning process, the suspicious motives for human cloning, and its potentially disastrous results.

The Link

Link the conclusion and the introduction with a fact, idea, or quotation from the opening.

Should human cloning be done? Maybe it can, as Richard Seed and other advocates would have us believe, help humankind solve problems such as infertility and disease. *But many scientists are skeptical. After assessing the potential costs of human cloning, they feel it should not be done.* Their opposition centers around the inefficiency of the cloning process, the questionable motives of the advocates for human cloning, and potentially disastrous results.

Prediction

Human cloning is likely to be a major focus of scientific and ethical debate in the twenty-first century. During the debate, scientists, researchers, and philosophers will doubtlessly line up on both sides of the question. *For now, though, such people seem to have more concerns about the process than supporting arguments.* In their opposing statements, they cite the inefficiency of the cloning process, the suspicious motives for human cloning, and its potentially disastrous results.

Recommendation

Because of these and other questions, the majority of scientists these days do not support human cloning. The major concerns they have involve the inefficiency of the cloning process, the suspicious motives for human cloning, and its potentially disastrous results. If so many scientists, researchers, and philosophers oppose human cloning, why then are we allowing it to happen? Maybe the federal government should ban this type of experimentation that allows humans to play God.

Besides bringing your essay to a close, you should make your conclusion meaningful and appropriate. Try asking yourself questions—"What do we learn by knowing this information?" or "How should this information change our way of thinking about this subject?" or "If this information is true, what are its implications and what can be done about it?" Often these questions will lead you to discover the best device for concluding your essay.

In an essay on domestic violence, for example, a recommendation on how to deal with this problem and perhaps prevent future incidents would probably be more meaningful and effective than simply echoing a statistic about battered women that you used to gain reader attention in the introductory paragraph. Rather than leaving the reader with a sense of hopelessness, you would close with suggestions of ways the reader could perhaps use the information in your essay to help recognize and deal with the national problem.

In short, the device that you use to close your essay, like the strategy or strategies that you used to begin it, should always be appropriate to the topic and, if possible, should draw meaningful conclusions from your support without bringing up any essentially new or unrelated issues.

The Completed 1-3-1 Essay

Once you have completed the five steps, you have succeeded in constructing a 1-3-1 essay from a paragraph, and you are now ready to combine the parts. The complete essay on Nelson Mandela would read as follows:

> During the past half-century, one man has led the fight against the oppression of South African apartheid, or *apartness*. The name Nelson Mandela has come to symbolize for people around the world the struggle for justice and freedom. As a lawyer, member of the African National Congress (ANC), and national leader, Mandela has worked tirelessly to gain equality for black South Africans.
>
> From his youth, Mandela dedicated himself to opposing apartheid, the government policy of racial segregation, by studying and practicing law under unfavorable conditions. Mandela's early interest in law was inspired by the cases that appeared before his father, Chief Henry Mandela of the Tembu tribe. In his father's court, he observed the legal processes that operated in Tembuland at the time. He also encountered firsthand the history and tribulations of his people. With this knowledge, he became determined to pursue a degree in law and to make a difference. Mandela started his higher education by attending the University College of Fort Hare, where he was suspended for joining a protest boycott. After his suspension, he moved to Johannesburg, completed his Bachelor of Arts degree by mail, and began to study for his law degree. In 1952, while he was confined to Johannesburg because of his political activities, Mandela took his attorney admission exam and was admitted to the profession. After finishing his education, Mandela opened a practice in Johannesburg, where his work put him in daily contact with blacks who were being displaced by new segregationist laws. These people were being removed from their land by the government even though their families had lived there for generations. In fact, Mandela and his law partner were also forced to move their practice from the city to a location where the bulk of their clients could not reach them.

Due to the oppression that Mandela observed as a young black growing up in South Africa and experienced as a lawyer, he became in 1944 an active member of the ANC, the country's major civil rights group. His first role in the ANC was that of organizer of the Youth League. In this role, Mandela led nonviolent protests against the Afrikaner government, despite persistent arrests. In response to an apartheid victory at the polls in 1948, Mandela and other Youth League leaders drew up the Programme for Action, which advocated boycott, strike, civil disobedience, and noncooperation, along with major reforms. When the ANC launched its Campaign for the Defiance of Unjust Laws in 1952, Mandela assumed his second major post, that of National Volunteer-in-Chief. In this position, he traveled South Africa organizing resistance to discriminatory legislation. Because of his role in the campaign, Mandela was brought to trial but was given a suspended prison sentence due to his advocating nonviolence. In the late 1950s, however, Mandela determined that his peaceful efforts at overcoming the oppression of apartheid were not working, so he assumed a third major post in the ANC: commander-in-chief of the armed branch of the ANC, the Umkhonto we Sizwe. Holding this position ultimately landed him in jail for twenty-nine years. After illegally leaving South Africa in 1961 to address a conference in Ethiopia and to arrange guerilla training for his Umkhonto we Sizwe members, he was arrested, tried, and sentenced to five years in prison. Then, while serving this sentence, he was tried again for sabotage, found guilty, and sentenced to life.

However, in the early 1990s, when South Africa went through major political and social changes, Nelson Mandela emerged from prison to become the nation's first black leader. Facing growing unrest at home and increased pressure from other countries, President F.W. de Klerk released Mandela and lifted the ban on the ANC in 1990. When he was released, Mandela took up where he had left off and plunged back into his work with the ANC. At the national convention of the ANC held in South Africa in 1991, Mandela was named its president. As ANC president, Mandela worked with de Klerk to end apartheid. For their efforts, Mandela and de Klerk shared the 1993 Nobel Peace Prize. Then in 1994, after the country's first multiracial elections, Mandela became the first black president of South Africa. His most notable achievement as president was to negotiate and finally sign in 1996 a new constitution for South Africa. This constitution, made possible by the efforts of one man to find justice for his people, ensures human rights and guarantees nondiscrimination.

When Nelson Mandela stepped down from the presidency of South Africa in 1999, certainly not all of that country's problems had been solved. Nonetheless, Mandela paved the way for a brighter future for his country, leaving behind a legacy of hard work, devotion, determination, and integrity. Perhaps there will be others who come after him who will transform his dream of true equality and harmony into a reality, but in the meantime we can remember the sacrifices he made as a crusading lawyer, as an ANC revolutionary, and as the first black president of his nation.

Writer's Checklist: Paragraph to Essay

_____ Have you selected from your portfolio (the collection of writing you have done so far in the course) a paragraph that you think would be a good candidate for expanding into an essay?

_____ Have you made your paragraph's topic sentence the thesis sentence of your essay? To be a strong thesis sentence, it must introduce the topic, state the main point you wish to make about the topic, and lend itself to development by specific details, facts, and evidence.

_____ Have you made each point of primary support in your paragraph the topic sentence of one body paragraph in your essay?

_____ Did you develop each body paragraph by making the secondary supports from your paragraph the primary supports in your essay? Have you written new secondary supports for your essay by asking yourself what additional details, facts, and evidence your readers need to be convinced?

_____ Have you added transitions where necessary between body paragraphs to smooth your reader's way?

_____ Does your introductory paragraph capture your reader's interest, state the thesis (main point) of the essay, and introduce the main divisions in the paper?

_____ Does your concluding paragraph echo the thesis and the divisions of the essay and bring the essay to an appropriate end without raising any major new issues?

_____ Have you reorganized your material into the 1-3-1 format and added transitional material between your final body paragraph and your concluding paragraph?

_____ When writing your draft, did you seek feedback from a friend, classmate, instructor, or tutor?

_____ Have you revised your draft for focus, unity, support, and coherence? (See Chapter 7.)

_____ Did you edit your work (see Chapter 8), and are you ready to submit a clean copy of your essay?

Summary

1. The 1-3-1 essay form consists of the following elements: an introductory paragraph, three body paragraphs, and a concluding paragraph. (See p. 175.)
2. Because the 1-3-1 form provides the writer with a skeleton in which to construct an effectively developed short essay, mastering this form is a useful way for students to learn how to write essays. A 1-3-1 essay can be written by expanding a general-to-specific paragraph into an essay. (See p. 178.)
3. The introductory paragraph of an essay should accomplish three objectives: capture the reader's interest, state the thesis of the essay, and introduce the divisions in the body paragraphs of the essay. (See p. 184.)

4. The body paragraphs should develop and support the main idea according to the divisions of the plan presented in the introduction. When turning a paragraph into an essay, you will find that the secondary supports in the original paragraph can often serve as primary supports in the body paragraphs of the essay. (See pp. 182–84.)
5. The concluding paragraph of a 1-3-1 essay should accomplish two main objectives: It should restate the thesis and the divisions of the essay using words different from those in the introductory paragraph and bring the essay to an end smoothly, without wandering into any new issues. (See p. 185.)

Writing Activities

Other Writing Activities

1. Read the following 1-3-1 essay carefully. On your own or with a small group of classmates, identify the thesis sentence and the three divisions in the body of the essay. Then discuss what technique the writer uses to capture the reader's attention. Finally, describe how the final paragraph in the essay functions as a conclusion. (For help with working as a team, see the "Guidelines for Working with Others" on page 26.)

Suicide and Its Causes

Every year hundreds of thousands of people not only attempt suicide but actually succeed in taking their own lives. This high suicide rate is influenced by a number of factors. Among them are psychological states, sociological conditions, and ineffective means of prevention. If we can learn to recognize these factors, we may become more successful at preventing suicide.

First, various psychological states may lead to suicide. One such state is depression, the most prevalent mental disorder in the world today. Depression itself is often caused by loneliness, loss of a loved one, or feelings of inadequacy. Depressed individuals may feel a sense of hopelessness and helplessness; they may feel that there is nothing they can do to make a real change for the better in their lives. Another psychological state that sometimes leads to suicide is intense guilt. People afflicted with such guilt sometimes believe that they have committed such unforgivable acts that they no longer deserve to be alive. A third mental state that often results in suicide—tension—may stem from a variety of causes. Pressure from deadlines, excessive work or family demands, or the unreasonable expectations that, for example, parents sometimes place on their children can produce such severe tension that some individuals are unable to cope with it. One source of tension especially noticeable these days is financial insecurity. Even in the midst of a booming stock market, some people are still not making ends meet. Overcome by anxiety, some of these people may end up taking their lives. The reason? The same that led to so many suicides during the Great Depression—fear of poverty.

Like economic insecurity, many psychological problems are rooted in sociological conditions. In fact, several sociological factors—including national or ethnic identity, race, sex, and age—play a role in the majority of suicides. For instance, the suicide rate in certain societies is high because of ancient traditions that support suicide as an honorable alternative to hardship. In the United States, recent studies have shown that suicide rates are increasing among minorities, particularly among blacks and Native Americans. Men and women also have different suicide rates. Women lead men in the category of attempted suicides, but men are apparently more successful when they do try. Their success is probably due to their tendency to use lethal weapons. While few children commit suicide, the rate of attempts among adolescents is steadily rising. The breakdown of the family structure and the increased availability of drugs and alcohol are contributors to this trend. Among adults, suicide attempts at middle age are most common; at the midpoint in one's life, escape from past failures often seems attractive. Those who survive middle age, however, are less likely to attempt to take their lives. With age, it seems, comes the ability to accept the stresses and disappointments of life.

Finally, perhaps the most disturbing factor contributing to the high suicide rate is the lack—or ineffectiveness—of suicide prevention. For several reasons, suicides are difficult to predict and prevent. First of all, in order for suicide to be prevented, the troubled individual must seek help. Since many people never seek aid, those who might be able to help never have the chance to do so. Even when distraught people contemplating suicide do call hotlines or friends, they may be so emotionally overwrought that they cannot tell the person on the phone where they are, even if they want to. And the problem does not end when one suicide attempt is prevented because there is no assurance that another attempt won't be made. In many cases, a person who has tried once to commit suicide eventually tries again. If the problems that person sought to escape are still present upon return to daily life, he or she is likely to make another attempt.

A better understanding of the main factors contributing to our high suicide rate—including psychological states, sociological factors, and ineffective means of prevention—is vitally necessary in our society. Perhaps as we become more aware of suicide as a growing problem and more knowledgeable about its contributing factors, we will be able to do more to prevent this wasteful tragedy.

2. Write an introductory paragraph and a concluding paragraph for the following three body paragraphs. To help you get started, we have provided the thesis sentence. Once you have created your introduction and conclusion, share them with a classmate. (For guidance in responding to another writer's work, see the "Guidelines for Giving Feedback" on page 49.)

Thesis Sentence: Winter temperatures need not be uncomfortable if one learns to dress properly.

Body Paragraph 1

Layering, or putting on two light garments instead of one heavy one, is the first way to dress properly for winter temperatures. It is not the thickness of a garment that keeps one warm but rather the garment's ability to trap air in its fibers; the air remains enclosed and is eventually warmed to the body's temperature. And layering garments on top of each other traps air between garments as well as within the garments themselves. Of course, some fibers trap more air than others, and garments made with such fibers naturally provide the best source of layering. Goose down, for example, is an excellent insulator because the feathers fluff up to two or three times their size, filling the spaces between them with warm air. Other effective insulators are duck down, polyester, wool, and cotton, in that order. Polyester and wool have the added advantage of providing insulation even when they are wet.

Body Paragraph 2

Wearing a hat and a vest is another way to protect against the cold. Most of the warm air in the body escapes through the top of the head and from the trunk (chest and abdomen). These areas of the body are vitally involved in maintaining warmth because the organs they contain are the source of body heat. The extremities—legs, arms, toes, and fingers—do not produce heat themselves; they are warmed by the heat that circulates through the body. Wearing a protective hat and a vest prevents heat from escaping from the head and the trunk and thus enables the bloodstream to distribute more heat to the extremities.

Body Paragraph 3

If clothing is properly layered and one is wearing a hat and a vest, the best way to keep the extremities from feeling the cold is to keep them moving and to insulate them with gloves and socks. By moving the fingers and toes, one forces blood to circulate through them, and, as was noted, circulation keeps them warm. Wearing gloves and mittens should prevent the warmth of the blood from escaping through the hands. And mittens, because they allow the fingers to warm each other by contact, are more effective than gloves. Wool socks are an excellent way to keep the toes warm because wool resists water, and feet tend to get wet if snow and slush are on the ground. For added insulation, moreover, mittens and socks can themselves be layered in the same way that coats and other garments are.

3. Expand one of the following paragraphs into an essay. Be sure that the paragraph you choose is on a topic that you know enough about to discuss effectively in an essay.

   A. Living in an apartment with roommates as my too-close neighbors has been enough to try my nerves. First of all, I have had no real privacy since I moved into the apartment. People are constantly bursting into my room to ask a question or just to chat. I cannot turn them away because I do not want to be rude or unfriendly. Second, at least once a day—and sometimes more often—I have to wait for something I need. The washer and dryer are always taken, and the shower seems to be in greatest demand whenever I am in the biggest hurry. And forget about getting a few minutes on the phone. By far the most irritating aspect of apartment dwelling, however, is the noise. I find it almost impossible to concentrate when music is blaring so loudly that the walls shake. And getting enough sleep is certainly difficult with all the talking and yelling I can hear through my room's paper-thin walls.

B. Regardless of the time of day or of the station, most television game shows have a predictable cast. First of all, every game show has a host. At the beginning of the show, the host jogs to center stage, smiles at the audience, makes a few jokes, and then introduces the guests. The host is usually dressed in the latest fashion: Male hosts wear well-cut suits, and female hosts wear designer dresses and pantsuits. When explaining the rules of the game, the host frequently speaks rapidly, using the catchy language of a radio disc jockey. Most game shows feature a guest star or two. Such a "star" is frequently an out-of-work actor or actress whose big series was canceled two or three years ago and who hasn't acted since. Like the host, the stars are dressed stylishly, and—also like the host—they have the ability to smile nonstop for an entire program. Finally, all game-show contestants tend to behave in similar ways. Favorite contestants are people who wear the most outrageous outfits or who easily become hysterical at the sight of a major prize. Whichever category the contestants fall into, they have trouble deciding which prizes to keep and which to give away.

C. Although high-school sports may not be important to everyone, most students who participate in them are favorably affected by the experience. One major advantage that students receive is the self-confidence they develop from performing before a crowd. This self-confidence contributes to the building of a positive self-image, which adults need in order to function successfully in society. Another benefit to be derived from participation in high-school sports is the friendship students form with the other players. Because they must cooperate with one another as a team, students learn to deal with and accept the ways of others. As a result, they develop a tolerance that should help them relate to people in later life. High-school sports also teach students the importance of discipline and determination.

4. Select a paragraph you have written from your portfolio to expand into a 1-3-1 essay. Follow the checklist on page 191. Place your completed essay in your portfolio. (For help with maintaining a writing portfolio, see the "Guidelines for Keeping a Portfolio" on page 61.)

Chapter 17

Writing an Essay from Scratch

Once you understand the format of the 1-3-1 essay and can expand a paragraph into an essay (see Chapter 16), developing an essay from scratch will be less of a challenge. This chapter will guide you through the process of writing a multi-paragraph paper, from the very early stages of determining purpose and audience and finding a topic. Keep in mind, however, that the process for writing an essay is very similar to the one you learned for writing paragraphs earlier in this book:

1. Determine your purpose and audience.
2. Find and explore a topic.
3. Write a thesis sentence with a controlling idea.
4. Develop support for the thesis.
5. Organize support and write a draft.
6. Revise and edit your draft.

(See Part One for more information on the writing process.)

Determine Your Purpose and Audience

You may remember from Chapter 2 that your **purpose** is your reason for writing, and your **audience** is the reader or readers you most want to reach with your writing. As you prepare to write, spend some time thinking about your reasons for writing and the audience that will read your essay. Doing so can help you make decisions about which details to include and how formal or informal to be at a later stage in your writing process.

CASE STUDY: Writing an Informative Essay

Jimmy Mendes, an exchange student studying nursing, was assigned to write an informative essay about a community health service or facility as part of his

Questions to Ask about Purpose and Audience

Purpose Why am I writing?

Am I writing to inform? To persuade? To entertain? To understand?

What is my topic?

What main point do I want to make about my topic?

What issues do I want my audience to think about as they read?

Audience Who will my readers be?

Are they informed or uninformed about the topic? What additional information can I provide?

Do my readers have strong feelings about this topic that I should be aware of?

Should my language and approach be formal or informal?

Community Health Topics class. Although he had not yet decided which community service or facility to explore, Jimmy knew from the start that his purpose was to inform his readers. He also knew that the audience for the paper would be broader than just his instructor and his classmates. His instructor had told the class that she was planning to include several student essays in the nursing program's monthly newsletter, which is distributed to all students and faculty in the nursing program and available online from the school's Web site.

This chapter follows Jimmy as he plans and writes his essay. Many of the steps he takes may seem familiar to you because of your earlier work in this course. The process for writing essays, after all, is very similar to the process for writing paragraphs. You can use his process and his final essay as a model for your own writing.

Find and Explore a Topic

In finding a topic for an essay, you should follow a similar approach to the one you used for choosing a topic for a paragraph (see Chapter 3). If you are free to choose a topic, select one that sincerely interests you or that you care about. Further, make certain the topic is one you know about, have experience with, or can find out about. If your instruc-

If your instructor has assigned a topic, think about what specific aspect of the topic interests you most or relates most closely to your experience.

tor has assigned a topic, think about what specific aspect of the topic interests you most or relates most closely to your experience.

Once you decide on a broad topic, a prewriting strategy can help you to accomplish two tasks:

- **narrow** a general topic, such as *cancer,* to a more specific topic, such as *treatment options for breast cancer patients,*
- **explore** that topic to make certain that it can be developed adequately in an essay.

Chapter 3 offers a detailed explanation of the following prewriting strategies, but here is a brief overview of each:

Brainstorming: Making a list of everything that comes to mind about a topic—facts, personal impressions, details, questions, quotations, emotions. (See page 35 for an example.)

Freewriting: Writing continuously about a topic for a specific period of time, not stopping to worry about grammar, sentence structure, spelling, and punctuation. (See page 36 for an example.)

Clustering: Grouping together related ideas about a topic in a visual format. (See page 38 for an example.)

Questioning: Asking and answering reporters' questions about a topic: *Who? What? Where? When? How?* and *Why?* (See page 39 for an example.)

Keeping a Journal: Responding to events, reacting to people or experiences, reflecting on personal situations or decisions in an informal way. (See page 41 for an example.)

Considering Audience: Thinking about the needs of the audience for a particular piece of writing.

As Jimmy Mendes thought about his assignment, he decided to try brainstorming to narrow his topic. He asked himself, *What health-related services or facilities exist in this community?* and wrote the following list in response:

free walk-in clinic in town

traveling flu-shot service in the public schools

community fitness center

local parks and recreation department

police department's DARE program

Council on Aging/Meals-on-Wheels program for seniors

local chapter of LaLeche league (offers breastfeeding information and support)

Since much of his work in his academic program had been related to sports health, Jimmy decided to write about the community fitness center located in the town in which he lived and attended school.

Activity

Using a Prewriting Technique to Narrow a Topic

Use a prewriting technique to narrow two of the following broad topics (letters A–E) to six more focused topics suitable for development in a 1-3-1 essay.

MODEL **Topic:** Student Life

final examinations

managing school and work

learning new technology

choosing courses

living off campus

paying for school

A. Health
B. Vacations
C. Television
D. Children
E. Computers

Write a Thesis Sentence for Your Essay

The thesis sentence in an essay, like the topic sentence in a paragraph, indicates the writer's narrowed topic and expresses a controlling idea (the main point, or *thesis*) that the rest of the essay will show, explain, or prove. In addition, the thesis sentence prepares readers for the rest of the essay. The strongest thesis statements, for example, have a built-in plan. In other words, the thesis sentence lets the reader know what to expect from the body of the essay and guides the writer in developing the essay.

Find a Happy Medium

Your controlling idea should be broad enough to develop within the structure of a 1-3-1 essay. It should not be so broad or vague, however, that you fail to say anything meaningful about your subject. While an essay gives you more room to write about a topic, you should aim to discuss a narrowed topic in detail rather than scratching the surface of a much larger topic. At the same time, your controlling idea should not be so focused that you find yourself unable to develop it when you begin to write the body paragraphs of your essay.

Read the following three possible thesis sentences for Jimmy Mendes's essay. Only the third example includes a controlling idea that is specific enough to be manageable yet broad enough to be well developed.

	Topic	Controlling idea
Too vague:	Community fitness centers	are great places.
Too focused:	Community fitness centers	are generally open from 6:00 or 7:00 A.M. to 8:00 or 9:00 in the evening.
Effective:	Community fitness centers	offer a wide variety of facilities and programs for the benefit of community members.

In writing your thesis sentence, you should look for a controlling idea that can be discussed fully in the space of several paragraphs.

Activity

Analyzing Thesis Statements

Read the following thesis sentences. For each sentence, describe what you expect of an essay developed from the thesis. Identify words in the sentence that lead you to this expectation.

A. My ideal job would include flexible hours, opportunities for travel, and an emphasis on helping others.
B. Raising a child with cerebral palsy often involves some degree of physical, emotional, and financial struggle.
C. The division of India to create a new country called Pakistan is as controversial today as it was in 1947.
D. Installing ceramic tile correctly takes time and patience.
E. Though only in her twenties, pop star Jewel Kilcher has had twenty years of experience performing for audiences.

Develop Support for Your Thesis Sentence

Once you have a working thesis sentence, you must develop the body of your essay by choosing points of support for it. Before you do so, however, you may find it helpful to decide which *method of development*—narration, example, cause and effect, process analysis, definition, comparison and contrast, or classification—you will use to write your essay. (These methods were covered in Part

Two.) Then you can continue to build support for the controlling idea expressed in your thesis sentence.

Decide on a Method of Development

Most essays, like most paragraphs, can be developed in a number of ways. Your controlling idea probably suggests one or more possible approaches. For example, let's say that you are writing an essay on the general topic of *blind dates*. The following thesis sentence lends itself to development by narration:

> My experiences on blind dates have taught me that compatibility means more than just shared interests.

You would tell the story of going on one or more blind dates to support your main point that shared interests do not automatically equal compatibility. On the other hand, the thesis sentence

> Blind dates arranged by mutual friends are far more successful than those arranged by computer dating services.

suggests a comparison or contrast essay. Further, the thesis sentence

> Preparing for a blind date involves following a familiar routine.

suggests development by process analysis. To be certain that the strategy you've chosen is the best one for your essay, run through the alternatives, and check to see whether any other method might offer a more effective way to develop your thesis sentence.

For his essay, Jimmy Mendes decided that example was the best strategy for developing his thesis sentence:

> Community fitness centers offer a wide variety of facilities and programs for the benefit of community members.

In an essay developed by example, the writer provides specific and convincing examples to illustrate his or her main point. The controlling idea in Jimmy's thesis sentence promises that he will present examples that show the *wide variety of facilities and programs* offered by community fitness centers.

Most essays, like most paragraphs, can be developed in a number of ways. Your controlling idea probably suggests one or more possible methods of development.

Choose the Best Support Points

In Chapter 5, we discussed the importance of building a solid foundation of support for your controlling idea. Support, remember, is any specific detail, fact, or evidence that you can use to show, explain, or prove your main point. Your task is to select points of support that are most likely to convince your reader. In a 1-3-1 essay, the writer includes three major points of support—one per body paragraph—and many other supporting details.

To find and choose support, return to your prewriting—any notes, brainstorming, freewriting, or other strategies that you used to discover your topic or to narrow and explore your topic. Cross out ideas that are unrelated to your thesis, and circle those that seem promising. As you examine your prewriting, ask yourself, *How else can I make my support more convincing?* You may find yourself doing some more prewriting to come up with additional details, facts, or evidence. Depending upon your topic, you may even want to do some research to gather additional support. (See Chapter 19 for more information on writing from sources.)

Jimmy Mendes's notes revealed some preliminary brainstorming that he had done to support his point that community fitness centers offer a wide variety of facilities and programs:

Facilities and programs offered by community health centers

pools

indoor track

aerobics classes

fitness services

basketball

fitness equipment (treadmills, stationary bikes, etc.)

health and nutrition counseling

gymnastics equipment

volleyball

martial arts classes

some stuff for groups

some stuff for individuals

Organize Your Support

Many writers—experienced writers as well as beginners—feel that they benefit from organizing their support in an outline or map before they draft. Doing so helps them to plan their draft. Writers who take this step can usually spot problems in unity (when the essay gets off track) or gaps in support (not enough evidence) before they begin to draft. They can also determine whether the order they have chosen—time, space, or importance—works to their advantage.

To be effective, an outline does not have to be elaborate. It should simply work as a guiding plan for you as you write, reminding you of the major divisions and supporting details within your subject. We will present two formats that may be helpful to you as you outline the support for your thesis sentence:

1. The traditional outline
2. The organizational tree

The Traditional Outline

You may be familiar with the traditional outline from high school or some other academic experience. Creating this sort of outline involves prioritizing your information and ideas and assigning numbers and letters that indicate the way in which you plan to present the support in your paper. The following shows you how to organize your ideas in a traditional outline:

Thesis Sentence: Write your thesis sentence here.

1. First major division of your essay
    a. Primary support for first major point
        1. Secondary support
        2. Secondary support
    b. Primary support
        1. Secondary support
        2. Secondary support
2. Second major division of your essay
    a. Primary support for second major point
        1. Secondary support
        2. Secondary support
    b. Primary support
        1. Secondary support
        2. Secondary support
3. Third major division of your essay
    a. Primary support for third major point
        1. Secondary support
        2. Secondary support
    b. Primary support
        1. Secondary support
        2. Secondary support

Traditional outlines come in two types: *topic* outlines and *sentence* outlines. In a topic outline, the writer includes only key words and phrases to indicate support points. In a sentence outline, which is closer to a draft, the writer writes complete sentences for each support point. Following is an outline that Jimmy

Mendes wrote as he continued to develop support for his thesis. It is a topic outline and does not include secondary supports. If your instructor requires you to submit an outline, ask him or her to be specific about the preferred format.

Thesis Sentence: Community fitness centers offer a wide variety of facilities and programs for the benefit of community members.

1. Competitive sports
   a. Basketball
   b. Volleyball
   c. Other sports (field and court)
2. Specialized group activities and programs
   a. Aerobics classes
   b. Toning and strengthening classes
   c. Martial arts
   d. Health- and fitness-related services
3. Facilities for individualized workouts
   a. Indoor track
   b. Swimming pools
   c. Fitness equipment
   d. Gymnastics apparatus

The Organizational Tree

An organizational tree contains the same information found in a traditional outline, but it is a strategy that appeals more to visual or graphical learners. It is called a "tree" because there is a "trunk" and there are "branches," though it actually resembles a tree turned upside down. Your controlling idea is the trunk of the tree, and your support becomes the larger and smaller branches of the tree.

"Treeing" is similar in appearance to "clustering," a strategy some writers use to generate ideas and facts and to visually map the relationships between those ideas and facts in the early stages (finding/narrowing/exploring a topic) of the writing process (see page 37). Although the two strategies look similar, the purpose of treeing (building and organizing support) is different. The tree version of Jimmy Mendes's outline is illustrated in Figure 17.1.

> Your controlling idea is the trunk of the tree, and your support becomes the larger and smaller branches of the tree.

While both traditional outlines and organizational trees accomplish the same results, you may find that you have a strong preference for one or the other. Choose whichever option works best for you, keeping in mind that the purpose of each is to help you map out the support for your main point and prepare you for writing your draft.

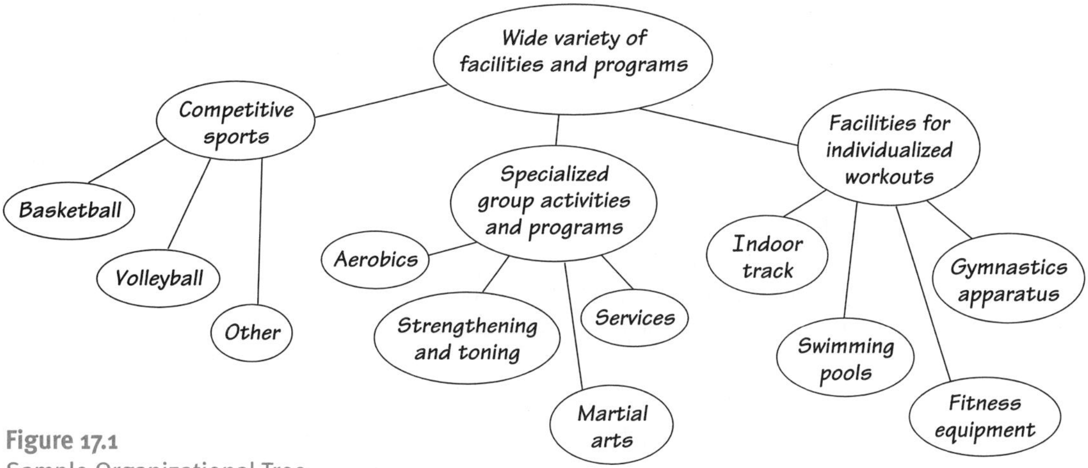

Figure 17.1
Sample Organizational Tree

Activity

Structuring Your Support

Write both a traditional outline and an organizational tree for the essay you are working on currently. Do you prefer one format over the other? What is it about each format that makes it more appealing or less appealing to you?

Checking for Order

If you have made an outline, chances are you have already decided on the most logical way to arrange the support for your thesis sentence. That is, you have decided which major support point to use in the first body paragraph, which to use in the second body paragraph, which to use in the third, and so forth. As you review your outline, consider the arrangement of your primary and secondary supports overall and within each paragraph to ensure that they are arranged effectively.

To review, the following are the most common ways to arrange support for a thesis sentence:

- time order (chronological order)
- space order
- order of importance (emphatic order)

Depending upon your topic, your purpose, and your audience, you may find that one works better than the others for your paragraph.

Time order (or chronological order) means that the points or events covered in an essay are arranged in the order in which they occurred or in which the reader would expect them to occur. Chapter 16 presents an example of an essay organized using time order. The writer supports her point that South African leader Nelson Mandela has done much to champion justice and freedom by offering a chronological look at his accomplishments. She begins with Mandela's childhood and early adulthood experiences, progresses through the 1940s and 1950s, and closes with Mandela's being elected to the office of president of South Africa in the 1990s.

Space order allows writers to organize support points according to some visual pattern. This is the organizational method that Jimmy Mendes chooses for his essay on community fitness centers. He walks his readers through a fitness center to see where the team sports are played, where the specialized classes are held, and where individuals work out on their own. Each of his body paragraphs is about a different area of a fitness center.

Finally, order of importance allows writers to arrange their supporting points from least to most convincing. Such an organization is often effective in persuasive writing. In Chapter 18, the student writer uses importance order to build her argument against tattooing.

You will have a chance to consider your organization again at the revising stage. It is helpful to look over your outline or plan before you draft, however, to see whether you are arranging your support in the most effective way.

Write, Revise, and Edit a Draft

Your draft is the first whole version of your essay. It includes your thesis sentence and all of the supporting details, facts, and evidence that you have chosen to show, explain, or prove your main idea. In your first draft, your ideas are fleshed out in full sentences and paragraphs. As you revise and edit that draft, you move toward a final version of your essay.

Write a Draft

Some writers draft their introduction first, their body paragraphs next, and their conclusion last. Although this approach works for many writers, we have found that many more students have better luck writing the body paragraphs first and then writing the introduction and conclusion. The following sections will help you, too, to write a draft "from the inside out" and then revise and edit it into final form.

Write topic sentences for the body paragraphs of the essay.

In a 1-3-1 essay, the writer supports the thesis statement with three (or more) major points. Working from your outline, turn each of your major points into a sentence that can serve as the topic sentence for one of the body paragraphs of your essay. Remember that the topic sentence of each body paragraph should directly support your thesis by helping to show, explain, or prove the point of your essay.

Student writer Jimmy Mendes wrote these three sentences based on his points of primary support:

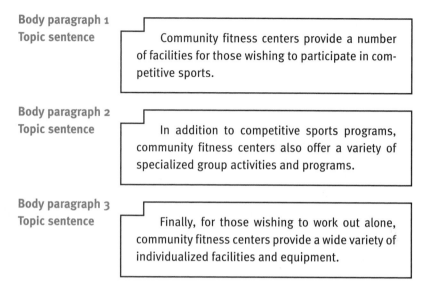

Body paragraph 1
Topic sentence

> Community fitness centers provide a number of facilities for those wishing to participate in competitive sports.

Body paragraph 2
Topic sentence

> In addition to competitive sports programs, community fitness centers also offer a variety of specialized group activities and programs.

Body paragraph 3
Topic sentence

> Finally, for those wishing to work out alone, community fitness centers provide a wide variety of individualized facilities and equipment.

Develop each body paragraph by adding details, facts, and evidence.
In developing the body paragraphs of your essay, refer to your outline for the details, facts, and evidence you chose for your sentences of primary support. Write out the primary support sentences, and then fill in secondary supports as needed. Keep in mind that primary supports are the strongest and most important details that you use to support your topic sentence. Secondary supports are additional details that answer the reader's challenge: *Tell me more.*

Effective body paragraphs often begin with transitional words or phrases that carry the reader smoothly from ideas presented in one paragraph to ideas presented in the next. For a list of common transitions, see page 84.

Write an introductory paragraph.
The introduction to an essay should accomplish three things:

1. Capture the reader's interest.
2. State the thesis.
3. Introduce the major divisions of the essay.

As we said in Chapter 16, most introductory paragraphs begin by attracting the audience's interest, and then go on to state the thesis and present the main points to be discussed in the body paragraphs of the essay.

Before you write your introduction, think about the various methods of catching a reader's interest: generalization, personal insight, anecdote, facts, quotation, questions (see pages 186–87 for an example of each). Decide which one works best for your topic and controlling idea. A helpful strategy is to write two different introductory paragraphs and then get feedback from a friend, classmate, or tutor on which is more effective. After all, if you are trying to hook your readers, why not try out some alternatives on a "live" audience before you submit your draft?

For his essay, student writer Jimmy Mendes chooses to get his reader's attention with facts and data about low levels of fitness among Americans of all ages. His completed essay appears on pages 209–11.

Write a concluding paragraph.

The conclusion is the writer's final words on a subject. Effective writers leave a reader with a reemphasis of the main point and, sometimes, a meaningful final insight or thought about the subject. A concluding paragraph in an essay should accomplish the following:

1. Repeat the thesis and divisions of the essay in different words.
2. Bring the essay to an appropriate end, without raising major new issues.

Your concluding paragraph is your chance to tie your entire essay together. Beyond restating the thesis, try to find some way to leave your reader with the impression of having read a well-developed and fully thought-out explanation, narrative, or argument. As you plan your conclusion, look back at the various strategies we presented in Chapter 16: generalization, link, prediction, recommendation (see page 189 for an example of each). Decide which one works best for your topic and controlling idea.

As demonstrated in his completed essay (pp. 209–11), Jimmy Mendes chooses to create a link from his opening paragraph to his closing paragraph and then to restate his thesis.

Revise and Edit the Draft

During and after the process of transforming an outline or organizational tree into the draft of the essay, the writer should be alert to ways in which the text can be revised and edited to make it better. For reminders on how to revise for stronger writing, see Chapter 7, which provides guidance on how to ensure that your essay is focused, unified, adequately supported, and coherent. For help with editing for grammar, punctuation and mechanics, word use, and ESL problems, see Chapter 8 and Part Five through Part Eight

Jimmy Mendes spent some time with his first draft, revising principally for coherence, grammar, and a few ESL challenges. After completing his revisions and editing, he took a break from his essay. The next day, with a fresh eye, he read it again. Assured that it was in the best shape possible, he printed it and submitted it to his instructor. His final draft follows.

Jimmy Mendes's Final Draft

According to recent reports, two-thirds of all American adults fall below recommended physical fitness levels, and more than half of all college students are either overweight or in poor shape. Experts agree that almost all Americans, from children to the elderly, would benefit from increased physical activity and especially from regular exercise. Unfortunately, many people overlook a valuable resource that is, in most communities, readily available and accessible. Community fitness centers offer a wide variety of facilities and programs for the benefit of community members.

People who wish to participate in competitive sports will find a number of facilities available at community fitness centers. "Pickup" basketball, for example, is a favored activity in many communities. Fitness centers almost always have one and often several indoor basketball courts that are available to all users. At larger centers, games may run continuously from early morning until the center closes. Games are typically short, and, as new players arrive, they usually have to wait only long enough for the current game to end before being able to join other newcomers in challenging the winners. In addition, many community centers provide one or more outdoor athletic fields for those wishing to organize pickup games in baseball, softball, soccer, and rugby, and they usually provide a number of courts for games like tennis, squash, handball, and racquetball. The unwritten rules for these activities resemble those for pickup basketball and are designed to give an opportunity to everyone who wishes to play. At some larger centers where demand for such facilities is quite high, participants may be able to reserve them a day or two in advance.

In addition to competitive sports programs, community fitness centers also offer a variety of specialized group activities and programs. These programs include high-energy activities like aerobics classes. The more strenuous aerobics classes often appeal mainly to younger members, but most centers make "low-impact" versions available for those wanting less stressful exercise. Many centers also organize anaerobic workout classes that focus on toning and strengthening major muscle groups and on improving flexibility. Some centers even provide instruction in martial arts, and several hold special self-defense classes for those eager to learn how to defend themselves. Community fitness centers also commonly work with local health-care providers to offer health-related services for the general population and for people with special needs. For example, various fitness programs may include instruction in nutrition and weight management. Even more specialized fitness programs are usually available for individuals with specific health problems like cardiovascular disease, arthritis, diabetes, and physical disabilities.

Finally, for those wishing to work out alone, community fitness centers provide a wide variety of individualized facilities and equipment. Most centers contain indoor tracks where users can walk, jog, or run. Some centers also make outdoor tracks available to their members. Almost all centers feature an indoor swimming pool, which is usually very popular. Most fitness center pools are reserved for swimming laps, and some may also have diving boards, but only a few centers allow purely recreational swimming. The goal is to maximize the use of the pool by swimmers who want to get the most possible exercise from them. Still another extremely popular feature in community fitness centers is free-standing exercise equipment for those who desire an individualized workout. Centers usually provide weight training with both free weights and weight machines, and most centers offer instruction in how to use this equipment effectively. Other exercise equipment commonly found at community fitness centers include stationary bikes, rowing machines, and stair steppers. Moreover, most fitness centers continue to support the most traditional activity of all: gymnastics. Although nowadays gymnastics is mostly practiced by specialists, many centers provide tumbling mats, pommel and vaulting horses, parallel bars, balance beams, and similar equipment for anyone who wishes to use them.

Most people admit that they pay too little attention to physical fitness and get less exercise than

```
they should. However, too many do nothing to correct
the problem. Many communities in America have excellent
local fitness centers. Among the many competitive sports
programs, group activities, and individualized resources
available at such facilities, almost anyone can develop
a fitness program that is both fun and beneficial.
```

☑ Writer's Checklist: Writing an Essay

_____ In planning your essay, have you determined your purpose (reason) and audience (readers)?

_____ Did you use a prewriting strategy such as brainstorming, freewriting, clustering, or questioning to find and narrow your topic? If the topic was assigned by your instructor, did you use a prewriting strategy to discover what aspect of the topic to write about?

_____ Does your thesis sentence include your narrowed topic and your controlling idea—the main point that the rest of the essay will show, explain, or prove?

- _____ Did you check to make sure your thesis sentence is neither too broad nor too focused?

_____ Have you developed adequate support for your thesis sentence?

- _____ Is the development strategy you've chosen (narration, example, cause and effect, process analysis, definition, comparison/contrast, or classification) best for your topic and controlling idea?
- _____ Have you returned to your notes or prewriting to discover specific details, facts, and evidence that you can use to show, explain, or prove your main point? If not, do additional prewriting or research to gather additional support for your thesis.

_____ Have you outlined your support points?

_____ Are your points arranged logically according to time order, space order, or order of importance?

_____ Have you written a draft using complete sentences and paragraphs?

- _____ Does each body paragraph have a topic sentence?
- _____ Have you developed each body paragraph by including primary supports that reinforce the topic sentence and secondary supports that give additional details about the primary supports?
- _____ Does your introductory paragraph capture your reader's interest, state the main point of the essay, and introduce the main divisions in the paper?
- _____ Does your concluding paragraph echo the thesis and the divisions of the essay and bring the essay to an appropriate end without raising any major new issues?
- _____ When writing your draft, did you seek feedback from a friend, classmate, instructor, or tutor?

_____ Have you revised your draft for focus, unity, support, and coherence? (See Chapter 7.)

_____ Did you edit your work (see Chapter 8), and are you ready to submit a clean copy of your essay?

Summary

1. Once you understand the format of the 1-3-1 essay and can expand a paragraph into an essay (see Chapter 16), writing one from scratch will be less of a challenge. To write a 1-3-1 essay, follow these steps:
   - determine your purpose and audience;
   - find and explore a topic;
   - write a thesis sentence with a controlling idea;
   - develop support for the thesis;
   - organize support;
   - draft, revise, and edit your draft.
2. Your purpose is your reason for writing. Your audience is your reader or readers. Determining purpose and audience early in the writing process can help you to make decisions about your essay as you write. (See p. 196.)
3. Of any potential topic, a writer should ask (a) Do I care about this topic? (b) Do I know something about it? (c) Do I have experience with it? and (d) Can I find out about it through research? A writer should answer *yes* to at least one of these questions before finalizing his or her topic. (See p. 197.)
4. Prewriting is helpful in narrowing a broad topic to one that is more specific and manageable in the space of a 1-3-1 essay. (See p. 199.)
5. A thesis sentence for an essay should present both the narrowed topic and a controlling idea that is neither too broad nor too focused to be developed effectively. (See p. 199.)
6. Writers develop support for a thesis by deciding which method of development to use and by choosing the most convincing details, facts, and evidence to reinforce the main point of the essay. (See p. 200.)
7. Creating an outline or organizational tree helps a writer plan a draft. By including main points, primary supports, and secondary supports, a writer can spot breaks in unity or gaps in support. (See p. 202.)
8. The following are the most common ways to arrange support in an essay: time order, space order, and order of importance. (See p. 205.)
9. Each body paragraph should begin with a topic sentence that relates directly to the thesis sentence and is then developed by the primary supports of the paragraph. (See p. 206.)

10. An introduction should (a) capture a reader's interest, (b) state the thesis or main point, and (c) introduce the major divisions of the essay. A conclusion should (a) restate the thesis and (b) bring the essay to an appropriate and meaningful close. (See pp. 207 and 208.)
11. Purposeful revision and careful editing are vital to the success of an essay.

Writing Activities

Other Writing Activities

1. With a small group of classmates, narrow each of the following general subject areas down to six different topics suitable for 1-3-1 essays. (See page 199 for a model.) (For help with working with others, see the "Guidelines for Working with Others" on page 26.)

   A. Music
   B. Public speaking
   C. Fashion
   D. Drugs
   E. Films
   F. Automobiles
   G. Education
   H. Parents
   I. Credit cards

2. Read the following sentences and identify which ones would make good thesis sentences, which ones are too narrowly focused for discussion within the framework of a 1-3-1 essay, and which ones are too broadly focused.

   A. At different stages in their lives, people regard Santa Claus differently.
   B. One reindeer, in particular, was Santa's favorite.
   C. Santa Claus is based on a number of myths and legends about both real and fictitious people.
   D. The computer center is really great.
   E. The computer center was constructed for one principal purpose.
   F. The campus computer center should have been built in a more convenient location.
   G. The life of a professional bowler can be extremely monotonous.
   H. A recent poll showed that most men wear size eleven bowling shoes.
   I. Hard-soled shoes are not permitted on bowling lanes.
   J. The new tennis court is finally finished.
   K. The new tennis court is unique.
   L. The new tennis court is surrounded by a twelve-foot fence.
   M. *Love,* in tennis, means "no score."
   N. The word *love* has many definitions.

O. There are many different types of discrimination.
P. Discrimination is the source of many recurrent social problems.
Q. Despite significant gains made during the turbulent sixties, discrimination is still alive and still horrible.
R. Soap operas are fun.
S. Soap operas are successful for a variety of reasons.
T. Most soap operas are on television between the hours of 1:00 and 4:00 P.M.

3. Write one thesis sentence for each of the following topics. Feel free to narrow the topics in whatever way you think best.

MODEL Topic: Student evaluations of the faculty

Thesis: Student evaluations of the faculty are important for several reasons.

A. Privatizing schools
B. Blizzards (or hurricanes, earthquakes, or tornadoes)
C. Teenage pregnancy
D. Breakfast cereals
E. An embarrassing accident
F. Political correctness
G. Health clubs
H. A life-changing experience

4. Write an outline for an essay based on one of the following thesis sentences.

MODEL Thesis Sentence: Tourists visit vacation resorts for various reasons.

1. Socializing
    a. meet different types of people from different backgrounds
    b. enjoy outings with other families
    c. meet members of the opposite sex
2. Activities
    a. sports
    b. amusement parks
    c. nightspots
3. Escape
    a. get away from family
    b. break away from daily routines
    c. get away from cities

A. Having to take basic courses in order to graduate from college can often be very frustrating.
B. Baby-sitting is a good job for a teenager to consider.
C. Living in the country (or city or suburbs) is better than living in the city (or country or suburbs).

5. Write topic sentences for each of the body paragraphs you outlined in Activity 4. Base your sentences on the notes in your outline.
6. Write a 1-3-1 essay based on your outline for the thesis sentence in Activity 4. When you begin writing, be sure to use the topic sentences that you wrote in Activity 5 for the body paragraphs of the essay.
7. Write a 1-3-1 essay on *one* of the following thesis sentences.

    A. Modern society is sold on the idea that the "new and improved" product is automatically the best.
    B. People cope with the monotony of everyday jobs in many different ways.
    C. Juvenile criminals should (or should not) be treated as adults.
    D. Money doesn't buy as much as it used to.
    E. Infidelity is a natural phenomenon.
    F. You can tell a great deal about instructors from the way they arrange and maintain their offices.
    G. Where students choose to sit in a classroom may reveal several facets of their personalities.
    H. You can tell New Englanders (Southerners, Westerners, Texans, and so on) by the way they talk.
    I. Building homes for people is the best form of volunteerism.

8. Write an essay on a topic of your own choosing. Be sure to follow the six steps we have given for writing a 1-3-1 essay from scratch. After you have finished your essay written from scratch and after your instructor has evaluated it, measure it against the essay you wrote that grew from a single paragraph. Which approach to essay writing do you prefer: developing a paragraph into an essay or writing the essay from scratch? Support your conclusion in a short essay, which can be shared with classmates and your instructor. Put this work in your portfolio. (For help with maintaining your writing portfolio, see the "Guidelines for Keeping a Portfolio" on page 61.)

Chapter 18

Writing a Persuasive Essay

Up to this point, much of this book has focused on writing that explains. In an explanatory paragraph or essay, you make a point about a topic by offering support for your controlling idea. The point you make is one that reasonable readers are likely to accept once you have explained it in detail. In this chapter you will learn about persuasive writing—writing that persuades or makes an argument.

What Is Persuasion?

To understand what persuasion is and how it differs from explanation, read two pieces of writing on the same topic: a paragraph that explains and a paragraph that persuades.

The following explanatory paragraph is developed by cause and effect:

> The estate of the late Emma Wiltshire is a good location for a city park for several reasons. In the first place, its location is perfect. Its central location makes it convenient for most city residents. Further, it is situated between two city bus lines, making it easy for people at the edges of the city to enjoy it. In the second place, it would make a great site for public and private gatherings. The setting is perfect for a family picnic ground. In addition, the park could serve as a site for outdoor plays. A nice hill on the land, known as "Battle Hill," is a natural seating place for audiences. Finally, and perhaps most importantly to some, the estate, if made into a park, would be an excellent place for citizens to exercise. The park would attract walkers, joggers, and cyclists because it is large enough to have trails through one of the most scenic spots in the county. For these people, the Wiltshire estate would be an ideal alternative to exercising on busy streets that sometimes do not have sidewalks.

This paragraph *explains* why the Emma Wiltshire estate is a good location for a city park. The writer assumes that the audience is reasonable people who need only a series of supporting statements to accept the point that this land would be *a good location for a city park for several reasons.*

In explanatory writing, the writer makes a statement and supports it. In persuasive writing, the writer takes a position and defends it.

But suppose the writer faced a different challenge. What if the writer's audience was not necessarily open to the idea of making the Wiltshire estate into a park? Perhaps some readers favor developing and zoning the land for business use. Others, perhaps, favor selling the land off for development of luxury homes. The writer then has to convince her audience that turning the estate into a park is something they *should* do. In other words, she must *persuade* her readers to agree with her point. The following is a persuasive paragraph on the same topic:

> Our city should buy the old Wiltshire estate and make it into a large city park. Buying this land for a park would solve many of the problems people in this town face when they want to exercise outdoors. In the first place, the property is far enough from the center of town and from heavy traffic so that residents do not have to risk injury just to exercise. The estate is large enough to provide trails for walking, jogging, and even cycling. The property would also answer the city's need for a good site for public and private functions. Equipped with tables, restrooms, and trash cans, it would be perfect for family picnics and even large group gatherings. Furthermore, the estate has a fine hill known as "Battle Hill," which could serve as an outdoor theater. Opponents of my plan suggest that the estate would require too much work at too high a cost for our city's budget. They point to the run-down state of the Wiltshire mansion, which sits in the middle of the property. In response to that argument, I suggest that we consider the possibility of making the mansion a center for meetings and conventions. Such a center would attract business to the area and pay for itself in a short time. Despite the argument of those who oppose my plan, I am convinced that turning the Wiltshire estate into a public area for the people of this town would be good for us all in the long run.

As you can see from these examples, persuasion differs from explanation in several important ways:

1. In explanatory writing, the writer makes a statement and supports it. In persuasive writing, the writer takes a position and *defends* it.
2. The controlling idea in the topic or thesis sentence of explanatory writing becomes more urgent in persuasive writing. In persuasive writing, the thesis is called the **proposition.** It is the place where the writer *proposes* an arguable position.
3. Persuasive writing assumes that the audience is against or hostile to the controlling idea, so the structure of a persuasive piece includes a built-in consideration or **refutation** of that opposing point of view.
4. Persuasive writing often concludes with a call to action.

Using Persuasion in Real Life

Most likely, you have had lots of experience persuading people to agree with you.

- You ask your instructor for an extension on a project deadline. He asks, "Why should I give you an extension?"
- You tell a friend that you believe violent video games should be banned. She asks, "How on earth could you support a ban?"
- At your annual town meeting, you argue that the town should increase property taxes to build a new high school. Another resident challenges: "What's your reasoning?"

The rest of this chapter will explain the structure of a persuasive essay and guide you through the process of writing one.

Activity

Writing Thesis Sentences and Writing Propositions

For three of the following topics, write a thesis sentence (narrowed topic + point you want to make about the topic) for an explanatory essay. Then turn each thesis sentence into a proposition (narrowed topic + your position on the topic).

MODEL

Topic: Pit bulls

Thesis Sentence: Pit bulls have a reputation for being more aggressive than many other breeds of dogs.

Proposition: Towns should require pit-bull owners to register their dogs.

A. Random unannounced locker searches in public schools
B. AIDS testing for couples applying for a marriage license
C. Bilingual education
D. Trapping animals for their fur
E. Adoption rights for gay couples
F. Recruitment of college athletes
G. High cost of college textbooks
H. Body piercing

The Structure of a Persuasive Essay

Persuasive essays can be structured in the same 1-3-1 format that we discussed for explanatory essays in Chapters 16 and 17. The main difference occurs in the body of the essay.

The Concession and Refutation

In an effective persuasive essay, one of the body paragraphs—either the first or the last—includes a **concession** and a **refutation**. The concession is the part of the essay where a writer politely recognizes the opposing point of view. The refutation is the writer's dismissal of the opposing position with even stronger evidence in support of his or her proposition. In the concession, the writer acknowledges, "Well, you've got a valid point there." In the refutation, the writer adds, "But consider this evidence."

In the concession, the writer acknowledges, "Well, you've got a valid point there." In the refutation, the writer adds, "But consider this evidence."

For example, let's say a student is writing an essay in which he argues *against* a dress code for public school students in grades K–12. His final body paragraph might begin with something like the following:

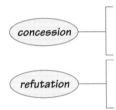

concession

Many of those who feel school dress codes are necessary have legitimate concerns about the health and safety of American schoolchildren. They argue that some students wear baggy pants and jackets to conceal weapons and drugs.

refutation

While this may be true of some students, restricting all students' civil rights is not the answer. Students and their parents must maintain the right to choose appropriate clothing. . . .

In this paragraph, the student recognizes the viewpoints of those who disagree with him (concession) and then goes on to respond to the opposing opinions with additional evidence in support of his proposition (refutation). Raising the opposition's claims—and then dismissing them with your own arguments—strengthens your essay. How? It makes you seem logical and rational, and it suggests that you have spent time thinking carefully about the issue before taking a position.

The Call to Action

Another major difference between the persuasive essay and many other types of essays is the **call to action** issued in the final paragraph. Since you are trying to persuade your readers, the call to action lets you end on a forceful note. In effect, the call to action is your way of saying, "Here is what I want done about this issue" and of inviting readers to act with you. For example, if your proposition is

Employers should offer on-site childcare options for employees with small children.

your call to action might suggest a new law that gives tax breaks to employers offering such programs. You might also urge readers to work together with their employers to explore the possibilities for on-site childcare. Including a call to action engages your readers and results in a fuller argument.

Putting It All in the 1-3-1 Structure

The following diagram shows you the form and function of the 1-3-1 persuasive essay:

Introductory Paragraph

Introduction
Proposition

The *introduction* captures the reader's interest in the issue. The *proposition* states the writer's position.

Body Paragraphs

First Body Paragraph

Topic sentence:
Reason #1
Evidence

The *topic sentence* offers the first reason readers should agree with the writer's proposition. The rest of the paragraph contains specific *evidence* to reinforce reason #1.

Second Body Paragraph

Topic sentence:
Reason #2
Evidence

The *topic sentence* offers the second reason readers should agree with the writer's proposition. The rest of the paragraph contains specific *evidence* to reinforce reason #2.

Third Body Paragraph

Concession
Refutation/Reason #3
Evidence

The *concession* is the writer's recognition of the opposing viewpoint. The rest of the paragraph *refutes* (dismisses or disproves) the opposition with the third and strongest reason and includes specific *evidence* to reinforce reason #3. Some writers present the concession/refutation in their first body paragraph.

Concluding Paragraph

Restatement of proposition
Call to action

The paragraph begins with a *restatement of the writer's proposition* (main point) and urges readers to *act* upon the proposition.

A Process for Writing a Persuasive Essay

The process for writing a persuasive essay is similar to the process you have been practicing throughout this book. If you need additional information about any step in the process, refer to the chapters in Part One.

Discover a Topic for a Persuasive Essay

If you are not assigned a topic by your instructor, finding a promising topic for a persuasive essay involves asking yourself what issues matter to you—in either your personal life, your academic life, or your professional life. Think about your daily conversations with friends, classmates, and coworkers: What are the topics or controversies on which you are most likely to take a position? Which issues do you feel strongly about? What angers you, excites you, or makes you skeptical? Use a prewriting strategy such as questioning, brainstorming, or freewriting to discover a topic that you know about or can find out about and—most importantly—that you care about (see Chapter 3 for more information about prewriting techniques). Keep in mind that you will need to narrow a broad topic, such as *violence,* to something more specific, such as *violence in prime-time television shows.* In addition, persuasive writing requires that you take a position on the issue you plan to write about.

Which issues do you feel strongly about? What angers you, excites you, or makes you skeptical?

Determine Your Purpose and Audience

In persuasive writing, a writer's purpose is always to persuade, or convince, a reader. Convincing readers depends in large part upon the writer's ability to analyze his or her audience. The writer of persuasion must always assume that the reader is on the opposite side of the issue. Not only does the writer ask, *What is my position on this issue?,* but the writer must also ask, *What is my reader's position on this issue?* Beyond knowing your audience's general opinion on or attitude toward the subject, it is also helpful to know how informed the reader is on the subject and how hostile he or she is to your position. What you are trying to do is convince your readers to change, or at least *open,* their minds.

In previous chapters on explanatory writing, we have asked you to decide on your purpose and audience first—before you discovered a topic. In persuasive writing, however, it makes more sense to choose what you'll write about before figuring out your purpose and audience for the essay. All of the steps we present can be helpful to you in your own writing process, but the steps do not necessarily have to be taken in this order. In fact, you may refine your purpose and audience throughout the writing process.

Write a Proposition

Your proposition is the statement of your position on an issue. Like a thesis sentence, it is the foundation for your entire essay.

An effective proposition

- states your narrowed topic and your position,
- is debatable—or, in other words, can be argued for or against.

Activity

What Makes a Good Proposition?

Examine the following sentences and decide which ones would make effective propositions. Of each sentence, ask yourself:

- Does it state a narrowed topic?
- Does it state the writer's position on the topic?
- Is the statement debatable?

MODEL Today's advertising images send a dangerous message about beauty to young people.

Narrowed topic: Advertising images

Position: Send a dangerous message

Debatable? Yes. Some would argue that advertising images send no message at all or a message that is not harmful to young people.

A. Students who pass basic English should earn credit for the course.
B. Microsoft offers new technology to public schools at a discounted rate.
C. The African nation Kenya covers an area of 225,000 square miles and has a population close to 29 million.
D. Antidepressants are overprescribed.
E. Scientists have classified seven types of viral hepatitis.
F. More medical research funding should be directed toward finding cures for viral diseases such as AIDS.
G. Hydroseeding is the best method of installing a new lawn.

CASE STUDY: Writing a Persuasive Essay

Sandrah Roth, a first-year writing student, found herself thinking very closely about the issue of tattooing. Many of her friends had recently been tattooed and were urging her to do it as well. Her choice of topic for a persuasive essay, *getting a tattoo*, grew out of personal interest.

She approached her proposition by asking herself a simple question: Is getting a tattoo a good idea? She did some freewriting to explore her ideas about the topic. In her freewriting, she also acknowledged the point of view of her audience: peers who favor tattooing.

From what I've heard, tattooing hurts! And it's not the safest process either. I don't think tattoo artists are even licensed in this state. A friend told me her procedure took over an hour and that she was sore for days afterward. Ouch! But tattoos are really "in" right now. They look neat and make a statement. Some of my friends are getting tattoos, and a few have asked me if I'd like to go along and do it too. What I really want to know is what people do if they get a tattoo when they're 25 and then regret the decision ten or twenty years later. I can't imagine being a grandmother someday and having my grandchild ask me about the roses around my ankle or the protest symbol on my shoulder. But they say that there are ways to remove tattoos. Laser surgery is one, and I think another one involves removing layers of skin. But I wonder which is more painful and risky, getting a tattoo or removing one? I don't think I want one, but I respect the rights of others to be tattooed if they want to. Overall, though, I think getting a tattoo is a bad idea.

The proposition that Sandrah derives from her freewriting *(Getting a tattoo is a bad idea)* can be used to introduce her topic and state her position, and it is debatable. In writing an essay against tattooing, the writer will need to counter the views of those who favor tattooing both by presenting better reasons for *not* getting tattooed and by directly refuting one or more opposing points.

Develop Support for the Proposition

Once you have written your proposition, you need to develop it by choosing the best, most convincing points of support. Just as in an explanatory essay, your main support points will become the topic sentences for your body paragraphs.

Choose the most convincing points of support.

Sandrah Roth looked back at her freewriting and at some notes she took as she talked to friends about their experiences. She decided to focus on three points that she felt were the most powerful reasons for not getting a tattoo:

health risks associated with tattooing
potential regrets (what's "in" now may be "out" or just plain undesirable in the future)
difficulties in removing tattoos

The writer found that the first two points were issues that most of her friends never seemed to question. They just assumed getting a tattoo was safe and that they would always like the design they had selected. Sandrah decided to address these ideas in her first and second body paragraphs.

After talking with friends, the writer discovered that most individuals in favor of tattooing ended their arguments by saying that it isn't an irrevocable process. In other words, tattoos aren't permanent. However, Sandrah's discussions with some people who had tried to have tattoos removed by various methods revealed that the removal process is expensive, painful, and not always successful. She chose to use the topic of tattoo removal to clinch her argument against tattoos because she knew it would be a strong refutation of readers' objections to her position.

Outline your major points and supporting evidence.

To develop your three (or more) major supports, try using a prewriting technique (see Chapter 3) or doing some research. In building a case for your proposition, you will need to reinforce each of your topic sentences with specific evidence. Evidence can come in the form of details, facts, or testimony (quotations) from experts or others familiar with the topic. Prepare to draft your body paragraphs by outlining your major points and the supporting evidence you will use to convince your audience to agree with your position.

Student writer Sandrah Roth chose to use an organizational tree to outline her body paragraphs (see Figure 18.1). Her tree shows her thesis statement, the major divisions of her argument, and the primary supports she will use to make her case. She also indicates the concession and refutation that she will use in her last body paragraph. (Her draft appears on pages 228–30.)

Three Ways to Organize Your Support

If you have made an outline, chances are you have already decided on the most logical way to arrange the support for your proposition. That is, you have decided which major support point to use in the first body paragraph, which to use in the second body paragraph, which to use in the third, and so forth.

The following are the most common ways to arrange support for your proposition: time order (chronological order), space order, and order of importance (emphatic order). Order of importance, which allows writers to arrange their supporting points from least to most convincing, is often the most effective way to organize a persuasive essay. Sandrah Roth's ordering of her points reflects their relative importance, with the most critical information about health hazards of tattooing appearing first on her tree, and two other areas of concern—potential regrets and difficult removal—coming in succession afterward.

Write, Revise, and Edit a Draft

Your draft is the first whole version of your essay. It includes your proposition and all of the supporting evidence that you have chosen to prove your main point. In a draft, your support points are arranged in the most logical order for your audience and purpose, and your ideas are fleshed out in full sentences and paragraphs.

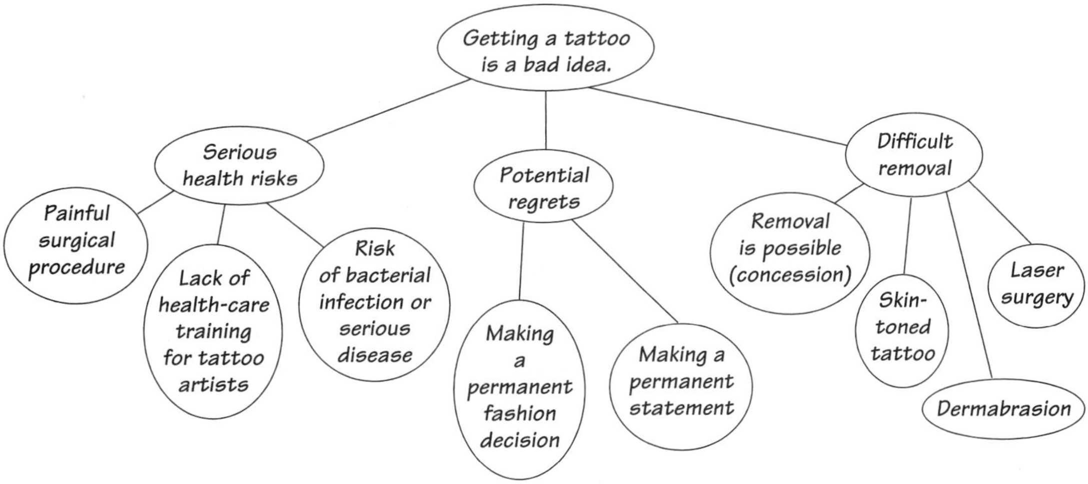

Figure 18.1
Sandrah Roth's Organizational Tree

Write a Draft

As we suggested in Chapter 17, many students find it is easier to write the body paragraphs of an essay first and then the introduction and conclusion than it is to write from start to finish. Drafting the body paragraphs first will help you to stay focused on building a solid support structure for your persuasive essay.

Write topic sentences for the body paragraphs of the essay.
In a 1-3-1 persuasive essay, the writer supports the proposition with three major points. Working from your outline, turn each of your main points into a topic sentence for one of the body paragraphs of your essay.

Sandrah Roth wrote these three sentences based on her organizational tree:

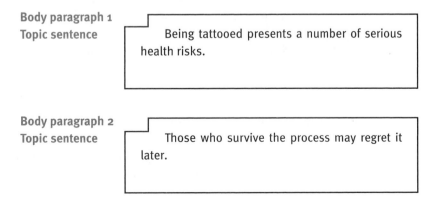

Body paragraph 1
Topic sentence

Being tattooed presents a number of serious health risks.

Body paragraph 2
Topic sentence

Those who survive the process may regret it later.

Body paragraph 3
Topic sentence (includes a concession)

> Despite the dangers to their health and the permanent effects on their bodies that tattoos involve, some people will undoubtedly argue getting a tattoo is not a bad idea because it can be removed.

Develop each body paragraph by adding specific evidence.

In developing the body paragraphs of your essay, refer to your outline for the details, facts, and evidence you chose for your sentences of primary support. Write out the primary support sentences, and then fill in secondary supports as needed. Keep in mind that primary supports are the strongest and most important details that you use to back up your proposition and to refute opposing arguments. Secondary supports are additional details that answer the reader's challenge: *Tell me more.*

Write an introductory paragraph.

The introduction to a persuasive essay, like the introduction to any 1-3-1 essay, should accomplish three things:

1. Capture the reader's interest.
2. State the proposition.
3. Introduce the major divisions of the essay.

As you write your introduction, remember the various methods of attracting a reader's interest: generalization, personal insight, anecdote, facts, quotation, questions (see pages 186–87 for examples). Other strategies for leading up to your proposition include providing background information on the issue or summarizing the controversy that surrounds it. Decide which lead works best for your topic, your purpose, and your audience. If, for example, you are trying to convince a supervisor to hire additional staff, including facts about declining productivity would be more effective than a personal anecdote about being stressed out.

> An effective opening improves the writer's credibility in the mind of the reader—and improves the chances that the reader will be convinced in the end.

For her essay, student writer Sandrah Roth chose to capture her reader's attention by briefly discussing the history of tattooing in American culture and its current upswing in popularity. Her completed essay appears on pages 228–30.

The best introductory paragraphs establish that the writer of the essay is knowledgeable, factual, straightforward, and able to think creatively about the topic. An effective opening improves the writer's credibility in the mind of the reader—and improves the chances that the reader will be convinced in the end.

Choosing Transitions for a Persuasive Essay

Effective body paragraphs often begin with transitional words or phrases that carry the reader smoothly from ideas presented in one paragraph to ideas presented in the next. These transitions are effective in writing that is developed by persuasion:

above all	consider that	in particular
also	especially	more important
another fact to consider	first (second, third)	most important
another reason	for example	remember
another thing	in addition	
best of all (worst of all)	in fact	

These transitions are effective in making a concession and refutation:

although (though)	it's true that	while
but	keep in mind that	yet
granted	nevertheless	
however	still	

Activity

Writing an Introductory Paragraph for a Persuasive Essay

For the persuasive essay you are currently drafting, write two introductory paragraphs using two of the different strategies outlined in Chapter 16 (generalization, personal insight, anecdote, facts, quotation, questions, background, or summary of the controversy) to lead into your proposition. Then describe to a friend, classmate, tutor, or instructor the purpose for your writing, the audience you intend to reach, and your main points of support. Ask him or her to read your two possibilities and tell you which is more effective.

Write a concluding paragraph.

The conclusion is the writer's final word on a subject. In a persuasive essay, ending on a clear, forceful, and convincing note is important. A concluding paragraph in a persuasive essay should include the following:

1. Restatement of the proposition
2. Call to action

Your concluding paragraph offers you the opportunity not only to remind your reader of your position on the topic but also to energize your reader to *do* something in response.

In her concluding paragraph, Sandrah Roth urges her readers to ask themselves several critical questions before deciding to get a tattoo. Her completed essay follows.

Sandrah Roth's Final Draft

Until recently, tattoos were never widely accepted in American culture. For much of the last century, tattoos have been most popular among groups of people who used them to show their independence from the mainstream. However, in recent years tattoos have become fashionable. Today anyone from a celebrity to a doctor or a schoolteacher might proudly wear one or more tattoos. Even students of high-school age or younger feel pressure to join large numbers of their peers in decorating their bodies with inked designs. Getting a tattoo is a bad idea. In fact, people should avoid getting tattooed for a number of reasons. Most importantly, they will be risking their health, they will likely regret their decision later, and they will find the decision very, very hard to undo.

Being tattooed presents a number of serious health risks. First of all, the procedure is painful. Tattoos are applied by inserting a needle and injecting ink into the deepest layers of the skin. For even a small design, this process may take an hour or more and require hundreds of painful punctures. Many subjects feel significant pain for days or even weeks and months afterwards. What people getting tattoos undergo is similar to minor surgery without the benefits of properly trained personnel or a suitable environment for such procedures. States generally require that tattoo artists be licensed; however, most have almost no training in health care, and few tattoo parlors could be called a clinical setting. Furthermore, many so-called tattoo artists practice without a license. Even in the best of circumstances, being tattooed creates a high risk of infection. The multiple punctures stress the whole area around the tattoo. Each needle prick is an open wound and an entry point for bacteria. The needles, the ink, the surroundings, and even the tattoo artist can be contaminated. Those who choose to get a tattoo risk minor bacterial infections and even serious disease. After the procedure, the subject may have to pay the tattoo artist and the doctor too.

Those who survive the process may regret it later. Being tattooed is a fashion decision. It is like choosing to get a new hairstyle or to pierce the ears. However, there is one big difference: Hair will grow back, and earrings will come out, but tattoos stay forever. Styles inevitably change, which means people's tastes change. People who want a tattoo should ask themselves a couple of questions. First, they should ask how they would feel about wearing the clothes they liked best five years ago. Then they should ask what design they would have picked for a tattoo five years ago and if they would choose that same design today. They might also ask if they would like to use that same design for the upholstery on their couch. If they like the design of their tattoo so much that they would permanently imprint it on their furniture, then they might not mind having it permanently imprinted on their bodies. Beyond being a permanent fashion decision, a tattoo may represent a permanent social or political statement. Individuals wanting to make a statement with a tattoo should think seriously about the permanence of the message. Will they feel so passionately twenty or thirty years from now? Chances are that they will not.

Despite the dangers to their health and the permanent effects on their bodies that tattoos involve, some people will undoubtedly argue that getting a tattoo is not a bad idea because it can be removed. However, although some tattoos can be removed, the options for removal are few, and none of them are good. Perhaps the cheapest and least painful option is to have the area tattooed over with skin-toned ink. Unfortunately, this process rarely works. In the best cases, the new tattoo actually covers the old one, but the likelihood of a perfect skin-tone match is low. Most people are left with an ugly, artificial-looking blotch that will become even more noticeable with time. One of the oldest methods of tattoo removal is dermabrasion. The technique is simple, but it is also expensive, dangerous, and extremely painful. In this process, the skin covering the tattoo is removed down to the deepest layers in a way similar to sandblasting. Dermabrasion almost always leaves extensive scarring and presents even greater risks of infection than tattooing. The most modern technique of tattoo removal is laser surgery. By burning away the ink under the skin, lasers can actually remove a tattoo completely without much scarring or blotching. However, the process requires many sessions and may take weeks or months to complete. It can also be extremely painful, and it usually costs thousands of dollars. And like dermabrasion, it can leave visible scars in place of the tattoo.

People thinking of being tattooed should ask themselves the following critical questions: Is this form of self-expression worth the many risks? How important is it to follow the current fashion of tattooing? Is the expression of style, taste, or individuality worth the pain or health risks associated with tattoos? Is a permanent tattoo compatible with changing personal tastes or personal values? People who are contemplating a tattoo should know that if they ever want to remove it, their only options will involve pain, suffering, and expense, and even then these options are not likely to be 100 percent effective. In short, they should decide not to be tattooed.

Revise and edit your essay.

Even experienced writers need to revise and edit their writing. As you learned in Chapter 7, revising requires questioning the focus, unity, support, and coherence of your essay. In the revising stage, writers ask themselves such questions as

Is my main point clear?
Does my essay go off track at any point?
Have I provided enough evidence to support my point?
Does the essay flow smoothly from one section to another?

Seek feedback to your draft from a friend, classmate, writing center tutor, or an instructor. Then revise. For more information about revising, see Chapter 7.

While revising involves making global changes, editing involves making changes to individual words and sentences for clarity and correctness. Refer to the editing checklist presented in Chapter 8 as you edit your essay.

☑ Writer's Checklist: Writing a Persuasive Essay

_____ Does my proposition state clearly my narrowed topic and my position? Is my position debatable?

_____ Have I carefully determined my purpose for writing? What am I trying to accomplish in my essay?

_____ Have I effectively identified my audience and anticipated any objections they may have to my proposition?

_____ Does my introductory paragraph draw the reader in to my subject and serve as a good lead into my proposition?

_____ Have I chosen the strongest and most convincing points of support for my proposition? Have I arranged my major support points from least important to most important?

_____ Does my final body paragraph include a concession (recognition of the opposing viewpoint) and a refutation (dismissal of the opposition with further support for the writer's position)?

_____ Have I developed the body paragraphs of my essay with specific evidence and additional details?

_____ Does my concluding paragraph restate my proposition and, if appropriate, issue a call to action?

_____ Have I revised my draft for focus, unity, support, and coherence (Chapter 7) and edited for clarity and correctness (Chapter 8)?

Summary

1. The persuasive essay differs from other forms of the essay in its purpose. The purpose of persuasion is to persuade, or convince, the audience to accept the proposition (thesis of the essay). (See pp. 216–17.)
2. The 1-3-1 format can be used for a persuasive essay. However, the first or final body paragraph in a persuasive essay should include a concession (recognition of the opposing viewpoint) and a refutation (dismissal of the opposition with further support for the writer's position). (See p. 219.)
3. An effective proposition states the writer's narrowed topic and position and is debatable. (See p. 222.)
4. The body paragraphs of a persuasive essay present the three strongest, most convincing points of support for the proposition. Writers generally arrange the points according to their order of importance. (See p. 223.)
5. In a persuasive essay, each body paragraph is further developed by specific evidence that reinforces the major support point presented in the topic sentence. (See p. 226.)
6. The introductory paragraph of a persuasive essay captures the reader's interest and leads the reader into the proposition. (See p. 226.)
7. The concluding paragraph restates the proposition and often includes a call to action. (See p. 227.)

Writing Activities

Other Writing Activities

1. For each of the following topics, write a proposition that states your position on the topic and is debatable. Imagine that your audience is a campus administrator or the editor of the college (or local) newspaper.

    A. Security on campus late at night
    B. Campus health-care programs
    C. Traffic
    D. Parking
    E. Campus food services
    F. Access to computer laboratories
    G. Eliminating a required course from the core curriculum

2. Write a persuasive essay based on one of the following propositions:

    A. College students without a reliable source of income should (should not) be given credit cards in their own names.
    B. Every student graduating from (insert name of the school you are attending) should (should not) be required to demonstrate proficiency in a second language.
    C. College authorities should notify parents of dependent students when grade point averages fall below 2.0.
    D. Physicians should (should not) lie to terminally ill patients.
    E. Single-sex dormitories on our nation's campuses should (should not) be a thing of the past.
    F. College athletes should (should not) receive stipends.
    G. Spanking is (is not) an effective form of punishment for small children.
    H. Traditional family values are (are not) essential to good political leadership.

3. Write a persuasive essay on a subject of your own choosing.
4. Break up into groups of four students each. As a group, select an issue as a topic for a persuasive essay. Keep in mind that the subject of the essay must be a debatable one. In other words, you should be able to write at least two different propositions. Have two people in the group develop an outline (or organizational tree) for a persuasive essay for one side of the argument, and have the two other people in the group develop an outline (or organizational tree) for an essay arguing an opposite position. Then share outlines. Compare each outline's reasoning and development; discuss possible ways to improve the structure of each argument. Then go back to your original partners and revise your outline. (For help with collaborating with classmates, see the "Guidelines for Working with Others" on page 26.)
5. Add a persuasive essay to your portfolio, and compare it to one of the explanatory 1-3-1 essays already in the portfolio. What are the main differences

between the two essays? How could you take the subject of the explanatory essay and convert it into a proposition for a persuasive essay, and how could you write an explanatory essay about the topic of your persuasive essay? What kind of changes would each of these conversions involve? (For help with maintaining a writing portfolio, see the "Guidelines for Keeping a Portfolio" on page 61.)

Part Four

Strategies for Completing Other Writing Tasks

You will likely find that you need strong writing skills outside of your writing course. Whether you are doing research writing for a nursing course, completing an in-class exam in Introduction to Psychology, communicating by e-mail on the job, or writing an effective résumé to land a job, Part Four presents strategies that will help you to complete a variety of writing tasks.

Chapter 19

Writing from Reading

Many times throughout college, you will be asked to respond in writing to something you have read. This chapter discusses academic assignments, but the strategies given here can be used beyond the classroom as well. In your career after college, you may be required to write a summary of a business report, or you may have to present your ideas and suggestions on something a coworker has written. To complete either a business assignment or an academic assignment effectively, you will need to follow a series of basic steps:

1. Read and understand the material.
2. Carefully plan your response.
3. Draft and revise your response.
4. Cite your sources.

This chapter includes several strategies to help you master each of these steps. It also includes a case study of the process one first-year writing student followed to write a paragraph response to a reading assignment.

Reading for Understanding

Here are some steps that will help you to understand assigned readings more fully and to write about them more successfully.

Prepare to Read

Efficient reading takes preparation. Some people can read in noisy situations and fully understand what they have read. However, most of us read best in quiet environments. Try to read alone at a table in the library or in your room, away from the hubbub. In a peaceful spot with good lighting, you can concentrate more fully and better understand what is on the page. To make sure that you are reading actively, you will need a pencil or a highlighter to make notes in the margins of the text or to underline important passages.

Skim First

If the reading assignment is short and mostly about information you need to know for a course, try to get its meaning by reading the opening paragraph and the topic sentences of the paragraphs that follow. If you're assigned a long text, examine the table of contents or chapter heads, if it has them. Then skim each section of the text before reading it. These initial skims will introduce you to the major ideas and help you to understand how each part fits into the organization of the entire work. Of course, if you are reading a literary work, like a short story or a poem, you'll want to skip the skim and jump right in. No need to ruin the ending! Get a feel for the rhythm of the language and the author's style. You don't have to pay attention to details just yet, but do try to identify your gut reaction to the basic ideas. This will help you to narrow down the position you want to take in your written response to the text.

Read a Second Time as an Active Reader

The second reading is perhaps the most important. This time, you read actively. Reading "actively" involves doing the following:

- making notes in the margin;
- highlighting important passages;
- marking vocabulary and references that you do not understand.

Making marginal notes and highlighting passages can help you to summarize the major points that you find in the text, plan responses to those points, and talk about ideas that the text has inspired. Taking the time to look up unfamiliar words or references in a dictionary will lead you to a better understanding of the writer's meaning. (If you would rather not write in your text, jot down your notes on a notepad or in a section of your notebook that you keep for just this purpose.) You will better understand what you read if you read actively. As you read and annotate (that is, take notes), think of yourself as having a conversation with the writer.

Once you have assembled an outline of the author's ideas, you not only have a key that unlocks the selection for a written response, but you also have a good model for organizing your own writing.

Summarize Major Points

Create a mini-outline or visual map of the reading from your marginal notes or notebook entries. The outline or map can reflect the writer's thesis (main point) and major divisions. The thesis usually appears in the opening or near the end of the work and is developed in the rest of the selection. To determine what the thesis is, you need to think of what, on the whole, the writer is trying to say. Next, locate the major divisions, which are the primary supports for the thesis. They may be developed in individual paragraphs or in a series of paragraphs. Once you have assembled an outline of the author's ideas, you not only have a key that unlocks the selection for a written response, but you also have a good model for organizing your own writing.

Identify Supporting Evidence

Develop your mini-outline or map more fully, including the supporting evidence and examples that the author gives for each major point. You don't need to use full sentences. Just jot down examples, causes, and comparisons that help you to understand the writer's ideas.

Respond to Ideas

Now it is time to add your thoughts and evaluation to the mix. Take time to react to all the ideas presented in the reading. In addition to thinking about the thesis, also look at the way in which the writer makes his or her points, the kinds of evidence presented, and so on. Reflect upon your first reaction: What was it about the text that made you feel this way? A good place to develop these ideas is in your writer's journal, if you keep one. If you have not started one, buy a small notebook to use for your thoughts on your reading, or start an electronic journal. Create a computer file just for responses of this kind, and update it with your reactions to each piece you read.

CASE STUDY: Writing a Response to a Reading

The following pages present the reading process that Jenny Hasek, a first-year writing student, followed as she read "Homeless Bound." You can read "Homeless Bound," Roy Rowan's first-person account of life among New York City's homeless population, on pages 256–65.

As a first step in the reading process, successful readers prepare to read. Knowing that the essay was not too long, Jenny quickly skimmed "Homeless Bound" before class. She read the first paragraph and then thumbed through the article, glancing at the topic sentences and noting when the writer moves from one experience to another. When Jenny came upon the section in which Rowan describes his stay at the McAuley Water Street Mission, she was hooked. Jenny had always been concerned about the homeless. As a volunteer at a local food kitchen, she had met people from many backgrounds who lived on the streets for reasons that were often a mystery to her. Once she had skimmed through the essay, she pulled a pen from her backpack and began reading from the beginning.

As she read, Jenny made notes in the margins, marking the major divisions of the essay. For instance, she noted each time Rowan went to a different shelter or met a new person. She also circled words and references she did not understand to look up later. In the first paragraph, for example, Rowan refers to Charon, the "Greek mythological ferryman." Jenny remembered that her instructor had handed out some thought questions along with this reading. One question focused on the references in the text to Greek myth. This question plus her own curiosity led Jenny to make a marginal note, and, after she finished the article, she looked for more information about Charon. In her dictionary she found that in Greek mythology, this figure rowed dead people across the River Styx to Hades, or hell. Jenny wondered why Rowan connects the homeless with the dead by mentioning Charon. Here is a section of the text with Jenny's notes:

> I parked my pack next to an old geezer and asked him if it was possible to spend the night in the terminal. "Yes," he said. "The cops usually don't bother you." He said his name was Philip Nachamie, and he had lived there for three weeks. "Once I worked as a clerk for E. F. Hutton," he explained, pointing in the direction of Wall Street. "Just a few blocks from here."
>
> I decided to board the next boat. Standing on the open bow with the cold wind whipping my face, I felt suddenly uplifted by the beauty of New York. The profusion of steel and glass soaring skyward from Manhattan's southern tip, Miss Liberty standing proudly with sun glinting on her gilded torch, the spidery span of the Verrazano Bridge stretching across the harbor's mouth—all striking human accomplishments in a city where thousands lived on the street.

Philip Nachamie held an important position at a top stock exchange firm and now has gone from success to struggle.

profusion: a great quantity

Hmmm. Miss Liberty symbolizes the dream of hope and opportunity, but the homeless do not share in this dream.

Rowan sees beauty in New York City even though he is on a ferry bound for a homeless shelter?

New York City is a place where people accomplish great things, but it is also a place where many people suffer. This difference seems unfair.

Since she knew she would have to write a paper about "Homeless Bound," Jenny decided that she needed to go back through the essay and pull out Rowan's major points. First, she pinpointed the thesis. Reading over the essay and her marginal notes, Jenny determined that the author's major point was about his own experience of homelessness and of a life without goals. Rowan ends the essay by stating that he could bear his two weeks of homelessness only because he knew his experience on the streets would end soon. So she phrased his main idea as follows:

> ***Perhaps the most devastating effect of homelessness is that it is a life without hope.***

Jenny then created an outline to identify all of the major divisions and supporting points that Rowan provides for his thesis:

Rowan's purpose
- *Wants to find out more about homeless*

Ferry to Staten Island
- *Philip, former E. F. Hutton clerk*
- *Project Hospitality, no bed available*
- *Sleeps aboard ferry*
- *New Englanders*

McAuley Water Street Mission
- *Has to attend Bible class to get bed and meal*
- *Collection of people, including garbage collector, bartender, sugar worker*
- *"Friends": Jimmy Pate, drunk who is ready to look for job, and Mark Fitzgerald, large Canadian, heart attack, offers to buy R. bus ticket*

Moravian Coffee Pot
- *Meets teachers, shopkeepers, actors, etc.*
- *They sit around in black and white groups. Complain about meals, rent cost; show little concern for one another*
- *R. wants to tell them to go get jobs*

"Hard Core" Experiences
- *Stays on street*
- *Sleeps on chairs*
- *Encounters mentally unstable people (e.g., Bill Roth, claims he could whip Mike Tyson)*
- *Goes to center where he feels threatened because of race*

Fulton Hotel
- *Panhandles*
- *Pays for small, cockroach-infested room*

Bellevue
- *Forced to wait with other "emergency" candidates*
- *The armed guards*
- *Old man who is not helped to go to the bathroom*
- *Forced to sleep on floor; thinks about loss of dignity*

Conclusion
- *Never again will see homeless people the same way*
- *Thinks you can live without money but not without plans*

If Jenny had created a visual map, it might have looked like Figure 19.1.

After creating her outline, Jenny recorded her reactions to Rowan's points in her journal. These ideas, she concluded, would help her to create a paragraph in response to the assignment. The following is an excerpt from her journal:

> *You know, what Rowan found out is right. What makes a difference in life is goals. I have a friend who is perfectly willing to go along in life without a clue about what he's going to do tomorrow. He is a college student, but won't be one*

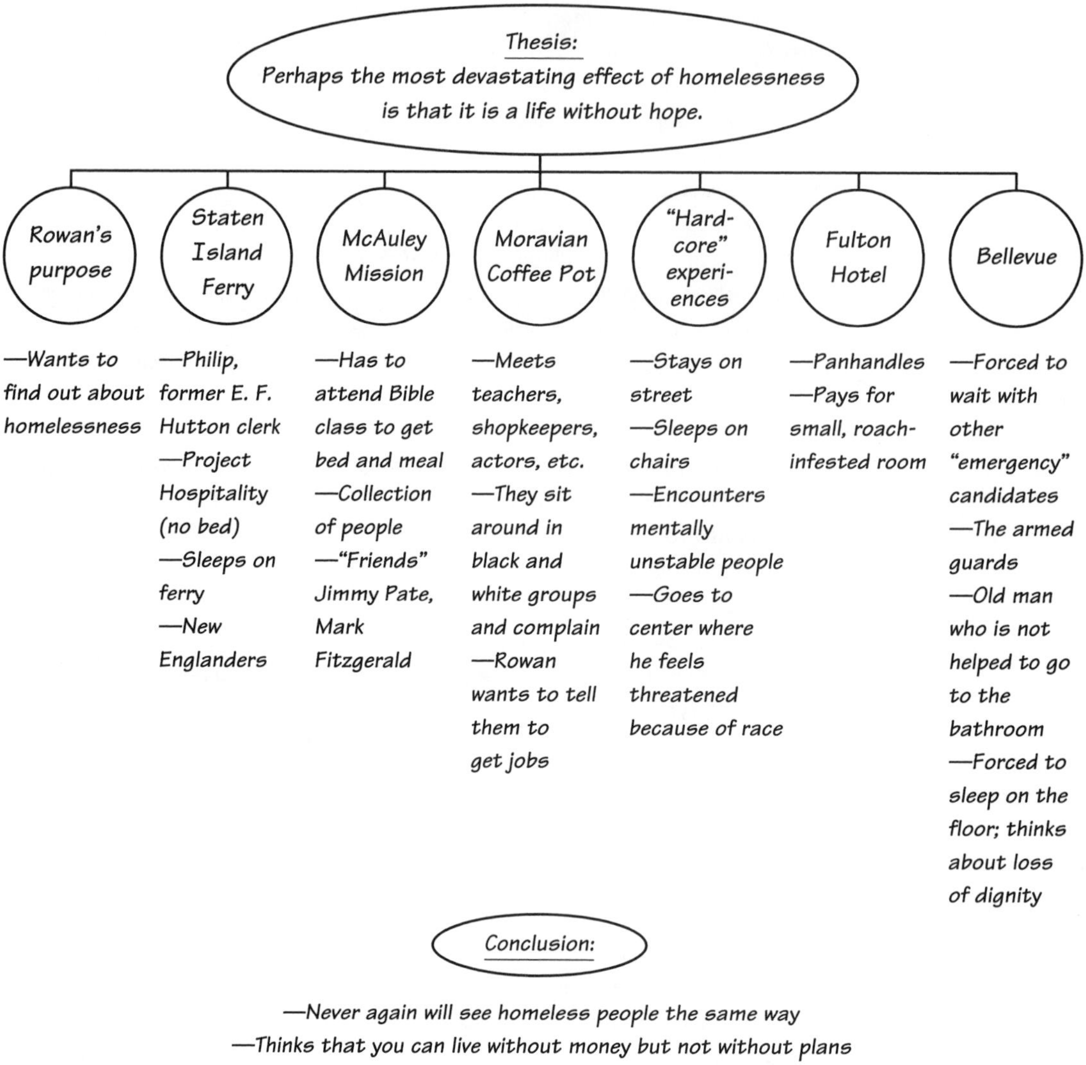

Figure 19.1
Visual Map of Rowan Essay

for long. He says that he is here because his parents are making him go. And all he really wants to do is party. He doesn't know what he wants to do apart from that. In a sense, he is homeless because he has no sense of himself. He has no idea about what he wants to be. He has no home. And if his parents ever get tired of supporting him, he may find himself on the Staten Island Ferry . . .

Planning Your Response

With an understanding of the text, you are ready to start your writing assignment. The following steps will help you plan your response to such an assignment.

Identify Key Words in the Writing Assignment

First of all, determine what type of response is required: a paragraph, a series of paragraphs, or an essay? Then reread the assignment statement or question and locate its most important words. A writing assignment that asks you to *explain,* for example, is far different from one that asks you to *argue* or *prove.*

Write a One-Sentence Response to the Assignment

Once you understand the assignment fully, the next step is to write a one-sentence response to the question after consulting your outline and the reading. If it is clear and well focused, this sentence can become your topic sentence or thesis.

For instance, an instructor might ask the following question about an essay you have read:

> In the article "Homeless Bound," one of the people author Roy Rowan encounters states, "You can live without money . . . but you can't live without plans." Do you agree? Support your answer with examples from the text of the essay as well as from your own experience.

Your one-sentence response might be as follows:

> I agree with the man at the Coffee Pot who states in Roy Rowan's article "Homeless Bound," "You can live without money . . . but you can't live without plans."

Or:

> I disagree with the man at the Coffee Pot who states in Roy Rowan's article "Homeless Bound," "You can live without money . . . but you can't live without plans."

Or even:

> I agree and disagree with the man at the Coffee Pot who states in Roy Rowan's article "Homeless Bound," "You can live without money . . . but you can't live without plans."

Whatever your opinion is, you can establish it clearly in this one-sentence response and use that sentence later as your topic sentence or thesis.

Develop Support for Your Topic Sentence or Thesis

Once your major idea is established, how are you going to support that idea? When you are responding to a reading, much of what you are reacting to or explaining will be in the text. So use your outline of the work to help you find support for your thesis or topic sentence. (For more information about developing support, see Chapter 5.)

Organize Your Response

As a final step in the planning phase, do a little organizing. Look at the evidence that you have to support your thesis or topic sentence. Use time order, space order, or importance order to organize your ideas. The result will be an outline for your response to the assignment. (See Chapter 6 for more information about organizing support.)

With her outline complete, student writer Jenny Hasek was ready to tackle the following writing assignment:

> Of the homeless people that Rowan describes in his essay "Homeless Bound," which ones does he prefer? Write a paragraph in which you contrast people he found admirable with those who angered or repulsed him.

The instructor wanted a paragraph on the Rowan article; that much Jenny could tell. But what did he want her to discuss in that paragraph? Jenny got out her pencil and underlined the following key terms: *homeless people, contrast, admirable, angered/repulsed.* As she thought about these words and the assignment, she realized that indeed there were some homeless people that Rowan "preferred" and even admired a bit. Then there were those who troubled him. Pulling out examples of both types from the essay would be easy. But she had to figure out what separated the admirable from the unadmirable.

That evening, after reading sections of the essay again, she decided that what Rowan liked about some of the people he met was their unwillingness to give in to their situation, their desire to take steps to get off the streets. For example:

> I returned to McAuley's three consecutive nights, making a couple of friends there whom I would be happy to meet again. One was Jimmy Pate, a highly intelligent black man with a close-cropped salt-and-pepper beard. He had managed a Salvation Army shop on Long Island and worked as a messenger in Manhattan. But as a periodic boozer, he would begin swigging gin and get fired. "I haven't had a drink for two weeks," he boasted. "Time to look for a job."

With this and other examples in mind, Jenny drafted the following one-sentence response to the question:

Of the homeless people that Roy Rowan describes in his article "Homeless Bound," the ones that he admires most are those who do not give up despite their circumstances.

She decided that her one-sentence response would make a good topic sentence for her paragraph. Now she had to assemble her primary and secondary supports. She gathered examples of homeless people who gave up and those who did not give up and organized those examples into this informal outline:

Topic Sentence: Of the homeless people that Roy Rowan describes in his article "Homeless Bound," the ones that he admires most are those who do not give up despite their circumstances.

1. *Those he admires have mainstream goals and values*
   a. *Jimmy Pate, giving up booze, looking for job*
   b. *Mark Fitzgerald, large Canadian, out-of-work oil worker*
   c. *The Fordham graduate and teacher, mental breakdown, a temporary walk on the downside, got to have goals*
2. *Those he does not admire—those who have given up*
   a. *The "angry bunch of men" at the Bellevue Shelter that give in to inhumane conditions*
   b. *The Coffee Pot clients—people from different backgrounds, some educated; draw social security benefits, but nobody seems sick; sit around in groups separated by race, complaining about their circumstances; Rowan wants to tell these people to get a job*

With her outline completed, Jenny was ready to move on to drafting her paragraph.

Drafting and Revising

Once you have an initial outline of your paper, the next steps include writing a draft; revising it for focus, unity, support, and coherence; and giving it a final edit.

Draft from Your Outline

Start drafting by turning the entries in your outline into complete sentences. If your assignment asks you to write a paragraph, begin with your topic sentence. (For more information on drafting a paragraph, see Chapter 6.) If your assignment requires you to write an essay, begin with your introductory paragraph, which should include your thesis statement. (For more information on drafting an essay, see Chapters 16 and 17.) Double-space your draft to leave room for revision.

Revise for Focus, Unity, Support, and Coherence

Think about how you might improve the focus of your draft. For example, is your topic sentence clear? Does it include your narrowed topic plus a controlling idea?

You can improve the unity of your paragraph by making sure that every sentence supports your controlling idea and that none of your details wanders off track. Add or reorganize primary and secondary support statements to reinforce your controlling idea or to further explain your points. Finally, be sure your paragraph is coherent and makes smooth transitions from point to point. Combine short sentences into longer sentences, and keep verb tenses consistent. (For more information on revising, see the Writer's Checklist in Chapter 7, How to Revise for Stronger Writing, on p. 90.)

Edit Your Work Carefully

Save editing for last. After you have finished drafting your paragraph or essay, go back over it carefully, correcting it by using the grammar, punctuation, and word-use guidelines in Chapters 23–44. Make sure that all of your sentences are grammatically and mechanically correct and that you have used proper punctuation throughout. Look over your word use, and, if English is not your native language, look for any common ESL troublespots.

Using her outline as a starting point, Jenny Hasek wrote the following first draft of her paragraph in response to her assignment on Roy Rowan's "Homeless Bound." Then she went back through her draft, revising for focus, unity, support, and coherence—and then editing for grammar and usage.

Of the homeless people that Roy Rowan describes in his article "Homeless Bound," the ones that he admires most are those who do not give up despite their circumstances. These people have goals and values that will eventually get them back into the mainstream of society.

One such person is — *who*

(transition) ^Jimmy Pate, "a highly intelligent black man," ^is

Another

(sentence combining) giving up booze and looking for a job. ^~~Mark Fitzgerald~~

is

~~is another~~ person who rises above his environment/^

Canadian

(capitalization) Mark Fitzgerald^ ~~is~~ a large ~~canadian~~ out-of-work

generously offers to share with Rowan a portion of his next welfare check.

(unity) oil worker, who^ ~~suffered a major heart attack~~.

A third person — *is*

(transition) ^Rowan says he would like to follow up with ^the Fordham graduate and teacher whose mental breakdown led him on a "temporary walk on the downside" and who expresses

In contrast, however,

(transitions) the importance of having plans. ^Rowan encounters many homeless people that he does not admire because they do

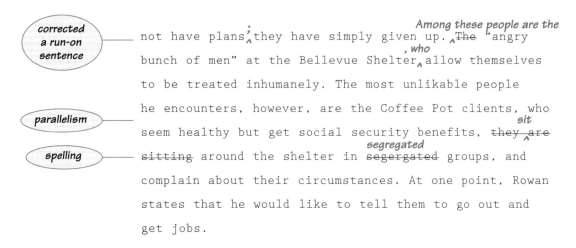

corrected a run-on sentence

parallelism

spelling

not have plans; they have simply given up. *Among these people are the* ~~The~~ "angry bunch of men" at the Bellevue Shelter*, who* allow themselves to be treated inhumanely. The most unlikable people he encounters, however, are the Coffee Pot clients, who seem healthy but get social security benefits, ~~they are~~ *sit* ~~sitting~~ around the shelter in ~~segergated~~ *segregated* groups, and complain about their circumstances. At one point, Rowan states that he would like to tell them to go out and get jobs.

Citing Sources

Writers in college and on the job have to name, or cite, the sources of their ideas and information. If they "borrow" words or information from other writers without giving those writers credit, then they are guilty of **plagiarism.**

Student writer Jenny Hasek gave proper credit to author Roy Rowan by including his name in her paragraph and by using quotation marks when she included the exact words from Rowan's article. She did not provide any other publication information in a footnote or list of sources because "Homeless Bound" was the only text being used for the class activity and her instructor knew the article Jenny was quoting from.

However, instructors may not always be familiar with your sources. In this case, instructors may not know whether the information you include in your writing is general knowledge that does not need a source citation. They also do not always know what ideas in your work are your own and what ideas or words you got from other people. Therefore, you need to develop honest research habits that will help you avoid plagiarism and inform your reader when you are using the ideas or words of others.

Develop an Organized Note-Taking Strategy

For longer assignments, and especially research papers, you need a note-taking strategy that clearly shows where you found your ideas and information. Some writers use note cards. On one side of the card, they carefully transcribe quotations within quotation marks and record other kinds of information as well that they got on their subject from a particular source. On the other side, writers enter the publication information for that source (that is, the author, title, date of publication, page number(s) for the quotes and information, URL, and so forth). Regardless of whether you use note cards, a notebook, a legal pad, or a computer, you need to include the right publication information for your source. This way, when you write your final paper, you will not mistakenly present another writer's hard work as your own. The Brief Documentation Guide on pages 250–55 will show you what publication information to include for different types of sources.

To Cite or Not to Cite

Sometimes it is difficult to decide whether to cite a source for information or ideas that you have found there. In fact, if you are tackling a topic that is totally new to you, you may feel that you owe everything in your paper to that source and perhaps others. The answer to this question is not to cite sources in every sentence of your paper, but to use your judgment. As you research your topic, ask yourself if the information and ideas you got from one source were also contained in at least two other sources that you read. If so, then the information can be considered "general knowledge," and their sources do not need to be cited. Save your citations for those sources that furnish you with unique information and, of course, direct quotes.

Develop Effective and Honest Summarizing and Paraphrasing Habits

Effective writing from reading often involves summarizing and paraphrasing a source, particularly when the information contained by that source is too long or complex to be directly quoted. A **summary** is a shortened version of a longer work. When you summarize a reading, you reduce several pages or whole chapters to a concise passage that meets your reader's needs. You accomplish this reduction by including only the controlling idea of the original, along with the major supporting points. Often, you will discover that you will not have to include all of the major points because only a few are needed to develop the point you are trying to make in your writing. But what you must always include when you summarize a writer's work is a clear and full citation of the source.

Like a summary, a **paraphrase** involves recreating what someone else has written. Only, in this case you are rephrasing in your own words a specific statement made by an author. Perhaps the writer's statement is too long and you need to pull out the key ideas. Or it may be that the writer's language is too technical for your audience and you need to translate. Or you may need to provide the reader with relief from a text that already has too many direct quotations. But beware when paraphrasing. Make certain that what you have written accurately reflects that author's meaning. Further,

Paraphrasing is rephrasing, in your own words, a specific statement made by an author when that author's original text is too long or too technical or when you need to provide the reader with relief from a series of direct quotations.

make sure when you paraphrase that you do not plagiarize by giving the impression that the ideas from the source are your own. One way to give credit is to include the author's name and even the source title in your paraphrase. Note how the following paraphrase tells the reader that the thought comes from the author, not from the writer:

> According to Rowan, he was apprehensive about living on the streets because of violent stories he had heard (257).

Follow Standard Citation and Documentation Models

Different areas of study—such as English, psychology, biology, and engineering—require different approaches to citing sources and documenting those sources in a paper. A short guide to source citation and documentation, based on the Modern Language Association's (MLA) *Handbook for Writers of Research Papers,* Fourth Edition, follows on page 250. Use this guide to cite outside sources when you write.

☑ Writer's Checklist: Writing from Reading

Reading

_____ Have you prepared yourself and found a quiet place to read efficiently?
_____ Have you skimmed the text to gain a general understanding of it?
_____ While reading the text a second time, have you taken useful notes and looked up unfamiliar words?
_____ After reading, have you created a brief outline or visual map of the text's major sections and ideas?
_____ Have you developed that outline or visual map more completely by adding specific details from the text to fill out the sections and support the ideas?
_____ Have you thought about your initial reactions to the reading and included them in your journal?

Writing

_____ Do you fully understand your writing assignment?
_____ Have you planned your response to that assignment effectively?
    _____ Identified key words in the assignment?
    _____ Written a one-sentence response?
    _____ Listed important information that supports your topic sentence or thesis?
    _____ Organized your written response into a clear outline?
_____ Have you created a good first draft of your response based on your outline?
_____ Have you revised and edited carefully?
_____ Have you cited and documented your sources fully and appropriately?

Summary

1. The first step in writing effectively about readings is to better understand what you read. (See p. 237.)
2. Once you understand the reading, the next step is to plan your written response to that reading. (See p. 243.)
3. After carefully planning your written response, you can then draft and revise. (See p. 245.)
4. Cite and document any outside sources you used to find the information and ideas contained in your paper, using accepted methods for your area of study. (See p. 247.)

Brief Documentation Guide

Let's say that in a conversation with a friend, you claim that the world's largest collection of preserved human brains—8,000—is in the basement of an English psychiatric hospital. Your friend looks at you a little funny and asks, "Where did you get that information?"

Whenever you use information from outside sources in your writing, you are responsible for answering your readers' questions: *Who said that?* or *Whose idea is this?* or *Where did these facts come from?* Writers **document** their sources to let readers know

1. which ideas or words in their essay come from another source, and
2. the exact publication information for each source.

Whenever you use information from outside sources in your writing, you are responsible for answering your readers' questions: *Who said that?* or *Whose idea is this?*

By documenting their research, responsible writers avoid plagiarism and give credit to other researchers. Careful documentation involves citing your sources (a **citation** is a reference to a source) in two places:

- within the text of your paper (this is called "in-text citation")
- in a list of works cited at the end of your paper

The MLA style is the most common format for documenting sources in the humanities (courses like English, art, foreign language, and philosophy). Refer to this guide when you are finding sources, taking notes, and drafting your essay.

MLA Format for In-Text Citations

You should provide an in-text citation every time you quote from (use exact words), paraphrase (use your own words to rephrase someone else's statements), or summarize an outside source. Your citation should appear next to the sentences in your paper that refer to the source information. Citations should include the name of the author and a page number, placed in parentheses. If you include the name of the source in a signal phrase, such as *Boston Mayor Thomas Menino told reporters . . .* or *According to a recent study by the American Cancer Society . . .*, you need only include the page number in parentheses. The in-text citation will lead your readers to the full citation that you include for each source in your list of works cited at the end of your paper (see page 252).

1. One Author

Enclose direct quotes in quotation marks

```
"As in the case of teenage child-bearing, the
most obvious link concerns the way an environ-
ment of constricted opportunity shapes the
alternatives that are available--or are per-
ceived to be available--in people's lives"
(Schwartz 118).
```

period is placed outside the citation

no comma

author's name and page number in parentheses

```
Concerning teenagers who have babies, Schwartz
states that "the most obvious link concerns the
way an environment of constricted opportunity
shapes the alternatives that are available--or
are perceived to be available--in people's
lives" (118).
```

signal phrase

page number is in paren-theses

2. Two or Three Authors In the case of three authors, use commas to separate the authors' last names.

```
"At present, there is more and more mistrust of their
leaders among younger voters" (Brown, Rinella, and
Randall 7).
```

3. Four or More Authors Use the last name of the first author followed by the Latin abbreviation *et al.*, meaning "and others."

```
Boys tend to get called on in the classroom more often
than girls (Oesterling et al. 243).
```

4. Corporate Author or Government Publication

```
The National Organization for Women reports an annual
increase in the amount of women in the workforce per
capita, each year (9).
```

5. Unknown Author If the author of the source is not known, use a shortened version of the title within the parentheses. The full title of this source, for example, is *A Guide to Eating Well.*

> Eating well can mean the difference between feeling well and feeling lousy (Guide 12).

6. Bible Abbreviate the title of any book longer than four letters ("Gen." for Genesis, "Sam." for Samuel, and so forth). Follow the name of the book with the chapter number, a period, and the verse number(s).

> The Lord is my shepherd; I shall not want (New American Bible, Ps. 23.1).

7. Source without Page Numbers If the source you are using does not have page numbers, such as an Internet source, cite only the author's name. Use the title if no author is given.

> "There is no definitive correlation between benign breast tumors and breast cancer" (Pratt).

8. Indirect Sources Sometimes you will want to use a quotation that your source has also used. If you cannot find the original source, you must label your citation as an indirect source. The abbreviation *qtd. in* stands for "quoted in." Note that the quotation within the quotation is enclosed in single quotation marks.

> "'People who had years of college can't find anything,' Nancy Muse, a resident of Northridge, California, told the New York Times" (qtd. in Schwartz 76).

MLA Format for a List of Works Cited

At the end of your paper, you must provide a list of the sources from which you quoted, paraphrased, or summarized. Put the entire list in alphabetical order using the author's last name first and the title as it appears on the title page of the source. (If your source has been written by more than one author or editor, all names after the first one should appear in regular order—first name, then last name.) If your source has no author, alphabetize it by the first main word of the title. Double-space your works cited page, and indent the second line of each entry five spaces.

Books

One Author

> Ash, Russell. Top 10 of Everything 2000.
>   New York: DK Publishing, 1999.

author listed last name first

title

second (and third, fourth, etc.) line indented five spaces

city

publisher

publication date

Two or Three Authors

Benedict, Jeff, and Don Yaeger. Pros and Cons: The Criminals Who Play in the NFL. New York: Warner, 1998.

Four or More Authors

Lee, Mary Price, et al. 100 Best Careers in Crime Fighting: Law Enforcement, Criminal Justice, Private Security, and Cyberspace Crime Detection. Updated ed. Foster City: IDG, 1999.

Unknown Author

National Geographic Atlas of the World. 7th ed. Washington, D.C.: National Geographic, 1999.

Editor or Compiler

Tanaka, Yukiko, ed. Unmapped Territories: New Women's Fiction from Japan. Seattle: Women in Translation, 1991.

Editor and Author

Pearson, Sam B., III. The Color of Racism: Understanding and Overcoming Discrimination. Ed. Donna G. Fricke. Chicago: Transformax, 1997.

Edition Numbers

The Chicago Manual of Style: The Essential Guide for Writers, Editors, and Publishers. 14th ed. Chicago: U of Chicago P, 1993.

Anthology

Halpern, Daniel, ed. The Art of the Story: An International Anthology of Contemporary Short Stories. Minneapolis: Viking, 1999.

A Work in an Anthology

Dagenais, Huguette. "Women in Guadeloupe: The Paradoxes of Reality." Women and Change in the Caribbean. Ed. Janet H. Momsen. London: James Currey, 1993.

Signed Article in a Reference Book

Tucci, Regis. "Voice of America." Historical Dictionary of American Radio. Ed. Donald G. Godfrey and Frederic A. Leigh. Westport: Greenwood, 1998.

Unsigned Article in a Reference Book

"Interest and Boredom." Cambridge International Dictionary of Idioms. New York: Cambridge UP, 1998.

Periodicals

Article in a Monthly Magazine

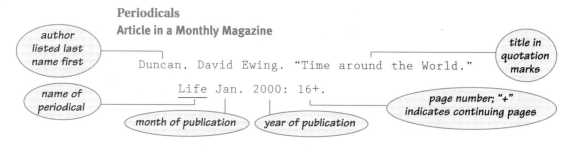

Duncan, David Ewing. "Time around the World." Life Jan. 2000: 16+.

author listed last name first
title in quotation marks
name of periodical
month of publication
year of publication
page number; "+" indicates continuing pages

Article in a Weekly Magazine

Bacon, John U. "Puck-émon: Hockey in Japan is Serious Business." ESPN the Magazine 13 Dec. 1999: 104+.

Article in a Newspaper

White, Diane. "What Underlies a Man's Fear of Shopping." Boston Globe 20 Dec. 1999: C7.

Unknown Author

"Doubts about Vitamin E." Associated Press. Washington Post 20 Jan. 2000: A4.

Editorial

"The Century Ends in Panama." Editorial. New York Times 18 Dec. 1999: A30.

Letter to the Editor

Flynn, Jennifer. Letter. Village Voice 9 Nov. 1999: 6.

Electronic Sources

Professional Web Site

Passport Services and Information. 21 Dec. 1999. U.S. State Department. 27 Jan. 2000 <http://travel.state.gov/passport_services.html>.

title of the Web site
date of publication or last update
sponsoring organization
date source was accessed
the URL (online address) in angle brackets (</>)

Personal Web Site

Brooks, Larry. Air Jordan. 6 Oct. 1999. 20 Dec. 1999 <http://www.unc.edu/~lbrooks2/jordan.html>.

Electronic Mail or Online Posting

Legarra, Debby. "On-line Writing Classes." 13 Oct. 1999. Online posting. Conference on Basic Writing. 19 May 2000 <cbw=l@tc.umn.edu>.

Mellor, Joseph. "Re: Book review." E-mail to Manan Ahmed. 5 Dec. 1999.

CD-ROM or Diskette Material without a Print Version

Generations Family Tree 6.0 Deluxe Edition. CD-ROM. Bellevue: SierraHome, 1999.

CD-ROM or Diskette Material with a Print Version

Griffin, Lauren. "Getting More out of Your 401k." Money Dec. 1998: 122-129. Infotrac. CD-ROM. M.E. Sharp, 1999.

Other Sources

Advertisement

LifeStyles. Advertisement. SPIN May 1999: 87.

Interview

Curley, Robert. Interview. The David Brudnoy Show. WBZ, Boston. 18 May 2000.

Pamphlet

American Psychiatric Association. Anxiety Disorders. Washington, D.C.: American Psychiatric Press, 1988.

Film or Video

The Blair Witch Project. Dir. Daniel Myrick and Eduardo Sanchez. Perf. Michael Williams and Heather Donahue. Artisan Entertainment, 1999.

Sound Recording

Madonna. Ray of Light. Warner Bros., 1998.

Television or Radio Program

New York: A Documentary Film. The American Experience. PBS, Boston. 20 Dec. 1999.

Readings

You can use the following selections to practice the strategies for writing from reading introduced in this chapter. Ranging in length from a page or two to ten pages, these essays deal with topics that affect us all, in one way or another, on a daily basis. The authors of these readings discuss social issues such as how we regard the homeless, the ways that we can misjudge people because of their race or job, and the differences between the sexes as demonstrated in males' and females' approaches to play. One essay examines the benefits of human cloning, a hotly debated issue. Another takes a light look at an interesting behavior that we may exhibit at one time or another, "tongue-showing." Before reading a selection, spend some time thinking about the "Preparing to Read" questions that come before it. Then, after you have read the essay, use the exercises on vocabulary and understanding to prepare yourself to write about the readings.

Homeless Bound

Roy Rowan

Roy Rowan, in this article first published in People *magazine in 1990, gives a vivid firsthand account of life among the homeless. Rowan uses sensory details of sight and touch to describe the harsh environment that homeless men and women endure in their daily lives.*

Preparing to Read

Think about the following questions as you read:

1. What attitude do people who live in the suburbs, like Rowan, have towards homeless people living on city streets? In what ways does Rowan reflect their attitudes?
2. What are your reactions to the individuals that Rowan meets? What traits do these people possess that make them more or less admirable than others?

A large crowd stands waiting for the Staten Island ferry. Hidden behind them, monopolizing the terminal's long wooden benches, are some sixty or seventy homeless men and women in various states—sitting and sleeping, drunk and sober, bearded and shaved, calm and agitated. A few days earlier a social worker had described this transportation hub in Manhattan as a "menagerie."[1] Today it is missing only the Greek mythological ferryman, Charon, to pole the damned across New York Harbor. Most of the people are not just homeless but are also drunks and druggies. An argument is raging 1

[1] **menagerie:** a collection of wild or foreign animals

between a black man and a drunk blond woman with a hip-high cast covering her left leg. She slashes at the man with one of her crutches until two policemen chase him away. Across the terminal, a loony, shoeless lad is menacing an Asian passenger. "Gonna knock your teeth out," he shouts. "You Jap guys stole my job." The same two cops lead him away, but blaring loudspeakers are now calling for police assistance elsewhere. "NYPD to the change booth!" echoes a plea to help a homeless man who had been knocked down by youths hurdling the turnstiles.

I hadn't come simply as a reporter to cover this stygian scene. Wearing faded jeans, a frayed corduroy jacket, vintage combat boots used in Korea, and with a beat-up pack strapped to my back, I was hoping to blend in with all the vagrants who had converted this old pier into a makeshift hotel. This was my first stop on a scary two-week journey into their murky, purgatorial[2] world. I wanted to report on what I had seen as one of *them.* 2

I had put off a haircut for several weeks and hadn't shaved for days. Still, I worried. Would this disguise really work? Could I make myself feel truly destitute, or would the safety of my just-temporary plight betray me? I fixed my gaze on a smartly dressed businessman tapping his shoes, impatient for the next boat to depart. He glanced everywhere except at me. That was a good sign. I had joined the estimated three million homeless who, it is said, have become "invisible" to most Americans. 3

I must admit that they had been largely invisible to me. On my way to work from suburban Greenwich, Connecticut, I would see the sleeping bodies sprawled over the cold marble or tucked into the recesses of Grand Central Terminal. In the evening as I headed home, these figures would come alive, rising like specters[3] out of a Hieronymus Bosch painting, dunning[4] us commuters with outstretched palms or empty coffee cups. But my personal involvement was very slight. 4

My knowledge of their problems was also slight. I knew that a preponderant number were black and that a large percentage were drug addicts, alcoholics, AIDS victims, or crazies turned loose from overcrowded psycho wards. And yet there were other homeless people, both black and white, who almost could have passed for fellow commuters. They were the ones who intrigued me most. Who were these seemingly sane, reasonably well-dressed drifters who languish in rail and subway stations, bus depots, bank vestibules, and stand like frozen statues on the street? How did they fall between the cracks of our affluent society? Could they ever climb back up? 5

I had decided to try to learn more about these victims of homelessness by stepping into their lives, and yet as that day approached, I felt myself 6

[2] **purgatorial:** relating to "purgatory"; a place or state of temporary suffering; [3] **specters:** ghosts; [4] **dunning:** begging

becoming more and more apprehensive. I had heard horror stories about the knifing and shooting of homeless men, mostly senseless attacks by marauding youth packs. One old man had been doused with gasoline and set afire. I had also heard about wild free-for-alls started by "crackheads" in the big armory shelters of Manhattan and Brooklyn. "Better sleep with your shoes on or they'll be stolen," I was warned. "Your glasses too."

The day was clear and crisp when I arrived at the Staten Island ferry ter- 7
minal. I had fifty dollars stashed in various pockets in small bills, but no house keys, checks, credit cards, driver's license, or any identification other than my Medicare card. To my wife's consternation I had removed my gold wedding band for the first time in thirty-seven years. Shorn of all these accoutrements,[5] I felt peculiarly weightless. Worse, the desolation made me feel that perhaps I had made a horrible mistake. Sharing a soldier's danger as a war correspondent, as I had done, was strangely exhilarating, yet the prospect of hunkering down with these derelicts seemed only demeaning.

I parked my pack next to an old geezer and asked him if it was possible 8
to spend the night in the terminal. "Yes," he said. "The cops usually don't bother you." He said his name was Philip Nachamie, and he had lived there for three weeks. "Once I worked as a clerk for E. F. Hutton," he explained, pointing in the direction of Wall Street. "Just a few blocks from here."

I decided to board the next boat. Standing on the open bow with the 9
cold wind whipping my face, I felt suddenly uplifted by the beauty of New York. The profusion of steel and glass soaring skyward from Manhattan's southern tip, Miss Liberty standing proudly with sun glinting on her gilded torch, the spidery span of the Verrazano Bridge stretching across the harbor's mouth—all striking human accomplishments in a city where thousands lived on the street.

I hadn't been to Staten Island for years, but a social worker had men- 10
tioned a place called Project Hospitality, a few blocks from the ferry. A sign on the door warned DON'T EVEN THINK OF DOING DRUGS HERE. A friendly woman at the front desk told me to sign in. "We'll be serving dinner in an hour," she said. "But you can have coffee now."

I still felt queasy in my new role, but I poured myself a cup and sat down. 11
About forty men and women filled the chairs that lined the room. Dinner consisted of mushy Swedish meatballs on a heaping mound of brown rice. Two peanut butter sandwiches were also doled out to each "client," as the homeless are referred to in drop-in centers like this. I pocketed mine for breakfast. "Sorry, but there are no beds available tonight on Staten Island," the woman at the front desk informed me.

I decided to spend the night crossing back and forth on the ferry. Its 12
throbbing engines lulled me right to sleep, but as the ferry docked, a cop

[5] **accoutrements:** equipment or clothing

rapped his club against the back of my seat. The police, I came to learn, are viewed by the homeless as both enemy and protector. I slipped into the terminal through an exit, then reboarded the boat without paying. By 5 A.M. I had made half-a-dozen round trips, snatching twenty-minute naps en route. Finally I joined the snorers slumped on the benches in the Manhattan terminal.

When the new day dawned, I was camped between a pair of talkative New Englanders. Anthony Joseph Robert Quinn proclaimed himself a lace-curtain Irishman from Boston. His downfall apparently came from growing up with too much money and an unquenchable thirst for whiskey. Having quit Boston College to join the army in World War II, he married a "very artistic lady" who eventually departed for Palm Beach with his and her money. But I couldn't pry loose the secret of what sent him into oblivion. "You don't have an extra shirt in that pack, lad?" he inquired. "There's nothing under this coat." I had two extra and gave him one. "Bless you. Care for an eye-opener?" he asked, pulling out a pint. 13

Cecile Sanscartier, an aging but still twinkly-eyed blond woman, was originally from New Bedford, Massachusetts. She moved to New York City, where her husband drove a taxi. One night, she says, he was parked in front of Metropolitan Hospital, and he was shot and killed by holdup men. For several years after his death, Cecile worked in a stationery store but kept falling behind in her rent. Reluctantly last summer she entered a city shelter, where she says, "I was scared of being robbed or raped, and felt like a prisoner. Here I can walk out through the turnstile any time I want." She had been living at the ferry terminal for two months. 14

After only one night there, I was eager to find a bed. My back ached, and I felt groggy from lack of sleep. I consulted the *Street Sheet*—a nonprofit annual publication, distributed free to New York's homeless, which lists the places they can go for food, shelter, clothing, medical assistance, and legal aid. It included the McAuley Water Street Mission. Within walking distance, it seemed like a good place to begin looking. At McAuley's, you must attend a midday, two-hour Bible class to get a ticket for dinner, a bed, and breakfast. "Food for the soul before food for the body," its homeless lodgers are told, although none seem eager for the religious nourishment. After the Bible class, I spent the rest of the afternoon at a nearby public library writing notes for this article. Warm, with clean bathrooms as well as books and newspapers, branch libraries are homeless havens. 15

Returning to McAuley's at 5:30 P.M., I joined about ninety men in the chapel. Most were young blacks. First we stored our belongings for the night in a padlocked closet. Then we were interviewed. I was "Roy Brown from Chicago," the cover I had decided to use. "No, I don't have any identification. My wallet was snatched at the bus terminal when I arrived." Many of the homeless, I knew, carried no identification. 16

Finally we filed downstairs for a thick meat soup that looked more like slabs of beef in gravy. Then everybody marched up to the dormitory, found their assigned bunks, and stripped for the communal showers. Hospital gowns were given out to sleep in because our clothes were hauled away on wheeled racks so they wouldn't be stolen. By seven-thirty everybody was in bed, the aged, handicapped, and grossly overweight having been awarded lower bunks. 17

Many men at McAuley's were regulars: some with jobs but no place to live, others out looking for work. But none had surrendered to homelessness. There was a laid-off garbage collector from the Bronx, an unemployed bartender from Ireland, a sugar worker from St. Croix whose home had been devastated by Hurricane Hugo, a political refugee from South Africa. "Why," he asked, "does a country like yours, that gives so much food to Africa, have so many hungry people?" 18

I returned to McAuley's three consecutive nights, making a couple of friends there whom I would be happy to meet again. One was Jimmy Pate, a highly intelligent black man with a close-cropped salt-and-pepper beard. He had managed a Salvation Army shop on Long Island and worked as a messenger in Manhattan. But as a periodic boozer, he would begin swigging gin and get fired. "I haven't had a drink for two weeks," he boasted. "Time to look for a job." 19

Another was Mark Fitzgerald, a gargantuan Canadian with a black beard so thick all you could see was a pair of blue eyes peeking out above it. He came from Churchill, on Hudson Bay below the Arctic Circle, where "polar bears," he said, "roam the streets like stray dogs." New York he called the "Trapezoid City. No matter what you do, you end up in a trap." 20

A linebacker in high school in Beaver, Pennsylvania, Fitzgerald once dreamed of a pro-football career. Instead he found work in a Canadian oil field. A series of job changes back in the United States followed, and with each he seemed to pick up more weight, until he tipped the scales at more than four hundred pounds. Finally, last December, at twenty-nine, he was hit with a massive heart attack in New York. "They jump-started me twice and kept me in intensive care for ten days," he reported. "That cleaned out my bank account." 21

Despite his own problems, Mark took pity on me. "I'll buy you a bus ticket to St. Christopher's Inn when I get my next welfare check," he promised. St. Christopher's, he explained, is a retreat in Garrison, New York, for homeless men. It bothered me not being able to level with Mark. But if word got out about what I was doing, it could have been dangerous. "How come you ask so many questions, man?" a McAuley regular had already wondered. My last night there, the director asked if I would like a permanent job manning the front desk. Clearly it was time to move on. 22

I had been spending my days trudging the streets, investigating different drop-in centers and soup kitchens listed in the *Street Sheet.* Some, I discovered, like the Holy Apostles Church in mid-Manhattan, serve hot, sit-down meals for one thousand men and women. *Voices to and from the Streets,* a free homeless newsletter published by the South Presbyterian Church in suburban Dobbs Ferry, even runs a column called "Dining Out with Rick C." that rates the soup kitchens for "atmosphere, service, and cuisine." Sunday breakfast at St. Bartholomew's Church on Park Avenue received a four-star rating in all three categories. "'Bum's Rush' is really unnecessary here," it reported, since "everyone has a ticket." But I found Saturday breakfasts at St. Agnes even better. "The coffee cake here is top shelf," commented a toothless table mate, who also advised me, "Stay out of Grand Central. Too many guys over there eager to cut up a white face." 23

After dinner I checked into the Moravian Coffee Pot, considered a safe haven for older homeless men and women. At first, the reverend in charge was pessimistic about my chances of being assigned to a shelter. But after spying my week-old whiskers and hearing my sad story about being robbed, I was put on a school bus bound for St. Clement Pope Roman Catholic Church in Queens. 24

During the next few days, I found many surprises among the hundred Coffee Pot clients. There were teachers with master's degrees, shopkeepers, file clerks, secretaries, chambermaids, day laborers, a lawyer, even a TV actor who played in *The Defenders,* and a former opera singer who now sang on Sundays in the First Moravian Church next door. Most were nicely spruced up, since two showers and long racks of donated clothing were available upstairs. Yet they sat around in segregated black or white cliques, complaining about everything from their free meals to the high rent and taxes that had driven them into the street. Consumed by their own misfortune, they showed little concern for each other. When it was announced that a woman there had died during the night, the news hardly caused a murmur. "I like rich people," a black woman confided. "Poor people are too cruel to each other." 25

Many Coffee Pot regulars, I was told, draw SSI (Supplemental Security Income) from the federal government for ailments that supposedly prevent them from working. But nobody appeared sick, except for the chronic, croupy cough that plagues practically all the homeless, and which I, too, had picked up. Several times I was tempted to stand up and shout, "Why don't you all go out and get jobs?" Instead, I'd go out myself, prowling the city till dark, seeking homeless people with more poignant[6] stories. I must have looked pretty grubby. Women, I now noticed, leaned away from me on buses and subways. 26

[6] **poignant:** deeply moving or touching the emotions

It was beginning to sink in that sitting around crowded, fetid drop-in centers, standing pressed together in long soup-kitchen lines, and sleeping side by side in shelters, the homeless had precious few moments alone. No wonder so many preferred the parks or streets, where even a cold packing crate to sleep in provided some privacy. 27

In four nights the Coffee Pot dispatched me to three shelters, each more comfortable than the last. Manhattan's famed Riverside Church, my final resting place so to speak, was called the "Helmsley Palace shelter." Pasta or some other tasty hot dish was served. The beds were well spaced in the men's choir room. There was a shower and a TV. 28

Already into my second week, the time had come to tough it out with the hard-core homeless in places like Tompkins Square Park on the Lower East Side, where police and squatters have been waging continuous warfare; Penn Station, dubbed the "Panama combat zone" because of a proliferation of drugs and guns; the Bowery; Brooklyn; and the big Bellevue shelter, converted from a hospital. 29

In Tompkins Square Park, with the temperature hovering around 20° F, I warmed myself over a trash-can fire with a group of shivering men, amusing themselves by reeling off their old penitentiary numbers. They eyed me suspiciously when I didn't chime in with mine. 30

That night I decided to stay on the street as long as my feet could take the cold. Dinner came from a Salvation Army mobile kitchen parked near City Hall. Too cold to sit around, I walked slowly up through Chinatown and SoHo back to the East Village. Along the way many men were leaning against buildings or slumped in doorways, waiting for the "Midnight Run," a church caravan from suburbia that distributes sandwiches and blankets. 31

"Be careful crossing the street," I kept reminding myself. The sleep deprivation that dims the consciousness of every homeless person was beginning to slow my own reactions. Quite a few street dwellers, I'd heard, get hit by cars. 32

Then I walked three miles back to the Battery. About 2 A.M. I decided to head for John Heuss House, a drop-in center for the chronically homeless and mentally ill, partly supported by Wall Street's Trinity Church. "You don't have a single scrap of paper with your name on it?" the night duty officer asked caustically.[7] Eventually he told me to shove some chairs together and stretch out, as others had done. Every time I reached for a chair, a mentally disturbed man grabbed it away. Only after the duty officer threatened to toss him into the street did I lie down. 33

Some of the mentally unstable homeless people, I found, sound deceptively sane. Bill Roth, thirty-three, a Long Island letter carrier for eight years, 34

[7] **caustically:** said sarcastically

was holding forth brilliantly in Grand Central about the collapse of communism in Eastern Europe, when he casually mentioned that boxing promoters were sure he could whip Mike Tyson, despite their eighty-pound difference. Later he admitted having been hospitalized for alcoholism and mental problems.

Deinstitutionalizing these troubled people, I realized, not only forces them to flounder helplessly, it also allows them to inflict their insanity on everyone around them—sometimes violently. Right after my homeless stint ended, a deranged man in a midtown subway station was pummeled[8] to death by a passenger he had accosted and spat on. 35

The next night I was determined to find a real bed. I went back to Staten Island, but with no success. I tried the nearly all-black drop-in center on Bond Street in Brooklyn. James Conway, a homeless chef, who had just been released from the hospital, warned me that a bloody battle royal had erupted there the previous day. I wasn't feeling too comfortable anyway. A black woman had pointed at me and yelled, "Hey, look at the macadamia nut," when I walked in. 36

Then I remembered that Mark Fitzgerald, my McAuley friend, had high praise for the Fulton Hotel in the Bowery. But a room there, he said, costs $6.50. (Bus, subway, and ferry fares, cough medicine, and repairs to my backpack had already used up thirty-five of my fifty dollars.) Finally I decided to try some panhandling—not an appealing idea, although a man at the Coffee Pot had boasted of picking up $240 in one day. 37

It was already dark when I arrived in Little Italy, a district of posh restaurants bordering on the Bowery. The streets were filled with fur-coated women from uptown. "Could you help a fella out?" I kept asking. In forty minutes I collected four quarters, a dollar, and a fiver, although my heart wasn't in it. I felt dishonest playing on the sympathy of strangers, knowing that I didn't really need their help. 38

The Fulton Hotel turned out to be a Chinese flophouse named Fu Shin, where a four-by-six-foot, windowless, tableless, chairless cubicle now costs $8.50. There was barely room to squeeze in between the wall and the bed, covered with a grimy green blanket showing worrisome brown burn holes. A light bulb hung from a false ceiling constructed of wrapping paper and chicken wire. 39

Here, at least, was a warm place of my own to shed my smelly clothes and sleep. But the cubicle, I discovered about 1 A.M., wasn't really all mine. That's when the cockroaches began running across my face. I sat up in bed the rest of the night reading a *New York Times* salvaged from a sidewalk trash can. By then I was almost looking forward to the Bellevue shelter with its thousand beds. 40

[8] **pummeled:** beaten

I wasn't sure they would let me into this city-run, older men's refuge. I lacked the required Human Resources Administration case number. But it was Martin Luther King, Jr.'s, birthday, and the place was down to a skeleton staff. I gave my real name and handed the man at the admitting office my Medicare card for identification. It was 5 P.M. "You'll have to wait till midnight for an emergency bed," he advised. He issued me a dinner slip and pointed down a long, dimly lit corridor to a waiting room where some fifty other emergency-bed candidates were congregated. 41

This was an angry bunch of men—mad at the armed guards there to keep order, mad at each other and at the world for the way it had treated them. "Sit up!" snapped a guard, prodding a skinny black fellow sprawled on the floor. "Go 'way, asshole," responded the man. "Is my lying down a security problem?" The guard prodded him again. "You don't even know why I'm lying here, asshole. I got two bullet holes in me." The guard finally gave up, and the bullet holes were never explained. 42

A trembly, eighty-year-old, bewhiskered white man kept trying to stand up and walk to the bathroom, only to fall back in his chair. The guards ignored him. So did the others in the room. I desperately wanted to offer a steadying hand. Yet, as a reporter, I also wanted to see what would happen. Finally I watched a dark wet spot spread across the old man's lap. Humiliated, he never looked down. 43

From time to time a woman came and called a few names—the lucky recipients of emergency beds. But at 1 A.M. about twenty of us were still waiting. "Okay, you guys are going to Post Five," barked one of the guards. He led us down two flights to an abandoned lobby and pointed at the marble floor. "Sleep here. You can go outside to pee." The price of homelessness, I had come to understand, is not the hard surfaces you sometimes have to sleep on or the soup kitchen meals that usually leave a strong aftertaste in your mouth. It is the dehumanizing loss of dignity. 44

After two weeks I felt saturated with these depressing sensations and ready to write. My grubbiness was also becoming unbearable. Sitting in the rear car of the train going home (where my neighbors never ride), I wondered if I would ever run into any of my homeless friends again. Would the deep chasm[9] separating us make such an encounter embarrassing, even though I now know there are talented, intelligent individuals out there among all the derelicts? Never again would I look away when a homeless person approaches. It might be somebody I know. 45

There are a few I would very much like to see. I would like to find out if Phillip Nordé, a handsome thirty-eight-year-old Trinidadian who says he 46

[9] **chasm:** a deep division or separation

was the first black man to model clothes on the fashion runways of Europe for Gucci, Valentino, Giorgio Armani, and Missoni, managed to stay off drugs. Having recently returned from a crack rehab center in Vermont, he lives at the Wards Island shelter under the Triborough Bridge. He fears that his problem is genetic. His father and grandfather were both alcoholics. "But crack," he says, "takes over your body, your mind, and your soul."

One man at the Coffee Pot, I believe, will surely break free. He's a Fordham University graduate and a teacher whose periodic mental breakdowns have left him homeless. Nevertheless, he calls his situation "a temporary walk on the downside" and feels his positive attitude won't permit him to stay stuck in that miasma.[10] "You can live without money," he says, "but you can't live without plans." That, I realized, is what had made two weeks of homelessness endurable for me. I always knew I would be going home. 47

After You Read

Developing Your Vocabulary

Using a dictionary, look up the following words and phrases that appear in the essay.

stygian (para. 2)
destitute (para. 3)
Hieronymus Bosch (para. 4)
preponderant (para. 5)
profusion (para. 9)
fetid (para. 27)
deinstitutionalizing (para. 35)

Understanding the Reading

1. Why do homeless people sometimes prefer staying outside to going inside a shelter for the night?
2. Though Roy Rowan disguises himself as a homeless person and spends two weeks on the streets, how is his experience different from the lives of those he observes?
3. According to Rowan, what do homeless people suffer from the most? What are some examples of this suffering?

Responding to What You Read

Paragraph Writing Assignments

1. How does Roy Rowan change as a human being during his two-week experience? Contrast the writer's attitude toward the homeless before his time on the streets with his attitude afterwards.

[10] **miasma:** a confusing atmosphere

2. Rowan describes the homeless at the beginning of his article as "invisible" to the rest of the population. Are there other "invisible" people that we do not want to see? If so, give examples to prove your point.

Essay Writing Assignments

1. According to the teacher who suffers periodic mental breakdowns and whom Rowan quotes near the end of his article, "You can live without money . . . but you can't live without plans." Do you agree? First explain what he means, given the context of the article. Then give evidence that supports your point.
2. Rowan encounters a political refugee from South Africa who asks, "Why . . . does a country like yours, that gives so much food to Africa, have so many hungry people?" How would you answer him? Develop an essay that responds to his question.
3. Do some research on the issue of deinstitutionalization (letting mentally ill people out of institutions to live among others). Does it work for the patients and for society? Or are there problems? Then develop an essay in which you detail your findings. Do not forget to cite your sources where needed in your essay and to include a list of those sources at the end.

Do I Look Like Public Enemy Number One?

Lorraine Ali

In her 1999 Mademoiselle *article "Do I Look Like Public Enemy Number One?" Lorraine Ali offers her personal account of growing up Arabic in America. Ali analyzes specific events in American culture that have increased prejudice against those of Middle Eastern heritage.*

Preparing to Read

Think about the following questions as you read:

1. Have you ever witnessed people being unfairly judged because of their nationality, race, or connections to a particular group?
2. Have you ever been influenced to distrust someone from another culture or country?

"You're not a terrorist, are you?" That was pretty much a stock question I faced growing up. Classmates usually asked it after they heard my last name: "Ali" sounded Arabic; therefore, I must be some kind of bomb-lobbing religious fanatic with a grudge against Western society. It didn't matter that just before my Middle Eastern heritage was revealed, my friend and I might have been discussing the merits of rock versus disco, or the newest flavor of Bonne Bell Lip Smacker. 1

I could never find the right retort; I either played along ("Yeah, and I'm going to blow up the math building first") or laughed and shrugged it off. How was I going to explain that my background meant far more than buzz words like *fanatic* and *terrorist* could say? Back in the '70s and '80s, all Americans knew of the Middle East came from television and newspapers. "Arab" meant a contemptible[1] composite of images: angry Palestinian refugees, irate[2] Iranian hostage-takers, extremist leaders like Libya's Muammar al-Qaddafi or Iran's Ayatollah Khomeini, and long gas lines at home. What my limited teenage vernacular couldn't express was that an entire race of people was being judged by its most violent individuals. 2

Twenty years later, I'm still trying to explain. Not much has changed in the '90s. In fact, now that Russia has been outmoded as Public Enemy Number One, Arabs have been promoted into that position. Whenever a disaster strikes without a clear cause, fingers point toward Islam. When an explosion downed TWA Flight 800, pundits prematurely blamed "Arab terrorists." Early coverage following the Oklahoma City bombing featured experts saying it "showed Middle Eastern traits." Over the next six days there were 150 documented hate crimes against Arab Americans; phone calls to radio talk shows demanded detainment[3] and deportation of Middle Easterners. Last fall, *The Siege* depicted Moslems terrorizing Manhattan, and TV's *Days of Our Lives* showed a female character being kidnapped by an Arabian sultan, held hostage in a harem, and threatened with death if she didn't learn how to belly dance properly. Whatever! 3

My Childhood Had Nothing to Do with Belly Dancing

Defending my ethnicity has always seemed ironic to me because I consider myself a fake Arab. I am half of European ancestry and half Arab, and I grew up in the suburban sprawl[4] of Los Angeles' San Fernando Valley. My skin is pale olive rather than smooth brown like my dad's, and my eyes are green, not black like my sisters' (they got all the Arab genes). Even my name, Lorraine Mahia Ali, saves all the Arab parts for last. 4

I also didn't grow up Moslem, like my dad, who emigrated from Baghdad, Iraq's capital, in 1956. In the old country he wore a galabiya (or robe), didn't eat pork, and prayed toward Mecca twice a day. To me, an American girl who wore short-shorts, ate Pop Rocks, and listened to Van Halen, his former life sounded like a fairy tale. The Baghdad of his childhood was an ancient city where he and his brothers swam in the Tigris River, where he did accounting on an abacus in his father's tea shop, where his mother blamed his sister's polio on a neighbor's evil eye, where his entire neighborhood watched Flash Gordon movies projected on the side of a bakery wall. 5

[1] **contemptible:** deserving scorn and pity; [2] **irate:** angry; [3] **detainment:** holding in custody; [4] **sprawl:** spreading urban development

My father's world only started to seem real to me when I visited Iraq the summer after fifth grade and stayed in his family's small stucco house. I remember feeling both completely at home and totally foreign. My sister Lela and I spoke to amused neighbors in shoddy sign language, sat cross-legged on the floor in our Mickey Mouse T-shirts, rolling cigarettes to sell at market for my arthritic Bedouin grandma, and sang silly songs in pidgin[5] Arabic with my Uncle Brahim. Afterward, I wrote a back-to-school essay in which I referred to my grandparents as Hajia and Haja Hassan, thinking their names were the Arab equivalent of Mary Ellen and Billy Bob. "You're such a dumbass," said Lela. "It just means grandma and grandpa." 6

At home, my American side continued to be shamefully ignorant of all things Arab, but my Arab side began to notice some pretty hideous stereotypes. Saturday-morning cartoons depicted Arabs as ruthless, bumbling, and hygienically[6] challenged. I'd glimpse grotesque illustrations of Arab leaders in my dad's paper. At the mall with my mom, we'd pass such joke items as an Arab face on a bull's-eye. She tried to explain to me that things weren't always this way, that there was a time when Americans were mesmerized by Arabia and Omar Sharif made women swoon. A time when a WASP girl like my mom, raised in a conservative, middle-class family, could be considered romantic and daring, not subversive,[7] for dating my dad. In effect, my mom belonged to the last generation to think sheiks were chic. 7

Not so in my generation. My mother tells me that when my oldest sister was five, she said to a playmate that her dad "was an Arab, but not a bad one." In elementary school, we forced smiles through taunts like, "Hey, Ali, where's your oilcan?" Teachers were even more hurtful: During roll call on her first day of junior high, Lela was made to sit through a 20-minute lecture about the bloodshed and barbarism[8] of Arabs toward Israel and the world. As far as I knew, Lela had never shed anyone's blood except for mine, when she punched me in the nose over a pack of Pixie Sticks. But that didn't matter. As Arabs, we were guilty by association, even at the age of twelve. 8

By High School, I Was Beginning to Believe the Hype

It's awful to admit, but I was sometimes embarrassed by my dad. 9

I know it's every teen's job to think her parents are the most shameful creatures to walk the planet, but this basic need to reject him was exacerbated by the horrible images of Arabs around me. When he drove me to school, my dad would pop in a cassette of Quran sutras (recorded prayers) and sing along in a language I didn't understand, yet somehow the twisting, weaving words sounded as natural as the whoosh of the Santa Ana winds through the 10

[5] **pidgin:** a simple speech used by people who speak different languages; [6] **hygienically:** related to health and cleanliness; [7] **subversive:** something that corrupts or overthrows; [8] **barbarism:** an offensive idea, act, or expression

dusty hills where we lived. His brown hands would raise off the steering wheel at high points of the prayer, the sun illuminating the big white moons of his fingernails. The mass of voices on tape would swell up and answer the *Emam* (priest), like a gospel congregation responding to a preacher. It was beautiful, but I still made my dad turn it down as we approached my school. I knew I'd be identified as part of a culture that America loved to hate.

My dad must have felt this, too. He spoke his native tongue only in the company of Arabic friends and never taught my sisters or me the language, something he would regret until the day he died. His background was a mystery to me. I'd pester him for answers: "Do you dream in English or Arabic?" I'd ask, while he was busy doing dad work like fixing someone's busted Schwinn or putting up Christmas lights. "Oh, I don't know," he'd answer playfully. "In dreams, I can't tell the difference." 11

Outside the safety of our home, he could. He wanted respect; therefore, he felt he must act American. Though he truly loved listening to Roberta Flack and wearing Adidas sweatsuits, I can't imagine he enjoyed making dinner reservations under pseudonyms[9] like Mr. Allen. He knew that as Mr. Ali, he might never get a table. 12

Desert Storm Warning

Fifteen years later, "Ali" was still not a well-received name. We were at war with the Middle East. It was January 16, 1991, and Iraq's Saddam Hussein had just invaded Kuwait. I will never forget the night CNN's Bernard Shaw lay terrified on the floor of his Baghdad hotel as a cameraman shot footage of the brand-new war outside his window. I was twenty-six and working for a glossy music magazine called *Creem*. When the news broke that we were bombing Baghdad in an operation called Desert Storm, I went home early and sat helpless in my Hollywood apartment, crying. Before me on the TV was a man dressed in a galabiya, just like the kind my dad used to wear around the house, aiming an ancient-looking gun turret toward our space-age planes in the sky. He looked terrified, too. With every missile we fired, I watched the Baghdad I knew slip away and wondered just who was being hit. Was it Aunt Niama? My cousin Afrah? 13

Back at work, I had to put up with "funny" faxes of camels, SCUD missiles, and dead Arabs. To my colleagues, the Arabs I loved and respected were now simply targets. Outside the office, there was a virtual free-for-all of racist slogans. Arab-hating sentiment came out on bumper stickers like "Kick Their Ass and Take Their Gas." Military footage even documented our pilots joking as they bombed around fleeing civilians. They called it a turkey shoot. A turkey shoot? Those were people. 14

[9] **pseudonyms:** fake names

Arabs bleed and perish just like Americans. I know, because two years 15
before we started dropping bombs on Baghdad, I watched my father die. He did not dissolve like a cartoon character, nor defy death like a Hollywood villain. Instead, chemotherapy shrunk his 180-pound body down to 120, turned his beautiful skin from brown to ashen beige, and rendered his opalescent[10] white fingernails a dull shade of gray. When he finally let go, I thought he took all the secrets of my Arabness with him, all the good things America didn't want me to know. But I look in the mirror and see my father's wide nose on my face and Hajia's think lines forming between my brows. I also see my mom's fair skin, and her mother's high cheekbones. I realize it's my responsibility to somehow forge an identity between dueling cultures, to focus on the humanity, not the terror, that bridges both worlds.

After You Read

Developing Your Vocabulary

Using a dictionary, look up the following words that appear in the essay:

composite (para. 2)
vernacular (para. 2)
deportation (para. 3)
emigrated (para. 5)
stereotypes (para. 7)
mesmerized (para. 7)
chic (para. 7)
exacerbated (para. 10)

Additional Vocabulary

The author makes references in the article to aspects of Arab culture and American culture and geography that may be unfamiliar to you. Use a dictionary, encyclopedia, or even an older friend or relative to track down the meanings or identities of the following:

Islam (para. 3)
sultan (para. 3)
Moslem (para. 3)
Baghdad (para. 5)
Flash Gordon (para. 5)
Bedouin (para. 6)
sheiks (para. 7)
Omar Sharif (para. 7)
Pixie Sticks (para. 8)
Santa Ana winds (para. 10)
Roberta Flack (para. 12)

[10] **opalescent:** reflecting a colored light

Understanding the Reading

1. How, according to Lorraine Ali, have Arabs become Public Enemy Number One for Americans?
2. What is racial stereotyping? What are some common racial stereotypes? How are Arabs stereotyped in American culture?
3. Why, according to the author, was it inappropriate to label her as an Arab terrorist?
4. Who was Ali's link to her Arabic heritage? Was she, as a youth, always proud of this heritage?
5. What does it mean to "act American"? In what ways did Ali's father preserve his heritage, and in what ways did he "act American"?
6. How did the Gulf War intensify anti-Arab feelings in the United States? What forms did this growing hostility take?
7. What point is Ali trying to make as she tells about her father's death?

Responding to What You Read

Paragraph Writing Assignments

1. Write a paragraph in which you define *stereotyping.*
2. Using examples, explore how the media have contributed to or countered racial stereotyping.

Essay Writing Assignments

1. In a country that prides itself on being a "melting pot" of immigrants, is it better for immigrants to leave their old culture behind and learn how to "act American," or should they try to hold on to as much of their heritage as possible? Present reasons for your position.
2. At the end of her article, Lorraine Ali describes herself as struggling to "forge an identity between dueling cultures." In this passage she shows that people of mixed heritage sometimes face identity crises. Write an essay in which you examine the causes and effects of such internal conflicts.
3. Have there been other flare-ups of racial hatred during wartime in U.S. history? Research, for instance, the treatment of Japanese Americans during World War II. Argue whether their treatment was appropriate or inappropriate.

What You Do Is What You Are

Nickie McWhirter

In her essay "What You Do Is What You Are," originally published by the Detroit Free Press, *columnist Nickie McWhirter examines how Americans classify one another by job title.*

Preparing to Read

Think about the following questions as you read:

1. What makes you who you are? Your personality? Your interests? Your work?
2. Describe a time when you or someone you know was judged by occupation.

Americans, unlike people almost everywhere else in the world, tend to define and judge everybody in terms of the work they do, especially work performed for pay. Charlie is a doctor; Sam is a carpenter; Mary Ellen is a copywriter at a small ad agency. It is as if by defining how a person earns his or her rent money, we validate[1] or reject that person's existence. Through the work and job title, we evaluate the worth of the life attached. Larry is a laid-off auto worker; Tony is a retired teacher; Sally is a former showgirl and blackjack dealer from Vegas. It is as if by learning that a person currently earns no money at a job—and maybe hasn't earned any money at a job for years—we assign that person to limbo,[2] at least for the present. We define such non-employed persons in terms of their past job history. 1

This seems peculiar to me. People aren't cast in bronze because of the jobs they hold or once held. A retired teacher, for example, may spend a lot of volunteer time working with handicapped children or raising money for the Loyal Order of Hibernating Hibiscus. That apparently doesn't count. Who's Tony? A retired teacher. A laid-off auto worker may pump gas at his cousin's gas station or sell encyclopedias on weekends. But who's Larry? Until and unless he begins to work steadily again, he's a laid-off auto worker. This is the same as saying he's nothing now, but he used to be something: an auto worker. 2

There is a whole category of other people who are "just" something. To be "just" anything is the worst. It is not to be recognized by society as having much value at all, not now and probably not in the past either. To be "just" anything is to be totally discounted, at least for the present. There are lots of people who are "just" something. "Just" a housewife immediately and painfully comes to mind. We still hear it all the time. Sometimes women who have kept a house and reared six children refer to themselves as "'just' a housewife." "Just" a bum, "just" a kid, "just" a drunk, bag lady, old man, student, punk are some others. You can probably add to the list. The "just" category contains present nonearners, people who have no past job history highly valued by society and people whose present jobs are on the low-end of pay and prestige[3] scales. A person can be "just" a cab driver, for example, or "just" a janitor. No one is ever "just" a vice-president, however. 3

We're supposed to be a classless society, but we are not. We don't recognize a titled nobility. We refuse to acknowledge[4] dynastic privilege. But we 4

[1] **validate:** to justify; [2] **limbo:** a state of uncertainty; [3] **prestige:** standing or position; [4] **acknowledge:** to recognize

certainly separate the valued from the valueless, and it has a lot to do with jobs and the importance or prestige we attach to them.

It is no use arguing whether any of this is correct or proper. Rationally it 5
is silly. That's our system, however, and we should not only keep it in mind, we should teach our children how it works. It is perfectly swell to want to grow up to be a cowboy or a nurse. Kids should know, however, that quite apart from earnings potential, the cattle breeder is much more respected than the hired hand. The doctor gets a lot more respect and privilege than the nurse.

I think some anthropologist ought to study our uncataloged system of 6
awarding respect and deference[5] to each other based on jobs we hold. Where does a vice-president–product planning fit in? Is that better than vice-president–sales in the public consciousness, or unconsciousness? Writers earn diddly dot, but I suspect they are held in higher esteem than wealthy rock musicians—that is, if everybody older than forty gets to vote.

How do we decide which jobs have great value and, therefore, the job- 7
holders are wonderful people? Why is someone who builds shopping centers called an entrepreneur while someone who builds freeways is called a contractor? I have no answers to any of this, but we might think about the phenomenon the next time we are tempted to fawn[6] over some stranger because we find out he happens to be a judge, or the next time we catch ourselves discounting the personal worth of the garbage collector.

After You Read

Developing Your Vocabulary

Using a dictionary, look up the following words that appear in the essay:

blackjack (para. 1)
discounted (para. 3)
dynastic (para. 4)
esteem (para. 6)

Understanding the Reading

1. When McWhirter says that "we" are supposed to live in a "classless society," what does she mean?
2. Why do we value some jobs over others? Does a job's value depend on who is doing the judging?
3. How does society judge an unemployed worker?
4. What is a "just a"? Can you name additional examples of "just a's" to those given in the essay?

[5] **deference:** honor an elder or superior; [6] **fawn:** to treat with flattery

Responding to What You Read

Paragraph Writing Assignments

1. Is the job you will be seeking upon graduation a "valued" profession, or not? Your controlling idea should be developed with reasons for your answer.
2. Using classification as a method of development, write a paragraph on what makes a job valued in our society. What characteristics must it have to be valued highly?

Essay Writing Assignments

1. Why do we value some jobs over others? Discuss the role that a job's importance to our daily lives plays in our opinion of its worth. You might also discuss the roles that the amount of education required and the amount of money one can earn play in determining a job's value. Can you think of any other reasons?
2. Are there more important qualities that we should value in human beings than their ability to hold a prestigious job? If yes, give some examples supporting your thesis. If no, disprove the possible arguments of someone who would argue differently.
3. Is the goal of equal employment opportunity realistic? That is, can job discrimination based on sex, race, or age be totally eliminated?

Welcome to the Tongue-Show

Jay Ingram

"Welcome to the Tongue-Show," written by Jay Ingram, first appeared in his 1989 book, The Science of Everyday Life. *This essay analyzes a specific aspect of human behavior—"tongue-showing"—and explores why it occurs.*

Preparing to Read

Think about the following questions as you read:

1. What is nonverbal communication?
2. How do you show people that you want them to leave you alone?

Try to remember the last time you had to do something with great control and precision[1] or concentration—like threading a needle or reading the instructions for your VCR. Was the tip of your tongue showing between your lips? If you're not aware of doing it yourself, think about the last time you saw a young child concentrating hard on connecting the numbered dots in a 1

[1] **precision:** exactness

puzzle. I'd bet you saw the tip of his or her tongue then. Behavioral scientists call this peculiar little phenomenon[2] "tongue-showing" (with their usual imaginative flair for naming), and it's a common and powerful form of nonverbal behavior.

There are many ways of showing your tongue. You can just stick the tip of it out between your teeth and leave it there or flick it in and out or leave it folded over between your teeth without sticking it out or even point it to one side or the other. No matter what specific form tongue-showing takes, it's always done to convey the message, "Don't bother me." What's intriguing is that the message is sent and received unconsciously[3]—neither the person showing his or her tongue nor the person at whom the display is aimed is aware of the intent or even the act itself. This immediately differentiates tongue-showing from sticking your tongue out at somebody or even running the tip of the tongue suggestively along the lips. These are both deliberate and conscious acts, and tongue-showing is neither. Yet it's a very common human signal, and it's possible to predict when someone will do it and what the effect will be on those that see it. 2

Children in nursery school tongue-show most often when they're involved in activities such as working with dough, drawing with crayons, or even kicking a ball. The greater the concentration needed, the more often the tongue appears. In one experiment, as children made their way to the top of an ever-narrowing set of steps, their tongues started to creep out. Even children who are not tongue-showing to begin with start to do so the moment they catch an adult watching them. 3

The tongue-showing of pool-playing fraternity brothers at the University of Pennsylvania correlated directly with the difficulty of the shot, and the poorer players tongue-showed more than the good players. Even gorillas follow the pattern—they show their tongues more when engaged in demanding tasks like balancing on an upturned wagon or hanging from chains. 4

There are many other situations where tongue-showing has been observed, but the explanation is the same: People (or gorillas) show their tongues when they don't want to be disturbed by others, usually because they're involved in something that's demanding their total attention. It's a subtle form of social rejection, a signal to stay away from the tongue-showing individual. The setting may be unusual: The most dramatic tongue-show I have ever seen was produced by a woman riding a bicycle down the center line of a busy downtown street in Toronto, her tongue fully extended. She was engrossed[4] in keeping her bicycle steady, and her tongue-showing worked as far as I could tell: Every car gave her as wide a berth as possible. 5

[2] **phenomenon:** an unusual event; [3] **unconsciously:** doing something without knowing; [4] **engrossed:** deeply involved

An experiment in Philadelphia illustrated how we rely on tongue-showing to keep others away. In this study a twenty-five-year-old white male sat at the top of a set of stairs leading into an office building. He stared intently at anyone who climbed the stairs to enter the building but did not threaten actual physical contact. A hidden observer recorded the reactions of all those who approached the building alone. Their reactions were predictably varied: Some looked away immediately, some smiled hesitatingly, others looked at their watches or brushed their hair. 6

But what was remarkable was the number that showed their tongues: Of fifty people, seventeen showed their tongues. While most of these did it within a few feet of the starer, some started tongue-showing more than ten feet away, and surprisingly, three began only *after* they'd passed the starer. (Although this may seem a little late to send a nonverbal "leave-me-alone" signal, the experimenters reasoned that they had their signals ready just in case the starer pursued them.) Obviously the signal can be used to avoid social contact even when the tongue-shower is not busy. The controls in this experiment were fifty people who passed the same man sitting in the same place on the stairs, but the man was reading, not staring. Only two tongue-showed. 7

The proof that the tongue-showing message is received comes from an experiment involving twenty-five male and twenty-five female college students. A student was seated at a desk facing the back of a room and was told to complete a reading comprehension test. He or she then received a test booklet and was warned that every question had to be answered in sequence. The supervisor then said that he was going to be transcribing[5] an audio tape and would wear headphones so as not to disturb the student. He sat at the front of the room, facing the student's back. 8

Page three had been removed from each booklet, and an observer hidden behind a two-way mirror noted each student's response as he or she made this unsettling discovery. Most students first swivelled in the chair and called out to the supervisor. He, of course, head bowed and ears covered with headphones—heavy, old-fashioned headphones—made no response. The student then either had to shout or to walk up to the supervisor's desk to get his attention. The supervisor continued to concentrate on his work but showed the tip of his tongue to half of the students who were trying to interrupt him. The observer timed how long each student hesitated before calling out loudly or even tapping the supervisor on the shoulder, and because the observer couldn't see whether the supervisor was tongue-showing or not, the experiment was truly "blind." 9

The results provided dramatic evidence that tongue-showing really does deter others. Those students who saw no tongue-showing waited, on aver- 10

[5] **transcribing:** making a written copy

age, 7.72 seconds before interrupting the supervisor; students who were shown his tongue waited 19.93 seconds (and one student, apparently inordinately sensitive to this sort of signal, waited 2 minutes). This average difference of 12 seconds is not only statistically significant, it's two and a half times longer, which in the circumstances would have seemed like an eternity.

The most curious part of the study was the post-experiment interview: Students were told the real purpose of the experiment and then asked to reproduce the facial expression of the supervisor. None depicted a tongue. Those who had actually seen tongue-showing by the supervisor denied they had seen it, although many of them admitted that they felt that the supervisor did not want to be disturbed. On the other hand, students who had *not* seen the supervisor tongue-showing reported feeling no reluctance to interrupt him. 11

So it seems that tongue-showing works, even though neither person involved is aware that the exposed tongue is sending a message. Why does the tip of the tongue convey the message, "Leave me alone"? Why not the nose or the eyebrows? One of the principal investigators in this area, Dr. Julia Chase of Barnard College, thinks it may have an early start. She observed a six-week-old infant lying in a crib with her tongue protruding.[6] The child's mother explained that the baby did that when she was finished breast-feeding—too weak still to pull her head away, she pushed the nipple out with her tongue. The baby then left her tongue visible for some time, discouraging her mother from further attempts at nursing. Charles Darwin observed a six-month-old doing the same thing with novel foods. While these are only anecdotal[7] accounts, they suggest that tongue-showing as a rejection signal might begin in infancy. 12

Once you are aware of it, you'll see tongue-showing everywhere, but note its variations: Sometimes it will be disguised in situations where showing the tongue might be deemed inappropriate. An example cited by researchers is the televised beauty pageant, where finalists are asked challenging questions to demonstrate their range of knowledge. The tongue makes its appearance on cue, not peeking out between the teeth, but busily moistening lips that need no moistening. 13

After You Read

Developing Your Vocabulary

Using a dictionary, look up the following words and phrases that appear in the essay:

behavioral scientists (para. 1)
intriguing (para. 2)

[6] **protruding:** sticking out; [7] **anecdotal:** based on unverified reports

differentiates (para. 2)
comprehension (para. 8)
inordinately (para. 10)
novel (para. 12)

Understanding the Reading

1. When, according to Jay Ingram, do people show their tongues?
2. Do we know we are showing our tongues when we concentrate? Do other people know?
3. Describe at least one experiment that is included in the Ingram article that demonstrates tongue-showing and what it means.
4. Why are "controls" important in an experiment?

Responding to What You Read

Paragraph Writing Assignments

1. Write a process analysis paragraph in which you give the steps to conducting a scientific experiment. Begin the paragraph with a clear topic sentence that gives an overview of the process.
2. Choose a message that you might want to send to your friends and family. Then write a paragraph in which you describe examples of nonverbal behavior that would get your message across. What example do you think would work best?

Essay Writing Assignments

1. Observe your classmates in class or during group leisure activities. Make notes on the nonverbal signs and signals that they exhibit. Why are they using those nonverbal motions and gestures? What are they saying without words? Write an essay that discusses your findings. Your thesis should summarize what you have observed.
2. A sign or gesture may have different meanings depending on the culture in which it is displayed. Write an essay in which you examine some gestures and body movements and the way they are interpreted in other cultures and in your own.
3. Conduct your own experiment to see if the findings on tongue-showing that Ingram presented are correct. Set up a situation that forces people to concentrate and to need to be left alone. Then observe them to see if they show their tongues. Don't forget to use controls to prove your findings. After you have conducted your experiment, report your findings in an essay written to your instructor. Include as your thesis whether or not your findings support the results Ingram reported.

"You Be the Monster and Chase Me": Children at Play

Deborah Tannen

Deborah Tannen, in her essay "'You Be the Monster and Chase Me': Children at Play," examines the gender differences in small children's playtime activity. This piece is excerpted from Tannen's 1998 book The Argument Culture: Moving From Debate to Dialogue.

Preparing to Read

Think about the following questions as you read:

1. How obvious are differences between the sexes when young children play?
2. Why do boys tend to irritate girls when they try to involve girls in their play?

A mother bought a toy for her three-year-old son that she remembered liking when she was a child. Called "A Barrel of Monkeys," it was a yellow plastic barrel containing bright red plastic monkeys with long arms shaped to hook into each other. The mother assumed her son would play with this toy as she had: looping the arms together to make a long strand of monkeys. But he had a different idea about how to play with this toy. He grabbed a bunch of monkeys in each hand, stood them up facing each other, announced, "These are the nice ones and these are the mean ones"—and set them upon each other in mock battle. 1

Watch small children at play. First of all, you'll see that girls and boys tend to play with other children of the same sex if they have a choice. And the way they play tends to be different. The girls spend a fair amount of time sitting together, and talking is a big part of their play: "Let's pretend," you hear. And "Wanna know a secret?" Most boys spend a lot of time roughhousing, grappling for toys, threatening or clobbering each other with toy weapons. These different ways of playing explain, in part, why they prefer to play with other children of the same sex. The boys find the girls' way of playing boring; the girls think the boys play too rough. And sometimes, so do the boys' mothers. 2

Few girls use their toys to set up battles between monsters and heroes. This is not to imply that little girls don't fight; of course they do. They struggle over rights to toys and have power struggles over who's in and who's out. But their disputes are more likely to be primarily (though certainly not exclusively) verbal, less likely to be primarily physical, all-out grappling to get what they want. Most important, girls don't tend to play-fight for fun. They are less likely to pick up whatever is at hand and turn it into a weapon. As the mother who bought her son A Barrel of Monkeys put it, "My friend has a lit- 3 tle girl the same age as my son. When her little girl wants to play, she says, 'You be the baby and I'll be the mommy.' When my little boy wants to play, he says, 'You be the monster and chase me!'"

Go into a kindergarten classroom, and you're likely to see this classic scene: A pair or group of little girls builds a structure in the block corner; then a pair or group of boys descends upon them and destroys it. The boys think it's hilarious; the girls are genuinely upset, even incensed. The girls think the boys are mean for having destroyed their creation. But the boys may be trying to include the girls in their play, setting up a mock[1] attack. 4

When I teach a course on gender and language, I ask the students in the class to keep a log of their experiences that relate to the course. One young man, Anthony Marchese, wrote about playing "Jenga," a game of blocks, with two friends: 5

> We played about three or four games and then we started building things with the blocks. It was really fun because we felt like little kids again. There were three of us building our own little structures, two guys and one girl, Alicia. We had each built a unique design, when suddenly the other guy threw a block at my structure to knock it over. It only glanced my building, and for the most part it stayed up. I then threw a block at his building, which prompted him to throw a block at Alicia's. She put her arms around her building to shield it from the flying blocks. While my friend and I destroyed each other's buildings, we couldn't get hers because we did not want to hit her with the blocks. Another guy in the room said to her, "Why didn't you throw blocks at them?" She said she did not like to play that way and she did not find our play very amusing. Honestly, it has been over ten years since I built anything with blocks, and I am sure it has been just as long for my male friend. But I can recall that when I played with blocks with my brothers, we would destroy each others' designs. Last Friday, I was just playing the way I used to play. . . . I did not want my building ruined, but I had a lot of fun throwing blocks at my friend's and destroying his.

Anthony's perspective sheds light on the kindergarten scene. It's not that the little boys are necessarily destructive, insensitive, and mean, though the girls may think so. It's a kind of game—it's fun. But they end up looking like bullies because of the way the girls react. This is not to say that boys are never mean: Both boys and girls can be exceedingly cruel to other children. But sometimes what is taken as being mean is simply an attempt to play in a way another child does not understand or appreciate—and this dynamic[2] is especially likely between boys and girls. 6

[1] **mock:** imitation; [2] **dynamic:** relationship

I saw this contrast one spring afternoon—and got a glimpse of the joyful spirit that can underlie what comes across as aggressive behavior. My husband and I were eating lunch at an outdoor table behind a fast-food restaurant adjoining[3] a large picnic area beside the ocean. It was Sunday, one of the first warm days of spring, and families had brought children who were running and playing as their parents ate. A little girl who looked about four or five was standing alone, absorbed in eating an ice cream cone, surrounded by a horde of boys of varying ages. One little boy, littler than she, was especially exuberant; he was skipping and running, waving his arms around: His joy was palpable. At one point he ran over to the little girl, whom he obviously knew, and clamped his hands on her hips. It wasn't even a shove, just a grab. Startled, she took a second or two to respond—by dropping her jaw, starting to cry, and heading straight for her father, who was sitting not far away. The girl soon stopped crying and went back to her ice cream cone. The boy continued to run around with the same look of excitement and pleasure on his face. Before long he ran up to an older boy and grabbed him in exactly the same way. The older boy at first ignored him but then allowed him to tumble into play. Soon they were roughhousing, pulling each others' jackets, pushing, shoving, and having a ball. It was clear as the warm spring day that by running up to the little girl and grabbing her, the boy was just trying to engage her in play—in a way she interpreted not as play but as an attack. 7

After You Read

Developing Your Vocabulary

Using a dictionary, look up the following words that appear in the essay:

incensed (para. 4)
exceedingly (para. 6)
horde (para. 7)
exuberant (para. 7)
palpable (para. 7)

Understanding the Reading

1. What research techniques does Tannen use to examine the behavior of children at play?
2. When Tannen observes boys and girls at play, what differences does she notice?
3. How, according to the author, do young boys try to include girls in their play? Are their attempts always successful?
4. Do play habits change as children grow into adults? In what ways?

[3] **adjoining:** next to

Responding to What You Read

Paragraph Writing Assignments

1. Write a narrative about an experience you have had, either as a child or as an adult, with conflicting approaches to play.
2. Compare and contrast your approach to play with that of a friend, brother, or sister.

Essay Writing Assignments

1. How are the differences between male and female play behavior reinforced by the media? By the toy industry? By other social influences? Support your thesis with good examples.
2. Does "play" take different forms as we grow older? Are there ways that men carry over their aggressive play behavior to their careers? How do women respond to this aggressive play behavior?
3. Is play behavior the result of biology or upbringing? Explore this topic by searching for a few relevant articles from online sources, magazines, books, or journals. Then take a position on the issue, give solid reasons to support your position, and argue your point.

The Case for Cloning

J. Madeleine Nash

"The Case for Cloning" first appeared as an online article for Time.com. J. Madeleine Nash argues that human cloning may be more helpful to medical science than lawmakers are willing to believe. Nash cites statistics and research in order to support her points.

Preparing to Read

Think about the following questions as you read:

1. How is human cloning ethically different from cloning a sheep?
2. Are there recently discovered benefits that make human cloning worthy of further research and development?

An elderly man develops macular degeneration, a disease that destroys vision. To bolster his failing eyesight, he receives a transplant of healthy retinal[1] tissue—cloned from his own cells and cultivated in a lab dish. 1

A baby girl is born free of the gene that causes Tay-Sachs disease, even though both her parents are carriers. The reason? In the embryonic[2] cell from which she was cloned, the flawed gene was replaced with normal DNA. 2

[1] **retinal:** relating to the retina of the eye; [2] **embryonic:** the state of being an embryo

These futuristic scenarios are not now part of the debate over human cloning, but they should be. Spurred by the fear that maverick physicist Richard Seed, or someone like him, will open a cloning clinic, lawmakers are rushing to enact broad restrictions against human cloning. To date, nineteen European nations have signed an anticloning treaty. The Clinton administration backs a proposal that would impose a five-year moratorium.[3] House majority leader Dick Armey has thrown his weight behind a bill that would ban human cloning permanently, and at least eighteen states are contemplating legislative action of their own. "This is the right thing to do, at the right time, for the sake of human dignity," said Armey last week. "How can you put a statute of limitations on right and wrong?" 3

But hasty legislation could easily be too restrictive. Last year, for instance, Florida considered a law that would have barred the cloning of human DNA, a routine procedure in biomedical research. California passed badly worded legislation that temporarily bans not just human cloning but also a procedure that shows promise as a new treatment for infertility. 4

Most lawmakers are focused on a nightmarish vision in which billionaires and celebrities flood the world with genetic copies of themselves. But scientists say it's unlikely that anyone is going to be churning out limited editions of Michael Jordan or Madeleine Albright. "Oh, it can be done," says Dr. Mark Sauer, chief of reproductive endocrinology[4] at Columbia University's College of Physicians and Surgeons. "It's just that the best people, who could do it, aren't going to be doing it." 5

Cloning individual human cells, however, is another matter. Biologists are already talking about harnessing for medical purposes the technique that produced the sheep called Dolly. They might, for example, obtain healthy cells from a patient with leukemia or a burn victim and then transfer the nucleus of each cell into an unfertilized egg from which the nucleus has been removed. Coddled in culture dishes, these embryonic clones—each genetically identical to the patient from which the nuclei came—would begin to divide. 6

The cells would not have to grow into a fetus, however. The addition of powerful growth factors could ensure that the clones develop only into specialized cells and tissue. For the leukemia patient, for example, the cloned cells could provide an infusion[5] of fresh bone marrow, and for the burn victim, grafts[6] of brand-new skin. Unlike cells from an unrelated donor, these cloned cells would incur no danger of rejection; patients would be spared the need to take powerful drugs to suppress the immune system. "Given its potential benefit," says Dr. Robert Winston, a fertility expert at London's 7

[3] **moratorium:** a waiting period; [4] **endocrinology:** the study of hormones; [5] **infusion:** an introduction of one thing into another; [6] **grafts:** the uniting of living tissue

Hammersmith Hospital, "I would argue that it would be unethical not to continue this line of research."

There are dangers, but not the ones everyone's talking about, according to Princeton University molecular biologist Lee Silver, author of *Remaking Eden* (Avon Books). Silver believes that cloning is the technology that will finally make it possible to apply genetic engineering to humans. First, parents will want to banish inherited diseases like Tay-Sachs. Then they will try to eliminate predispositions to alcoholism and obesity. In the end, says Silver, they will attempt to augment normal traits like intelligence and athletic prowess.[7] 8

Cloning could be vital to that process. At present, introducing genes into chromosomes is very much a hit-or-miss proposition. Scientists might achieve the result they intend once in twenty times, making the procedure far too risky to perform on a human embryo. Through cloning, however, scientists could make twenty copies of the embryo they wished to modify, greatly boosting their chance of success. 9

Perhaps now would be a good time to ask ourselves which we fear more: that cloning will produce multiple copies of crazed despots,[8] as in the film *The Boys from Brazil;* or that it will lead to the society portrayed in *Gattaca,* the recent science-fiction thriller in which genetic enhancement of a privileged few creates a rigid caste[9] structure. By acting sensibly, we might avoid both traps. 10

After You Read

Developing Your Vocabulary

Using a dictionary, look up the following words that appear in the essay:

cultivated (para. 1)
maverick (para. 3)
infertility (para. 4)
coddled (para. 6)
predispositions (para. 8)
obesity (para. 8)

Text References for Further Investigation

Look up these names and titles on the World Wide Web or in library reference sources to understand them and Nash's essay better:

Tay-Sachs disease (para. 2)
Richard Seed (para. 3)
Madeleine Albright (para. 5)

[7] **prowess:** skill and bravery; [8] **despots:** rulers with absolute power; [9] **caste:** a social class

Dolly, the cloned sheep (para. 6)
The Boys from Brazil (para. 10)
Gattaca (para. 10)

Understanding the Reading

1. What, according to Nash, are the two main ways in which human cloning can help researchers in the field of medicine?
2. Why should states and the federal government *not* outlaw experiments in human cloning?
3. Why do people respond negatively to the idea of human cloning?
4. Are there real dangers associated with human cloning?

Responding to What You Read

Paragraph Writing Assignments

1. What are three major medical benefits of human cloning? Write a paragraph in which you provide examples gained from Nash's essay and from an additional source on the subject.
2. If you could have a child cloned from any person living or dead, who would that be and why? Write a paragraph in which you give reasons for your choice.

Essay Writing Assignments

1. Is cloning humans "playing God"? If you believe it is, write an essay in which you define "playing God" and make comparisons between the two acts. If you do not believe the two acts are similar, write an essay that also defines "playing God" but contrasts it with human cloning.
2. As Nash states, Congress is considering a bill that would "ban human cloning permanently." Should the federal government have the power to control scientific research? Or should researchers be allowed to experiment when and however they please? Write an essay in which you discuss both sides of this issue to determine which argument is stronger.
3. Human cloning is not the first scientific breakthrough that was greeted with a mixed reaction. Through the ages, many scientific discoveries have been feared at first by scientists and the general public. Research this topic, and write an essay in which you explore two or three major discoveries that were at first unappreciated.

Chapter 20

Writing Timed Paragraphs and Essays

At some point in many of your courses, you will be asked to write in class. In-class writing often includes timed quizzes and exams that test your knowledge of a subject. To receive a high mark on your quiz or exam, you will need to write a paragraph or essay that discusses the topic in a clear, organized, and efficient manner.

Writing an answer to a discussion question under pressure can be challenging, though. Organizing and writing a paragraph or essay in a short space of time can cause a writer to panic. Panic can bring about writer's block, which leaves writers staring at blank paper and racking their brains for an idea. Following a process can help you to avoid writer's block. This chapter presents a process for writing timed paragraphs and essays.

Before you begin, you may find it comforting to know that most instructors don't expect in-class writing to be as complex and polished as writing done out of class or over a long period of time. However, they do want you to present a topic or thesis sentence with a clear controlling idea. They also expect you to explain your approach to the topic in a clear and orderly way, with as much supporting information as possible. By writing well-structured paragraphs and essays, you make it easy for your instructor to see how well you know the material.

How to Recognize a Discussion Question

One way to decide whether a question requires a paragraph or essay response is by eliminating other types of questions.

- You already know that a **"true-false"** or **"multiple-choice"** question simply requires that you check a correct answer from among answers provided for you.
- A second kind of question you can rule out is the **"ID" (identification)** question to be answered in several sentences or sometimes in a single sentence.

Usually the directions will say "Identify briefly" or "Comment briefly" and will list various terms or topics. In such cases the instructor is checking to see whether you know the most significant information about the items listed. He or she does not want a long discussion.

- A third type of question asks you to **"list"** certain items or facts. The instructions may say, "List three types of medieval chants" or "What are George Polya's four steps for problem solving?" or "List five psychosomatic disorders." Such questions do not call for full discussion, and answering them does not involve writing a paragraph or an essay.

Questions that do require essay or paragraph answers include a keyword or phrase in the directions. The following words and phrases often signal that a paragraph or essay is expected:

analyze	summarize
describe	what
discuss	what do you think
do you think	which
explain	why
how	why do you think

In some courses, instructors include brief situations or cases for you to respond to on a quiz or exam. These cases are meant to test how well you know and understand the course material by giving you an example to think and then write about. For instance, a psychology instructor might put the following situation on a test and ask you to write a coherent, thoughtful response to the questions that follow it:

> You have noticed that the women you know achieve higher grades in their English courses than do the men. You wonder if this is true for most women in your college. You suspect that there are developmental or social factors that contribute to an increased verbal abilities in women, so you decide to conduct a study.
>
> 1. How would you do the study?
> 2. What would be the limitations of your study?

In other courses, a discussion question might be introduced with a quotation from a noted authority. In such a situation, you are usually called upon to either explain what the quotation means or to respond to that quotation by agreeing or disagreeing. The following question could appear on a macroeconomics test:

> The economic theorist Edwin Ford states in his landmark book *The Future of the American Economy,* "If one firm cuts its price, it will make more money, so if all firms cut their price, they will make more money." Agree or disagree.

Recognizing discussion questions is not always easy. In general, a question requires an essay or paragraph answer if it asks you not only to supply facts but also to develop an explanation or position on a topic. Once you have determined that a question calls for written discussion, you can follow three basic steps to answer it:

1. **Understand.** Make sure that you understand what the question asks you to do.
2. **Collect.** Mentally collect and then jot down any facts that may be useful to your answer.
3. **Organize.** Organize and write your answer, using the techniques for structuring paragraphs and essays discussed in this text.

Understanding the Question

The way a question is worded should suggest the following:

- whether a paragraph or essay is appropriate;
- the method of development you should use in your paragraph or essay.

Paragraph or Essay?

In a discussion question, the instructor will usually indicate whether the response should be a paragraph or essay. The question might state, "In an essay, explore the . . ." or "Write a paragraph describing . . ." If the question does not contain such direct instructions, then you need to decide which is the most appropriate form. Base your decision on the amount of time you have, the complexity of the question, and how much you know. You might also ask the instructor what he or she expects.

How much time do I have?

When the class is fifty minutes long, you will probably have no more than forty minutes left in which to think and write after the instructor has given out the assignment and answered students' questions. On the other hand, if you are taking a final examination, you may have nearly two hours remaining. Let us suppose that you are taking a test in a fifty-minute class period. You see that you have to answer ten true-false questions, followed by two discussion questions. Spending just a minute each for the true-false questions, you will have thirty minutes left for the discussion part, or about fifteen minutes for answering each of the discussion questions. Obviously, you will not have enough time to write two five-paragraph essays. In this case, the time schedule suggests that a paragraph response to each question will be sufficient and appropriate.

How complex is the question?

As you consider whether to write one paragraph or more for each answer, you should also think about the nature of the question. How complex is the question?

If it asks for examples and you know that you can give those examples briefly and concisely, one well-developed paragraph may be enough. On the other hand, you may need to explain causes or effects and you may know that each cause or effect is fairly complicated. In this case, if you have the time, you should write a short essay, devoting one whole body paragraph to each cause or effect.

How much do I know?

Finally, how much you write will depend on how much you know. If you are eager to answer a particular question, you may have thought more about that issue, and you may be prepared to treat it more fully in an essay.

What Method of Development?

Frequently, a discussion question will suggest an appropriate method of development for your paragraph or essay answer. It may ask you to do one of the following:

1. Provide a *narration.*

   Sample Question: As a part of the service component for this course, you have been required to tutor a high-school student in mathematics. Describe your first tutoring session, including your efforts at establishing a relationship, your testing techniques, and your teaching strategies.

2. Give *examples* to support a point.

   Sample Question: Discuss the following statement: Christopher Columbus was probably not the first European to "discover" and visit the Americas.

3. Give the *causes and effects* of an event or a situation.

   Sample Question: What events in society can lead to political isolationism?

4. Detail a *process.*

   Sample Question: How is glucose oxidized?

5. *Define* a term or a series of terms.

   Sample Question: What is *self-actualization*?

6. *Compare or contrast* two persons, things, events, or ideas.

   Sample Question: How do "accounts payable" and "notes payable" differ?

7. *Classify* people, things, or ideas.

   Sample Question: Discuss the three types of classical arches: Doric, Ionian, and Corinthian.

Learning how to pick up on cues from the question and to understand what method of development would be the best to use is important. This skill will contribute to the success of your answer and to your getting a good grade on your exam.

CASE STUDY: Writing a Timed Essay

Lakeysha Jones, a first-year student studying American history, faced the following question on her final exam:

> *Question:* What conditions in Salem Village, Massachusetts, in 1692 caused the series of "witch" trials to occur? In your response, be sure to discuss various theories that have been advanced to explain the phenomenon of the trials.

Because the instructor had spent so much time in class on the Salem witch trials, Lakeysha had expected that the test would include at least one discussion question about it. She had therefore reviewed the information about the trials the night before, and she was ready. But before she started writing, she read the question carefully to make sure she understood what the question was asking her to do.

She realized the keywords of the question were "what caused" and "discuss various theories." In other words, the instructor wanted her to examine different reasons why the event occurred, and so she would be writing an answer that would focus on *causes.* Lakeysha recalled from her reading and lecture notes that there were at least three or four major theories about why the trials occurred. To explain all of them would take some time and space. An essay response, therefore, would be appropriate. Since she had two hours to complete the exam, and the identification and short-answer questions would take her only about forty-five minutes, she decided that she had plenty of time to develop and draft the essay.

Collecting Facts

As soon as you think you understand exactly what your instructor expects, you will have to get together the information you will need to write an answer. First, brainstorm for any facts you feel might be useful. Do not try to decide now what you can use; jot down everything that seems to offer possibilities. Because you know what the question asks of you, you have already narrowed your topic.

First, brainstorm for any facts you feel might be useful. Do not try to decide now what you can use; jot down everything that seems to offer possibilities.

Lakeysha Jones decided to tackle the identification and short-answer questions first on her history exam. However, completing those shorter questions took a bit longer than she expected. By the time she was ready to start her essay, an hour had gone by. She would now need to make the best use of the remaining hour. After reviewing the topic and requirements of the written assignment, Lakeysha brainstormed for facts that would answer the question. In fifteen minutes she came up with the following list of facts and thoughts:

> *—Theories of why the witch trials occurred—physical illness, economic problems, and the most unlikely—that witchcraft was actually being practiced*
>
> *—Need to provide some background in introduction. Salem Village, 20 men and women killed, others jailed. The problem: don't know why trials occurred—mass hysteria? What? Happened sometimes in the past century—when people let their superstitions get the best of them.*
>
> *—Sickness/physiological-psychological—weather contributes to insanity: hot weather*
>
> *—Hysteria among the young women—maybe caused by lead poisoning as well as weather—paranoia and hallucination*
>
> *—Could have been caused by the rye fungus*
>
> *—Econ—problems faced by Salem people in 1680s and 90s: economic insecurity, money was losing value, land prices were increasing. People wanted each other's property: what better way to get it than to claim your neighbor is a witch.*
>
> *—Under Mass. law, convicted witches' property went to the crown and was publicly auctioned.*
>
> *—Actually witchcraft was being practiced. There are people around today who think they're witches.*
>
> *—16th and 17th centuries—there were documented covens of witches and warlocks in Europe, so why not in Salem as well?*

In Lakeysha's brainstormed list she had already started to group her thoughts around the causes for the Salem witch trials that she was going to explore in her essay: physical, economic, and supernatural. A thesis sentence was also developing from her brainstorming. Her next steps were to establish her thesis, weed out what she would not need, add information where there were gaps, and organize the parts into an effective whole before drafting. Time was ticking away—she had fifty-five minutes left.

Organizing and Writing the Paragraph or Essay

After brainstorming and accumulating the facts and ideas that are needed to answer the in-class discussion question, it is time to plan and draft your paragraph or essay. This final stage involves

- creating a topic or thesis sentence;
- organizing your information into a rough outline;
- writing the draft.

As you develop your skills in writing and become more comfortable with in-class assignments, you will be able to shorten the steps described in this section. But in the meantime, mastering this process can help you build confidence and lessen the stress of a timed writing situation.

Creating a Topic Sentence or Thesis

Your topic or thesis sentence in your in-class paragraph or essay should contain a controlling idea that does the following:

- responds directly to the question being asked;
- shows your method of development;
- previews your supporting evidence.

For example, suppose that a question on a sociology exam asks you to "Define the term *family* and discuss the different forms it takes in today's society." If you are going to write a one-paragraph response, your topic sentence might be

Topic — Controlling idea

The family, a basic social group united by kinship or marriage, takes various forms in today's society.

This sentence directly responds to the topic. It also indicates that the rest of your paragraph will focus on examples of family types, including "extended," "single-parent," "step," "childless," and "same-sex."

The same exam question might ask you to write an essay in response. To plan an essay, you will still follow the same guidelines, but you will set up a discussion that is more developed. Your thesis, which would appear in a brief introduction, might be the following:

Topic

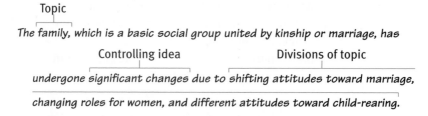

The family, which is a basic social group united by kinship or marriage, has

Controlling idea — Divisions of topic

undergone significant changes due to shifting attitudes toward marriage, changing roles for women, and different attitudes toward child-rearing.

This thesis statement would set up more than a presentation of family types. It would start an essay-length discussion of the important changes that the traditional family has undergone and *why* these changes have occurred. Each reason, or division of topic, would need its own body paragraph.

Organizing Information

As you reexamine the facts and ideas from your brainstorming that you will use to support your topic sentence or thesis, ask yourself, "Can I group these in a meaningful way?" One speedy technique for organizing that information is to cluster your points by numbers. If several items on your list are related, you might put a "1" by each. If other items seem to relate to another point, you can put a "2" by each of these, and so on. See the following example of a student's strategy for grouping information from her brainstormed list in response to the question on types of families in today's society:

The old notion of the family (nuclear) as a mother and father and children is changing (1)

Nuclear family, the traditional notion of the family (1)

The type that is very common these days—single parent (2)

Family size has decreased in the past century—partly because of the increased accessibility of birth control (1?)

More and more families headed by a single mother (2)

Single-parent families headed by father are not as frequent but still face challenges (2)

Extended families have been declining in numbers because of pensions and social security (3)

Cost of health care for aging results in grandparents being taken care of by their baby-boomer children (3)

Grandparents doing more of the raising of children these days (3)

When the single parent gets married, the result: stepfamily (4)

Stepmothers for instance may have difficulty with husband's children (4)

Some people prefer not having children of their own—for various reasons, including career (5)

Other couples postpone having children until later (5)

Same-sex marriages involve gay couples—marriages not recognized in many states (6)

The number of same-sex families is increasing (6)

Many same-sex married couples adopt children or go through in vitro fertilization (6)

Result: a new kind of family structure (6)

After you use the number system to group facts and ideas, the next step is to write a summarizing sentence for each group. If you are writing a paragraph response, these summarizing sentences will serve as primary supports for the controlling idea in your topic sentence. In the case of an essay, they can serve as topic sentences for the body paragraphs of your essay in direct support of your thesis. The student writing on the question of types of families created the following sentences as primary supports to represent the groups of facts and ideas from her brainstorming:

1. *The traditional concept of the family as a "nuclear family" with a mother and father and their biological children has undergone significant change, particularly in the twentieth century.*
2. *Along with the dramatic social change of the past century has come an increase in the number of single-parent families.*
3. *Extended families, which consist of many possible combinations of related adults and children, are perhaps one of the oldest variations of the nuclear family.*
4. *When a single parent marries, the result is a stepfamily.*
5. *Another different concept of family that has become more common is the childless family.*
6. *Same-sex families are perhaps the newest form that the family is taking.*

Once you have written your primary supports, arrange these major points in an effective order. Then add your major points as primary supports under your topic sentence or thesis statement. Next bring in the facts and ideas from your brainstormed list that can be used to develop those primary supports. Include those facts and ideas as secondary supports under the primary supports. The result—once you have your topic sentence or thesis, primary supports, and secondary supports listed—is a rough outline of your answer to the question. Don't be afraid to leave out some of your data if you feel it is not strong support for your response to the question.

Don't be afraid to leave out some of your data if you feel it is not strong support for your response to the question.

With her brainstorming completed, student writer Lakeysha Jones started to draft her thesis. She reviewed the discussion question and her brainstorming list briefly and came up with the following thesis sentence:

> *Many types of theories have been presented as possible explanations for what actually occurred in Salem and what really led to the witch trials.*

This statement, she decided, was appropriate for her in-class essay because it directly responded to the question. She could follow it up with a sentence that introduced her method of development and previewed her supporting evidence, such as this one:

These theories fall into three categories: physical, economic, and supernatural.

Once again going back to her brainstormed list, Lakeysha numbered her details according to their connection with the major divisions: physical, economic, and supernatural. After grouping her information around her major points, she wrote the following topic sentences for her supporting paragraphs:

1. *A group of theories about the Salem witchcraft trials explains them in terms of physical factors.*
2. *One group of theories explains the witchcraft trials according to economic tensions and problems that the citizens of Massachusetts, especially the citizens of Salem Village, were experiencing during the late 1680s and early 1690s.*
3. *Another group of theorists simply claims that witchcraft was actually being practiced in Salem Village.*

As she developed her rough outline by listing supporting facts and ideas under each of her topic sentences, Lakeysha decided to rearrange her points. Since the economic theory would be the most convincing to her instructor, she decided to put it last, after theories about supernatural and physiological causes. The following is her rough outline:

1. *One group of theorists simply claims that witchcraft was actually being practiced in Salem Village.*

   —accounts of supernatural events in village

   —16th and 17th centuries—there were documented covens of witches and warlocks in Europe, so why not in Salem as well?

2. *Another group of theories about the Salem witchcraft trials explains them in terms of physical factors.*

   —sickness/physical health-mental health—weather contributes to insanity: hot weather

   —hysteria among the young women—maybe caused by lead poisoning as well as weather—paranoia and hallucination

   —could have been caused by the rye fungus

3. *Still another group of theories explains the witchcraft trials according to economic tensions and problems that the citizens of Massachusetts, especially the citizens of Salem, were experiencing during the late 1680s and early 1690s.*

—problems faced by Salem people in 1680s and 90s

—like today, economic insecurity fed other insecurities

—their money was decreasing in value; land prices increasing

—therefore, people wanted each other's property

—what better way to get it than to claim your neighbor is a witch?

—under Mass. law, convicted witches' property went to the crown and was publicly auctioned

Drafting from the Rough Outline

After assembling your rough outline, it is time to turn words into sentences and sentences into paragraphs. When writing an essay response to a discussion question, do not spend a great deal of time and space writing a long introduction to your thesis. A sentence or two introducing the thesis is sufficient. Similarly, an effective concluding paragraph would restate your thesis and include one or two sentences explaining how you supported it.

Whether you are drafting an essay or a paragraph, make sure that you connect your sentences coherently. Usually you will not have a chance to revise a rough draft or edit thoroughly for spelling, grammar, and mechanics. If time permits, examine what you have written for problems of coherence, and take time to edit closely.

Lakeysha Jones realized that she had only a rough outline and that she would have to supply more facts and details as she went along. She would also need to ensure that the points connected smoothly. But it was time to start her draft. As she began her introduction, she went back to her notes. Her instructor would not want an elaborate introduction, but she decided she would have to give some background to the witch trials as a lead-in to her thesis. Her resulting introduction and the rest of her essay follows:

During the summer of 1692, a series of events took place in Danvers, Massachusetts (then called Salem Village), that eventually led to the deaths of more than twenty innocent men and women and the imprisonment of many others. Remembered today as the Salem witchcraft trials, these events have both fascinated and puzzled generations of historians. Many types of theories have been presented as possible explanations for what actually occurred in Salem and what really led to the trials. For the most part, these theories fall into three categories: supernatural, physical, and economic.

One group of theorists simply claims that witchcraft was actually being practiced in Salem Village. Pointing to the court records, these theorists say that the events that occurred in Salem Village have no explanation other than a supernatural one. Believable witnesses, they say, supported stories told of people and objects floating in the air, people twisting their bodies into unnatural shapes, and other such seemingly supernatural occurrences. They also state that some of the accused admitted to practicing witchcraft and refused to take it back, even in the face of death. Moreover, covens of witches and warlocks were common in Europe throughout the sixteenth and seventeenth centuries, and so the existence of such covens in New England was, these theorists insist, a real possibility.

A second group of theories about the Salem witchcraft trials explains them in terms of physical factors. One theory points to the fact that the winter before the trials was long and cold and the summer was very hot and humid. According to this theory, extremes in weather made the citizens of Salem uncomfortable and paranoid, so they turned their attention to witchcraft. Another theory based on physiological data concludes that the young women who began the hysteria suffered from a form of lead poisoning that made them paranoid and caused hallucinations. People who make this argument have pointed out that the Puritans usually lined their cooking pots with lead. Yet another theory in this category argues that the people of Salem were suffering the effects of a fungus that grew on rye and produced paranoia and hysteria in humans who ate it. The Puritan farmers in the Salem area used rye as an everyday part of their diet, and the type of fungus that could have infected them tends to grow during hot and humid summers like the one Massachusetts experienced at the time of the trials.

Finally, a third group of theories explains the witchcraft trials according to economic problems that the citizens of Massachusetts, especially the citizens of Salem, were experiencing during the 1680s and early 1690s. According to this line of thinking, serious economic uncertainties made the people of Salem nervous and insecure. Because of problems between the colonial government and the government of England, the value of New World currency had decreased. The farmers and merchants of Salem had difficulty supporting themselves and their families. Land prices skyrocketed, and as a result some people wished they could own neighboring farms. Under Massachusetts law, individuals convicted of witchcraft gave up their estates to the crown, and these estates were sold at public auction. Accusing neighbors of practicing witchcraft became an easy way to expand one's farm and get additional land at a reasonable price. Most of the people executed for witchcraft were in fact wealthy landholders with jealous neighbors.

Most likely the Massachusetts witchcraft trials will never be fully understood or explained. Much of the existing evidence is contradictory, and no amount of historical investigation seems to get to the bottom of it. In the meantime, historians and sociologists continue to explain what happened at the trials in terms of factors that are mostly supernatural, physiological, or economic in nature.

Lakeysha finished her essay with five minutes to spare. As she edited it, she corrected a few misspellings and subject-verb agreement problems. All in all, she was proud of her work. She was relieved that she went into the exam organized.

Writer's Checklist: Writing Timed Paragraphs and Essays

_____ Do you understand the discussion question?

_____ Is a paragraph or essay required?

_____ What method of development is being suggested?

_____ Will your list of brainstormed facts and ideas provide enough information to answer the question and support your topic sentence or thesis?

_____ Have you created an appropriate topic sentence or thesis in response to the question?

- _____ Does it directly answer the question being asked?
- _____ Does it show your method of development?
- _____ Does it preview your supporting evidence?

_____ Have you organized your supporting facts into groups that support your topic sentence or thesis?

_____ Have you created primary supporting sentences representing those groups?

_____ Does your rough outline include convincing evidence that supports the topic sentence or thesis and develops your primary supports?

_____ Have you checked your rough outline for organization and unity?

_____ As you draft your response to the discussion question, are you connecting your points coherently?

_____ Have you left time for a final edit?

Summary

1. Following a series of steps can help you in answering a discussion question. (See p. 286.)
2. Before you begin to organize an answer, you must determine exactly what the question asks you to do. (See p. 286.)
3. Once you understand the question, jot down any facts and ideas you can recall that seem relevant to the topic and approach suggested by the question. (See p. 290.)
4. Write a topic sentence or thesis for your answer. (See p. 292.)
5. Group your supporting material, and develop supporting sentences to represent those groups. (See p. 293.)
6. Create a rough outline from the topic or thesis sentence, the primary supporting sentences, and information that develops those sentences. (See p. 295.)
7. Be sure that the points included in your outline are unified and ordered effectively. (See p. 295.)

8. Write your draft from your outline, making sure your points connect smoothly and coherently. (See p. 296.)
9. After completing your draft, revise and edit it as needed during the time remaining. (See p. 298.)

Writing Activities

1. Read each of the following questions carefully. Decide

   - what each asks you to do;
   - what method would be the most useful in developing an answer.

   A. Explain what is meant by the term *polyphony.* (music)
   B. In an essay explore how governmental policy can affect a nation's economy. (economics)
   C. What is the constitutional procedure for appointing a Supreme Court justice? (political science)
   D. What effect has the growing concern for consumer welfare had on business? (business)
   E. What are the major parts of the animal cell? What is the principal function of each? (biology)
   F. Explain the purposes of dreaming. (psychology)
   G. What is "revenue"? How is it measured? (accounting)
   H. What is hydrolysis? (biology)
   I. What is the difference between the Theory X and Theory Z management styles? (business)
   J. In Shirley Jackson's story "The Lottery," how does the author build suspense? (English)

2. Clip three or four articles from magazines or newspapers, selecting articles devoted to one problem or issue. Develop a question based on your reading of the articles. Now, jot down a list of ideas that might be useful to you if you were asked to write a paragraph or essay answer to your question. Add the articles and your list to your portfolio for later use.
3. In a small group, share the magazine or newspaper articles that you collected for Activity 2. Discuss one of these articles. Then write a discussion question that an instructor might ask about the article on an exam. As a group, list information that you might consider important if you were asked to write a paragraph or essay in response to your group's question. Share your reasons for including each idea or fact in your list.
4. On your own, write an essay answer to one of the essay-length discussion questions in Activity 1 or to a question given you by your instructor, allowing yourself only forty minutes to complete it. Include your essay in your portfolio.

Chapter 21

Writing Online

Both in and outside of the classroom, writing online is becoming common and necessary. The Internet and the World Wide Web make it easier than ever to share your ideas with others in writing. A basic knowledge of e-mail programs and Internet capabilities will help you to communicate online with your teachers and classmates. However, you should follow rules of etiquette, style, and format in order to express yourself acceptably and effectively. Keep in mind that as you write online, whether to a teacher or to a classmate, you must be considerate of your audience and purpose, just as if you were writing a paper for class or having a face-to-face conversation.

Taking Advantage of the Internet and the World Wide Web

These days most people know the Internet chiefly as the provider of the World Wide Web. Through its special computer servers that are connected at points to the Internet, the Web offers pictures, sound, and video in addition to text. When you visit a site on the Web, you can read the information that it contains and experience it in a number of other ways as well.

The Web offers practical advantages for the college writer. You probably know, for example, that the Web can be used as a research tool for finding information on a variety of topics. What you may not know is that it can also be used as a powerful tool for communicating and collaborating with your classmates and instructors.

Electronic Mail

One of the most convenient ways to share your writing on the Internet is through electronic mail, or "e-mail." When used appropriately, e-mail is an effective and efficient way to connect with others. If you do not have an e-mail account, check with your instructor about getting an account on your school's server.

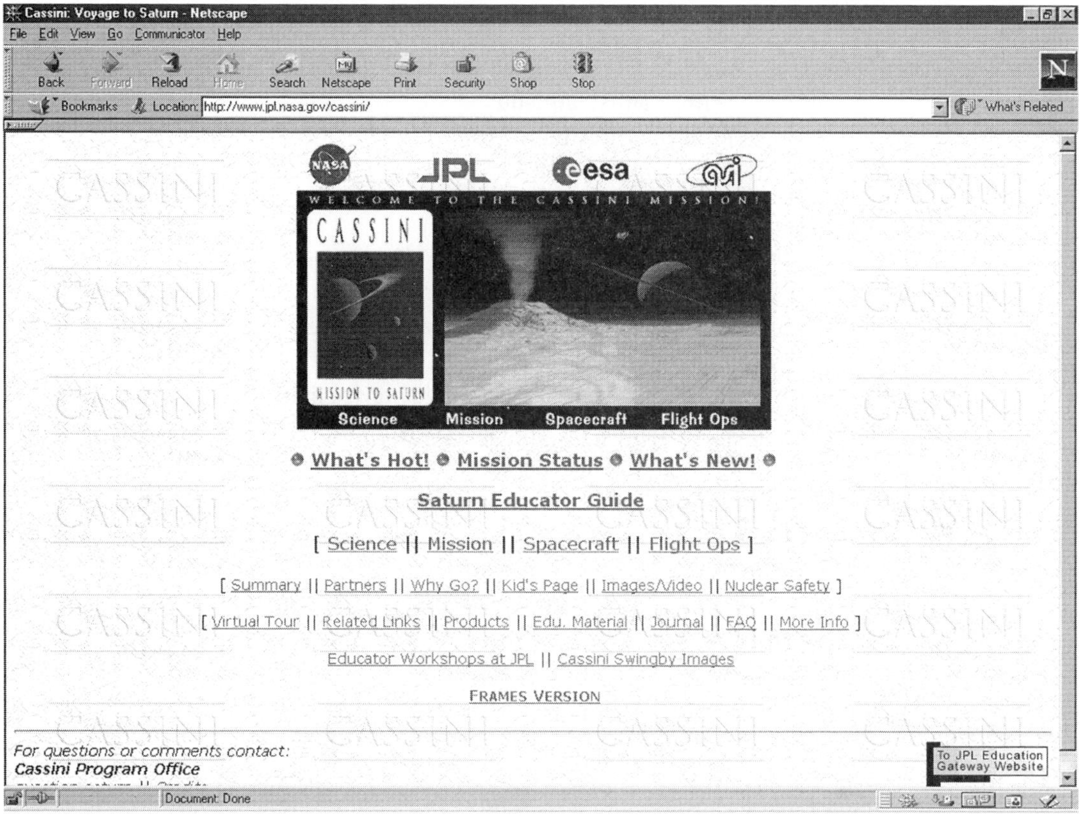

Figure 21.1
Example of a Web Page, from the NASA Web Site

E-mail as a Tool in the Classroom

Many college courses require you to work with others. In English or history, for example, you may be asked to brainstorm together for an upcoming essay. In a biology class, you may have to work with lab partners to write a report. Whatever your assignment, e-mail can connect you with your fellow collaborators. If your schedules conflict and arranging a face-to-face meeting is difficult, you can send your ideas to your partners' mailboxes. Later, when they have the chance to read your e-mail, they can respond with feedback to your ideas and with ideas of their own. The exchange can continue until you have settled on an approach to the assignment and assigned responsibilities to each group member.

In the following example, Sakinah, a first-year student, checks in with Carlos and Brian, her classmates. The three have been assigned a group project on Mary Cassatt, an American painter.

To: carrojo@frostburg.edu
bsullivan@frostburg.edu
Subject: Class project schedule

Dear Carlos and Brian,

I thought our meeting in the library after class was very productive. We got a good headstart on the class presentation on Mary Cassatt.

Carlos, you agreed to search the database at the library for a few short articles on her contributions to art in general. Could you bring those listings to our meeting tomorrow? Brian, you said you would browse museum Web sites, look for the locations of her paintings, and even come up with a few possible images for our presentation. Can you manage all of this by Friday? Meanwhile, I am going to research Mary Cassatt as a female artist in a world dominated by male artists.

Maybe there's an angle there. I hope to have that research completed by the end of the week.

Well, I hope all is going well with you. Don't forget, we're meeting at 2:00 on the 4th floor of the library tomorrow. See you then.

Sakinah

Of course, once you start creating drafts of your written work, you can exchange them with collaborators and peer evaluators using e-mail. Generally, you have two options for getting your work through cyberspace:

- You can copy the text of your draft from a word-processing file and "paste" it into an e-mail message.
- You can send the word-processing file as an attachment to your e-mail message.

If you send the file as an attachment, be certain that your recipient has the software for opening and reading that file. If you don't know how to send attachments, check out the "Help" function within your e-mail program.

If you don't know how to send attachments, check out the "Help" function within your e-mail program.

You may also have the opportunity to use e-mail to share drafts with your instructor. You may even be allowed to submit the final form of your paper by e-mail. E-mail enables instructors to have immediate access to your work so that they can give you their feedback in a more timely manner. In some cases, you could submit your draft at 4 A.M. after a long night of writing and receive feedback by noon (but don't consider this a rule of thumb). Of course, you may be asleep when your computer chimes, "You've got mail," but the message will be waiting for you when you wake up.

For instructors, the increased opportunity for participating in their students' drafting process is not the only advantage of using the Internet. They can have online conferences with their students, put their syllabi and assignments on their Web pages, set up bulletin boards for class announcements, establish chat rooms for informal discussions of ideas raised in class, and even post sample drafts and final papers. Knowing your way around the Internet may be essential to your success in your courses.

To: nadspa@frostburg.edu
Subject: Your Paper on *South Park*

Dear Nadia,

I wanted to share a few thoughts with you about your first draft of the paper on the television program *South Park*. Your paper gave me valuable information, both interesting and disturbing, about the violence in *South Park*.

Your thesis seems clear and straightforward: *SP*'s violence is acceptable because the show is targeted toward an audience that is mature enough to put the violence in its proper perspective. You even point out in your first body paragraph that the government rating on the show (TV MA) appears before each show, and you argue that the 11 P.M. slot makes it less possible that younger viewers will watch it. Your second body paragraph tackles a major issue: that the action of the program is exaggerated. The more extreme or strange the events, you write, the less likely the "mature" viewer is going to take the program seriously. Finally, in your third body paragraph, you make a good effort to show that the plots of *SP* would not appeal to a younger, less mature audience.

While your divisions are clear and your points developed, I wonder how well reasoned some of those points are. For instance, do all "immature" youths go to bed before 11 P.M.? How do you define an "adult audience"? Are you sure that there aren't some viewers out there, even among the "mature" viewers, that won't try to imitate the strange happenings on this very controversial show? You don't need to change your topic, but you may need to modify your thesis.

Good luck with the second draft. Drop by during my office hour if you are having difficulty.

Dr. Parks

E-mail Basics

E-mail has many advantages. It is much quicker than traditional mail (which some call "snail mail") and often much cheaper than a telephone call. But it is only effective when used correctly. To get the most from your e-mail communication, follow these guidelines:

1. Address your e-mail accurately. If you understand how an e-mail address is constructed, you can avoid writing the wrong address. A small mistake can make your message undeliverable.

Online addresses usually consist of the following:

fparks	@frostburg	.edu
(username)	(server)	(domain)

The username might be the first initial and last name of the person you're writing to joined together in lowercase. It could also be any other set of letters or numbers assigned by his or her Internet provider. Be sure to type the address correctly because craig.robinson@gilette.com is not the same as craigrobinson @gillette.com.

The @, or "at" sign, separates the username from the rest of the address. The server name is the name of your recipient's Internet provider. It can be the abbreviated or full name of a college, a business, a provider—such as Hotmail, MindSpring, America Online (AOL), or Prodigy—or any number of groups that have been licensed to offer Internet service.

Finally, the last three letters of the address stands for the major "domain" for that Internet provider. The domain name shows that the provider is one of the following institutions or organizations: educational (.edu), commercial (.com), nonprofit organization (.org), network (.net), military (.mil), or government (.gov).

2. Learn how to use special features. Most e-mail programs allow you to send one message to several addresses, so you won't need to create a copy for each recipient. In addition, many programs include an address book in which you can store frequently used e-mail addresses. The address book is useful when the e-mail address you need is very long or when you have a number of e-mail addresses to remember. Another benefit of most e-mail programs is the REPLY function. This capability lets you respond to a message directly without having to rewrite the correspondent's address or add a new subject line.

3. Use the subject line. You can help the recipient of your e-mail, in most cases, by filling in a clear subject for your message in the "Subject:" blank on the e-mail form. When you are writing to a busy instructor, boss, colleague, or classmate, you need to be considerate and provide a clear but short subject line summarizing your e-mail message.

Use keywords from your message in your subject line. For instance, if you are e-mailing your instructor to ask for an appointment to discuss your last paper, your subject line might be: "Appointment Request." When your instructor sees this subject heading among the list of e-mail that she has received that day, she will know how important it is to read and respond quickly to your message.

4. Attach files correctly. Most e-mail systems include an attachment feature that can be an effective way to share drafts and to submit final papers. When you send an attachment, your e-mail message will serve as a cover letter for your longer document. As a cover letter, your message should refer to the assignment, provide an overview of the paper, and tell the reader how to provide feedback. The heading of the e-mail message will show that the longer file containing the paper has been attached to the e-mail message. To read your paper, the receiver has to click on the highlighted file name. Usually the document will be opened as a word-processing file.

E-journals

You may be assigned to keep an electronic journal, or e-journal, for a course. Your instructor may ask you either to maintain such a journal on your own or to add entries to an ongoing class journal. Journals are often used in writing classes because they help students explore their ideas and experiences. Later, students may find topics for papers in their entries. An e-journal is particularly effective because it is convenient and easily shared. You can make entries in your e-journal word-processing file on a daily basis, and when you are asked to hand in the journal, you can do so by either printing it out or attaching it to an e-mail message.

Anna Antoniolli
Journal Entry—October 14, 2000

Topic: If you were asked to sign a pledge to stop using offensive language on campus, would you do it?

If I were asked to stop using offensive language on campus, I would do so. Doing away with racist, sexist, and other offensive speech does not restrict freedom of speech. All of our individual freedoms under the Constitution end where the rights of others begin. After I graduate from college, I want to be a newspaper reporter. As a news gatherer, I will have the right to collect and publish information about people that is truthful. But my right to report the story and my reader's right to know will always be limited by my subject's right to privacy. So if I publish a story that wrongfully accuses someone of something and they suffer financial loss or psychological harm because of it, my victim will have the right to sue me and my newspaper for libel. The same goes for hate language. A person's freedom of speech ends where it starts hurting others. If I make a racist or sexist statement or yell out profanities, then I am hurting someone else or at least making others feel uncomfortable. Therefore, I cross the line between acting on my freedoms to violating those of others. At that point, I lose those freedoms. Now, I know some people will disagree with me . . .

Collaborative Tools on the Internet

Asynchronous means "without regard to time"; *synchronous,* on the other hand, means "in real time."

In addition to e-mail, the Internet and World Wide Web provide other tools and opportunities for learning, collaboration, and writing. Among these are asynchronous and synchronous forms of communication. *Asynchronous* means "without regard to time"; *synchronous,* on the other hand, means "in real time." Asynchronous communication tools allow you to post messages for other users to read whenever they have the chance. Synchronous tools, such as chat rooms, are used by instructors of online distance-education courses. Chat rooms allow users to hold conversations and exchange ideas as though they were in the same room or talking on the telephone.

Online Distance-Education Courses

Many colleges offer online courses. Because they exist entirely on the Web, these courses are convenient for students whose busy schedules conflict with the times when courses are offered on campus. Such courses often go beyond presenting content. Programs supporting online courses allow students to take quizzes and tests, brainstorm in a chat room with fellow students about assignments, and communicate with their instructor by e-mail. To take distance-education courses, students must have access to a computer, an Internet connection, and a Web browser (such as Netscape Navigator or Internet Explorer). The students' online writing skills are often the only way to communicate in the course—and to make an impression on the instructor. For this reason, distance-education students must use effective writing strategies for each online interaction.

Figure 21.2 shows a Web page outlining the distance-education course offerings at two Georgia institutions.

Chat Rooms

You can participate in chat rooms, or Internet Relay Chat, and have discussions with people from around the world on a specific topic. You enter the "room" from your Web browser by logging onto a server that is about your topic. After entering the room, you can see who is there and who is ready to chat, including who is serving as "host" for the conversation. The host is the person who manages the flow of the discussion. Once you have entered the conversation, everything you and the others in the room type is recorded and communicated without any time delay. People who love chat rooms hold thousands of conversations each day on topics from Stephen King novels to Formula 1 race cars.

You will soon find that chatters have their own set of phrases and symbols. For instance, they are fond of abbreviations such as BBL, which stands for *be back later,* and LOL for *lots of laughs.* They also like to use symbols, like <s> (for *smile*) and <:)> (for *smiley face*), to show the facial expression that goes along with their words.

ENGLISH 101 CHAT ROOM	Who's in the Room
The Prof says: I thought the last assignment went well.	The Prof (Host)
	Adam
Nora: Hi, Adam.	Nora
Adam: Hi, Nora ;o)	Raj
Chris has joined the conversation.	Chris
Chris says: I felt I did better on my editing this time.	Stephanie

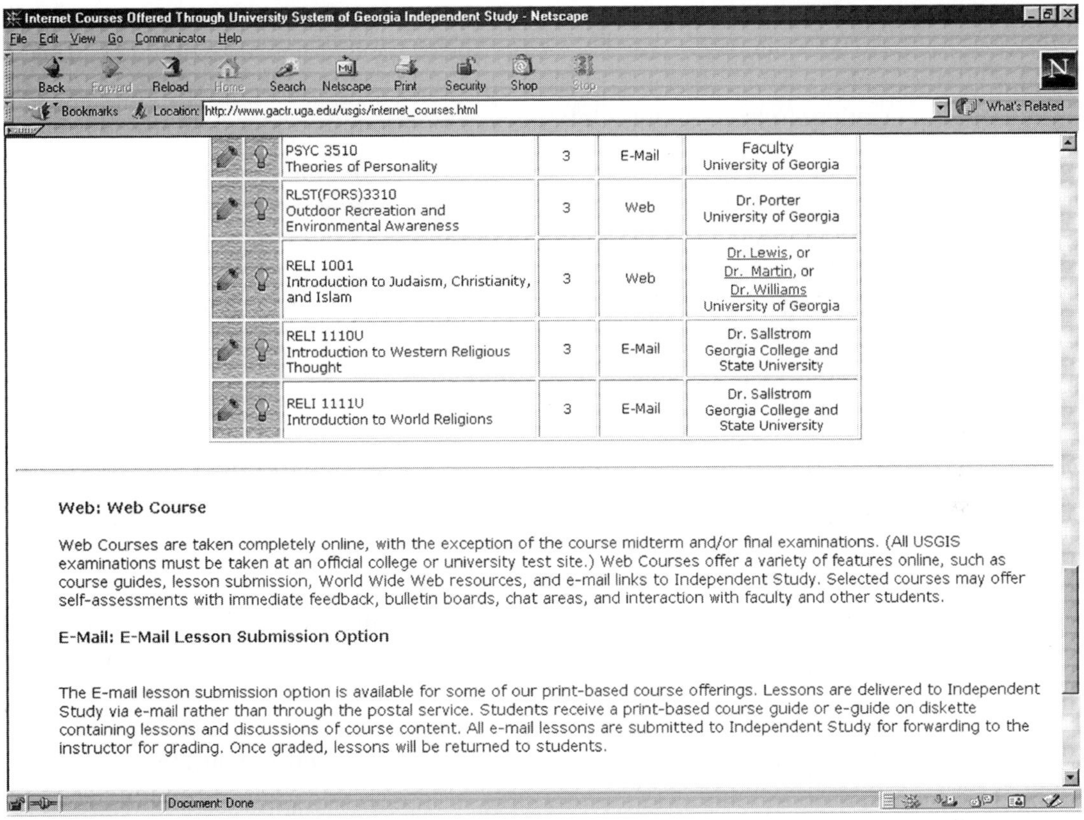
Internet Courses Offered Through University System of Georgia Independent Study - Netscape

File Edit View Go Communicator Help

Back Forward Reload Home Search Netscape Print Security Shop Stop

Bookmarks Location: http://www.gactr.uga.edu/usgis/internet_courses.html What's Related

PSYC 3510 Theories of Personality	3	E-Mail	Faculty University of Georgia
RLST(FORS)3310 Outdoor Recreation and Environmental Awareness	3	Web	Dr. Porter University of Georgia
RELI 1001 Introduction to Judaism, Christianity, and Islam	3	Web	Dr. Lewis, or Dr. Martin, or Dr. Williams University of Georgia
RELI 1110U Introduction to Western Religious Thought	3	E-Mail	Dr. Sallstrom Georgia College and State University
RELI 1111U Introduction to World Religions	3	E-Mail	Dr. Sallstrom Georgia College and State University

Web: Web Course

Web Courses are taken completely online, with the exception of the course midterm and/or final examinations. (All USGIS examinations must be taken at an official college or university test site.) Web Courses offer a variety of features online, such as course guides, lesson submission, World Wide Web resources, and e-mail links to Independent Study. Selected courses may offer self-assessments with immediate feedback, bulletin boards, chat areas, and interaction with faculty and other students.

E-Mail: E-Mail Lesson Submission Option

The E-mail lesson submission option is available for some of our print-based course offerings. Lessons are delivered to Independent Study via e-mail rather than through the postal service. Students receive a print-based course guide or e-guide on diskette containing lessons and discussions of course content. All e-mail lessons are submitted to Independent Study for forwarding to the instructor for grading. Once graded, lessons will be returned to students.

Document: Done

Figure 21.2
Example of a Web Page for Online Courses Offered at Two Georgia Institutions

Raj says: I felt like I did too. Whoops! BBL
Raj has left the conversation.
The Prof says: What problems did
you solve this time?

Message Boards, or Bulletin Boards

You can also post messages and have ongoing discussions online by writing on a message board (sometimes called a "bulletin board"). Message boards are similar in purpose to chat rooms, but they work asynchronously. This means that you can take part in a conversation—by "posting" and reading messages—but at your own convenience. Your instructor may have established a message board for members of your class to use to comment on readings or on class discussions.

Netiquette

To write effectively online, you must follow the Internet's own etiquette, or social rules, called "netiquette." Following these guidelines will make your communications welcome to most Internet users.

1. Be brief. Respect others' time by keeping your messages and postings short.
2. Learn and follow the social rules of online tools. For instance, when needed, ask if you may join an online conversation before you express an opinion.
3. Make sure your choice of type font can be read easily.
4. Send attachments with care. Before sending one, ask whether your recipient has software that can open and read the attachment.
5. Don't use all capitals or all lowercase letters. Sending a message in capitals seems like shouting and makes your message difficult to read. Using only lowercase, on the other hand, creates a less effective message. Your reader will think that you wrote too quickly and without much thought.
6. Don't "flame" your reader. Flaming, or using obscene or abusive words online, usually is caused by immaturity or the failure to think about how such language will affect the other person. Try to impress people, even in your e-mail, with the quality of your thinking.
7. Respect others' words and ideas. If you borrow information for a paper from a source on the Internet, be certain to document that source. (See Chapter 19.)
8. Be aware that you have no privacy online. Write every message as though it were a public one, whether you are writing personal e-mail or in a public chat room.

Sending a message in capital letters seems like shouting and makes your message difficult to read.

Strategies for Effective Writing Online

Since writing is the chief way to communicate online, you must develop effective writing strategies in order to get the most from the Internet and Web. Many messages you will write for the Internet will be brief and will not need much planning. However, your online communications for school and for your job will require the same care and thought that writing a paper calls for. To write effectively online, use the strategies that you learned in the earlier chapters of this text.

The following case study is a brief guide to writing online. Justin Barnes, a first-year writing student, has been assigned to attend a campus lecture and then write about it. The case study of his writing process may help you as you prepare to write online.

Consider Your Audience and Purpose

Think about your audience ahead of time, and be aware of their expectations. Before you write, decide on the amount of detail your readers will need and the right level of formality. In tone, be friendly and conversational but respectful. Also, be aware that an electronic communication may not always best serve your purpose. For instance, a formal proposal for your boss or a controversial thesis for your instructor may be better communicated on paper or in a personal conversation than in an e-mail message.

CASE STUDY: Writing an Online Review

Justin Barnes, a first-year college student, was assigned by his composition instructor to attend one campus lecture during the semester and to report on it. First, Justin glanced through the college newspaper to see what interested him. On the front page was an article about an upcoming lecture by Bill Gates, the founder of Microsoft. The lecture, sponsored by the business program, was going to be downlinked from a satellite and shown on a monitor in one of the business department's large classrooms. The topic of the lecture was to be "Succeeding in the Digital Age." Justin e-mailed his instructor to get his approval for reviewing the Gates lecture. In his reply, the instructor approved the topic and suggested that Justin submit his review by e-mail.

During the lecture, Justin took notes not just on what was said but also on his own reactions to the speaker's points. Back at his apartment, he spread out his notes on his desk and started to organize them. At first he thought he would log on to the e-mail system, write a quick review, and be done with it. But then he thought about the reaction that his audience—his instructor—might have to such a review. First of all, Justin had seen four classmates at the lecture, and he knew the instructor was going to get a number of reports on what Gates said. To make his report stand out, he would have to spend some time strengthening it. Also, because the instructor might not know a lot about the computer software business, Justin would have to avoid technical language as much as possible. Finally, Justin's goal was to get off on the right foot with his instructor and to get a good grade on the assignment, so he figured he needed to make this message thoughtful and well structured. He decided to spend some time organizing and drafting the review before submitting it.

Brainstorm for Ideas before Starting to Write

Whether you are preparing to write online or offline, prewriting can help. Try jotting down a list of all of the points you need to cover in your message. Once you have a complete list, go back through the items and decide what additional information is needed and which points are not relevant before you start writing.

The notes that Justin Barnes took during the Gates lecture covered six pages of notebook paper. They ranged from the major points made by the speaker to Justin's own impressions. As he read back over his notes, he began to jot down the information that he felt he could use in his review. The following list is based on his notes:

—Gates—informally dressed for the head of such an important company

—Looks like a kid, but when he speaks about the direction of business in the future, people listen

—Lecture based on his book Business @ the Speed of Thought

—Introduced speech with a comparison—the digital infrastructure and a nervous system

> *—Technology is like a healthy nervous system: able to run smoothly and efficiently, to respond quickly to emergencies, to quickly get information to people, to make decisions*

—Says "the successful companies of the next decade will be the ones that use digital tools to reinvent the way they work"

—Points for managers:

> *—E-mail can increase personal initiative and responsibility; therefore, insist that employees communicate through e-mail*
>
> *—"Know your numbers"—keep on top of sales figures by using online data [Gates used a lot of examples from successful corporations throughout his lecture: Coca Cola, McDonald's, Ford, Intel, etc.]*
>
> *—Share online data with middle managers so that they can act; don't just give it to upper management*
>
> *—Stress collaboration and use digital tools to create and support teams of thinkers*
>
> *—Replace paper with electronic forms—for instance, sales reports and other routine administrative forms [I agree, there seems to be too much paper used these days—think of all the trees we would save if routine reports and correspondence were done online]*
>
> *—Get away from the idea of "one-dimensional," assembly-line jobs—workers shouldn't be cogs in the wheel; should be in touch with the whole process through digital tools [interesting point—I never thought about this before, but sometimes we work our part of the job without knowing what others are doing; companies like Saturn, for instance, have moved away from that limited idea]*

—Regularly reevaluate your business processes—technology allows this evaluation

—Use e-mail and other technologies to answer customer complaints—and do so quickly

—Technology can help managers connect with outside suppliers of products and services and bring them inside

—Increase speed and efficiency of delivery of your products through the use of technology

—Use the Web to sell your products and to eliminate go-betweens

—Strengthen customer relations through the Internet—not just sales, but contact, problem solving, etc.

Focus and Structure Your Message

As with all good writing, you need to focus and structure your ideas and information. Working from your brainstormed list, you can establish your main point and supporting ideas. The following is the basic structure used in business letters and most academic writing: a clear introduction, a developed body, and a summary or evaluating close. The beginning should establish the focus of your message and the reason for the communication. The middle provides the organized support for the thesis. Then the closing summarizes or reacts to the points and brings the message to an end.

Student writer Justin Barnes had his major points listed. Now he had to organize them. As he thought about his organization strategy, he knew that he would need

- a beginning that would introduce the lecturer and lecture as well as give a little background on both;
- a body paragraph that would focus on Gates's twelve points;
- a closing paragraph that would contain his own evaluation of the lecture.

With this general organization in mind, Justin set about organizing his review. After working and reworking the material, he was certain that the points he had chosen were unified behind his general idea and purpose. He then wrote the following rough outline:

Introduction

Summary of assignment

The lecture title and information about when the lecture was held

Introduction to Bill Gates, his job, and his accomplishments

Based on his book Business @ the Speed of Thought

The importance of the lecture topic in today's world

Body

Says "the successful companies of the next decade will be the ones that use digital tools to reinvent the way they work"

Outlines 12 points for managers

Closing

An inspiring lecture

Some excellent points

Increased communication and collaboration through digital tools

Paper flow reduced by technology

Making workers more than cogs in the machinery

Answering consumer demand quickly and keeping in touch with customers

One confusing point—eliminate middlemen? [Amazon.com, for instance]

But overall a valuable learning experience

Draft and Revise Your Message

With your outline established, you have a solid foundation for a first draft. At this stage, do not edit your writing too closely as you go through your first draft. However, aim for smooth, connected sentences as you write. When you revise, you should evaluate your writing for focus, unity, support, and coherence. (See Chapter 7 for revision tips.) Once you are satisfied with your ideas, edit carefully for grammar, punctuation, mechanics, word use, and any ESL problems. You now have a final draft to turn in online.

Justin Barnes decided that he would draft his review on his computer. After revising it, he would send it to his instructor by attaching it to an e-mail message. He knew his instructor would be able to open the attachment because the instructor had said he could.

Justin started his draft and found that his outline was very helpful. Even though he had to reorder and even eliminate some of the information in the outline, he wrote what he thought was a successful review. What follows is his final draft:

Gate-way to Success in the Digital Age

On October 3, I attended a lecture given by Microsoft founder Bill Gates on the topic of "Succeeding in the Digital Age." The lecture was simultaneously sent to over one hundred locations around the world via satellite. Gates's focus was how business can use technology to compete more effectively in the next decade. His presentation was based on the ideas put forth in his latest book, Business @ the Speed of Thought. While he mostly discussed the benefits that businesses can gain from using technology, most of his modern ideas seemed to be based on good old-fashioned common sense.

Gates mentioned that many businesses are already following the twelve points he suggests in his book. The first idea, using e-mail to increase employees' initiative and responsibility, is already a reality in many organizations. His second and third suggestions are that businesses should keep sales figures online and use digital tools to share important information with middle managers. According to my Introduction to Business instructor, these techniques are also being used already by businesses to empower their decision-makers. However, it seems to me that four of Gates's other ideas have not been adopted widely. These suggestions are replacing paper with electronic forms, getting important services and products from other businesses, reevaluating business processes regularly, and getting away from the idea of "one-dimensional" jobs. Where I work part-time, the boss is always talking about these improvements, but it is a lot of lip service with not much action. Gates's final four points seem to be his most innovative. He realizes that a business needs customers to keep it alive. For this reason, Gates recommends using e-mail and other digital tools to sell one's products, to increase the speed of delivery, to deal with customer complaints, and to stay in touch with customers between sales. These ideas would be useful to any manager, particularly mine.

Overall, I found Bill Gates's lecture clear and inspiring. He made some excellent points. I was especially interested in his ideas about using technology to increase communication and collaboration, to reduce paper flow, to make workers feel like more than cogs in the machinery, and to respond quickly and positively to customers' needs. However, I was a bit confused by his discussion of businesses' using digital tools such as the World Wide Web to eliminate the "distributors," a

```
term invented to define people or companies that deliver
products from the manufacturer to the buyer. After all,
some of the most successful Internet-based companies--
Amazon.com and eBay.com--are "distributors." Despite
this confusing point, however, I found the lecture very
interesting and informative.
```

Writer's Checklist: Writing Online

_____ Have you considered your audience's needs?

- _____ Is electronic communication suitable for your purpose?
- _____ Have you addressed your e-mail message correctly?
- _____ Did you provide a useful subject line?
- _____ Have you attached files correctly and written a message as a cover letter?

_____ Have you used a prewriting technique to create a list of facts and ideas to support the message?

_____ Is the organization of your electronic communication effective?

- _____ Have you provided a clear introduction?
- _____ Is the body of your message informative and convincing?
- _____ Do you conclude appropriately?

_____ After you drafted the message, did you revise and edit carefully?

- _____ Is the message unified and coherent?
- _____ Have you edited carefully for grammar, punctuation, mechanics, word use, and any ESL problems?

_____ Did you reread your document for netiquette? (See p. 308 for guidelines.)

Summary

1. The Internet and World Wide Web provide valuable opportunities for communication and collaboration. (See p. 300.)
2. E-mail is often used in the classroom to improve communication among students and between students and their instructor. (See p. 301.)
3. When sending an e-mail message, address the message properly, use the subject line, and attach files of separate documents correctly. (See p. 303.)
4. Other online tools for learning, collaboration, and writing can be *asynchronous,* without regard to time, and *synchronous,* in real time. (See p. 305.)
5. Regardless of the online communication tool that you are using, always practice good netiquette. (See p. 308.)
6. Because writing is the chief means for online communication, use the strategies for effective writing outlined in this text for planning, drafting, and revising your important e-mail messages. (See p. 308.)

Writing Activities

Writing Activities

1. Visit your instructor's Web site, if he or she has one. What does he or she include? Is the course syllabus online? Does the site include personal information? Are there links to other sites? Everyone can benefit from suggestions, so give your instructor a polite review of the Web site and make suggestions, if appropriate, for additional information that he or she might include.
2. Send an e-mail message to a classmate. In the message, review a first draft of a classmate's assignment. Mention both its strengths and weaknesses. Be sure to follow all of the rules for sending e-mail efficiently. Also, practice good netiquette, and use the strategies for online writing described in this chapter.
3. Start an e-journal. Set up a file on your computer to use for regular journal entries. In the journal, describe and reflect on your most recent experiences, respond to recent class discussions, or do both. Include the date on each entry. Save your e-journal and submit it to your instructor.
4. Rewrite the following online message so that it will follow the rules of netiquette:

   Dear Elana,

   I have read your paragraph responding to Christine Gorman's article "Sizing Up the Sexes" and quite frankly am ASTOUNDED AND DISAPPOINTED BY IT.

   First of all, your topic sentence is a bunch of rubbish. How can you claim that "Men have a higher sex drive because of nature"? This statement suggests that female sexuality isn't important. So what, portions of the male hypothalamus are larger than the female's. WHAT DOES THAT PROVE? Do the autopsies of 41 brains performed at the Salk Institute prove conclusively that men have a stronger sex drive? Where's your crap detector? And what's your next conclusion: If women had larger hypothalamuses, they would have the same sex drive as men?

   My suggestion is that you RETHINK YOUR CONCLUSIONS. I certainly hope your next draft is better than this one.

5. Review an event on campus or a news program on TV that is about a topic of interest to you. Send your review to your instructor by e-mail. Remember that your instructor may not know a great deal about the event or topic, so be certain to give a clear description or summary of it. Also record your thoughts and reactions. Follow the rules of e-mail and netiquette and the process for creating effective online writing.
6. Write an e-mail message to yourself, describing the progress you have made in your writing thus far this term. Also, detail improvements that you need to make. Even though your audience is yourself, still observe rules of e-mail and netiquette, and use the process for creating effective online writing. Print your completed message and place it in your portfolio.

Chapter 22

Building Career Communication Skills

When applying for a job, you must show that you have strong career communication skills. Planning and creating convincing job-related documents will help you to stand out from other applicants. These documents include an application (or "cover") letter, a résumé, and follow-up letters.

Planning Career Communication

A valuable step to take when preparing to apply for a job is to *plan* the documents that you will send to a potential employer. As a part of this planning process, you can benefit from performing a personal inventory and analyzing more closely the employer's needs.

Performing a Personal Inventory

When you seek a job that you are qualified for and truly want, your chances for success are better than when the job is not closely matched to your interests and background. Therefore, when you are on the job market, be aware of the kinds of employment that fit your education, skills, and interests.

One way to gain this awareness is to perform a personal inventory (see page 317). Many people use a personal inventory to match their interests and experience with a number of jobs. This process can sometimes reveal a career interest you didn't expect. It also can serve as a resource later when you are putting together a résumé.

Answering the Employer's Need

Planning career communications means knowing yourself and also knowing what the audience (potential employers) wants. One way to learn about what they want is to examine job ads in your field of interest.

An employment advertisement, or job ad, is an official statement that a job is available. It is usually found in the classified section of a newspaper, online

Personal Inventory

Name: Date:

1. What kind(s) of job(s) are you going to apply for?
2. In what type of position do you see yourself in five years? In ten years?
3. What sources of information will you use to learn of the jobs available in your field?
4. Do you prefer to live and work in a particular city, state, or part of the country? If so, where?
5. What personality traits do you have that are suited to the career you have chosen?
6. Have you prepared yourself educationally for the career you have chosen? If so, list relevant degrees, courses taken, and other relevant educational experiences.
7. Do you have any *relevant* work experience? If no, go to #8. If yes, list the most recent job first. Include for each job the dates of employment, the organization's name, the location of the organization, your job title, and your responsibilities.
8. What skills have you gained and used on the job? For each skill, list names of organizations, your position at each, and your responsibilities. (For example, *Management skill:* Wendy's Restaurant, Shift Manager; managed shift of twelve workers, dealt with problems of scheduling, evaluated employees; President, social fraternity; organized community service p rojects.)
9. Have you been actively involved in professional, campus, or community activities? If so, list the name of each activity, the organization, years of involvement, your role and accomplishments.
10. What skills have you gained and used while involved in professional, campus, or community activities? For each skill, list the organization, your position, and your responsibilities. (For example, *Financial Management:* Student Government Association, Treasurer; oversee purchases, prepare annual budget, and so on.)
11. Have you received any honors, awards, special recognitions, or scholarships? (Do not forget academic recognitions such as a high grade-point average or the Dean's List.) If so, list them below with the most recent first. Include in each entry the distinction, along with the location and year.

at a Web site, or in a professional publication. Besides providing information about the job, the job ad also gives you insights into the audience—the potential employer.

Besides providing information about the job, the job ad also gives you insights into the audience—the potential employer.

An effective job ad should include information about the employer, the open position, the qualifications being sought, and how to respond. The following ad for a full-time bookkeeper includes this information:

BOOKKEEPER—FULL-TIME
Rapidly growing design firm in downtown Washington, D.C., seeks an energetic, organized, team-oriented bookkeeper responsible for accounts payable, accounts receivable, bank reconciliation, and financial reports run from Mind Your Own Business (MYOB) accounting software. Good written and verbal communication skills, the ability to work independently in a small office, and proficient skills in MS Word/Excel required. (Mac experience a plus.) Send or e-mail application, along with salary requirements, to Kelly Bland, Personnel Director, Capitol Graphics, 1610 17th Street, NW, Washington, D.C. 20009 or to kbland@capgraph.com. Deadline for applications is February 2, 2001.

Because every word costs money, many businesses are concise in their job ads, but they do want to say enough so that they do not receive a lot of applications from unqualified people.

A person with a background in bookkeeping who plans to apply for the job at Capitol Graphics can gain all of the necessary information from that company's ad to plan an effective response. First of all, the ad says that Capitol Graphics is small but "rapidly growing." This implies that the applicant might be asked to perform a number of different duties, some perhaps that are not listed. Also, the pressure might at times be intense. However, the close-knit environment of a small company that encourages a team approach might make up for those occasional pressures by providing her with personal rewards.

Secondly, the graphics firm does not have the space to detail fully what a bookkeeper's job involves. But they do list the most important responsibilities: "accounts payable, accounts receivable, bank reconciliation, and financial reports run from Mind Your Own Business (MYOB) accounting software." They also include the background requirements that they expect from their applicants. The successful candidate should be able to show that she has "the ability to work independently in a small office," so some office experience—and best of all experience in a small office—would have to be documented on the résumé. Further, she would have to have been trained in or had work experience with standard bookkeeping procedures as well as particular software programs and computer platforms. But there is no indication of level of education or number of years of experience that this company is expecting. The field is open for candidates with many different work experiences and educational backgrounds.

What this company seems to emphasize most in their ad are the personal skills that they expect candidates to have. However, personal skills are more difficult to document on a résumé. The company describes their ideal bookkeeper as "energetic, organized, [and] team-oriented" with "the ability to work independently" and "good written and verbal communication skills." How does an applicant prove that she has these personal skills and traits? Obviously, the company is not going to interview someone who does not show that he or she has these requirements. The writer will have to reexamine her personal inventory for evidence that she can meet these expectations. She might find such evidence in her past projects as a worker, volunteer, or organization member. She might also refer to her success in a composition or speech course as proof of her ability to communicate well.

The person who wants to apply for the bookkeeper's job at Capitol Graphics can gather many hints on how to construct a successful application for the job—just from the ad. Because skills and personal traits are more important to this firm than job history and education, she would plan an application letter that focuses on her background as a self-starter and team player. Her résumé would take a "functional" format (see pp. 329–30) to stress her skills and personal traits over her past jobs and educational background.

After putting together her letter and résumé, she would then send them to the address listed in the ad by the deadline.

Ethical Considerations

As you fill out a personal inventory and think about how you can meet potential employers' needs, you have to be honest about your qualifications. In your response to ads for attractive positions, you might be tempted to exaggerate or "fudge" your abilities, background, or training a bit in order to land an interview. At this point, you must recognize the difference between lying and "creative truth-telling."

Lying in an application letter or résumé involves claiming or even implying that you have skills or a background that you don't actually have. For example, you should not say that you have earned a degree when in fact you have not—or say that you have had certain kinds of work experience when in fact you have not. Employers usually try to check the truth of such information before offering someone a job.

However, candidates can make the most of what they *do* have. Through "creative truth-telling," the job seeker puts her skills, traits, and background in the best possible light. Let's say a job ad is seeking a registered nurse for a network of health-care providers. The ad lists the following requirements:

State licensure
CPR certification
1–2 years current Emergency Department experience preferred

A recent graduate who is very interested in the position may be worried that she won't be considered for the job because she hasn't had the required experience in an emergency department. However, she did volunteer at a local hospital while in high school, and she completed training in emergency procedures during her nursing program. With this background, she believes she can perform the necessary functions of an ER nurse. Therefore, she doesn't hide the fact that she hasn't been a full-time nurse in an emergency setting, but her application letter and résumé emphasize the similar experiences she has had.

Application Letters That Get Results

Career counselors often say: "Those who get jobs are not always those most qualified, but they are usually the ones who have the know-how to get jobs." A big part of this "know-how" is knowing how to write effective application or cover letters. Employers usually read these letters before they look at résumés.

Besides following the suggestions for form and content made in this chapter, you can make sure that your letters have a chance by

- finding out to whom you are writing;
- using nonsexist language;
- maintaining a personal but not "chummy" tone; and
- choosing a clear and appropriate format.

Unsolicited Application Letters

Each day companies and organizations receive unsolicited, or not requested, letters of application from job seekers. Most unsolicited letters get filed and are never read seriously. The letters that successfully catch the reader's attention do so through their language, appearance, and the qualifications they present.

Beginnings of Unsolicited Application Letters

Unsolicited application letters should be kept brief to avoid taking up the reader's valuable time. But to be of any value, even unrequested letters must contain a certain amount of information. They must state an interest in a specific desired position.

In today's job market, most organizations need employees with specialized skills. For this reason, job candidates should not send a general letter of interest that forces the company to determine which position the writer might fill. The excerpt that follows is from the beginning of a general letter of interest:

> I am interested in any positions in human resources that may be open now. Since my education has been broad, I believe I could serve your company in a variety of work roles.

This job seeker has a serious problem, though he or she may not know it. The letter lacks a sense of focus and suggests that the writer has not yet decided on a specific career goal. A company is not likely to interview such a person.

The next letter excerpt is much more specific and is more likely to get a response:

> Is your company looking for a human resources assistant—someone who has skills as an effective employee liaison?
>
> For the past two years, I . . .

Although no details are given yet, the reader of this letter gets a sense of a qualified person in a specific field. The organization may have no openings for someone with experience with employee benefits and concerns, but at least the reader of the letter will be able to respond.

Notice that the second letter opening begins with a question. Asking a question is an attention-getting device. Most employers would prefer crisp, direct letters, without attention "grabbers." Sometimes, though, the uniqueness of a job candidate might be shown in a creative opening to a letter.

If an attention-getter seems inappropriate to the organization and situation, a better opening may be a simple statement of inquiry—that is, a sentence asking about job openings. For example:

> I am writing to inquire about current or potential openings in your organization for legal assistants. If such a position is open or anticipated, I would like to be considered for it.
>
> My educational background includes . . .

Supporting Sections of Unsolicited Application Letters

The supporting sections that make up the body of an unsolicited job letter should be brief. The body summarizes major accomplishments, such as college degree work and any related work experiences. In general, the body should satisfy the audience's appetite for information about the candidate. The letter introduction above might continue with a body paragraph like this:

> My educational background includes an associate's degree in office technology, with a focus on legal assistance, from Briarsmith Community College. I graduated from Briarsmith with a cumulative grade point average of 3.8 (on a 4.0 scale). My work experience during college includes two years as an administrative assistant for Wal-Mart, Inc., in the Jonesboro, Arkansas, office and one year as a receptionist at the law firm of Samuelson Associates, also in Jonesboro.

The last items in an unsolicited job letter should be

- a reference to an enclosed résumé,
- a polite closing,
- a request for further action from the potential employer, such as further information, a follow-up letter, or even an interview.

With a conclusion added, these two sections would create a complete unsolicited job letter that would look like Figure 22.1.

Figure 22.1
Example of an Unsolicited Job Letter

223 Wabash Boulevard
Maclean, VA 23109
April 23, 2001

Mr. Robin Stone
Director of Personnel
McDougal, Donne, Smith, and Lopez, Esqs., Inc.
45 Elite Drive
Memphis, TN 38101-3999

Dear Mr. Stone:

I am writing to inquire about current or potential openings in your organization for legal assistants. If such a position is open or anticipated, I would like to be considered for it.

My educational background includes an associate's degree in office technology, with a focus on legal assistance, from Briarsmith Community College. I graduated from Briarsmith with a cumulative grade point average of 3.8 (on a 4.0 scale). My work experience, during college, includes two years as an administrative assistant for Wal-Mart, Inc., in the Jonesboro, Arkansas, office and one year as a receptionist at the law firm of Samuelson Associates, also in Jonesboro.

I have included my résumé for your review. If you would like to discuss further my employment at McDougal, Donne, Smith, and Lopez, I can be reached at 901-555-1234 weekdays from 9:00 A.M. to 5:00 P.M. I look forward to your reply.

Sincerely,

Sandra Keene

Note that the conclusion of this letter does not call for an interview because the writer does not know if a position is open. However, since the cover letter and résumé in an unsolicited situation are brief, the employer may be interested in calling or writing back to the candidate for more details. In some cases, depending on the strength and perseverance of the candidate and the needs of the employer, new positions may even be created.

Solicited Application Letters

Solicited application or cover letters are those that answer a public announcement or advertisement. Solicited letters do not differ much in structure from unsolicited job letters, but they usually contain more detail.

Beginning a Solicited Application Letter

Solicited application letters should begin with a clear statement of the job opening for which you are applying and where you found that job opening or announcement. For example:

> **TRAVEL COORDINATOR**
> National Systems Resources, Inc., a national leader in the area of computer system development and integration, has an immediate opening for a travel coordinator to arrange corporate travel, provide back-up for receptionist, and order supplies.
> Candidates for the position should have a minimum of two years secretarial or customer-service experience and a familiarity with the Internet and Web browsers. Applicants should also be able to handle multiple tasks in a busy professional environment.
> Interested applicants should forward their résumés and the names of three references to: Emily Chou, Personnel Director, National Systems Resources, Inc., 4908 Bridgeway Court, Manassas, VA 20109.

In response to the job advertisement, one job-seeker began his application letter in the following way:

> I am responding to your recent notice in the March 12 issue of the *Washington Post* for a travel coordinator. Please accept this letter and the accompanying résumé as my application for the position.

By citing the job title and source of the ad in the opening of the letter, the applicant is giving valuable information to the employer. Organizations often advertise a number of openings at one time. Naming the vacancy that this letter addresses allows the receiver of the letter to hand the letter on to the person in the company who is in charge of the search for a travel coordinator. Also, including the source of the job ad—in this case, the *Washington Post*—helps the employer to determine the best place to advertise for employees in the future.

Supporting Sections of Solicited Application Letters

The supporting section or body of a solicited letter also has a unique function. In an unsolicited letter, the supporting section is mostly a brief personal summary.

In a solicited letter, on the other hand, its purpose is to get the candidate an interview by answering the ad or announcement point by point.

Successful job seekers show how their skills and background meet the employer's needs by arranging them in the body according to the order in which those qualifications are listed in the ad. The following is a good example of how one applicant organized the supporting section of his application letter for the travel coordinator position.

Successful job seekers show how their skills and background meet the employer's needs by arranging them in the supporting section, or body, according to the order in which those qualifications are listed in the ad.

> I recently graduated from Manassas College with a degree in recreation and leisure studies. This program has helped me to understand the travel industry as well as to develop the organizational skills that would be required of a travel coordinator.
>
> In addition, while working my way through college, I was employed as a customer service representative for custombuilt.com, a national online business that provides custom-made furniture and household fixtures for its customers. My duties included responding to customer questions and complaints, both over the phone and online. Sometimes my office logged as many as one hundred very challenging calls each day. It was perhaps the busiest office in the custom-built organization. Despite the hectic pace, multiple requests, and sometimes conflicting demands that were placed on me, I was rated highly by supervisors for quality of service and patience.

The writer demonstrates an understanding of what the employer wants by following the sequence of the requirements as stated in the ad. He demonstrates first the relevance of his educational background to the job. Then he states how he meets the work experience qualification in customer service. While discussing his work experience, he touches on his online skills and describes how he can successfully deal with several tasks. Responding in this manner sends a signal to the prospective employer that he is seriously interested in this particular job.

Conclusions of Solicited Application Letters

The conclusion of a solicited job letter is also unique. In the unsolicited job letter, further communication is all that can be expected, since the writer is uncertain if a position is even open.

In a solicited letter, however, besides referring to an enclosed résumé, the conclusion is the place to request an interview. Since the main purpose of the solicited job letter is to get an interview, extra thought should be put into this part of the letter to ensure the best results. An effective conclusion, such as on page 326, would include the specifics of when and where the candidate can be reached. Figure 22.2 shows the complete solicited application letter.

Figure 22.2
Sample Complete Solicited Application Letter

1701 Stonewall Court, #85B
Manassas, Virginia 20109
February 17, 2001

Emily Chou, Personnel Director
National Systems Resources, Inc.
4908 Bridgeway Court
Manassas, VA 20109

Dear Ms. Chou:

I am responding to your recent notice in the March 12 issue of the *Washington Post* for a travel coordinator. Please accept this letter and the accompanying résumé as my application for the position.

I recently graduated from Manassas College with a degree in recreation and leisure studies. This program has helped me to understand the travel industry as well as to develop the organizational skills that would be required of a travel coordinator.

In addition, while working my way through college, I was employed as a customer service representative for custombuilt.com, a national online business that provides custom-made furniture and household fixtures for its customers. My duties included responding to customer questions and complaints, both over the phone and online. Sometimes my office logged as many as one hundred very challenging calls each day. It was perhaps the busiest office in the custom-built organization. Despite the hectic pace, multiple requests, and sometimes conflicting demands that were placed on me, I was rated highly by supervisors for quality of service and patience.

I believe, therefore, that my credentials and strong interest in your company make me an ideal candidate for the position of travel coordinator. I have included my résumé, which also indicates where my written recommendations may be obtained.

I would be more than happy to meet with you at your convenience to discuss further the possibility of my joining the National Systems Resources team. I can be reached for an interview weekdays during the day at 555-3344 or evenings at 555-3221.

I look forward to hearing from you.

Sincerely,

Robert M. Byrd

I believe, therefore, that my credentials and strong interest in your company make me an ideal candidate for the position of travel coordinator. I have included my résumé, which also indicates where my written recommendations may be obtained.

I would be more than happy to meet with you at your convenience to discuss further the possibility of my joining the National Systems Resources team. I can be reached for an interview weekdays during the day at 555-3344 or evenings at 555-3221.

I look forward to hearing from you.

Strategies for Writing Effective Résumés

If an application letter has met its purpose, the next step in the job placement process for an employer is to review a candidate's résumé carefully. Often employers will first skim a résumé for specific information. Therefore, résumés must have a format that clearly highlights relevant information. And, of course, your résumé should be neat and arranged well on the page.

Like job letters, résumés must also be tailored to a specific audience. You cannot write one résumé and expect to use it successfully time and time again. In an application to one company, you may need to emphasize one set of qualifications. In an application to another organization, you may wish to emphasize another set.

In an application to one company, you may need to emphasize one set of qualifications. In an application to another organization, you may wish to emphasize another set.

If possible, the best strategy is to have your résumé on computer disk. Then you can easily reorganize it to match the specifics of the job ad. Another possibility is to create two or three versions of your résumé in advance. Each one could highlight a different set of skills.

Your choice of *language* in a résumé also plays an important role in communicating your strengths. Though your personal history cannot be changed, the words used to describe that history can help to get you an interview. For example, in contrast to weak phrases such as *worked as,* powerful action verbs such as *directed, managed, developed,* and *initiated* can go a long way in presenting yourself as a candidate worth attention. Such words express strong commitment and active involvement in the work of an organization.

An effective résumé is like a good sales pitch. What is being sold is your "self." The résumé is perhaps the only document an employer can use to get a sense of the "self" behind a list of credentials, skills, and work experiences. Résumés can reflect a person's creativity as well. At the very least, they should be accurate and concise and use language forcefully.

In general, there are two kinds of résumés: *chronological* and *functional*. Each works differently.

- Chronological résumés are summaries of candidates' education, training, work experiences, and related items arranged according to time.
- Functional résumés focus on the skills that candidates have gained from their background.

Chronological Résumés

In a chronological résumé, information about education or work experience is ordered according to time, such as dates of degrees awarded or dates of employment. Information can be arranged from past to present or according to reverse chronology, beginning with most recent and moving to the past. Reverse chronological order is preferred because it lists the candidate's most recent accomplishments first. Usually, your most recent experience would be important to a potential employer.

The chronological résumé on page 328 was written as a reply to this ad for a marketing assistant position:

> **MARKETING ASSISTANT**
> Large software developer in the Boston area seeks a highly energetic individual to team up with our marketing department. Responsibilities include creation and preparation of marketing flyers and packages, distribution and tracking of marketing materials and sales proposals, management of marketing database, and coordination of team meetings, special projects, and various administrative tasks as needed. Qualified candidates will possess a BA/BS degree and/or 1+ years in a related position, strong verbal and written communication skills, and a working knowledge of Microsoft applications. Send résumé to Kenneth Krauss, AMB Technologies, 4 Heritage Plaza, Brookline, MA 02445 or kkrauss@amb.com.

Felicia Martin chose the chronological résumé format because she has had relevant job experiences while attending college. Her work experience section includes her latest jobs, which are similar to the one she is applying for. She places these work experiences ahead of her educational background because the ad focuses more attention on the kinds of skills the applicants should have than on their college degrees.

Other situations may call for putting education or training up front. For many graduating students, education and training will certainly be their most recent experiences. Sometimes education will be all that can be offered to the employer. If you don't have an impressive work history, you can highlight other skills, such as those demonstrated in extracurricular activities, to make up for this lack.

Figure 22.3
Example of a Chronological Résumé

Felicia J. Martin
4301 Revere Way
Ipswich, Massachusetts 01938
978-555-4567
fmartin@mindspring.com

OBJECTIVE	A marketing assistant position leading to career growth
WORK EXPERIENCE	
Summer 2000	Marketing Intern, National Security Life Insurance Company, Boston, Massachusetts • Designed marketing flyers • Worked with team to create national advertising campaign • Provided support for meetings and special events • Developed a database of addresses for marketing purposes
1998–present	Assistant Manager, Publication Services Department, Staples, Inc., Ipswich, Massachusetts • Supervise three employees during shift • Provide advice for customers with special projects • Design and produce reports, brochures, and newsletters
1996–1997	Customer Service Representative (part-time), Publication Services Department, Staples, Inc., Fairfield, Connecticut • Processed orders from customers in person and over the phone • Completed document design projects using Microsoft software applications • Chosen as "Employee of the Month" for two months
EDUCATION	
December 2000	B.A., Northeastern University, Boston, Massachusetts. (GPA=3.64.) Major: Business Administration; Concentration in Marketing
May 1997	A.A., Fairfield Community College, Fairfield, Connecticut. Scholarship recipient.
REFERENCES	Career Placement Office Northeastern University Boston, Massachusetts 02115-0195

Functional Résumés

Functional résumés look different from chronological résumés because they serve a different purpose. While the chronological résumé summarizes a candidate's history according to time, a functional résumé emphasizes key skills that would be sought by the potential employer.

The same information found in a chronological résumé may be included in a functional résumé. However, the information is presented in a form that stresses skills and expertise, not time and accomplishment. Some common skills areas are

- communication,
- management/supervision,
- leadership,
- technical expertise,
- teamwork.

Any of these areas can be arranged in a functional résumé to fit the audience's needs. Details within each section can come from both work and educational experiences because it is the skill itself that is being stressed. Education and a brief list of work experiences can be listed separately, as can honors and awards.

In fact, the beauty of the functional résumé is that it combines all areas of experience and training to provide a good profile of the candidate. Many students who lack relevant job experience find that a functional résumé is the best way to represent their abilities.

Figure 22.4 is a functional résumé for another candidate for the marketing assistant position listed earlier. Since William Lopez does not have any work experience related to the job, he translates other experiences he has had into qualifications for the position.

William Lopez faces the difficult challenge of convincing a potential employer that even though he has not had relevant job experience he is qualified for the position. Therefore, he emphasizes the skills that would be required of a marketing assistant. Examining the ad closely, he sees that AMB Technologies is looking for a person who not only knows the specialized field of marketing but who also has good communication, teamwork, and technology skills. The functional format allows William to show that he has these skills by referring to his various experiences on the job, in school, and through extracurricular activities. As he gathers evidence from his background and organizes these experiences under the skill areas, he is careful to use active verbs. Strong verbs, such as *develop, design,* and *manage,* reinforce the impression that Lopez is, as the ad specifies, a "highly energetic individual."

Figure 22.4
Example of a Functional Résumé

William R. Lopez
43 Hampshire Street
Cambridge, Massachusetts 02138
(617)555-8023
wlopez@aol.com

OBJECTIVE	Marketing Assistant position leading to management opportunities
RELEVANT SKILLS	
Marketing	• Conducted extensive marketing study for Marketing Practicum class • Hosted marketing professionals who spoke at marketing club meetings • Marketed fraternity programs and activities to university community • Participated in marketing task force at community college
Communication	• Developed and delivered marketing presentations for classes • Made presentations, conducted meetings, and worked on team projects as president of marketing club • Focused on communication techniques and practices in community college program • Currently manage a staff of twelve workers as shift manager at fast-food restaurant • Deal with the general public on a regular basis at restaurant
Computer Technology	• Designed reports for marketing classes using Microsoft Word and Excel • Created brochures and flyers for fraternity activities using page design software • Made presentations using Microsoft PowerPoint
EDUCATION	
December 2000	B.S., University of Massachusetts, Boston, Massachusetts Major: Business Administration. Concentration: Marketing and Advertising
1997	A.A., Bunker Hill Community College, Boston, Massachusetts Concentration: Communication
WORK EXPERIENCE	
1999–Present	Shift Manager. Wendy's Restaurant. Newton, Massachusetts
Summer 1998	Landscape Worker. Bonneville Garden Center. West Newton, Massachusetts (part-time)
1997–1999	Counter Waiter and Cashier. Wendy's Restaurant. Newton, Massachusetts
EXTRACURRICULAR ACTIVITIES	
1999–2000	President, Marketing Society, University of Massachusetts, Boston
1998–1999	Chair, Special Programs Committee, Alpha Gamma Delta fraternity, University of Massachusetts, Boston
1996–1997	Chair, President's Student Advisory Board, Bunker Hill Community College
REFERENCES	Career Placement Office University of Massachusetts, Boston Boston, Massachusetts 02129

Follow-Up Letters

If a strong application letter and résumé have earned you an interview, what comes next? After the interview, the successful job candidate follows up with a polite letter to both the personnel director and the supervisor of the position she is applying for. In this letter she can thank these people for the interview and, if appropriate, express greater interest in the position. The follow-up letter offers yet another chance for the job candidate to express continued interest in the position and to keep the dialog with the potential employer going a bit longer.

The follow-up letter should be pleasant, professional, and brief. The writer might also want to thank a particular interviewer who was thoughtful or helpful during the visit to the organization.

The follow-up letter should be pleasant, professional, and brief.

Generally, the content of the letter can follow the standard letter outline given for solicited and unsolicited application letters:

1. **Beginning**—Expresses thanks for the chance to interview for the position. It refers to the job title and the date of the interview.
2. **Supporting section**—A positive reaction to the interview, interviewers, and the location along with a restatement of interest in the position.
3. **Conclusion**—A friendly ending that compliments the people at the organization, a hope of hearing from them in the near future, and a willingness to supply any further information.

Here is an example of a follow-up letter:

I am writing to thank you for the opportunity to interview last Thursday for your position of Assistant Manager of Purchasing.

I greatly enjoyed my day at Price-Day headquarters. I was especially pleased to be able to tour the facility and to visit the purchasing department. Everyone there was warm and supportive. My experience only increases my desire to become a member of the Price-Day team.

I wish you and your coworkers continued success. In the meantime, if you have further questions, please do not hesitate to contact me immediately. I look forward to hearing from you.

☑ Writer's Checklist: Building Career Communication Skills

_____ Have you completed a personal inventory?

_____ Has the job for which you are applying been advertised? Or are you sending an unsolicited application?

_____ Can you honestly match your skills and background with the requirements for the position?

_____ Does your application or cover letter contain a clear beginning, convincing supporting section, and purposeful conclusion?

_____ Have you chosen an appropriate format for your résumé? Is it chronological or functional?

_____ Does your résumé present important information about you and emphasize skills and experience that qualify you for the position?

_____ Are your application letter and résumé neat and clearly arranged on the page?

_____ Would your follow-up letter enhance your chances of getting the job?

Summary

1. Career communication includes application letters, résumés, and follow-up letters. (See p. 316.)
2. When planning career communication, the applicant can explore his or her strengths and weaknesses by performing a personal inventory. (See p. 317.)
3. To plan career communications, you also have to understand what the audience, or potential employer, needs. (See p. 316.)
4. Letters of application serve as cover letters for résumés. They are either solicited by an ad or announcement or unsolicited. (See p. 320.)
5. Résumés follow one of two forms: chronological or functional. (See p. 327.)
6. The follow-up letter should express the applicant's thanks for the chance to interview, a continued interest in the position, and a hope for future communication. (See p. 331.)

Writing Activities

Writing Activities

1. Now that you have the necessary strategies for writing effective application letters and résumés, write your own job package materials. To complete this assignment you will, most likely, have to do some career planning first.

   A. Conduct a personal inventory.
   B. Find a specific position or job opening to which you can respond.
   C. Analyze the ad carefully, searching for key organizational needs that can be addressed in your letter and résumé.
   D. Design a résumé and application letter tailored specifically to the position. (You may use either the chronological or functional résumé format. Since you are responding to an ad for a real position, your letter can be considered "solicited.")
   E. Use the Writer's Checklist to help you revise your work.

2. Choose a career field that might interest you in the future. Do some research to determine what qualifications a person has to have to get an *entry-level* position in that field. Then write an unsolicited application to a personnel director of a firm where people in your chosen profession are employed. In the letter, ask if positions are open and make a case for your worthiness as an applicant. To be convincing, you will have to give evidence showing that you have the necessary qualifications for the job.
3. With a classmate, create a brief profile of a company in your community. The profile should contain a description of the business's history and products. To get information, you might consult the organization's annual report and employee handbook. Also, you will want to interview someone who works at the company. Prepare your profile in the form of a short essay for your instructor.
4. You have become so good at preparing résumés that you decide to provide the service for others. You have named your business The Gourmet Résumé. You plan to offer your services to fellow classmates, family members, and friends. Your job, therefore, will have many parts. You will have to interview your clients to get information on their background and skills as well as the positions they are seeking. Once you have this information, you will have to decide whether their résumés should be chronological or functional. Finally, you will have to prepare the final copy so that it is clear, brief, targeted, and attractive.

   To test out your new business, select an individual who needs an up-to-date résumé and go through your process with him or her. While putting together the résumé, ask for feedback from your client.
5. You are the personnel director at Venus Aerospace. Recently, your firm advertised for an accountant in local and regional newspapers, as well as in professional journals. (A copy of the job ad follows.) On looking through the stack of applicants, you come upon a résumé from Jeffrey Bandulla, which is included here. Would you invite Jeffrey for an interview based on his résumé? What are its strengths and weaknesses? Would you have any suggestions for Jeffrey?

   The ad reads as follows:

VENUS AEROSPACE CORPORATION NEEDS AN
ACCOUNTANT-BOOKKEEPER

Duties include accounts receivable/payable and payroll. Candidates should be college graduates with experience in overseeing a budget. Annual salary: $33–37K. Send letter and résumé to: Personnel Director, Venus Aerospace Corporation, 75816 Aeronautical Boulevard, Atlanta, GA 30306-4402.
Venus Aerospace is an equal opportunity employer. Deadline for applications: November 21, 2000.

Jeffrey's résumé:

Jeffrey Bandulla
33312 Harcourt Road
Decatur, GA 30348

Career Objective:	—To obtain a position as an accountant in a firm where I can advance to a managerial level
Education:	—University of Georgia, B.S., Accounting, May 2000 —Major coursework completed: Introductory Accounting, Cost Accounting, Auditing, Advanced Tax Accounting, Principles of Marketing, Principles of Management, Economics
Activities:	—Disc jockey for WUGA, the campus radio station —UG Basketball team member —Treasurer, Film Society 1998–2000
Work Experience:	
June 1999 to Sept. 2000	Microlabs Systems, Winterville, Georgia: maintenance position
May 1998 to Aug. 1999	Weavers Caretaking, Athens, Georgia: yard work and mowing (seasonal)
References:	Furnished on request

Part Five

Editing Sentences for Grammar

Diagnostic Test for Part Five: Editing Sentences for Grammar

Use this test to check your grammar skills. Answers appear on page 477.

A. Label each of the following sentences *F* for fragment, *RO* for run-on, or *S* for sentence.

1. The long trail ended in the heavy underbrush.
2. Where the trail ended and disappeared in thick vegetation.
3. We decided to turn around and go back, it was too hard to continue.
4. After hiking up to the peak of the hill, we looked down into the valley.
5. We had never seen anything so beautiful the dew on the flowers reflected the sunlight.
6. Trudging back down toward the road and being careful not to lose each other.
7. We finally made it to the camp, tired and exhausted from the hike.
8. Determined to hike another hill tomorrow, we decided to get some much-needed rest.

B. Each of the following sentences contains a problem with verbs—either subject-verb agreement or verb form or tense. Correct each incorrect verb.

9. Either my mother or my grandmother cook Thanksgiving dinner each year.
10. My uncle and my grandfather always watches one of the football games on TV.
11. Every year I help out with the clean-up, but I hated it more than the other chores.
12. One of my least favorite memories are when my aunt spilled leftover gravy all over me.
13. My cousins have came over to our house for the last ten years and have never helped out once.

C. Choose the correct form of the pronoun in each of the following sentences, and write it in the blank.

14. Evan was earlier than _____ in arriving at the bus depot. (*me* or *I*?)
15. Jennifer and _____ arrived at the same time. (*he* or *him*?)
16. Anyone who showed up late had to carry _____ bags on the bus. (*their* or *his or her*?)
17. I decided to sit with Genevieve, _____ I knew from work. (*whom* or *who*?)
18. Many students made _____ spring break reservations early. (*their* or *his or her*?)

D. Choose the letter of the sentence that uses the adjective or adverb correctly.

19. (A) Professor Smyser is a helpful physics teacher.
    (B) Professor Smyser is a helpfully physics teacher.
20. (A) He knows how to give examples that illustrate the ideas well.
    (B) He knows how to give examples that illustrate the ideas good.
21. (A) My roommate performed bad on the last major test in that class.
    (B) My roommate performed poorly on the last major test in that class.
22. (A) He should study different next time, or he will not improve.
    (B) He should study differently next time, or he will not improve.
23. (A) When I compared our two grades, I saw that mine was the better.
    (B) When I compared our two grades, I saw that mine was the best.

E. Label each of the following sentences *C* for clear or *U* for unclear in its use of modifiers. Some of the sentences contain a dangling or misplaced modifier; others use modifiers clearly and correctly.

24. After changing the tire, the car was moved off the roadway's edge.
25. The driver only meant to take a short trip to the store and go by the post office.
26. Monitored closely and filled up frequently, the driver had been watching that tire for some time.
27. While at the auto parts store, the air gauge was purchased to keep from overinflating the tire.
28. The tire made it to almost 40,000 miles before the tread separated.

F. In each of the following sentences, identify the part of the sentence that contains faulty parallelism.

29. The 1999 Academy-award-winning movie *American Beauty* was dark, unusual, and it was well-directed.
30. Kevin Spacey starred as a middle-aged American man who loses his job, beginning to engage in uncharacteristic activities, and fantasizes about a younger woman.

31. His wife was played by Annette Bening, an actress who is known for her strength, her beauty, and she is very intelligent.
32. Rose petals became a symbol for what the father dreamed, what he believed, and they could also symbolize his feelings and emotions.

Chapter 23

Fragments

What Is a Fragment?

A sentence is a group of words that has a subject *and* a verb *and* expresses a complete thought. A **fragment** is a group of words that is missing a subject, missing a verb, or does not express a complete thought. A fragment is only a piece of a sentence.

SENTENCE I work out at the gym on weeknights and ride my bike on the weekends.

FRAGMENT I work out at the gym on weeknights. *And ride my bike on the weekends.*

And ride my bike on the weekends has a verb *(ride),* but it is missing a subject *(I),* and it doesn't express a complete thought. In other words, the meaning of this word group is not clear without the help of other sentences around it.

Common Types of Fragments

You can identify fragments in your writing if you know the most common types:

- dependent word fragments;
- prepositional phrase fragments;
- *-ing* verb fragments;
- explanatory fragments.

Dependent Word Fragments

A **dependent clause** is a group of words that cannot stand independently as a sentence because it lacks a complete thought. A dependent clause begins with a **dependent word.** This list includes some common dependent words.

Common Dependent Words

after	even though	until	which, whichever
although	if	what, whatever	while
because	since	when, whenever	who, whoever
before	unless	where, wherever	

A dependent clause is always a part of a sentence. It is never a sentence by itself.

EXAMPLE My son was sent home from day care today. Because he had a high fever.

Because he had a high fever is a dependent clause that starts with the dependent word *because.* This word group is a fragment because, by itself, it doesn't express a complete thought. When you proofread your writing, be on the lookout for word groups that begin with dependent words. When you find one, check for a subject, a verb, and a complete thought.

To correct a fragment that begins with a dependent word, connect the fragment to the sentence either before or after it:

because
My son was sent home from day care today~~.~~ ~~Because~~ he had a high fever.

or leave out the dependent word to create a complete thought:

He
My son was sent home from day care today. ~~Because he~~ had a high fever.

Prepositional Phrase Fragments

A **preposition** connects a noun, pronoun, or verb with other information in a sentence. A preposition is the first word in a **prepositional phrase.** This list includes some common prepositions.

Common Prepositions

about	before	from	out (outside)	up
above	behind	in (inside)	over	upon
across	below	into	past	with
after	beside	like	since	within
against	between	near	through	without
along	by	next to	to	
among	down	of	toward	
around	during	off	under	
at	for	on	until	

A prepositional phrase is always a part of a sentence, never a sentence itself.

EXAMPLE Christopher Reeve is making a Hollywood comeback. With the support of his family.

With the support of his family is a prepositional phrase that starts with the preposition *with.* This word group is a fragment because it is missing a subject and a verb. When you proofread your writing, be on the lookout for word groups that begin with a preposition. When you find one, check for a subject, a verb, and a complete thought.

To correct a fragment that begins with a preposition, connect the fragment to the sentence before or after it:

> Christopher Reeve is making a Hollywood comeback~~.~~, ~~With~~ with the support of his family.

Or you can rewrite the fragment, adding the missing subject and verb:

> Christopher Reeve is making a Hollywood comeback. He has ~~With~~ the support of his family.

-ing Verb Fragments

A verb that ends in *-ing (studying, eating, driving)* is never by itself a complete verb in a sentence. When you proofread your writing, watch for sentences that begin with *-ing* verbs. When you find one, check for a subject, a verb, and a complete thought.

EXAMPLE The senator appealed to working parents. Hoping to generate support for her new childcare bill.

Hoping to generate support for her new childcare bill is a fragment because it lacks a subject and a verb.

To correct a fragment that begins with an *-ing* verb, connect the fragment to the sentence before or after it:

> The senator appealed to working parents~~.~~, hoping ~~Hoping~~ to generate support for her new childcare bill.

Or you can rewrite the fragment, adding the missing subject and verb:

> The senator appealed to working parents. She hoped ~~Hoping~~ to generate support for her new childcare bill.

Explanatory Fragments

Sometimes writers create fragments when they try to explain something or give an example of something in a previous sentence. When you proofread your writing, watch for word groups that give added information after a complete sentence.

EXAMPLE Advertisements for jeans target American youth. Especially those between fifteen and nineteen years old.

Especially those between fifteen and nineteen years old is a fragment because it lacks a subject, a verb, and a complete thought.

To correct a fragment that begins with an example or explanation, connect the fragment to the sentence before or after it:

> Advertisements for jeans target American youth~~.~~, especially ~~Especially~~ those between fifteen and nineteen years old.

Or you can rewrite the fragment, adding the missing sentence elements:

> Advertisements for jeans target American youth. ~~Especially those between fifteen and nineteen years old.~~ *These ads target fifteen to nineteen-year-olds especially.*

Summary

1. A **fragment** is a group of words that is missing a subject, missing a verb, or does not express a complete thought. A fragment is only a piece of a sentence.
2. Most fragments begin with either a **dependent word** (see p. 340), a **preposition** (see p. 341), an ***-ing* verb** (see p. 342), or an **example or explanation** (see p. 342).
3. To correct a fragment, either connect it to the sentence before or after it, or rewrite the fragment, adding the missing sentence elements.

Editing Activities

Identify and Correct Sentence Fragments

Practice 23-A (Answers appear on p. 477.)

Decide whether the following items are complete sentences or whether they contain a sentence fragment. Label each complete sentence with an *S*. Label items containing fragments with an *F*, and then rewrite them to make complete sentences. You may combine sentences, add words, or delete words as necessary to make each item a complete sentence.

EXAMPLE __F__ Many people refuse to see a doctor for chronic pain~~.~~*,* ~~Hoping~~ *hoping* that the pain will go away on its own.

1. The number-one health and safety problem in the American workplace is RSI. Which stands for Repetitive Strain Injury.
2. According to the U.S. Bureau of Labor Statistics. RSI is now responsible for more than 60 percent of all workplace-related illnesses.
3. Repetitive Strain Injuries involve damage caused by misuse or overuse. Of certain nerves, muscles, and tendons.
4. RSI affects workers whose jobs involve performing repetitive tasks. For example, computer operators, postal workers, and musicians.
5. The condition can lead to numbness, tingling, and pain. These sensations most often occur in the wrists, arms, neck, and shoulders.
6. Many people who do a lot of keyboard typing and mouse clicking have suffered severe damage in their wrists. Because of constant, repeated compression of certain nerves.
7. You may be familiar with some of the most common forms of RSI. Especially carpal tunnel syndrome and tendonitis.

8. American workers had a difficult time proving that RSI was a work-related injury. Since these types of injuries develop over time.
9. According to the RSI Center at the Massachusetts Institute of Technology, you may be at risk for developing an RSI. If your job involves repetition of small, rapid movements.
10. Many companies are investing in ergonomic solutions for their employees. Ergonomics is the science of changing working conditions to suit the needs of the worker.

Practice 23-B **(Answers appear on p. 477.)**

Each of the following groups of words is a sentence fragment. Edit each one, adding or changing whatever you need in order to create a complete sentence. You may even combine two of the items into one sentence.

EXAMPLE Some of the most interesting and terrifying tales of medical catastrophes^ *are true stories.*

1. *The Hot Zone* by Richard Preston, a terrifying but true story that presents the account of an outbreak of the Ebola virus in the early 1990s.
2. The author, admitting that he changes some of the names but insisting that the facts are true.
3. For example, that many of the events took place in Reston, Virginia, and Washington, D.C.
4. The Ebola virus, which is named for the Ebola River, a tributary of the Congo or Zaire River in Africa.
5. Because of the location of the virus's origin, its formal name Ebola Zaire.
6. Which is a "level 4" virus, called a "hot" virus, with an incubation period of less than twenty-four days.
7. Whose symptoms include bleeding out of body openings and a breakdown of almost all of the body's tissues.
8. Helping to isolate and control the virus, Major Nancy Jaax, an Army veterinarian, and her husband, Major Gerald Jaax, also a veterinarian.
9. Since the virus had originated in monkeys being used for research.
10. Preston's book, an interesting and compelling story of the outbreak that introduces readers to one of nature's deadliest mysteries.

Practice 23-C

Edit the following paragraph, fixing all sentence fragments. You may combine sentences, or you may delete or add information as needed to correct the errors. Punctuate your new sentences correctly.

In 1996 James McBride published a book called *The Color of Water.* Which, as the subtitle says, was "a black man's tribute to his white mother." McBride, who grew up in Brooklyn, New York, a child of a Jewish mother and an African-American father.

He tells the story partly from his point of view and partly from his mother's point of view. Because he wants readers to experience the hardships his mother endured. Suffering discrimination from both whites and blacks. He explains how his mother tried hard to protect him and his siblings from the cruelty of others. Because of their mixed-race status. Throughout normal and sometimes extreme conditions of McBride's childhood. We see how he comes to love and respect his mother for her determination and courage. Taking his title from something his mother said about God. McBride makes an important point about race: "God is the color of water. Water doesn't have a color." One of the most moving parts of the book is at the end when McBride lists the names of his eleven brothers and sisters along with their accomplishments so far in life. Including becoming doctors, lawyers, musicians, and teachers. Helping us to appreciate what his mother overcame to make a decent life for her family.

Edit Your Own Writing for Sentence Fragments

1. Perhaps your instructor has marked sentence fragments in some of your writing. Rewrite the piece, eliminating the sentence fragments and creating complete sentences. Watch your punctuation. Resubmit the piece or file it in your portfolio as your instructor directs you.
2. Write a short essay describing someone you know who has influenced you in a positive way. Include such dependent words as *because, which,* or *who* and transitional phrases such as *for example* and *for instance.* Proofread your writing carefully for sentence fragments. One trick is to read your piece beginning with the last sentence first. Continue reading your writing "backwards" until you get to the first sentence. Make sure that each word group that you have punctuated as a sentence has a subject and a verb and expresses a complete thought.

Chapter 24

Run-Ons: Comma Splices and Fused Sentences

What Is a Run-On?

An independent clause, like a sentence, is a group of words that has a subject *and* a verb *and* expresses a complete thought. When two independent clauses are run together in one sentence without appropriate punctuation, the result is a **run-on.** There are two types of run-ons:

- A **comma splice** joins two independent clauses with only a comma and no conjunction (for example, *and, but, or*).

Independent clause 1 / Independent clause 2

COMMA SPLICE — Funding for space exploration was cut, NASA protested the decision.

- A **fused sentence** joins, or "fuses," two independent clauses with no punctuation.

Independent clause 1 / Independent clause 2

FUSED SENTENCE — TV programs mirror society the reflection is often exaggerated.

When you proofread your writing, read one sentence at a time and listen for pauses. If you pause in the middle of a sentence, look for two subjects and two verbs. If the two subjects and verbs are linked by a conjunction or a dependent word (see p. 340), then you have written a complete sentence. However, if two independent clauses are joined without any punctuation or connecting word, or with only a comma, you have written a run-on sentence.

Four Ways to Correct Run-Ons

You can correct run-ons in your writing in one of four ways:

- adding a period,
- adding a comma and coordinating conjunction,

- adding a semicolon,
- adding a dependent word.

Correct a Run-On by Adding a Period

The easiest way to correct a run-on sentence is to separate the two independent clauses with a period and capitalize the first word after the period. You will have created two separate sentences.

EXAMPLE Funding for space exploration was cut. NASA protested the decision.

Corrected this way, each of the independent clauses *(Funding for space exploration was cut* and *NASA protested the decision)* becomes its own sentence. Be careful not to use this method too often, however. If you do, your writing may become full of short, choppy sentences. Try to use different ways to correct run-ons when you find them.

Correct a Run-On by Adding a Comma and Coordinating Conjunction

A second way to correct a run-on is to add a coordinating conjunction. Separate the two independent clauses with a comma (a comma splice has one already) and add one of these joining words: *and, but, or, so, yet, nor, for.* Choose the word that best expresses the relationship between the two independent clauses.

EXAMPLE TV programs mirror society, but the reflection is often exaggerated.

Inserting a comma and the coordinating conjunction *but* separates the first independent clause *(TV programs mirror society)* from the second *(the reflection is often exaggerated).*

Correct a Run-On by Adding a Semicolon

Another way to correct a run-on is to use a semicolon (;) to separate two independent clauses. Semicolons are like periods in that they separate two clauses that could stand on their own as sentences. However, writers might choose a semicolon over a period if the ideas in the two independent clauses are closely related.

EXAMPLE A search engine is a program that helps you find information on the Internet; some common search engines are AltaVista, Yahoo!, and Infoseek.

The second independent clause *(some common search engines are . . .)* offers examples to support what the writer says in the first independent clause *(A search engine is a program that helps you find information on the Internet),* so correcting with a semicolon is a logical choice.

Correct a Run-On by Adding a Dependent Word

A fourth way to correct a run-on is by making one of the independent clauses a dependent clause. You do this by adding a dependent word such as *although, because, since,* or *when.* (See the list on p. 340 for other dependent words.)

EXAMPLE Although my
~~My~~ car has 156,000 miles, I have never had a problem starting it.

EXAMPLE Renée signed up for a public speaking course because she thought it would boost her confidence.

When the dependent clause comes at the beginning of a sentence, you should use a comma after it. When the dependent clause comes at the end of a sentence, however, there is generally no need for a comma before it. The exception: Use a comma before *though, although,* and *even though* when they appear in a dependent clause at the end of a sentence.

Summary

1. A **run-on** is two independent clauses (clauses that can stand alone as complete sentences) punctuated as one sentence. There are two types of run-ons:

   A **comma splice** joins two independent clauses with only a comma and no conjunction. (See p. 346.)

   A **fused sentence** joins, or "fuses," two independent clauses with no punctuation. (See p. 346.)

2. To correct a run-on, separate the independent clauses with a **period** (see p. 347), a **comma and coordinating conjunction** (see p. 347), a **semicolon** (see p. 347), or by adding a **dependent word** (see p. 348).

Editing Activities

Identify and Correct Run-Ons

Practice 24-A (Answers appear on p. 478.)

Edit each of the following run-on sentences (comma splices and fused sentences) using one of the four correction strategies presented in this chapter. Use each correction strategy at least twice.

EXAMPLE Many cities and towns now make it easy for residents to recycle; ~~,~~ used newspapers, cans, and bottles can be put out alongside the weekly garbage for collection.

1. The earth as we know it took hundreds of millions of years to evolve, it balances itself over time.

2. Modern society has harmed this balance it has introduced chemicals and radiation into the environment.
3. Between 1945 and 1960 alone, over 200 synthetic chemicals were introduced into the environment these chemicals were manufactured by humans.
4. America generates four pounds of solid waste, or garbage, per person per day, much of this waste is recyclable.
5. The Environmental Protection Agency calls for four steps to help with the landfill problem, they include reducing waste and recycling.
6. The EPA also recommends burning waste when possible then the rest goes into a landfill.
7. Recycling saves up to 95 percent of the energy and water used to make goods from raw materials, it creates up to 90 percent less water and air pollution.
8. Many companies are finding that recycling pays off, AT&T recycles twenty-five truckloads of metals and plastics every day.
9. An organization called Planet Ark includes information called "Fifteen Ways to Save the Planet" on their Web site it is located at www.planetark.com.
10. One example is to use water wisely, by turning the tap off while brushing your teeth, another involves walking or using public transportation whenever possible.

Practice 24-B **(Answers appear on p. 478.)**

Each of the following word groups is a run-on sentence. Rewrite each one twice, using two of the correction strategies from this chapter.

EXAMPLE

While some
~~Some~~ people learn better when information is presented visually, others prefer written instructions.

, yet
Some people learn better when information is presented visually others prefer written instructions.

1. People are not always successful in college, some experience difficulties during the first year.
2. One of the main difficulties is time management inefficient use of time keeps students from getting everything done.
3. Students also have problems understanding professors' vocabulary, they may not be used to academic language.
4. Students should try to stay with the course, often they begin to understand with more exposure to the concepts.
5. Reading the textbook can also be hard textbooks are sometimes written in academic language.
6. Students are often not ready for the reading load of a college course, they do not allow enough time in their schedules to get everything done well.
7. Some students try to work too much they need the extra money.

8. Students should do their best to limit working hours, trying to do too much adds more stress to their lives.
9. Finally some students can become bored, they just cannot relate to a class.
10. Finding ways to apply the course content to life can help, seeing education as a route to a better job also keeps people in college.

Practice 24-C

Edit the following paragraph, eliminating all run-on sentences. Hint: Not all of the long sentences in the paragraph are run-ons.

> Martin Luther King, Jr.'s "I Have a Dream" is one of the most famous and important speeches in the English language, it was delivered in 1963. He spoke to 250,000 civil rights protesters they had come to the Lincoln Memorial in Washington, D.C. King was a preacher; his speech uses elements of African-American religious language. For example, he repeats certain words and phrases, this creates an emotional response in his listeners. He says, "Now is the time to lift our nation from the quicksands of racial injustice to the solid rock of brotherhood," and he repeats "Now is the time" several times in a row. Another phrase he repeats is "We cannot be satisfied"; he does this to emphasize his course of action. Most famous is his repetition of "I have a dream" these words communicate his vision for a better America. This new America would be a land where everyone would enjoy freedom, not just those privileged by their race and class. King's speech has touched the hearts of Americans everywhere they have understood that the American dream should be open to all who want to dream it.

Edit Your Own Writing for Run-Ons

1. Look through your portfolio to find a paragraph or essay in which you have made run-on sentence errors—comma splices and/or fused sentences. Rewrite each of those sentences, using one of the four correction strategies discussed in this chapter.
2. Two social issues surfaced in these exercises: environmental responsibility and racial equality. Write a detailed paragraph discussing one of these as you see its importance for the twenty-first century. Use many longer, more complex sentences; however, be careful to punctuate them correctly so that you do not end up with any run-ons.

Chapter 25

Subject-Verb Agreement

What Is Subject-Verb Agreement?

A verb must agree with, or "match," its subject in number. A singular subject (one person, place, or thing) requires a singular verb; a plural subject (more than one person, place, or object) requires a plural verb.

SINGULAR   [My company]Subject [offers]Verb a terrific benefits package.

PLURAL   [Many companies]Subject [offer]Verb medical and dental benefits.

A verb must also agree with its subject in person. The following chart shows the present-tense forms of some common verbs *(be, have, do, walk,* and *study).*

	Singular	Plural
1st Person	I am	We are
	I have	We have
	I do	We do
	I walk	We walk
	I study	We study
2nd Person	You are	You are
	You have	You have
	You do	You do
	You walk	You walk
	You study	You study
3rd Person	He/she/it is	They are
	He/she/it has	They have
	He/she/it does	They do

He/she/it walks	They walk
He/she/it studies	They study

Five Common Troublespots

Sometimes writers are unsure of the real subject of a sentence, and so making the verb agree becomes difficult. You can identify problems with subject-verb agreement in your writing if you are aware of five troublespots:

- words that separate the subject and verb;
- compound subjects;
- indefinite pronouns;
- collective nouns;
- a verb that comes before the subject.

Trouble When Words Separate the Subject and Verb

Writers sometimes lose sight of a subject when several words come between the subject and the verb in a sentence. Most often, a subject and verb will be separated by a prepositional phrase or a dependent clause. When the word group that is between the subject and verb contains a noun, you might mistake that noun for the subject of the sentence.

INCORRECT The rise in violent crime in our nation's public schools worry many parents.

To correct problems in subject-verb agreement when words separate the subject and verb, cross out any prepositional phrase or dependent clause. The subject of a sentence is never in these word groups. Then, find the subject of the sentence by asking yourself who or what is doing the action in the sentence.

EDITED The rise ~~in violent crime in our nation's public schools~~ worries many parents.

In this example, it is the *rise* in crime that worries the parents, not the *schools*. The verb *worry* must agree with the singular subject, *rise*.

Trouble with Compound Subjects

Some sentences have more than one subject. When two or more subjects are joined by the conjunction *and*, they are called a **compound subject.** A compound subject is a plural subject and requires a plural verb.

EXAMPLE My sister and her husband ^live ~~lives~~ in the British Virgin Islands.

Sometimes writers will want to make the verb agree with the nearest noun *(husband)*. In this sentence, the verb must agree with the entire subject, *my sister and her husband.*

Trouble with Indefinite Pronouns

Indefinite pronouns do not refer to specific persons, places, or things. Here is a list of common indefinite pronouns that are *always singular:*

Indefinite Pronouns: *always singular*

anybody	each	everyone	nobody	somebody
anyone	either	everything	no one	someone
anything	everybody	neither	nothing	something

EXAMPLE Each of my neighbor's dogs digs ~~dig~~ in my vegetable garden.

Each is the subject of the sentence. The verb should agree with the singular subject *each,* not with the plural noun *dogs.*

Here is a list of common indefinite pronouns that are *always plural:*

Indefinite Pronouns: *always plural*

both	many	several
few	most	some

EXAMPLE Many of the doctors in my healthcare network make ~~makes~~ Saturday appointments.

Many is the subject of the sentence. The verb should agree with the plural subject *many,* not with the singular noun *network.*

Trouble with Collective Nouns

Collective nouns are tricky. Depending on how they are used, they can require either singular or plural verbs. Here is a list of common collective nouns:

Common Collective Nouns

committee	crowd	group	range
couple	faculty	jury	staff
crew	family	number	total

Subject Verb

SINGULAR My family is proud of its Cuban heritage.

Subject Verb

PLURAL An increasing number of suburban families are returning to the cities.

Hint: If you are unsure whether the collective noun is singular or plural, ask yourself whether it refers to a single unit acting together or to parts acting individually.

Trouble When the Verb Comes before the Subject

Subjects usually come before their verbs. When they do not, the number of the verb is sometimes difficult to determine. Proofread for agreement by turning the sentence around, putting the subject first.

EXAMPLE There ~~is~~ *are* nearly seven thousand students on this campus.

Subject: Nearly seven thousand students — Verb: are

Nearly seven thousand students are on this campus.

EXAMPLE Among the problems autistic children face ~~is~~ *are* language difficulties.

Subject: Language difficulties — Verb: are

Language difficulties are among the problems autistic children face.

Summary

1. A verb must agree with, or "match," its subject in **number** and in **person.** (See p. 351.)
2. Making the verb agree with its subject is difficult if the subject is hard to identify. Many writers have trouble identifying the subject when

   words separate the subject and the verb (see p. 352)
   the subject is a **compound subject** (see p. 352), an **indefinite pronoun** (see p. 353), or a **collective noun** (see p. 353)
   the verb comes before the subject (see p. 354)

Editing Activities

Identify and Correct Errors in Subject-Verb Agreement

Practice 25-A (Answers appear on p. 479.)

Each of the following sentences contains an error in subject-verb agreement. Identify the subject in each sentence, and then edit the sentence by changing either the subject or the verb.

EXAMPLE Someone who holds the copyright to written materials ~~own~~ *owns* the legal rights to them.

1. The Copyright Law of 1976, which was written by lawmakers, protect owners of copyrighted material.
2. A number of members of Congress recognizes that this law needs to be updated.
3. With the rise of technology like the Internet comes new problems with how to balance creative protection with public interest and access.

4. For example, modifying computer programs and copying compact disks is now easy tasks because of new technologies.
5. Many members of the American workforce wonders who owns the material that exists on their company's computer network.
6. A committee including members from academia and the publishing world have helped to create new guidelines about using copyrighted material.
7. Students and their professor is allowed to use copyrighted material for educational purposes.
8. Students in a computer class studying the Internet is not allowed to copy copyrighted material onto their own Web sites.
9. Several new laws, like the 1998 Digital Millennium Copyright Act, updates the 1976 law to include new technologies, like distance education.
10. Though they may copy protected works, a student and her teacher is held liable if they use the work for personal gain outside the classroom.

Practice 25-B (Answers appear on p. 479.)

Some of the following sentences contain errors in subject-verb agreement. Edit the sentences that have errors. Write "correct" beside those sentences in which the subjects and verbs agree.

EXAMPLE Most Americans who watch Olympic and professional sports ~~is~~ *are* aware of the use of steroids by some athletes.

1. The use of performance-enhancing drugs are becoming more and more of a problem every year.
2. With more advances in drug development, officials in various organizations are having a tougher time detecting illegal substances.
3. Erwan Mentheour, a French cyclist, admit that he took several drugs before being caught in 1997.
4. "Doping," as it is called among world-class athletes, have become a serious threat to the integrity and appeal of sports.
5. Charles Yesalis of Penn State University, an expert on drug use in the Olympics, claim that the International Olympic Committee has known about the problem for forty years.
6. Athletes across the sports spectrum is getting caught; however, many others are not.
7. Many of the newer performance-enhancing drugs can have deadly effects.
8. Human growth hormone and erythropoietin (EPO) often causes severe heart problems.
9. Unnatural levels of testosterone is known to cause liver cancer and impotence.
10. Better drug-detecting methods and technology is a beginning to help sports clean up its act.

Practice 25-C

Edit the following paragraphs, fixing all errors in subject-verb agreement. Underlining the subject of each sentence may help you to edit.

Each year, a large number of professional athletes gathers at Mark Verstegen's International Performance Institute (IPI) in Florida. Among this group is tennis player Mary Pierce and Boston Red Sox shortstop Nomar Garciaparra. Verstegen, who uses the best techniques in sports, train athletes to make the most of their potential. According to Verstegen, one of the most valuable parts of the training programs involve sports psychology. Anyone with athletic abilities lose focus from time to time. The Verstegen philosophy allows athletes to regain their focus on the skills they can improve. Verstegen, along with his six associates, formulate a specialized training plan for each athlete.

Everyone who works with athletes at IPI understands sports medicine and physics. Along with weight training comes nutrition education and an emphasis on understanding the science of the sport. Verstegen and his staff is helping super athletes become even better with a combination of knowledge and hard work.

Edit Your Own Writing for Subject-Verb Agreement Errors

1. Look over your portfolio or previous writing to find places where you might have made an error in subject-verb agreement. Do you see where you went wrong? Using the correction strategies from this chapter, rewrite the sentences in which subjects and verbs do not agree. Hand in your revisions to your instructor.
2. Two of these exercises discussed sports and the ways in which athletes are trying to get better, stronger, and faster. Write a paragraph in which you discuss sports today (professional or recreational) and the kinds of pressures associated with competing. Use some of the following indefinite pronouns in your paragraph: *each, everyone, no one, anything, most, many,* and *few.* Be sure to use the correct verb form (singular or plural) with them.

Chapter 26

Verb Forms and Verb Tenses

What Are Verb Forms and Verb Tenses?

In writing, using the wrong form of a verb is an error that readers will notice. Using verbs correctly means choosing the correct form and tense. **Verb form** refers to the different ways a verb can be spelled and pronounced. **Verb tense** tells when the action of a sentence takes place. All verbs in English (except for *be*) have five basic forms:

Forms of English Verbs

Present tense	work	I **work** three days a week.
Present tense -*s* form	works	She **works** full-time.
Past tense	worked	I **worked** an extra day last week.
Present participle	working	I **am working** to pay for college.
Past participle	worked	I **have worked** at Wal-Mart for two years.

The irregular verb *be* has eight forms:

Forms of the Verb *Be*

Base form	**be**
Present tense	I **am** he/she/it **is** we/you/they **are**
Past tense	I/he/she/it **was** you/we/they **were**
Present participle	**being**
Past participle	**been**

Using Verbs Correctly

You will be able to edit your writing for problems with verb forms and verb tenses if you know how to use two types of verbs:

- regular verbs
- irregular verbs

Regular Verbs

Verbs that form their tenses in similar ways according to similar rules are called **regular verbs.** Most verbs in English are regular.

Present and Past Tense Forms for Regular Verbs

The **present tense** is used to describe events happening at the present moment or to describe habitual actions (things that happen all the time). Use an *-s* ending when the subject is *he, she, it,* or a singular noun such as *the dog* or *Professor Garcia* or *the library.* The **past tense** is used to describe events that have already happened. Use an *-ed* ending for regular verbs in the past tense. The **future tense** is used to describe events that haven't yet happened but will happen in the future. Use *will* before regular verbs to form the future tense.

Present tense	I **walk** three miles a day. The library **closes** at 9:00 tonight.
Past tense	I **walked** downtown yesterday. The library **closed** early last night.
Future tense	I **will walk** to class tonight. The library **will open** at 8:00 in the morning.

Present and Past Participle Forms for Regular Verbs

Present participles (*-ing* ending) and past participles (*-ed* ending) are often used with helping verbs like *be* or *have.* A form of *be* + a present participle forms the **progressive tense,** which describes ongoing or continuous action or action "in progress" at a certain moment in time. A form of *have* + a past participle forms the **perfect tense,** which describes action completed before a more recent past event.

Be + Present Participle = Progressive Tense

Present progressive	I **am walking** more often now that the weather is warmer.
Past progressive	I **was walking** near the lake when I saw the car accident.
Future progressive	I **will be walking** to work when I start my new job.

***Have* + Past Participle = Perfect Tense**

Present perfect	The library **has closed** for the evening.
Past perfect	The library **had closed** early twice before.
Future perfect	The library **will have closed** for the winter break by the time renovations begin.

As you proofread your writing, ask yourself whether the action you are describing in each sentence is happening now (or on a regular basis), has happened in the past, or will happen in the future. You may also need to determine whether the action is in progress or was completed before another more recent past action.

EXAMPLE She ^showed ~~show~~ her bad temper at work yesterday. [The action being described *(showing)* happened in the past, so *showed* is the correct form of the verb.]

EXAMPLE I can't meet you for dinner tonight because I ^will be studying ~~study~~ for an exam. [The action being described *(studying)* will be in progress at a particular moment in time *(tonight)*, so *will be studying* is the correct form of the verb.]

EXAMPLE We ^had lived in that house for twelve years before we sold it in June. [The first action being described *(living in that house)* was completed before the more recent past action *(selling the house)*, so *had lived* is the correct form of the verb.]

Irregular Verbs

Some verbs in English are **irregular,** which means that they do not follow a standard pattern for creating their various forms. Until you memorize the forms of irregular verbs, consult the following list when you proofread your writing for correct verb use. (See p. 357 for the forms of the irregular verb *be.*)

Partial List of Irregular Verb Forms

Present tense	Present tense -*s* form	Past tense	Present participle	Past participle
begin	begins	began	beginning	begun
bite	bites	bit	biting	bitten
blow	blows	blew	blowing	blown
break	breaks	broke	breaking	broken
bring	brings	brought	bringing	brought
build	builds	built	building	built
buy	buys	bought	buying	bought

catch	catches	caught	catching	caught
choose	chooses	chose	choosing	chosen
come	comes	came	coming	come
dive	dives	dived, dove	diving	dived, dove
do	does	did	doing	done
draw	draws	drew	drawing	drawn
drink	drinks	drank	drinking	drunk
drive	drives	drove	driving	driven
eat	eats	ate	eating	eaten
fall	falls	fell	falling	fallen
fly	flies	flew	flying	flown
freeze	freezes	froze	freezing	frozen
get	gets	got	getting	gotten
give	gives	gave	giving	given
go	goes	went	going	gone
hang (to suspend)	hangs	hung	hanging	hung
have	has	had	having	had
know	knows	knew	knowing	known
lay	lays	laid	laying	laid
lead	leads	led	leading	led
lie	lies	lay	lying	lain
lose	loses	lost	losing	lost
make	makes	made	making	made
pay	pays	paid	paying	paid
put	puts	put	putting	put
quit	quits	quit	quitting	quit
ride	rides	rode	riding	ridden
ring	rings	rang	ringing	rung
run	runs	ran	running	run
see	sees	saw	seeing	seen
set	sets	set	setting	set
shake	shakes	shook	shaking	shaken
shrink	shrinks	shrank (shrunk)	shrinking	shrunk
sing	sings	sang (sung)	singing	sung
slay	slays	slew	slaying	slain
slide	slides	slid	sliding	slid
speak	speaks	spoke	speaking	spoken
steal	steals	stole	stealing	stolen
sting	stings	stung	stinging	stung
swim	swims	swam	swimming	swum
swing	swings	swung	swinging	swung
take	takes	took	taking	taken

tear	tears	tore	tearing	torn
throw	throws	threw	throwing	thrown
wear	wears	wore	wearing	worn
write	writes	wrote	writing	written

Summary

1. **Verb form** refers to the different ways a verb can be spelled and pronounced. All English verbs except *be* have five basic forms. *Be* has eight forms. (See p. 357.)
2. **Verb tense** tells when the action of a sentence takes place. (See p. 357.)

   Use the **present tense** to describe events happening now or happening regularly. (See p. 358.)
   Use the **past tense** to describe events that have already happened. (See p. 358.)
   Use the **future tense** to describe events that haven't yet happened. (See p. 358.)
   Use the **progressive tense** (*be* + present participle) to describe an action in progress. (See p. 358.)
   Use the **perfect tense** (*have* + past participle) to describe action completed before a more recent past event. (See p. 358.)

3. Verbs that form their tenses in similar ways according to similar rules are called **regular verbs.** In the present tense, regular verbs take an *-s* ending with *he, she, it,* or a singular noun like *the dog* or *Professor Garcia.* In the past tense, regular verbs take an *-ed* ending. (See p. 358.)
4. **Irregular verbs** do not follow a standard pattern for creating their forms. Until you memorize the forms of irregular verbs, consult the chart on pp. 359–61.

Editing Activities

Identify and Correct Verb Problems

Practice 26-A (Answers appear on p. 479.)
Each of the following sentences requires at least one form of the verb *be.* Fill in a correct form of the verb for each blank, making sure that the verb matches the subject and is in a suitable tense.

EXAMPLE My favorite movie <u>had been</u> *The Graduate* before I saw *Pulp Fiction.*

1. The American Film Institute _____ responsible for causing a controversy in 1998 when it published its list of the best 100 films of the twentieth century.
2. *Citizen Kane,* starring Orson Welles, _____ the first film on the list.
3. *The Wizard of Oz* and *Gone with the Wind,* in the top ten, _____ both made in 1939.

4. One controversy surrounding the list _____ that the cut-off date for consideration _____ 1996.
5. *Titanic,* therefore, _____ not eligible for the list.
6. Film critics _____ _____ complaining that the rules for choosing films _____ inconsistent.
7. Only American films _____ considered, for instance, but that definition _____ vague.
8. *The English Patient* _____ included, although its director, writers, and cast _____ European.
9. The American Film Institute _____ _____ criticized even now for the way in which it created the list.
10. Whenever anyone creates a list of this kind, it will most likely _____ questioned and challenged.

Practice 26-B **(Answers appear on p. 479.)**

Each of the following sentences contains an incorrect form of an irregular verb. Edit each sentence using the correct form of the irregular verb. Check the chart on pages 359–61 if you need help.

EXAMPLE Just yesterday, my husband ~~speaked~~ *spoke* about planning a family vacation.

1. In 1999 millions of Americans drived to the beach for a family vacation.
2. While many people have flied on airplanes, cars remain the choice for cheap transportation.
3. The beach has took the prize for years for the top vacation destination for families and individuals.
4. Many people enjoy laying in the sun or romping in the waves.
5. Who hasn't shaked sand from shoes and blankets at some time or another?
6. Even the threat of skin cancer has not shrank the numbers of people at beaches.
7. MTV's "Spring Break" has saw tremendous increases in attendance over the past couple of years.
8. Beach vacation packages have broke records recently in numbers of trips booked.
9. The beaches have got more crowded, but people still go.
10. The beach has gave families and individuals of all ages a place to go for nature, relaxation, and fun.

Practice 26-C

Edit the following paragraph, correcting all errors in verb form and verb tense. (The errors are printed in *italics.*) Make sure that all the verbs remain in the past tense, present perfect, or past perfect tenses because the events described happened in the past or continue to have an impact on the present. Refer to the examples of these tenses on pages 358–59 if you need to.

One of the most shocking events of the late twentieth century *occurs* on April 20, 1999. Two young men dressed in black trenchcoats *were opening* fire on classmates and teachers at the Columbine High School in Littleton, Colorado. Before killing themselves, they *will kill* twelve students and a teacher. America *tracks* this event on television and in the papers anxiously and nervously. Many "copycat" incidents *will be occurring* throughout the country in the weeks following the shooting. This event *had affected* schools across the country. Many schools *react* to the shooting by strengthening security. Congress *will* even *react* by introducing new gun legislation. The discussion surrounding the event *centers* on what caused these two students to lash out in violence. Parents, society, gun laws, peer pressure, rock groups, video games—all *had been blamed* for this tragedy.

Edit Your Own Writing for Verb Problems

1. Look in your portfolio or recent writing for a paragraph or essay in which you misused verb forms or verb tenses. Read over your writing carefully, and then use the strategies you learned in this chapter to edit your writing. Hand in your revisions if your instructor asks you to.
2. What do you think is the cause of school shootings like the one at Columbine? In your opinion, which is more to blame for such tragic events: parents, society, gun laws, peer pressure, rock groups, or video games? Or do you think other reasons cause teens to become violent? Write a detailed paragraph expressing your opinion on this topic. Pay special attention to your use of verbs as you revise. Have you used appropriate verb tenses? Are forms of regular and irregular verbs spelled correctly?

Chapter 27

Pronouns

What Is a Pronoun?

A **pronoun** is a word used in place of a noun. Writers use pronouns in order to avoid awkward repetition.

> Gregor is really funny. *He* ~~Gregor~~ is also a good cook.
>
> Karina left *her* ~~Karina's~~ sandals by the pool.
>
> Tragedy is easier to bear if something good comes out of *it* ~~tragedy~~.

Using Pronouns Correctly

As you proofread your writing, make sure that you

- make pronouns and antecedents agree;
- make pronoun references clear;
- use the correct pronoun case.

Make Pronouns and Antecedents Agree

A pronoun must agree with the noun it refers to or replaces. This noun is called the **antecedent.** If the antecedent is singular, for example, the pronoun must also be singular.

> *Carlos* made his choice, and now *he* has to live with it. [*He* refers to *Carlos.*]

If the noun is plural, the pronoun must also be plural.

> *Anya and Eva* decided not to go to the play. *They* went to a movie instead. [*They* refers to *Anya and Eva.*]

Singular and Plural Forms of Common Pronouns

	Singular	Plural
Personal pronouns (refer to specific persons or things)	I, me, you, she, her, he, him, it	we, us, you, they, them
Possessive pronouns (indicate ownership)	my, mine, your, yours, her, hers, his, its	our, ours, your, yours, their, theirs
Demonstrative pronouns (identify nouns)	this, that	these, those

Some writers get into pronoun agreement trouble when the antecedent seems to refer to many people when in fact it includes only one person. Words that cause this difficulty are indefinite pronouns and collective nouns.

Indefinite Pronouns

Indefinite pronouns (words like *anyone/anybody, each, either/neither,* and *everybody/everyone*) do not refer to specific people, places, or things. Instead, they are often used to make generalizations. Most indefinite pronouns are singular. (See p. 353 for lists of common indefinite pronouns.)

EXAMPLE *Each* of the women in the carpenters' union carries ~~their~~ *her* membership card proudly.

EXAMPLE *Anyone* who drives recklessly should lose ~~their~~ *his or her* license.

Traditionally, *he* was used with indefinite pronouns to refer to a person of either sex. However, it is no longer thought to be appropriate to use a masculine pronoun *(he/him/his)* to refer to words that could include females as well as males. One way to revise such sentences is to use the phrase *his or her* instead of *his,* as in the previous example. Another way to revise such sentences is to make the subject plural:

EXAMPLE *Employees* ~~*Each* of the employees~~ will pay for ~~*his*~~ *their* own life insurance.

Collective Nouns

Collective nouns also pose problems for some writers. Words like *committee, crowd, jury,* and *staff* can sometimes "feel" like plural words when, in fact, they are singular. (See p. 353 for a list of common collective nouns.)

EXAMPLE The school committee will make ~~their~~ its decision by Friday.

Make Pronoun References Clear

Pronouns are handy because they help writers avoid repetition, but if it isn't clear what word a pronoun refers to, your reader may misunderstand your meaning.

EXAMPLE Ivan told Louis that the scores had been posted and that *he* had passed the exam. [*Who* passed the exam—Ivan or Louis?]

EDITED Ivan told Louis that the scores had been posted and that *Louis* had passed the exam.

In general, writers make three common pronoun-reference errors: ambiguous reference, broad reference, and weak reference.

Ambiguous Reference

An *ambiguous reference* occurs when there are two or more possible nouns a pronoun could refer to.

EXAMPLE Sharon and Katja went shopping on Saturday. Later, *she* said *she* didn't like what *she* had bought. [Who said? Who didn't like? Who bought?]

EDITED Sharon and Katja went shopping on Saturday. Later, *Katja* said she didn't like what *Sharon* had bought.

Broad Reference

A *broad reference* occurs when a pronoun refers to an entire statement rather than to a specific noun or nouns.

EXAMPLE Both Renaldo and Angela agreed to follow their parents' traditions for their wedding day. *This* made for an overly long wedding ceremony. [What does *This* refer to?]

EDITED Both Renaldo and Angela agreed to follow their parents' traditions for their wedding day. *Following these traditions* made for an overly long wedding ceremony.

Weak Reference

A *weak reference* occurs when the antecedent is a noun that cannot logically be replaced by the pronoun.

EXAMPLE Before I finished mowing the lawn, *it* ran out of gas. [What does *it* refer to?]

EDITED Before I finished mowing the lawn, *the lawn mower* ran out of gas.

Use the Correct Pronoun Case

Pronouns take different forms depending on the purpose they serve in a sentence. In other words, pronouns have different spellings when they are used as subjects, as objects, or to show possession. The three **cases** are listed below.

Pronoun Cases

	Subject pronouns	Object pronouns	Possessive pronouns
Singular			
1st person	I	me	my, mine
2nd person	you	you	your, yours
3rd person	he, she, it, who	him, her, it, whom	his, her, hers, its, whose
Plural			
1st person	we	us	our, ours
2nd person	you	you	your, yours
3rd person	they, who	them, whom	their, theirs, whose

Some writers have trouble determining which case is needed in some sentences.

Subject Pronouns

Use a subject pronoun when the pronoun is the subject of a verb.

Subject Verb

She speaks Chinese and English.

Subject Verb

He has lived in four different countries.

Compound Subjects. Use a subject pronoun in a compound subject (two or more elements joined by the conjunction *and*).

EXAMPLE James and ~~me~~ *I* skipped the review and then failed the test.

Hint: If you are not sure which pronoun to use in a compound subject, try each one alone in the sentence. "*I* skipped the review and failed the test" is correct. "*Me* skipped the review" is clearly incorrect.

Comparisons. Use a subject pronoun in comparisons that include *than* or *as.*

EXAMPLE Rashid is taller than ~~her~~ *she*. *[Implied:* Rashid is taller than *she is.]*

EXAMPLE We don't watch as much TV as ~~them~~ *they*. *[Implied:* We don't watch as much TV as *they do.]*

To make sure you are using the correct pronoun case, say the sentence out loud, adding the implied word or words.

Object Pronouns

Use an object pronoun when the pronoun is the object of a verb or the object of a preposition.

Verb Object

I told *her* to apply for the management position.

Preposition Object

She went with *him* to the career seminar.

Compound Objects. Use an object pronoun in a compound object (two or more elements joined by the conjunction *and*).

EXAMPLE The teacher told Shane and ~~I~~ *me* to see him during office hours.

Hint: If you are not sure which pronoun to use in a compound object, try each one by itself in the sentence. "The teacher told *me* to see him during office hours" is correct. "The teacher told *I* to see him during office hours" is incorrect.

Choosing between *Who* and *Whom*

Choosing between these two relative pronouns is tricky. Some writers mistakenly believe that *whom* is used only for formal situations and that *who* is the more casual, more widely used pronoun. As you proofread your writing, remember that *who* is always a subject pronoun and *whom* is always an object pronoun.

Who left the door open? *[Who* is the subject of the verb *left.]*

For *whom* are you voting? *[Whom* is the object of the preposition *for.]*

Hint: To make sure you are using the correct case, try to substitute *he* or *she* (also subject pronouns) wherever you see *who*. You may have to change the word order a bit. If *he* or *she* makes sense, then the correct choice is *who*. You can also try substituting *him* or *her* (also object pronouns) for *whom*. If *him* or *her* makes sense, then the correct choice is *whom*. If the sentence is a question, try answering it using either *he* or *him*.

EXAMPLE Janelle, ~~whom~~ *who* left the company in March, is doing very well. [*She left the company in March* . . . sounds right, so *who* is correct.]

EXAMPLE I just saw someone ~~who~~ *whom* I dated briefly in college. [*I dated him briefly in college . . .* sounds right, so *whom* is correct.]

EXAMPLE With ~~who~~ *whom* should I leave this package? [*I should leave the package with him* sounds right, so *whom* is correct.]

Possessive Pronouns

Possessive pronouns are used to show ownership.

Enrique carved *his* initials into the desk.

The white car is *ours;* the red one is *theirs.*

Be careful not to confuse the possessive pronouns *its, whose, theirs,* and *your* with the contractions *it's, who's, there's,* and *you're.* (See Chapter 32, Apostrophes, for more information about contractions.)

EXAMPLE ~~Theirs~~ *There's* no business like show business. [This sentence does not indicate possession, so a possessive pronoun should not be used.]

EXAMPLE The *Miami Daily News* lost ~~it's~~ *its* best movie critic. [This sentence does indicate possession—the *newspaper's* critic—so a possessive pronoun should be used.]

Summary

1. A **pronoun** is a word used in place of a noun. Writers use pronouns in order to avoid repetition. (See p. 364.)
2. A pronoun must agree in number with its **antecedent,** the word it refers to or replaces. Writers often have difficulty determining whether **indefinite pronouns** (see p. 365) and **collective nouns** (see p. 365) are singular or plural.
3. **Pronoun references** should be clear because readers will be confused if they cannot understand which word the pronoun is replacing. In general, writers make three common pronoun-reference errors: **ambiguous reference** (see p. 366), **broad reference** (see p. 366), and **weak reference** (see p. 366).
4. Use the proper **pronoun case.** (See p. 367.)

   Use a **subject pronoun** in a compound subject (see p. 367), in a comparison using *than* or *as* (see p. 367), or when the pronoun is the subject of a verb (see p. 367).

Use an **object pronoun** in a compound object (see p. 368) or when the pronoun is the object of a verb or preposition (see p. 368).

Who is a subject pronoun; *whom* is an object pronoun. (See p. 368.)

5. **Possessive pronouns** are used to show ownership. (See p. 369.)

Editing Activities

Identify and Correct Pronoun Errors

Practice 27-A (Answers appear on p. 479.)

The following sentences contain no personal pronouns. Edit the sentences, substituting pronouns for nouns where appropriate and making the pronouns agree with their antecedents. A few of the sentences may need more than one change.

EXAMPLE American television viewers are very loyal to ~~the viewers'~~ *their* favorite shows and characters.

1. *TV Guide* magazine frequently publishes *TV Guide*'s lists of favorite TV shows and characters.
2. Recently, *TV Guide* published a feature article called "TV's 50 Greatest Characters Ever!"
3. Number one on the list was Louie DePalma, a character on the show *Taxi* known for the character's meanness.
4. Lucy Ricardo is rated number three for Lucy's zany, crazy antics on the *I Love Lucy* show.
5. A more recent TV character, Roseanne, made the list for Roseanne's "ferocious humor."
6. Editors of the magazine listed Kramer of *Seinfeld* as the editors' 35th pick for Kramer's "vibrating, head-shaking, arm-waggling" entrances.
7. Xena is listed for Xena's being a "bodacious battle-ax," and Xena is cited as being a "prehistoric Sipowicz."
8. Of course, Andy Sipowicz of *NYPD Blue*, known for Sipowicz's harshness and insensitivity, also made the list at number 23.
9. Even a cartoon character, Homer Simpson, made the list for Homer's being a "coarse, oafish, self-involved, oblivious, overgrown child."
10. And would anyone doubt that Steve Urkel would make this kind of list for Steve Urkel's annoying nerdiness on *Family Matters*?

Practice 27-B (Answers appear on p. 480.)

Each of the following sentences contains one or more pronoun errors. Edit the sentences, correcting the errors in pronoun agreement, pronoun reference, and pronoun case.

EXAMPLE Many books are available for parents to read about ~~her~~ *their* child's development.

1. Everyone seems to have their own opinion about how to raise children.
2. My husband and me have been criticized for letting our son use a pacifier.
3. This bothered us for a while, but we realized it was right for us and for our baby.
4. Some parents feel that its okay to let their young children sleep with them.
5. For those parents whom have trouble sleeping, sharing a bed with an infant may not be the smartest idea.
6. Many parents today favor letting a child cry themselves to sleep.
7. Letting our infant son cry himself to sleep was not a practice that appealed to my husband and I, though.
8. Our baby would fall asleep when one of us sang to him or rocked him. This made us all happy.
9. Whenever my mother and I discuss parenting styles, she always says that she was much more strict than me.
10. However, I remember when my mother let my baby sister eat a whole box of cookies because she was tired.

Practice 27-C

Edit the following dialog for any errors in pronoun agreement, pronoun reference, or pronoun case.

"Me and Jeremy want to do our research on physician-assisted suicide," explained Leo.

"Our group wants to do it's paper on Internet censorship," said Terese. "We think Nick and her want to write about bilingual education."

"Well, give your proposals to Dr. Lewis or I," said Janine, the teaching assistant.

"Do you want our's to be turned in Monday or Wednesday?" asked Terese.

"Monday would give I, at least, more time to consider your ideas," explained Janine.

"Everyone in our group has his done already," said Sheri.

"This is great," said Janine. "I'm proud of you're work."

"Nobody is prouder than me!" exclaimed Sheri. "This was hard!"

Edit Your Own Writing for Pronoun Errors

1. Look through your portfolio to find a paragraph or essay in which you have made some pronoun errors. Using the strategies you learned in this chapter, edit your writing. Resubmit as your instructor directs.
2. Do you think that people should have the right to die? Do you think censoring material on the Internet is a good idea? Choose an issue on which you have a strong opinion. Write a detailed paragraph giving reasons for your opinions. Pay close attention to your pronoun use, proofreading closely for pronoun agreement, reference, and case.

Chapter 28

Adjectives and Adverbs

What Are Adjectives and Adverbs?

Adjectives and adverbs are modifiers—words that describe or give more information about other words in a sentence. **Adjectives** modify nouns and pronouns and answer the questions *which one? what kind?* and *how many?*

The young boy picked daisies for his mother.

We are tired from our trip.

Two bald men got on the bus at Madison.

There were several protesters outside the theater.

Adverbs modify verbs, adjectives, or other adverbs and answer the questions *when? how?* and *how much?*

We drove to Baltimore today.

Chandra hoped to do well on her exam.

The customer's request put me in an extremely awkward position.

She looked very carefully at the old photograph.

Using Adjectives and Adverbs Correctly

This chapter will help you to

- choose between adjectives and adverbs;
- use adjectives correctly in comparisons;
- use *good* and *well* correctly.

Choose between Adjectives and Adverbs

Writers sometimes mistakenly use an adjective where an adverb is needed or use an adverb where an adjective is needed. The words themselves can be confusing because many adjectives become adverbs simply by adding an *-ly* ending: *honest/honestly, positive/positively, slow/slowly.* As you proofread your writing for errors in adjective and adverb use, focus on the word being modified. Someone can be a *careful* driver (adjective), but that person drives *carefully* (adverb). An *annual* celebration (adjective) is a celebration that happens *annually* (adverb).

EXAMPLE You will have to walk ~~quick~~ quickly in order to catch that bus. *[Quickly* describes the verb *walk.]*

EXAMPLE A retriever is a ~~real~~ really smart dog. *[Really* describes the adjective *smart.]*

EXAMPLE I met a ~~poorly~~ poor woman named Rita at the church soup kitchen. *[Poor* describes the noun *woman.]*

Use Adjectives Correctly in Comparisons

Use the **comparative** form of an adjective to compare two things. The comparative form of a one-syllable adjective generally has an *-er* ending. If the adjective has two or more syllables, its comparative form begins with the word *more* or *less.*

EXAMPLE The Ford Excursion is *larger* than the Chevy Suburban.

EXAMPLE The Olympus digital camera is *more expensive* than the Toshiba model.

Use the **superlative** form of an adjective to compare three or more things. The superlative form of an adjective generally has an *-est* ending (for one-syllable words) or begins with the word *most* or *least* (for adjectives with two or more syllables).

EXAMPLE The Ford Excursion is the *largest* sport utility vehicle on the market.

EXAMPLE The Nikon 950 is the *most expensive* digital camera that I have seen.

It is incorrect to use a double comparative (more + adj. or adv. ending in *-er*) or a double superlative (most + adj. or adv. ending in *-est*).

EXAMPLE My Spanish is ~~more~~ better than my English.

EXAMPLE Kira is the most ~~smartest~~ intelligent person I know.

The following chart lists the irregular comparative and superlative forms of common adjectives.

Irregular Forms of Common Adjectives

Adjective	Comparative	Superlative
bad	worse	worst
good	better	best
little (in amount)	less	least
many/much	more	most
well	better	best

Use *Good* and *Well* Correctly

Many writers confuse *good* and *well.*

Use *good* as an adjective.	Use *well* as an adverb.
She is a *good* cook.	She cooks *well.*
Mark did a *good* job painting the fence.	Mark painted the fence *well.*
They are *good* at avoiding phone calls.	They avoid phone calls *well.*

Use *well* as an adjective when you refer to someone's health, as in *My grandmother is not well today.*

Summary

1. Adjectives and adverbs are modifiers—words that describe or give more information about other words in a sentence. **Adjectives** modify nouns and pronouns and answer the questions *which one? what kind?* and *how many?* (See p. 372.) **Adverbs** modify verbs, adjectives, or other adverbs and answer the questions *when? how?* and *how much?* (See p. 372.)
2. Use the **comparative** form of an adjective to compare two things. The comparative form of an adjective generally has an *-er* ending (for one-syllable words) or begins with the word *more* or *less* (for adjectives with two or more syllables). (See p. 373.)
3. Use the **superlative** form of an adjective to compare three or more things. The superlative form of an adjective generally has an *-est* ending (for one-syllable words) or begins with the word *most* or *least* (for adjectives with two or more syllables). (See p. 373.)
4. Use ***good*** as an adjective and ***well*** as an adverb. (See p. 374.)

Editing Activities

Identify and Correct Adjective and Adverb Errors

Practice 28-A (Answers appear on p. 480.)

The following sentences contain no adjectives or adverbs. Edit the sentences, adding at least one adjective or one adverb per sentence to clarify or to expand the sentences. The questions that follow the sentences are designed to help you think of some possible adverbs or adjectives that might fit the sentence. You do not have to answer all the questions for each sentence.

EXAMPLE *Grocery shopping* ^ ~~Shopping~~ is one of my least favorite things to do. [What kind of shopping?]

1. Every Saturday morning, I sit at my table to make a list. *[Which table? What kind of list?]*
2. After writing down things like *milk, butter,* and *eggs* on my list, I look through the refrigerator and cabinets for items to add. *[What kind of "things" are milk, butter, and eggs? How would someone look through the refrigerator and cabinets?]*
3. I then check the newspaper to see if there are coupons that will help me to save money. *[How would someone check the newspaper? What kind of newspaper is it? What kind of coupons?]*
4. I always go to the farmstand first for tomatoes, corn, apples, and bananas. *[Which farmstand? What kind of tomatoes? Corn? Apples? Bananas?]*
5. At the supermarket, I travel up and down the aisles listening to the chatter of other shoppers. *[How would someone travel in a supermarket? What kind of chatter would one hear?]*
6. A woman at the fish counter was telling a man how to make a marinade for swordfish. *[What sort of woman? What sort of man? How was she telling him? What kind of marinade?]*
7. I found myself in the awkward position of reaching over the woman for a bottle of marinade. *[How awkward was the position? What kind of marinade?]*
8. In the cereal aisle, a mother was trying to stay in control with kids reaching out for everything they saw. *[What kind of mother? How was she trying? How many kids? How were the kids reaching?]*
9. While in the cleaning products aisle, I try to choose the brands. *[When does the shopper try? Of all the brands, which does the shopper try to choose?]*
10. The last thing I do before I check out is recycle my cans and bottles, and then I congratulate myself on a job done. *[How was the job done? What kind of cans? What kind of bottles?]*

Practice 28-B (Answers appear on p. 480.)
In each sentence, choose the correct word in parentheses.

EXAMPLE Jason just took a (good/well) job as an e-business consultant.

1. Today, many positions are being created to meet (new/newly) demands.
2. Today, for example, a person who thinks (visual/visually) can get a job as a Web site designer.

3. Ten years ago, companies were not as (aggressive/aggressively) in using the Web as a business solution.
4. (Recent, Recently), careers in media and communications have boomed.
5. Some of the (better/best) jobs in the year 2005 will be in the field of medical technology.
6. As the baby-boomers age, they will (certain/certainly) need health care.
7. Another (real/really) booming field is the service industry.
8. More and more people can afford to hire others to perform the (less desirable/least desirable) tasks.
9. However, my housecleaner, who advertises her services online, earns a (better/best) salary than I do!
10. With new technology, more and more American workers are (extreme/extremely) interested in working from home.

Practice 28-C

The paragraph that follows contains many errors in the comparative and the superlative forms of adjectives and adverbs. Edit the paragraph, substituting the correct forms.

> One of the more scariest sexually transmitted viruses affecting women today is the papilloma virus. It is the more common infection in the United States and Europe, affecting 75 percent of sexually active women. It is even more easier to transmit than gonorrhea or HIV. The virus spreads most thoroughly than others because a condom does not stop it. One of the disturbingest aspects of the papilloma virus is that it seldom produces obvious symptoms. Although a Pap smear can detect it, this test is least reliable than many tests. A three-year study of Rutgers University women revealed that more than 40 percent contracted the virus, which is a more higher percentage than other STDs. A shockinger fact about papilloma is that is it connected with 95 percent of cervical cancer cases. Although it is least prevalent in men, papilloma can also cause penile cancer. The more complete treatment for papilloma virus would involve a yet undiscovered vaccine.

Edit Your Own Writing for Adjective and Adverb Errors

1. Look through your portfolio to find a paragraph or essay that could be strengthened by more careful use of adjectives and adverbs. Edit your writing and submit it as directed by your instructor.
2. Write a detailed paragraph in which you compare two jobs you have had or would like to have. Include things that are similar and different, better and worse, about the two jobs. Be sure to include a number of adjectives and adverbs in your writing to make it more descriptive for your reader.

Chapter 29

Misplaced and Dangling Modifiers

What Is a Modifier?

A **modifier** is a word or phrase that describes or gives more information about other words in a sentence. For a sentence to be clear, the reader must know which word or words the modifier refers to. Sometimes, however, a modifier is too far away from the word it is describing to be clear. Other times, the word to which the modifier refers is not even in the sentence. As you proofread your writing, make certain that modifiers and the words they describe are close together.

Avoiding Misplaced and Dangling Modifiers

This chapter will help you to identify and correct

- misplaced modifiers;
- dangling modifiers.

Misplaced Modifiers

Modifiers should be placed at the point in a sentence where their meaning is clearest. A **misplaced modifier** describes the wrong word or words in a sentence because it is incorrectly placed. Especially troublesome are limiting modifiers (such as *almost, nearly, only, just,* and *hardly*), prepositional phrases, and *-ing* phrases.

Misplaced Limiting Modifiers

The following misplaced modifiers may sound correct when spoken, but they are incorrect in formal writing.

EXAMPLE The speaker almost talked the entire hour. *[Almost* should modify *the entire hour,* not *talked.]*

EXAMPLE The waiter nearly made $70 in tips last Saturday. *[Nearly* should modify *$70,* not *made.]*

Rewritten with the modifiers closer to the words they describe, these sentences are clearer.

EDITED The speaker talked almost the entire hour.

EDITED The waiter made nearly $70 in tips last Saturday.

As you proofread, look for limiting modifiers (words like *almost, nearly, only, just,* and *hardly*). Make sure that each limiting modifier is close to the word or words it describes.

Misplaced Prepositional Phrases and *-ing* Phrases

Some writers have difficulty placing modifiers, especially when the modifier is a phrase. As you read these sentences, ask yourself who was *in the nude* and who was *yelling in Japanese.*

EXAMPLE Kenneth couldn't answer the door to pay the pizza delivery boy in the nude.

EXAMPLE Mrs. Kinjo chased away the dog yelling in Japanese.

Rewritten with the modifiers closer to the words they describe, these sentences are clearer.

EDITED Kenneth, in the nude, couldn't answer the door to pay the pizza delivery boy.

EDITED Yelling in Japanese, Mrs. Kinjo chased away the dog.

Dangling Modifiers

A **dangling modifier** is a phrase that cannot logically describe another word in the sentence. When a sentence opens with a modifier, the reader expects the modifier to be followed by the word it modifies. When the modifier is not followed by the word it modifies, it "dangles." Dangling modifiers are often hard to recognize in your own writing because, to you, the meaning of the sentence may be perfectly clear. The following sentences contain dangling modifiers.

EXAMPLE Before closing shop, the lights were turned off.

EXAMPLE While on the telephone, the scrambled eggs burned in the pan.

EXAMPLE To pass the nursing board exam, long hours of study are necessary.

In each of these sentences, the introductory phrase seems to modify the subject of the sentence. Common sense tells us, however, that *lights* don't *close shop;* that *scrambled eggs* do not talk *on the telephone;* and that *long hours* do not pass the *nursing boards.*

To correct a dangling modifier, add the word that is being modified to the sentence. You can make the word the subject of the sentence, or you can add the word to the opening phrase. Either method of revising makes the sentence clearer.

EDITED Before closing shop, ^Phil turned the lights ~~were turned~~ off.

EDITED While ^I was on the telephone, the scrambled eggs burned in the pan.

EDITED To pass the nursing board exam, ^students must study long hours. ~~long hours of study are necessary.~~

Summary

1. A **modifier** is a word or phrase that describes or gives more information about other words in a sentence. For a sentence to be clear, the reader must know which word or words the modifier refers to. (See p. 377.)
2. A **misplaced modifier** describes the wrong word or words in a sentence because it is incorrectly placed. Especially troublesome are limiting modifiers (such as *almost, nearly, only, just,* and *hardly*), prepositional phrases, and *-ing* phrases. As you proofread, make sure that each modifier is close to the word or words it describes. (See p. 377.)
3. A **dangling modifier** is a phrase that cannot logically modify another word in the sentence. When an opening modifier is not followed by the word it describes, it "dangles." To correct a dangling modifier, add the word that is being modified to the sentence. You can make the word the subject of the sentence, or you can add the word to the opening phrase. (See p. 378.)

Editing Activities

Identify and Correct Misplaced and Dangling Modifiers

Practice 29-A (Answers appear on p. 480.)

Each of the following sentences contains a misplaced modifier. (Remember that a modifier can be a single word or a phrase.) Edit the sentences, moving the modifiers to an appropriate place so that the meaning is clear.

EXAMPLE I have ~~only~~ found ^only three articles about stress management for my research paper.

1. Stress almost affects everyone at one time or another.
2. A little stress actually is helpful in that it channels resources of the body.
3. Thinking and memory get better during moments in the body of stress.
4. The sense of pain is dulled during stressful events also.
5. More blood is sent to the brain and muscles carrying oxygen. [Hint: Blood carries oxygen.]

6. The immune system cannot keep infection from taking a harmful toll on the body after a long period of stress.
7. Delayed stress nearly affects all people who work in naturally stressful occupations.
8. Chronic stress results from setting off the stress response too often on the body.
9. Cortisol, a substance only created during stress, can become toxic to brain cells.
10. More and more diseases are being linked to chronic stress like heart disease and digestive disorders.

Practice 29-B (Answers appear on p. 481.)

Each of the following sentences contains a dangling modifier. Edit each sentence to make the meaning clear. As in the examples in this chapter, you may need to add or change words to fix the dangling modifier. This may mean changing the subject of the sentence.

EXAMPLE Writing ten papers per semester, ~~a computer had to be added~~ *I had to add a computer* to my budget.

1. Before writing a research paper, the Internet should be consulted as a source of information.
2. Varying in the quality of information it contains, writers must evaluate each Internet source for its reliability.
3. To evaluate an Internet site for reliability, the author of the site must be identified.
4. While surfing the site, any clues about the author's expertise will help evaluate the source.
5. Before using information on a site, the facts must be verified.
6. Because of their research expertise, sites hosted by university faculty are usually reliable.
7. Though containing advertisements and promotional material, many organizations sponsor sites that are professionally checked.
8. Before quoting or copying information from a commercial Web site, the company should be contacted.
9. When reprinting a company's Web site logo, the company must give permission to do so.
10. Using borrowed information, the Internet can be a great source if research writers know how to cite electronic sources properly.

Practice 29-C

Edit the following paragraph, correcting all misplaced and dangling modifiers. You may have to add or change words as you edit.

For couples to stay close, always they need to do little things for each other. To keep the spark alive, flowers are given on special and not-so-special occasions. Giving space and freedom, special interests are encouraged by some partners. Before getting married, the romance should give way to smaller acts of kindness by couples. Instead of complaining about a lack of attention, communication should be open. Often one partner feels nearly as though all of the giving is one-sided. Couples often have trouble opening up to a therapist with their problems. They just should make a point to talk and to spend time together every day. Giving a back rub or buying a silly present, relationships are often saved by couples who keep each other important.

Edit Your Own Writing for Misplaced and Dangling Modifiers

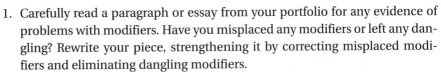

1. Carefully read a paragraph or essay from your portfolio for any evidence of problems with modifiers. Have you misplaced any modifiers or left any dangling? Rewrite your piece, strengthening it by correcting misplaced modifiers and eliminating dangling modifiers.
2. Write a detailed paragraph about one of the topics in this chapter's exercises: stress, the Internet, or relationships. For example, which do you think you have the most difficulty coping with? Proofread your paragraph carefully for misplaced or dangling modifiers.

Chapter 30

Parallelism

What Is Parallelism?

Your writing will be clearer and more effective if you use parallel structure. **Parallelism** means that all similar elements in your sentence—such as items in a list or items being compared—have the same grammatical form. Sentences that are not parallel sound a bit off-balance, as in the example below.

NOT PARALLEL — Julia is trustworthy (adj.), reliable (adj.), and knows (verb) her job well.

PARALLEL — Julia is trustworthy (adj.), reliable (adj.), and *knowledgeable* (adj.).

Making Sentences Parallel

To make a sentence parallel, be sure that the parts of your sentence share the same form when they are joined in one of the following ways:

- with a coordinating conjunction;
- with a correlative conjunction;
- with *than* or *as* in a comparison.

Putting nouns with nouns, verbs with verbs, and phrases with phrases will ensure balance in your sentences.

Parallelism with Coordinating Conjunctions

Writers often use the coordinating conjunctions *and* and *or* to present pairs and lists. When you use these words in your writing, check to see that what comes before *and* or *or* has the same grammatical form as what comes after it.

EXAMPLE Soccer involves endurance, skill, and teamwork ~~the team plays as a unit~~.

EXAMPLE Marta checked her rearview mirror, put on her blinker, and switched ~~she was switching~~ lanes.

EXAMPLE We knew that we could advertise our business on the Internet, ~~putting it~~ in the local paper, or on the town's cable channel.

Parallelism with Correlative Conjunctions

Correlative conjunctions come in pairs.

either . . . or	*both . . . and*
neither . . . nor	*not only . . . but also*
whether . . . or	

When you use correlative conjunctions, be sure the items you join are parallel in structure.

EXAMPLE *Whether* studying for an exam *or* meeting ~~to meet~~ her sales goals at work, my mother always does ~~puts forth~~ her best. ~~effort~~.

EXAMPLE Cigarette smoking is *not only* a health hazard *but also* ~~it can be~~ an expensive habit.

Parallelism with *Than* or *As*

Writers often use the words *than* or *as* to make comparisons. If you use one of these words to compare items, check to make sure that the items are expressed in parallel form.

EXAMPLE I find it easier to draft a paper in stages than to write ~~writing~~ it all at once.

EXAMPLE On the basketball court, Lara finds offense as exciting as ~~playing~~ defense.

Summary

1. **Parallelism** means that all similar elements in your sentence have the same grammatical form. Putting nouns with nouns, verbs with verbs, and phrases with phrases will ensure balance in your sentences.
2. When you use the coordinating conjunctions *and* and *or* to present pairs and lists in your writing, check to see that what comes before *and* or *or* has the same grammatical form as what comes after it.

3. When you use a correlative conjunction pair *(either/or, neither/nor),* be sure the items you join are parallel in structure.
4. If you use *than* or *as* to make a comparison, check to make sure that the items you are comparing are expressed in parallel form.

Editing Activities

Identify and Correct Sentences That Are Not Parallel

Practice 30-A (Answers appear on p. 481.)

Each of the following sentences presents a pair or list using a coordinating conjunction. Edit each sentence to make it parallel in structure. You may have to add words or change words in order for your sentences to make sense.

EXAMPLE My goals this semester include improving my math grade, seeing the writing tutor once a week, and ~~to learn~~ *learning* more about the Internet.

1. Successful students know how to manage their time, how to deal with professors, and reading skills.
2. They take notes effectively, know when to listen carefully, and organization.
3. Three problems students encounter with time are taking too much time on unimportant tasks, spontaneous activities, and not building some flexibility into their schedules.
4. Effective students are organized, efficient with time, and know how to set goals.
5. Studying for the hard subjects first, knowing your best time of day, and a good study place all help a person be a better student.
6. A successful student also takes risks, is able to focus attention, and curious.
7. To lessen stress, a successful student laughs, relaxes, or physical activity.
8. No matter what courses you take, it's important to set positive goals, establish study patterns, and keeping track of achievements.
9. Other pieces of advice from effective students include learning to say "no," getting enough rest, and how to do two things at once.
10. While being a successful student may seem difficult, being prepared, positive, and determination will certainly help.

Practice 30-B (Answers appear on p. 481.)

Complete the following sentences by adding material that correctly forms a parallel structure. Add any information that makes sense in the sentence. You may use the information hints provided by the questions that follow the sentences.

EXAMPLE I recently discovered that working at Disneyland is more exciting than *bussing tables in Los Angeles*.

1. Tourist locations like Florida and California are home to both wealthy people and _____. *[What is the opposite of wealthy?]*

2. People are either getting rich or _____. *[What is the opposite of getting rich?]*
3. Wealthy developments drive up housing costs both for the ones who can afford it and _____. *[Who are the opposite of those who can afford it?]*
4. People who need to work in tourist areas find it more difficult to find housing than _____. *[What are people who need to work trying to find?]*
5. Jobs in busy areas are plentiful for people with higher level job skills and _____. *[Who are the opposite of people with higher level job skills?]*
6. The problem is both being able to afford to live in busy areas and _____. *[What might be another challenge for people without a lot of money?]*
7. According to the National Coalition for the Homeless, it takes either a job paying $8.89 an hour or _____ for the single mother to afford a one-bedroom apartment. *[What else might a single mother need to be able to afford an apartment?]*
8. Whether they are restaurant employees or _____, many entry-level workers cannot afford adequate housing today. *[What is another occupation that might be plentiful in tourist areas?]*
9. Since jobs are easy to find in tourist areas, many high-school graduates believe it is better to go straight to work than _____. *[What is one alternative to going straight to work after high school?]*
10. College, however, provides not only an education but also _____. *[What else does college provide besides a good general education?]*

Practice 30-C

Edit the following paragraph, correcting sentences that are not parallel. You may have to add words to make your meaning clear.

> One of the most popular actresses in the last fifteen years has been Meg Ryan. Starring both in *Top Gun* and shocking viewers in *When Harry Met Sally,* Ryan captured viewers' attention early in her career. Both her perkiness and being intelligent have become qualities associated with Ryan. She met up with Tom Hanks in the movie *Sleepless in Seattle* and starring in *You've Got Mail.* Their on-screen chemistry has proved to hit it big at the box office and creating many fans. She has been called both a private person and loyal to friends. When not in front of the camera, she either wears jeans or sporting casual clothes. She finds it more challenging to be a normal wife and mother than acting. Ryan claims that part of her appeal has been her adorableness and that she is liked by both men and women.

Edit Your Own Writing for Faulty Parallelism

1. Look through your portfolio to find a paragraph or essay in which you have made mistakes in parallelism. Also look for sentences which you could combine effectively using compound elements with parallel structure. Revise your work and submit as your instructor directs.

2. Write a short essay in which you compare and contrast your experience in high school (or in the work world) with your experience in college so far. Use *than* or *as* as you compare elements of both experiences: for example, studying, social life, expectations of teachers or professors, your own growth. Proofread carefully for parallel structure when you are finished.

Part Six

Editing Sentences for Punctuation and Mechanics

Diagnostic Test for Part Six: Editing Sentences for Punctuation and Mechanics

Use this test to check your punctuation and mechanics skills. Answers appear on page 482.

A. Each of the following sentences needs a comma, an apostrophe, a semicolon, a colon, or a hyphen. Correct each sentence as needed.

1. Bring the following items to the meeting a notebook, a calendar, and a list of ideas for how to improve the student senate.
2. One of the first time members of the committee recently made the suggestion that we design a student senate Web site.
3. One of President Wegners goals for the campus is to have a stronger student government.
4. Perhaps Lena Mejía our writing lab director can recommend a good designer.
5. The student senate helps to coordinate activities during the year it also advises the administration on school policy.
6. Our group can be an important link among students faculty and administrators.
7. We try especially hard to meet commuter students needs.
8. Though being a student senator takes time it offers a valuable opportunity for building leadership skills.
9. Please come to next weeks meeting.

B. Punctuate the following conversation, inserting quotation marks, commas, and periods where necessary.

10. Why are we studying these things in writing class Jess asked
    Learning to be a better reader will improve your writing Professor Creager replied
    But Jess continued what does reading have to do with writing?

For starters Professor Creager explained if you become a better reader of other people's writing, it's likely that you will be a better reader of your own writing. Being a better reader of your own writing means you will more easily spot problem areas and make revisions.

Jess thought about this idea and then added Yeah, then I could put myself in my reader's shoes.

C. Each of the following sentences contains one or more words that need to be capitalized. Correct each sentence, adding capital letters where necessary.

11. We turned down canal street once we approached the french quarter in new orleans.
12. The organizer of our trip, rev. banserick, had been to the city last spring and thought it would be a good place for our choir from our lady of mercy church to perform.
13. In the course many of us took last term, music appreciation, we learned about dixieland jazz and the music produced in the famous preservation hall.
14. As a fundraiser, our church choir began performing jazz numbers for area dinner clubs in the detroit, michigan, area.
15. Going to new orleans seemed like a good way to expand our musical horizons.
16. Strolling down bourbon street, however, opened up some unexpected horizons.
17. We had never seen people walking down the street with open budweisers and open blouses before!
18. While we did hear some good music by people like pete fountain and johnny adams, we think that maybe this city is not the city for a church choir trip.

Chapter 31

Commas

Commas (,) help readers understand the meaning of a sentence. Consider the differences in the following sentences:

> When you bake Marcus you always make a mess.
>
> When you bake**,** Marcus**,** you always make a mess.

When you use, misuse, or leave out commas, your meaning isn't always clear. This chapter will help you to understand when and how to use commas in several common situations:

- commas to separate items in a series;
- commas in compound sentences;
- commas to set off introductory word groups;
- commas to set off nonessential modifiers;
- commas to set off a direct quotation;
- other uses of commas.

Commas to Separate Items in a Series

When you create a series, or list, of three or more single words or word groups, use commas to separate each item. Some writers omit the comma between the last two items in the series (just before the word *and*). However, you should include that comma for clarity.

EXAMPLE My local grocery store sells food, books, stamps, and greeting cards.

EXAMPLE We listed our home for sale in the newspaper, on the Internet, and on our town's cable channel.

EXAMPLE The library's new floor plan improves access to the reference area, provides more space for quiet study, and allows for seven more computer stations.

Commas in Compound Sentences

An independent clause can stand on its own as a complete sentence. A compound sentence contains two independent clauses separated by one of these joining words: *and, but, or, so, nor, for, yet.* Use a comma before the joining word (also called a coordinating conjunction) in a compound sentence.

EXAMPLE Kristen started her new job last week, and she has already mastered the accounting system.

EXAMPLE Marika can take the statistics course at night, or she can complete the course online.

Commas to Set Off Introductory Word Groups

Writers use a comma to separate certain introductory words from the main part of the sentence. The words that follow the comma should be able to stand alone as a sentence.

EXAMPLE Therefore, I favor mainstreaming as a way to improve education. [*I favor mainstreaming as a way to improve education* can be punctuated as a complete sentence.]

EXAMPLE To enter the system, you must type your password.

EXAMPLE When babies are teething, they may drool a lot or run a slight fever.

Commas to Set Off Nonessential Modifiers

A modifier describes or gives more information about another word or words in a sentence. If a modifier is **nonessential** (not necessary) to the meaning of the sentence, set it off from the rest of the sentence with commas. (Think of it this way: You could grab onto the commas to lift the nonessential material out of the sentence.) If the modifier is **essential** to the meaning of the sentence because it provides information necessary for understanding the sentence, do not use commas.

You can tell whether a modifier is essential by taking it out of the sentence and checking to see if the sentence still makes sense. Take a look at these sentences:

My grandmother, who lives in Dallas, owns six Dalmatians.

My grandmother owns six Dalmatians.

If the writer has *two* grandmothers—one who lives in Dallas and one who lives in Seattle—the reader is left wondering which one owns the Dalmatians. In this case, the modifier is essential to the meaning of the sentence, and so the writer should not use commas. However, if the writer has only one grandmother, the modifier *who lives in Dallas* is nonessential because the remaining sentence is clear and makes sense. In that case, the writer needs to include the commas. Using commas correctly makes the meaning of a sentence clear.

EXAMPLE The Connecticut River, which separates Vermont and New Hampshire, was recently designated an American Heritage River. [There is only one Connecticut River.]

EXAMPLE My landlord, who lives above me, plays country music all day long. [I have only one landlord.]

Commas to Set Off a Direct Quotation

When you use a direct quotation—someone's exact words—in your writing, use commas to set off the quotation from the rest of the sentence. At the end of the quotation, the comma always appears *inside* of the quotation marks. (For more information about using quotation marks, see Chapter 34.)

EXAMPLE "Listen for a rattling sound in the tailpipe," said the mechanic.

EXAMPLE My mother asked, "Do you have to go out looking like that?"

EXAMPLE "One way to solve the problem," she responded, "is to fill the hole and paint over it."

Other Uses of Commas

Dates

Put a comma in between the day and year when writing a specific date.

The *Titanic* sank on April 15, 1912.

Addresses

Use a comma to separate parts of an address included in a sentence. Note that there is no comma between the state and the zip code.

Northern New Mexico Community College is located at 1002 North Onate Street, Espanola, NM 87532.

When a date or address appears in the middle of a sentence, place a comma after it.

EXAMPLE December 1, 2012, is the date on which all of my student loans will be paid off.

EXAMPLE 64 Roland Avenue, Baltimore, Maryland, is the site of my grandmother's childhood home.

Names

Use commas when you are addressing someone by name.

Petra, can you make the game tonight?

Summary

1. Use **commas** to separate items in a series (see p. 391), to separate the day from the year in a specific date (see p. 393), and to separate the parts of an address included in a sentence (see p. 393).
2. Use a comma before the joining word (like *and, but,* or *or*) in a compound sentence. (See p. 392.)
3. Use a comma to set off certain words or word groups from the main part of a sentence:

   introductory word groups (see p. 392)
   nonessential (unnecessary) modifiers (see p. 392)
   direct quotations (see p. 393)
   dates, addresses, and names (see p. 393)

Editing Activities

Identify and Correct Comma Errors

Practice 31-A (Answers appear on p. 482.)

Edit each of the following sentences, adding commas where needed.

EXAMPLE More than 1.5 million American, British, and Canadian soldiers crossed the English Channel in the summer of 1944.

1. One of the most important battles ever fought occurred on the beaches of Normandy France.
2. Referred to as D-Day this battle began the Allied invasion to free Europe from Hitler's Nazis.
3. Dwight D. Eisenhower who later became president of the United States was the Supreme Commander of the Allied troops.
4. Occurring on June 6 1944 the D-Day invasion led to many deaths on the beaches.
5. Thousands of Allied soldiers died but the area was finally won.
6. Once the Allies were securely in France they could move on to Paris and ultimately to Berlin.
7. Steven Spielberg's Oscar-winning movie *Saving Private Ryan* which begins with the Normandy invasion takes a harsh look at war.
8. The movie features Tom Hanks Matt Damon and Ted Danson.
9. The first half-hour which presents some of the most realistic battle scenes ever filmed shows the attack on the Normandy beaches.
10. The movie portrays the heroism the struggles and the senselessness of war.

Practice 31-B (Answers appear on p. 482.)

The dialog that follows contains no commas. Edit the sentences, placing commas where needed.

EXAMPLE "I'm here today to offer the services of the Community Career Center," said the career counselor.

1. The career counselor asked the class "How many of you know what career field you want to enter?"
2. "I would like to be a computer programmer" replied Joshua "because they make a lot of money."
3. "You will have to take math and science" the counselor explained.
4. "That's okay" Joshua replied "since I like those subjects."
5. "I just wanted to make sure that you understand the requirements of a job you're interested in" the counselor said.
6. Li Xian then asked "What kinds of courses do I need in order to become a nurse?"
7. "You will also need to take lots of science courses" the counselor answered.
8. "If I'm not so great at science" Jerome asked "what are my options?"
9. The counselor replied "That depends on your talents and your interests."
10. "You might want to read *What Color Is Your Parachute?* by Richard Nelson Bolles in order to explore your interests and to find a career path" she advised.

Practice 31-C

Edit the following paragraph by adding commas where they are needed.

Called an American dynasty the Kennedy family has been regarded as American royalty. When John and Jackie Kennedy lived in the White House people referred to it as Camelot. President Kennedy's untimely assassination which occurred in November 1963 sent the nation into mourning. "John-John" and his famous salute at his father's funeral captured America's hearts and it caused most Americans to feel as if they knew this family. When Robert Kennedy President Kennedy's brother was killed in 1968 the nation mourned again with this ill-fated family. On his way to becoming president himself Robert was killed for his political beliefs. Most recently John F. Kennedy Jr. his wife Carolyn and her sister Lauren were killed tragically in a plane crash. Again the nation watched as the Kennedy family who seem like us and yet above us grieved. Many had thought that John Jr. who had attained a law degree would follow his dad and uncles into politics. Senator Edward Kennedy said of his nephew in his eulogy "like his father he had every gift but length of days."

Edit Your Own Writing for Comma Errors

1. Comma usage challenges many writers. Look through your portfolio to find a paragraph or essay in which you have made comma errors. Using the skills you learned in this chapter, edit your writing to eliminate comma problems. Submit your revision as directed by your instructor.
2. Write a detailed paragraph in which you discuss the career you are pursuing. Why have you chosen it? What kind of preparation will you need to get a job in this field? (If you are already employed in this field, talk about the skills required in your position.) Include in your paragraph at least one compound sentence, one sentence with introductory elements, and one with a nonessential modifier, as explained in this chapter. Proofread your paragraph for correct use of commas.

Chapter 32

Apostrophes

Writers use an **apostrophe** (') to show possession (ownership) or to indicate that a letter or letters have been left out to form a contraction.

> Frank's bike is in the shop for repairs. [The bike belongs to Frank.]
>
> He hasn't been able to ride to school this week. *[Hasn't* is a shortened form of *has not.* The apostrophe takes the place of the *o* left out of *not.]*

Some writers also use apostrophes to make letters, numbers, and abbreviations plural.

If you misuse or fail to use apostrophes in your writing, your meaning may be unclear to your reader. This chapter will help you understand how to

- use apostrophes to show possession;
- use apostrophes in contractions;
- use apostrophes with letters, numbers, and abbreviations;
- avoid unnecessary apostrophes.

Apostrophes to Show Possession

Add **'s** to singular nouns to show possession. Add **'s** even if the singular noun ends in *s,* unless the pronunciation would be too awkward. In that case, a simple apostrophe at the end of the word would be acceptable.

> The neighbor's cat is stuck in our tree.
>
> His business's reputation suffered.
>
> Ulysses' ship was caught in a storm.

To make a plural noun ending in *s* possessive, add just an **'**. For a plural noun ending in something other than *s* (for example, *men*), add an **'s.**

The computers' hard drives have been crashing all week.

My children's school is being renovated over the summer.

Hint: When proofreading your writing for use of apostrophes, carefully think about your meaning. If you are not sure where to place the apostrophe, reword your sentence using an *of* phrase in place of the possessive noun. For example, *the girl's computer* refers to the computer of *the girl* (one girl). *The girls' computers* refers to the computer of *the girls* (two or more girls).

When you are showing ownership by two people or things (called joint possession), make the last noun possessive.

Caryl and John's condo went on the market last week.

For time expressions, follow the rules for punctuating possessive nouns.

Today's newspaper is at the front desk. [Think: the newspaper *of today.*]

It cost me two weeks' pay to replace that broken window. [Think: the pay *of two weeks.*]

Apostrophes in Contractions

Use an apostrophe to show a contraction of two words into one.

There's = *there is* haven't = *have not*
Don't = *do not* I'll = *I will*

Many writers confuse *it's* and *its.* Remember to use the contraction *it's* only in situations where you could also use *it is. Its* (with no apostrophe) is a possessive pronoun.

It's amusing to watch a dog chase *its* own tail. [You can say ***it is** amusing,* but *chase **it is** own tail* is incorrect.]

Apostrophes with Letters, Numbers, and Abbreviations

Use an apostrophe to make letters, numbers, and abbreviations plural.

The 1040's are in the file marked "tax forms."

The V's and U's look alike on our monitor.

The bartender looked carefully at their I.D.'s.

Unnecessary Apostrophes

Do not use apostrophes with nouns that are plural but not possessive.

EXAMPLE Their wedding ~~photo's~~ ^photos^ are beautiful.

EXAMPLE Our company has two Web ~~site's~~ ^sites^.

Do not use apostrophes with possessive pronouns *(his, hers, its, theirs, ours, yours).*

EXAMPLE The magazines in the back seat are ~~her's~~ ^hers^.

Summary

1. Writers use an **apostrophe** to show possession, to form a contraction, and to make letters, numbers, and abbreviations plural. (See p. 397.)
2. To make a **singular noun possessive,** add *'s,* even if the singular noun ends in *s.* (If the *-s's* pronunciation is too awkward, as in *crisis's,* it is acceptable to add only an '.) (See p. 397.)
3. To make a **plural noun possessive,** add just an ' if the noun ends in *-s.* If the noun ends in something other than an *-s,* add an *'s.* (See p. 397.)
4. Use an apostrophe to show a **contraction** of two words into one. (See p. 398.)
5. ***It's*** is short for *it is. (It's on the shelf = It is on the shelf.)* **Its** is a pronoun used to show possession. *(Its name* = the name belonging to *it.)* (See p. 398.)
6. Use an apostrophe to make letters, numbers, and abbreviations plural. Do not use an apostrophe with nouns that are plural but not possessive. (See p. 398.)

Editing Activities

Identify and Correct Apostrophe Errors

Practice 32-A (Answers appear on p. 483.)

Edit each of the following sentences, adding apostrophes where needed to show possession, to indicate contractions, or to form plurals.

EXAMPLE ~~Ive~~ ^I've^ often wondered whether I have a learning disability.

1. Many students suffer from a learning disability called dyslexia, and they cant distinguish among certain letters or make meaning from words.
2. Theyll often switch certain letters, like ts and rs.
3. Dyslexic students might not be able to read a teachers instructions on the board because such students cant form images from the words.
4. One of dyslexic students major problems is that they read very slowly.
5. Theyre often so used to the problem that they don't realize they have it.
6. Dyslexias other name is Development Reading Disorder, or DRD.
7. One of DRDs side effects is that mathematics is often difficult.

8. Students arent able to translate the symbols into thought.
9. A students self-esteem suffers when he or she suffers from DRD.
10. Although learning disorders tend to run in families, early intervention can help students achievement.

Practice 32-B (Answers appear on p. 483.)

Edit each of the following sentences, taking out unnecessary apostrophes and adding apostrophes where needed to show possession, to indicate contractions, or to form plurals.

EXAMPLE Camp Horizon is one of many camps founded recently to help children with medical ~~challenge's~~ *challenges*.

1. Outside Millville, Pennsylvania, Camp Horizons campers arrive ready for a week full of fun.
2. These campers suffer from skin disease's like psoriasis and alopecia.
3. Begun in 1995 by Dr. Howard Pride, Camp Horizon gives kids with special problem's a camp experience.
4. Here these kids do craft's, enjoy water activities, and meet new friends.
5. Amy Paller, M.D., who works and teaches at Northwestern Universitys Children's Memorial Hospital in Chicago, says that these kids need to be around other kids who have skin problems.
6. Kids get daily skin treatment at Camp Horizons Med Shed.
7. Campers who admit that they have few friends at home meet other's who need companionship.
8. Two other diseases common among these camper's are ichthyosis and ectodermal dysplasia.
9. Its hard to imagine having scales or not being able to sweat; these children, however, are used to peoples stares and comments.
10. Camp Horizon gives them a week to enjoy the outdoor's and the understanding friendship of other children.

Practice 32-C

Edit the following paragraph for apostrophe errors. Not every sentence will contain an error, and some sentences may contain two.

The 1960s were turbulent in many ways. Society was changing at a rapid pace, and peoples' goals and values shifted. The protests over the Vietnam War kept everyones anxiety levels high. As soldiers came home, they werent always welcomed warmly. College campus's were full of turmoil and sometimes violence as students challenged authority. Pop music also changed faster in this decade than perhaps any other time. Music of the fifties' sounded nothing like the music of the sixtie's. The Civil Rights' Movement finally took hold in this decade with the passage of the Civil Rights Bill in 1964. Three important assassination's—those of John F. Kennedy, Martin Luther King, Jr., and Robert Kennedy—added to societys tension. America went through growing pains' in the sixties, and this growth changed the culture.

Edit Your Own Writing for Apostrophe Errors

1. Look through your portfolio for a paragraph or essay to scan for errors in apostrophe use. Edit your paper, and resubmit it as your instructor directs.
2. Think over your own life and the many changes you have witnessed. Write a detailed paragraph describing some of the major changes that have affected you in areas such as technology, education, music, sports, or health. Use possessives and contractions so that you can practice your use of the apostrophe. Review your work carefully to see if you used the apostrophe correctly before handing it in.

Chapter 33

Semicolons

Using a **semicolon** (;) correctly is a challenge for many writers. The semicolon has two basic functions:

- to separate items in a long or complicated series;
- to join independent clauses.

Semicolons in a Series

Writers usually use commas to separate items in a series. For example, *I brought soda, chips, and pickles to the party.* When a series is long or the items contain commas, however, use semicolons to separate the items. Otherwise, your reader may find it difficult to tell where one item ends and another begins. In the following example, the writer tells about meeting three new people—Jorge, Luis, and Marlena—but without semicolons, it sounds as if the writer has met *six* new people.

EXAMPLE At the party, I met Jorge, my sister's new boyfriend; Luis, Jorge's older brother; and Marlena, Jorge's wife.

Semicolons with Independent Clauses

When you have two independent clauses that express closely related ideas, you can use a semicolon to join them in one sentence.

Amy was promoted this week**;** she is now the manager of her group.

Our air conditioner is not working right**;** it never got below 80° in the kitchen last night.

When a conjunctive adverb (a transitional word such as *however, furthermore, meanwhile, therefore, otherwise*) connects two independent clauses, use a semicolon before the conjunctive adverb. You must also use a comma after the transitional word, unless that word contains only one syllable (example: then).

Professor Shea is ill this week; however, her T.A. will teach the class.

Note that you *can* punctuate these examples as complete sentences. (It is correct to write: *Professor Shea is ill this week. However, her T.A. will teach the class.*) Using only a comma to separate two independent clauses will create a run-on sentence (see Chapter 24).

Summary

1. When a **series** is long or complicated, use **semicolons** to separate the items. (See p. 402.)
2. Use a semicolon to **join two closely related independent clauses,** especially when the second independent clause begins with a transitional word such as *however* or *furthermore.* (See p. 402.)

Editing Activities

Identify and Correct Semicolon Errors

Practice 33-A (Answers appear on p. 483.)

Each of the following pairs of sentences could be joined with a semicolon. Rewrite them, adding an appropriate conjunctive adverb *(however, furthermore, meanwhile, therefore, otherwise)* for five of the sentences and joining five others with only a semicolon.

EXAMPLE

My brother prefers to use a road map when driving to a new place; I prefer using written directions.

My brother prefers to use a road map when driving to a new place; however, I prefer using written directions.

1. Howard Gardner's theory of multiple intelligences explains why some people are better than others at learning in certain ways. Everyone is successful in a different area.
2. Gardner has described eight types of intelligence. Some people may be good in several areas.
3. Two of the types are *musical* and *visual.* These are not normally thought of as intelligences but as talents.
4. Gardner makes a distinction between a talent and an intelligence. He claims that an intelligence is natural, not learned.

5. Two other intelligences are *interpersonal* and *intrapersonal.* These abilities involve dealing with others and understanding one's self.
6. Another type of intelligence involves physical activity. This does not necessarily mean athletic ability.
7. *Verbal* and *mathematical* are two easily accepted types of intelligence. People who do well on standardized tests like the SAT probably have one of these abilities.
8. The *naturalist* intelligence explains why some people have "green thumbs." Others cannot grow plants no matter how hard they try.
9. Understanding that people possess different intelligences is important. School and work situations should be changed to suit these differences.
10. We all need to understand ourselves better. We should try to determine our own intelligences or strengths.

Practice 33-B (Answers appear on p. 484.)

Each of the following sentences contains a long, complicated list of items with commas. Each sentence needs semicolons to separate the items. Substitute semicolons for some of the commas as you rewrite each sentence correctly.

EXAMPLE During our family's visit to Florida, we visited Venice, a city on the Gulf coast; Boca Raton, a city on the east coast; and Isla Morada, one of the Florida Keys.

1. Destin, Florida, South Padre Island, Texas, and Ocean City, Maryland, are all cities with popular tourist beaches.
2. Cities that draw tourists for other attractions are San Antonio, Texas, Anaheim, California, and Washington, D.C.
3. Orlando, Florida, is home to Disney World, maybe the world's most popular theme park, Universal Studios, a busy theme park devoted to movies, and Epcot Center, a combination entertainment and learning park.
4. Many cities such as Chicago, Illinois, Atlanta, Georgia, and San Diego, California, draw large numbers of travelers for conferences.
5. The Art Institute of Chicago, one of the world's most famous museums, the United Center, the arena that is home to the Bulls, and the Magnificent Mile, a famous shopping area, are three reasons Chicago is a popular place to visit.
6. Three of the largest cities in the United States are New York, New York, Los Angeles, California, and Houston, Texas.
7. Coastal Maine, famous for lobster, New Orleans, Louisiana, location of the French Quarter, and Memphis, Tennessee, Elvis Presley's famous birthplace, attract their share of tourists each year.
8. Texas Stadium, home of the Dallas Cowboys, Fenway Park, Boston's famous ball field, and Three Rivers Stadium, located in the heart of Pittsburgh, bring visitors to their cities regularly.

9. Even smaller towns, such as Sedona, Arizona, Martha's Vineyard, Massachusetts, and Petoskey, Michigan, enjoy a lively tourist trade.
10. Gettysburg, Pennsylvania, Tombstone, Arizona, and Charlottesville, Virginia, draw visitors every year because of their historical significance.

Practice 33-C

Edit the following paragraph, inserting semicolons where needed. Some semicolons may be needed in lists; others may be needed in sentences that should be joined correctly. Not every sentence will need a semicolon.

> Shawna Parizo, a "sensory analyst" for Ben & Jerry's ice cream, Ellen Sirot, a "parts model" with attractive hands and feet, and Jackie Stathis, a "seatfiller" for awards shows have unusual jobs that they love. One is from Waterbury, Vermont, another is from Westchester County, New York, and one works in Victorville, California. All three women followed their talents or desires into jobs that fill a special need. Shawna began as an ice cream scooper with sensitive taste buds, Jackie was attending an awards show when she got the idea for her service, Seatfillers and More. Ellen was auditioning to model her legs, someone spotted her attractive feet and hands and offered her a job. Laura Simpson's job involves "talking" to animals, people call her a pet psychic. She began as a social worker for human beings. Mickie McGowan laughs for a living, she also does all kinds of funny voices. All of these women advise finding what you are good at and following it to the right job for you.

Edit Your Own Writing for Semicolon Errors

1. Look through your portfolio for a paragraph or essay in which you might have used semicolons incorrectly or a piece in which the use of semicolons might strengthen your writing. Revise and then hand it in, as your instructor directs.
2. Think of your ideal job. Write a detailed paragraph in which you describe this job and what you would do in it. How would your job be unique? What would make you good at it? How can you prepare yourself to follow this desire into a career? After you have written a draft, look back over your paper and find several places where you can join sentences effectively using semicolons.

Chapter 34

Quotation Marks and Italics

Writers use **quotation marks** (“ ”) or ***italic type*** to give words, phrases, titles, and direct quotations special treatment. This chapter will tell you when to use:

- quotation marks;
- italics.

Quotation Marks

Quotation marks are used to enclose direct quotations and the titles of certain short works.

Quotation Marks with Direct Quotations

Use quotation marks to set off a direct quotation, the exact words of another speaker or writer. Do not use quotation marks with an indirect quotation, in which you restate someone's ideas in your own words. (See Chapter 19 for more information about how to include direct and indirect quotations in your writing and how to give credit to the original source.)

Direct quotation	“That was the easiest exam ever!” Zach exclaimed.
Paraphrase	Zach told us that the exam was easy.
Direct quotation	According to the Chamber of Commerce, “Auto racing is the lifeblood of our tourist industry. Each year, the sport draws more and more Americans—from all corners of the nation—to our state.”
Paraphrase	The Chamber of Commerce reports that auto racing, which brings in tourist dollars from all over the United States, continues to increase in popularity in our state.

Titles of Short Works

Use quotation marks to refer to titles of articles, essays, chapters within longer works, poems, short stories, songs, and specific episodes of television shows.

My article, "The Ten Best Places to Eat in Minneapolis," was published in yesterday's paper.

Ricky Nelson's song "Garden Party" has nothing to do with Katherine Mansfield's short story "The Garden Party."

When you include a quoted title within a direct quotation (a quotation within a quotation), the inside quotation marks become single quotation marks.

Jed asked, "Have you read 'The Lottery' by Shirley Jackson?"

Using Punctuation with Quotation Marks

Always place commas and periods inside quotation marks. Always place colons and semicolons outside.

"There is talk," the boss said, "about unionizing within the company."

The employee replied, "I would never vote for a union here at Westco"; after thinking it over for a moment, she added, ". . . almost never."

Question marks and exclamation points can be placed inside or outside quotation marks. If only the quoted material is a question or exclamation, place the punctuation inside the quotation marks.

The reporter inquired, "Do you expect lawsuits as a result of the tragedy?"

If the entire sentence is a question or an exclamation, then the end punctuation should be placed outside the quotation marks.

Didn't T. S. Eliot say, "It's not wise to violate the rules until you know how to observe them"?

Italics (Underlining)

Italic type resembles handwritten script and is used to make words and phrases stand out from the rest of the text. Most typewriters and word processors come with italic capabilities. If your machine doesn't print italics, you can use underlining instead.

Use Italics for Certain Titles

Use italics for titles of the following types of works:

Books: *Chicken Soup for the Soul, The Client*

Magazines: *Newsweek, Popular Mechanics*

Newspapers: the *New York Times,* the *Charlotte Tribune*

Films: *The Blair Witch Project, The Perfect Storm*

Plays: *Death of a Salesman, Hamlet*

Television and Radio Programs: *Frasier, Sesame Street, Morning Edition*

Legal Cases: *Craft v. Metromedia*

Software: *Quicken, Word*

Use Italics for Letters as Letters, Words as Words

Aardvark has three *a*'s in it.

The word *short* is longer than the word *long.*

Summary

1. Writers use quotation marks (" ") and *italic type* to give words, phrases, titles, and direct quotations special treatment. (See p. 406.)
2. Use quotation marks to enclose a **direct quotation,** the exact words of another speaker or writer. Do not use quotation marks with an indirect quotation, in which you restate someone's ideas in your own words. (See p. 406.)
3. **Quotation marks** are also used to enclose titles of short works, including newspaper and magazine articles, essays, poems, short stories, songs, and chapters of books. (See p. 407.)
4. Using **other punctuation** with quotation marks is tricky. Commas and periods always go inside of quotation marks. Colons and semicolons always go outside. Question marks and exclamation points go inside unless they apply to the entire sentence. (See p. 407.)
5. Use **italics** for titles of longer works and certain other specialized material, including books, magazines, newspapers, films, plays, TV programs, legal cases, and software. (See p. 407.) Italics is also used when representing letters as letters and words as words. (See p. 408.)

Editing Activities

Identify and Correct Problems with Quotation Marks and Italics

Practice 34-A (Answers appear on p. 484.)

Edit each of the following sentences, adding quotation marks and italics (underlining) where necessary.

“Who ?”

EXAMPLE Who has finished the book The Awakening asked the professor?.

1. The professor asked Who has begun the research project on The Great Gatsby?
2. You might begin with the journals American Literature and Studies in the Novel, found in our library she advised.
3. A good source for the history of the period she explained would be the New Yorker magazine, which began the same year that the novel was published.
4. What about looking in the Encyclopedia Britannica? Ciro asked.
5. You should not use general encyclopedias for academic research papers she explained except for very general information.
6. The professor told the students about some other sources they could use for research on the novel and on F. Scott Fitzgerald's short story Babylon Revisited.
7. Kevin said that he had found an informative article called Platonism in The Great Gatsby in the journal Midwest Quarterly.
8. Can we compare The Great Gatsby to Adventures of Huckleberry Finn? asked Keisha.
9. You may do that answered the professor if you have developed a solid thesis.
10. Be sure to document all of your information, using the MLA Handbook for Writers of Research Papers she added.

Practice 34-B (Answers appear on p. 484.)

Edit the following sentences so that they are direct rather than indirect quotations. You will need to change a few words, capitalize the first word of the direct quotation, and add quotation marks where they are needed. You may also need italics.

“Sleep will help you to think better.”

EXAMPLE My mother always says, ~~that sleep will help me to think better.~~

1. Prevention magazine claims that sleep isn't the only way to feel more rested.
2. Dr. Kristine Clark says that people should eat their heaviest meal at breakfast for more energy during the day.
3. She says that digesting food late at night takes energy, which should be used for sleeping well.
4. The magazine article Get More Energy states that iron is an important element for creating energy.
5. In his book The Promise of Sleep, Dr. William C. Dement claims that a sleep diary is a good way to calculate how much sleep a person really needs.
6. Dr. James Maas says that people should add fifteen minutes to their sleep time until they feel totally rested the next day.
7. His book Power Sleep claims that almost everyone should add at least one more hour to their current sleep time to feel their best.
8. Drinking lots of water can also boost energy, claims Dr. Clark.

9. Dr. Diane Wetzig says that learning to deal with daily stresses better can boost our energy levels.
10. In the book Strength Training by Dr. Wayne Westcott, the author claims that physical exercise stimulates the release of hormones that affect your brain and make you feel more energized.

Practice 34-C

Edit the following paragraph for correct use of quotation marks and italics.

Recently, Entertainment Weekly magazine published the book The 100 Greatest TV Shows of All Time. It contains chapters called Top 10, Comedies, and Guilty Pleasures. Other chapters are Game Shows, Dramas, Talk/Variety, and Miniseries. Put together by the editors of the magazine, the book describes these TV shows and contains a short feature called Just the Facts. Of Seinfeld, the show that ranked second, the book claims The original idea was about a stand-up comedian and how everyday situations supply the material that ends up in the monologue. The animated show The Simpsons appears in the top twenty, and the book claims that it takes one hundred animators six months to produce one episode. Another show in the top twenty, 60 Minutes, has produced over $1 billion for CBS and has won over sixty Emmys in its twenty-plus years on the air. Star Trek, also in the top twenty, had a second pilot episode called Where No Man Has Gone Before. The book calls Saturday Night Live the best variety show ever, even though an early review by the New York Times claimed Quality is an ingredient conspicuously absent from the dreadfully uneven comedy efforts of the new series. Helen Mirren, who played Jane Tennison in PBS's Prime Suspect, one of the best dramas ever, learned from London detectives Never let them see you cry. Lonesome Dove, based on Larry McMurtry's book, is listed in the Miniseries chapter as one of the best ever.

Edit Your Own Writing for Problems with Quotation Marks and Italics

1. Look through your portfolio to find a paragraph or essay in which you have made errors in using quotation marks and/or italics. Or you may find something in your portfolio to which you can add direct quotations or italicized words to make it better. Resubmit your writing if your instructor asks you to.
2. In order to practice using quotation marks and italics correctly, write an imaginary dialog between two people who are discussing important events of the twentieth century. These could include works of art (books, plays, movies), news events (think about wars, disasters, inventions, accomplishments), and legal cases *(Brown v. Board of Education* or *Roe v. Wade)*. Include as many titles or phrases that need italics as possible. Proofread for correct use of quotation marks and italics.

Chapter 35

Other Punctuation

Marks of punctuation serve as important road signs for your reader, signaling when to stop, go, or pause and then continue. When you misuse punctuation, you may confuse your reader or send a message that isn't what you wanted to say. This chapter presents five commonly misused punctuation marks:

- colon :
- dash --
- hyphen -
- parentheses ( )
- brackets [ ]

You can identify and fix punctuation errors in your writing if you know the correct use of each punctuation mark.

The Colon :

A colon acts as a spotlight for something else in a sentence. Writers use a colon to introduce a list, an explanation, or a multisentence quotation. A complete sentence should come before the colon.

> These people have volunteered to plan the American Cancer Society's annual 10K road race: Susan Dziadek, Liu Tan, and Jacob Horner.
>
> My uncle Bradner had a single goal in life: to make a lot of money.
>
> The governor stated: "I am withdrawing from the senatorial race. My health comes first."

Notice that in each of the first two examples, you could replace the colon with a period, remove the list or explanation, and you would still have a grammatically correct sentence.

These people have volunteered to plan the American Cancer Society's annual 10K road race.

My uncle Bradner had a single goal in life.

If the words before the colon cannot stand on their own as a complete sentence, remove the colon—unless what follows the colon is a quotation.

EXAMPLE For dinner, we had/ lasagna, Italian bread, and salad. [*For dinner, we had* is a sentence fragment.]

The Dash --

Writers use dashes for emphasis or dramatic effect or to set off additional information. To set apart words or phrases appearing in the middle of sentences, writers use a pair of dashes—one at each end of those words or phrases. To type a dash, press the hyphen key (-) twice (--).

I left for the airport at 9:00 A.M. sharp--without my airline tickets.

The final project--worth 40 percent of your grade--is due on the first of May.

The talk-show host set an informal tone--the kind of tone that causes guests to relax and say too much.

Dashes can also be used to set off a long appositive phrase. (Appositives are words and phrases that rename nouns.) If the appositive phrase has commas within it, use a dash to show where the appositive begins and ends.

The branches of the United States military--the air force, the army, the navy, and the marines--work from a shared budget.

The Hyphen -

Use a hyphen to join words that act as a single description of a person, place, or thing.

Sugar-coated cereals are popular among children and teens.

Her boss handed her a top-priority project at 3:00 on Friday afternoon.

If the description follows the person, place, or thing, do not use a hyphen.

Children and teens prefer cereals that are sugar coated.

Her boss said the project was top priority.

Also use a hyphen to divide a word at the end of a line when part of the word must go on the next line. Divide the word between syllables. Check a dictionary if you are unsure of where to break a word.

Migraine headaches are often triggered by caffeine, chocolate, or fatigue.

Parentheses ( )

Writers place parentheses around words and phrases that are not essential to the meaning of a sentence but that are helpful. Parentheses are often used for interruptions, examples, and explanations. Parentheses are always used in pairs.

INTERRUPTION My English teacher (by far the best teacher I've had at this school) showed us how to use a new writing-process software program today.

EXAMPLE I told him that there were lots of reasons (his cheating on me, for example) I was breaking up with him.

EXPLANATION "Twiggy" Lawson (born Lesley Hornby) was the ultimate ultrathin supermodel of the 1960's.

Parentheses can also be used to present a numbered list within your sentence.

This report will (1) explain our technology problems at the St. Louis facility, (2) propose a plan for solving these problems, and (3) present a budget for this plan.

Unless the punctuation is part of the material in parentheses, place commas and periods outside of parentheses.

After you make the orange glaze (see page 158), begin rolling out your pastry dough.

For more specific comments about the visit to the new factory site, please see my trip summary (attached to this memo).

Brackets [ ]

Writers sometimes need a way to include editorial comments, corrections, or clarifications within someone else's word-for-word statement. Use brackets to enclose words that you have added to or changed in a direct quotation.

"This is a significant change for [the London Stock Exchange]," Chairman John Kemp-Welch said in a recent interview.

The original text reads, "This is a significant change for us." The writer has, for the reader's sake, clarified who the *us* is by enclosing her own language in brackets.

Summary

1. A **colon** acts as a spotlight for something else in a sentence. Use a colon to introduce a list, an explanation, or a multisentence quotation. (See p. 411.)

2. Use a **dash** for emphasis or dramatic effect or to set off additional information. (See p. 412.)
3. Use a **hyphen** to join words that act as a single description of a person, place, or thing or to divide a word at the end of a line of text. (See p. 412.)
4. Place **parentheses** around words and phrases that are not necessary to the meaning of a sentence but that are helpful. Parentheses are often used for interruptions, examples, and explanations. (See p. 413.)
5. Use **brackets** to enclose words that you have added to or changed in a direct quotation. (See p. 413.)

Editing Activities

Identify and Correct Punctuation Errors

Practice 35-A (Answers appear on p. 485.)

Edit each of the following sentences, inserting a colon where needed. If a sentence is already correct, write "correct" next to it.

EXAMPLE Many Americans' favorite dishes are classic Mexican foods: burritos, tacos, and enchiladas.

1. Several college courses are considered difficult by most students physics, calculus, and statistics.
2. Others, however, find courses such as philosophy, psychology, and literature difficult.
3. Taking language courses challenges many students for one basic reason their listening skills need improvement.
4. Writing gives students difficulty in several areas sentence structure, poor mechanics, and shallow topics.
5. Many students in college take skills-boosting courses such as Basic Writing and Developmental Math.
6. Many majors can require five years to complete education, business, or science.
7. Some students take courses for one reason to get a good job.
8. They see their college careers as training for a job in computers, in business, or in education.
9. A college education, however, should mean more than job training it should prepare students for life.
10. The best students are those who become lifelong learners, who have positive attitudes about all subjects, and who learn to manage time effectively.

Practice 35-B (Answers appear on p. 485.)

Edit each of the following sentences, adding punctuation (a colon, dash, hyphen, or pair of parentheses) where necessary.

EXAMPLE Sarah attended one of the top-notch schools in the East for a semester.

1. Are kids today especially kids of baby-boomer parents spoiled by having too many possessions?
2. Do today's children expect to have the best of everything and this includes toys, clothes, computers, and cars even when their parents cannot afford it?
3. Many blame television for giving kids the I want it all attitude.
4. Writer Martha Fay her article "Sedated by Stuff" appeared in the magazine *Civilization* in 1999 says that kids learn early that stuff equals acceptance.
5. Fay claims that it's easier for parents to say yes than to say no they really do not want to disappoint their children.
6. She says that in her case and in the case of many others certainly "going overboard" has to do with trying to make up for not spending enough time with her kids.
7. Fay claims that our culture has no agreed upon value except money.
8. Psychiatrist Annie Boland says that we are a consumer society buying things is one of our highest priorities.
9. The parents of these baby-boomer parents grew up in the Great Depression the time in American history when we were the poorest as a nation.
10. Many think the current consumerism and spoiling of our children is a natural progression from hard fought battles against poverty.

Practice 35-C

Edit the following paragraph, in which the various marks of punctuation discussed in this chapter are used incorrectly. In each case, supply the correct punctuation.

The professor: student relationship can be one of the most important relationships in a person's life. Students who make it a point to get to know their professors reap important benefits-they gain a mentor, for example. Mentors: named after the Greek who advised Telemachus in *The Odyssey:* can teach more outside the class than in. Mentors help students in many ways by teaching from experience, by teaching one on one, and by teaching through trust. When a mentor relationship develops, both people (professor and student) benefit. The student benefits by learning more than classroom based knowledge. The professor benefits by passing on experience: by feeling needed and appreciated. Mitch Albom, in his book *Tuesdays with Morrie,* recounts his relationship with his former professor mentor. Professor Morrie Schwartz died from ALS: Lou Gehrig's disease: but not before he passed on his life lessons to Mitch. Through Morrie, Mitch learned important lessons about many subjects–love, marriage, and death. Mitch learned that a good mentor-and we all need one—is one of life's more significant relationships.

Edit Your Own Writing for Punctuation Errors

1. Look through your portfolio to find a paragraph or essay in which you have made mistakes with such punctuation as the colon, the dash, the hyphen, parentheses, or brackets. Or, find some writing that could be improved by editing with the use of these punctuation marks. Submit to your instructor as directed.
2. Write a detailed paragraph about someone in your life who has served as a kind of mentor. Edit your paragraph by combining or adding sentences that use the dash, the colon, parentheses, or brackets. Also, use at least one hyphenated word. Proofread your paper to see whether you have used each of these punctuation marks correctly.

Chapter 36

Capitalization and Abbreviation

Writers sometimes have difficulty determining when and what to capitalize and how to abbreviate words. This chapter will give you some guidance about

- using capital letters;
- using standard abbreviations.

Using Capital Letters

When you speak, you don't have to worry about remembering capitalization rules. When you write, however, you must capitalize

1. the first letter of the first word in every new sentence,
2. names of specific people, places, things, and dates, and
3. certain words in titles.

Capitalize the First Word in a Sentence

Capitalize the first letter of the first word in a new sentence. You must also capitalize the first letter in the first word of a direct quotation, even if the quotation does not begin the sentence.

> **M**y sister recently asked, "**A**re you planning to have more children?"

Capitalize Names of Specific People, Places, Things, and Dates

Remember that while general words and categories are not capitalized, specific (also called "proper") words and categories are. For example, in the sentence *My Uncle Otto was a violinist,* the word *uncle* is capitalized because it is the proper name of a specific person. In the sentence *My uncle was a violinist,* the word *uncle* is not capitalized.

People

Capitalize names of specific people and their titles.

Specific	General
Governor Christine Todd Whitman	the governor
Professor Ingrid Schreck	our professor
Dr. Normand Tanguay	my doctor
Kristin Abruzzese	my neighbor

For family relationships and other titles, capitalize the word only if you could substitute a proper name for it.

I set the table because Mother asked me to. = Jane asked me to.

I set the table because my mother asked me to. ≠ my Jane asked me to.

Places

Capitalize the names of specific countries, regions, states, cities, towns, streets, and buildings. You should also capitalize specific geographical areas.

Specific	General
Mexico	that country
Santa Clara, California	my hometown
the West	the western part of the country
the Bronx	our neighborhood
the Sears Tower	the tower
Cuesta Verde Boulevard	this street
the Pacific Ocean	the ocean
Badlands National Park	a national park

Names that come from the names of countries are generally capitalized. The names and languages of groups of people indicating their continents, races, religions, and tribes are also capitalized. Classifications based on color, however, are usually—but not as a rule—written in lowercase.

Yoshiko is Japanese but speaks fluent French.

He was raised in Montreal and considers himself Canadian.

Nimmi's parents are Hindus, but she is a Muslim.

Lauryn does not see herself as black or white.

Things

Capitalize the names of specific government agencies, companies, groups, and products. Also capitalize the names of specific schools, courses, historical events, and ships or spacecraft.

Specific	General
the National Transportation Safety Board	the agency
Procter & Gamble	our company
the League of Women Voters	the group

Pampers	diapers
Introductory Algebra	my algebra class
Kennedy Memorial High School	our high school
the Persian Gulf War	this war
the *Titanic*	the ship

Dates

Capitalize the names of days, months, holidays. The names of seasons are generally presented in lowercase.

Specific	General
Friday	yesterday
February	next month
Valentine's Day	our anniversary
May 1	spring

Capitalize Certain Words in Titles

Capitalize all of the important words in titles of documents, books, periodicals, newspapers, articles, movies, television programs, and so on. You should not capitalize *the, a, an,* or prepositions (such as *at, by, to, on*) unless they are the first word in the title.

Journalists, clergymen, and merchants protested the Stamp Act.

Tina highly recommended *Twenty Thousand Leagues under the Sea.*

Salon is a great online magazine.

Have you read her essay "A Day in the Life of an E.R. Nurse"?

Abbreviations

The English language contains many abbreviations—shortened forms of titles, common words and phrases, Latin words, and date and time references.

Titles

Use standard abbreviations for titles used before and after proper names.

Ms. Norma Rogan	John F. Kennedy, Jr.
Mr. Chet Skidmore	Melody Graulich, Ph.D.
Dr. Carolyn Sedor	Sanjiv Singh, M.D.
Rev. Jesse Jackson	Carmela Ramírez, C.E.O.
Prof. Nikola Rozik	

Familiar Abbreviations

Abbreviations of word groups most often are made up of the first letters of the words in the group or phrase. Frequently used and familiar multiword abbreviations appear in all capital letters and without periods. Multiword abbreviations that are pronounced as words—for example, AIDS or NASA—are called *acronyms.*

AIDS (Acquired Immune Deficiency Syndrome)
CD (Compact Disc *or* Certificate of Deposit)
CIA (Central Intelligence Agency)
ESL (English as a Second Language)
NASA (National Aeronautic and Space Administration)
NBA (National Basketball Association)
PBS (Public Broadcasting System)
PC (personal computer)
RSVP (*Réspondez s'il vous plaît, or* Please respond)
YMCA (Young Men's Christian Association)

If you use an unfamiliar abbreviation in your writing, write out the full name followed by the abbreviation in parentheses the first time you include it. After that, you may use only the abbreviation throughout the rest of your paper.

Advances in digital signal processor (DSP) technology have improved wireless communications. The annual DSP Design Conference is being held in San Jose this year.

Common Latin Abbreviations

Some Latin words and phrases are often abbreviated in text.

ca. *(circa,* meaning *about, approximately)*
e.g. *(exempli gratia,* meaning *for example)*
etc. *(et cetera,* meaning *and so forth)*
P.S. *(post scriptum,* meaning *postscript)*

Dates and Times

400 B.C. *(before Christ)* or 400 B.C.E. *(before the common era)*
A.D. 1066 *(anno Domini,* meaning *in the year of our Lord)* or 1066 C.E. *(the common era)*
8:30 A.M. or 8:30 a.m. *(ante meridiem,* meaning *before noon)*
6:00 P.M. or 6:00 p.m. *(post meridiem,* meaning *after noon)*

Summary

1. **Capitalize** the first letter of the first word in every new sentence (see p. 417); names of specific people, places, things, and dates (see p. 417); and certain words in titles (see p. 419).
2. Use standard **abbreviations** for titles, common words and phrases, Latin words, and date and time references. (See p. 419.)

Editing Activities

Identify and Correct Problems with Capitalization and Abbreviations

Practice 36-A (Answers appear on p. 485.)
Edit each of the following sentences, capitalizing where necessary.

EXAMPLE When we look back on the twentieth century, we will remember important events such as the ~~great depression~~ Great Depression, the ~~holocaust~~ Holocaust, and the ~~aids~~ AIDS epidemic.

1. Though many people are aware of the holocaust, few are aware that nearly 1.5 million armenians were slaughtered by the turks in the early part of the twentieth century.
2. Important people, such as rev. martin luther king jr., mahatma gandhi, and nelson mandela, changed the course of history.
3. World war I and world war II, the boer war, and the vietnam war were all important conflicts that changed world maps.
4. In fact, many new countries were born in the last century: zimbabwe, the people's republic of china, and the czech republic.
5. Important companies like ford motor company, microsoft, and sega made millions as they changed transportation, technology, and entertainment.
6. Symbols of twentieth-century progress include the empire state building, the channel tunnel that links england and france, and the *apollo* moon landings.
7. The warsaw treaty, the suez canal, and china's cultural revolution all made an impact on the century.
8. Disasters, like the sinking of the *titanic,* the burning of the *hindenburg,* and the oklahoma city bombing will be well remembered into the twenty-first century.
9. Sports figures like jim thorpe, nadia comaneci, and michael jordan helped to make the century memorable.
10. The wright brothers' flight at kitty hawk, the soviet union's *sputnik,* and *soyuz*'s orbiting of the earth all marked tremendous advancements for flight in the twentieth century.

Practice 36-B (Answers appear on p. 486.)
Each of the following sentences contains at least one word or phrase that should be abbreviated. Edit the sentences, substituting the abbreviation.

EXAMPLE ~~Doctor~~ Dr. Getherall is my advisor this year.

1. Gregg Jonas, Junior, spoke at our student-organized conference this past weekend on current issues.
2. He said that the National Association for the Advancement of Colored People continues to gain strength as a voice for equality and fairness.
3. Another speaker was Dolores Lopez of the Federal Bureau of Investigation, formerly of the Internal Revenue Service.

4. Her topic was white collar crime in the age of personal computers and facsimile machines.
5. A man from the audience, Jesse Okampa, Certified Public Accountant, agreed with Agent Lopez.
6. The ante meridiem sessions were held in the university auditorium.
7. For the sessions after lunch we met in the distance learning classroom and watched a Video Cassette Recorder tape of a presentation.
8. Sergeant Sherry Bates of the United States Army addressed us about world matters.
9. She explained that the European Union must work at better cooperation among member states, especially between the United Kingdom and France.
10. As an expert on the former Union of Soviet Socialist Republics, she helped us to understand those countries' current economic challenges.

Practice 36-C

Edit the following paragraph, capitalizing where necessary and using appropriate abbreviations.

My family is a busy group of people who live in springtown, texas. My cousin, doctor jerry stabler, junior, works as a computer science professor at west plains university. He has developed new programs for using electronic mail and has worked for netscape on their browser technology. My aunt, who is a registered nurse, volunteers at the local young men's christian association as a health consultant. She also collects money for the red cross and the american cancer society. My uncle, a retired business executive for international business machines, now consults for the international monetary fund. My father edits books for purepress incorporated in neighboring edgeport. My mother, a science teacher at grove high school, researches the effects of acquired immune deficiency syndrome on young children. Lastly, my sister volunteers for Mothers Against Drunk Driving and works at the Atlantic & Pacific grocery store in town.

Edit Your Own Writing for Capitalization and Abbreviation Errors

1. Search through your portfolio for a paragraph or essay in which you might have misused capital letters or abbreviations. Edit your work, correcting your mistakes. Submit your revisions to your instructor as directed.
2. Write a detailed paragraph in which you describe people and places that have been meaningful to you in some way. Think of relatives, teachers, and coaches. Remember vacation spots, places you have lived, or places you have visited. After you complete your paragraph, edit it carefully for capitalization and (if you used any) abbreviations.

Part Seven

Editing Sentences for Word Use

Diagnostic Test for Part Seven: Editing Sentences for Word Use

Use this test to check your word-use skills. Answers appear on page 486.

A. In each of the following sentences, identify any clichés or slang.

1. Last week I got a letter from my grandmother, who is one in a million.
2. She was writing from the depths of despair because of her old man's health.
3. My step-grandfather and I have yet to bury the hatchet, but I know that she will love him to the bitter end.
4. In this day and age, it's rare that a couple stays together through thick and thin.
5. To make a long story short, she is bummed at the thought of being alone.
6. I hope that we can all breathe a sigh of relief when doctors find out what's up with his heart.

B. The following italicized phrases are too wordy. Rewrite the sentences, cutting down on the wordiness by substituting a more concise word or phrase.

7. We read an article in the paper *on the subject of* the short supply of special education teachers.
8. *Due to the fact that* many programs require more than four years' training, special education is a hard field to staff adequately.
9. Some universities and school districts are now being creative *with regard to* preparing teachers for special education.
10. They are creating training programs *for the purpose of* retraining classroom teachers for the responsibilities of special education.

C. Combine each of the following pairs of sentences to avoid choppiness.

11. Jane is my roommate. She is majoring in criminal justice.
12. She wants to work as a prison official. She wants to organize daily activities for the inmates.

13. Her father was a police officer. He was commended on several occasions for meritorious behavior.
14. She is a very determined person. She knows that she can make a difference in the world.

D. Correct each misspelled word that follows, without consulting a dictionary or computer. If a word is spelled correctly, leave it alone.

15. decieve
16. relys
17. submiting
18. loveable
19. calendar
20. irresistable
21. embarrased
22. conscience

E. Fill in the blank with the correct word.

23. We were _____ to go when the trip got cancelled. (all ready, already)
24. Take my _____; don't ever start smoking. (advise, advice)
25. With proper early intervention, we will have _____ cases of sexually transmitted disease. (less, fewer)
26. My cousin is older _____ I by six months. (then, than)
27. Her mother is the one _____ career takes her to Europe once a month. (whose, who's)

F. Identify any sexist language in the following sentences.

28. Please contact your congressman about the e-mail legislation.
29. A male nurse admitted her when she arrived at the emergency room.
30. I bought the shoes although they were made of man-made materials.

Chapter 37

Word Choice

When you revise your writing, carefully examine your choice of words. Choose words that are precise and appropriate for your purpose. To be clearly understood by your audience, you should avoid using the following:

- slang;
- clichés;
- wordy language;
- vague language.

Avoid Slang

To be clear, writers have to use language that their audience understands. **Slang**—the informal words and phrases that you use mostly when you are talking with your friends—is inappropriate in college writing.

To eliminate slang from your writing, the first step is to identify the word or phrase you have used as slang. If you are unsure, look in a current dictionary. Once you have identified a word or phrase in your writing as slang, replace it with a word or phrase that would be understandable to a larger audience.

EXAMPLE The opposing players ~~talked trash to~~ *harassed* each other.

EXAMPLE The boss was ~~uptight~~ *nervous* until we ~~nabbed one~~ *made a sale*. Then he started to ~~chill.~~ *relax.*

EXAMPLE My friend is ~~bummed out~~ *depressed* because he ~~has issues.~~ *feels guilty about cheating on his girlfriend.*

Avoid Clichés

Effective writers choose words that are clear and fresh to express their ideas. They avoid using **clichés,** which are recurring phrases in speaking and writing that have become stale and predictable from overuse.

To make your writing clear and lively, you need to eliminate clichés whenever possible. You have two options:

1. Replace clichés with clearer and fresher word choices.
2. Eliminate the clichés and rewrite the sentence for clarity and specificity.

EXAMPLE

In 1998, 81 million *were sold.*
~~At the present time,~~ rap and hip-hop CDs ~~are selling like hotcakes. Going~~
Sounding unlike any other kind of music,
~~against the tide in the music industry, the~~ rap and hip-hop music has ~~climbed the~~
gained a wider audience, *Regardless of rap's success,*
~~ladder of success,~~ leaving country and rock music in its wake. ~~Be that as it may,~~
to further broaden their appeal
many music critics argue that rap musicians still have ~~a hard row to hoe~~ before they will be taken seriously.

Avoid Wordy Language

Effective writing is concise—that is, it uses the fewest words possible to express its meaning. Good writers aim for economy when they are drafting and revising their paragraphs and essays. They realize that readers become impatient with writing that is filled with repetitious, empty language, which takes up their time and is often unclear.

To make your writing more concise:

1. Eliminate repetition.
2. Weed out wordy phrases.
3. Avoid *it is, there is,* and *there are* constructions.

Eliminate Repetition

Most people agree that writers should not say the same thing twice, but sometimes the words that they choose do just that. Reduce repetitive phrases by eliminating extra words.

Repetitious phrase	Edited
red in color	red
the period of one year	one year
small in stature	small
join together	join
exact same	same
past history	history

Weed Out Wordy Phrases

Some writers mistakenly assume that using more words is more effective. Eliminate or reduce wordy phrases so that the meaning of your sentences is clearer.

Wordy phrase	Edited
despite the fact that	despite
in my opinion	(omit this phrase)
in the event that	if
for the purpose of	for (*or* use *to* form of verb)
make contact with	contact
is able to	can
people of Cambodian descent	Cambodians
one and the same	the same

Avoid *It is, There is,* and *There are* Constructions

Sentences beginning with *it is, there is,* and *there are* are often longer than they need to be. Delete these phrases from your writing. As you rewrite the sentences, emphasize the most important words.

EXAMPLE ~~It is difficult to choose~~ between studying and watching TV~~.~~ [inserted: *Choosing* … *is difficult*]

EXAMPLE ~~There is a bicycle~~ I would like to own~~.~~ [inserted: *that bicycle*]

EXAMPLE ~~There are many~~ people ~~who~~ disagree with me. [inserted: *Many*]

Avoid Vague Language

When your instructor writes the word *vague* on your paper, it means that you have chosen words that are too general when more specific information is required. To avoid vague language in your writing, you should:

1. Be able to recognize the difference between general terms and specific terms.
2. Rewrite a sentence using specific language.

General terms are words and phrases that express broad categories of people, objects, and actions. Specific terms, on the other hand, describe individual people, objects, and actions. The rule of thumb for good writing is to always try to be specific in your writing.

EXAMPLE Machines cannot do the job people can.

EDITED Computers cannot grade essays the way instructors can.

EXAMPLE He needs good computer skills for his job.

EDITED He needs Internet search skills for his job as a marketing assistant.

EXAMPLE That television show is bad.

EDITED The *Jerry Springer Show* offers poor role models for young adults.

Summary

1. When you write, choose words that are precise and appropriate for your purpose. To be clearly understood by your audience, avoid using slang, clichés, wordy language, or vague language. (See pp. 427–28.)
2. **Slang** is the informal words and phrases that you use mostly when you are talking with your friends. Think about your audience as you revise. (See p. 427.)
3. **Clichés** are recurring phrases in speaking and writing that have become stale and predictable from overuse. Revise your writing using words and phrases that are original and precise. (See p. 427.)
4. **Wordy language** is tiresome to readers, who often want to get to the point of your writing quickly. Revise your writing to eliminate repetition (see p. 428), weed out wordy phrases (see p. 428), and eliminate *it is, there is, there are* constructions. (See p. 429.)
5. Choosing specific terms, facts, and details over general ones is the best way to avoid **vague language.** (See p. 429.)

Editing Activities

Practice Choosing Words Carefully

Practice 37-A (Answers appear on p. 486.)

Edit each of the following sentences, removing slang (language specific to a small group) and clichés (overused language). Rewrite the sentences, substituting words or phrases for the slang or clichés. You may have to add information to make your meaning clear.

EXAMPLE

girlfriend ended our relationship

My last ~~girl gave me the slip~~ because I couldn't dance.

1. Here at the turn of the century swing dancing has become the cream of the crop in dancing for some people.
2. A club in Manhattan, for example, offers nearly forty different classes on a new tight trend—dances from the 1930s and the 1940s.
3. A 1998 commercial for khaki pants is partially credited with swing's resurgence, making many hot to trot to learn the new craze.
4. Certain movies and new retro rock bands, like the Brian Setzer Orchestra, have also introduced people to this sweet craze.
5. Although some people think swing dancing is a piece of cake, instructors explain that even though "flying" is way cool, learning the basics is first and foremost the way to go.
6. Needless to say, swing dance instructors in larger cities like New York and Boston are sitting pretty these days, helping swing wanna-bes learn moves like the East Coast Swing.

7. Another, more challenging, dance is the Lindy Hop, a cool dance first practiced by Harlem African Americans.
8. Famous swing artists of the 1930s, such as Jimmie Lunceford, Chick Webb, and Benny Goodman, made audiences want to shake a leg.
9. Interestingly, at that point those in the know warned against this hip new dancing because of its "dangerously hypnotic influence."
10. Modern swingers are drawn, like, to the same rocking rhythms and just good clean fun that this kicky dancing provides.

Practice 37-B (Answers appear on p. 487.)

In each of the following sentences, wordy or vague phrases are underlined. Edit each sentence by eliminating the wordy or vague phrase and making the sentence more concise, clear, and exact. You may have to add words (to make a sentence more specific) as well as remove words. You may also find that you have to invent some information.

EXAMPLE *Thirty-eight million* ~~Lots of~~ people living in the United States were born in another country.

1. In today's current society there are people of just about every nationality living in the United States.
2. From the original beginning of this country's founding throughout its entire history, immigrants have come here for the purpose of making a new life.
3. It is possible that your family was originally from Asia, Europe, or South America, or that they may be of African descent.
4. Unless you are of the Native American race, your ancestors who came before you were from another home country.
5. As it turns out, this great country of ours is made up of a vast and large number of uniquely different ethnicities.
6. Immigrants have a tendency to join together in cities in the event that good jobs become available to them and in order to meet others of their same culture.
7. Due to the fact that many new residents of the United States have trouble with English, good jobs are often unavailable and they find themselves in a bad situation.
8. Often immigrants from other countries find themselves doing jobs that many others do not want.
9. There are other challenges and frustrations for new immigrants, such as finding acceptance and fitting in with the established population who already lives in the United States.
10. It is sometimes frustrating for recent immigrants to overcome many people's racial intolerance and their fear of change and new things.

Practice 37-C

Edit the following paragraph for word choice, making your new paragraph more concise, specific, and clear. Each sentence contains at least one of the problems discussed in this chapter—slang, clichés, wordiness, and vague language. You may have to invent details as you revise.

There is something interesting about England's Sarah Ferguson, the Duchess of York. This carrot-top celeb has captivated the imaginations of both the British and the American public at large. Despite the fact that she has split from Prince Andrew, Queen Elizabeth's son, she is still viewed as royalty. It is weird how the public can't get enough of the facts of her life. She hit all the papers in the early 90s when a tabloid caught her sucking face with her financial advisor. The press also has dogged her about her weight continually without letting up. They have bad-mouthed her for not fitting in to the royal mold. Sarah herself admits that she has screwed up on a lot of occasions by spending and eating out of control. Her goal now is to get back on her feet due to the fact that she wants her two daughters to have a good life. She is now the mouthpiece for Weight Watchers and the host of her own talk show. Her new life has helped her to wipe out two kinds of pounds: extreme debt and excess weight.

Edit Your Own Writing for Poor Word Choice

1. Look through your portfolio for a paragraph or essay that you have already completed, or use a draft that you are currently working on. Where could your writing be more exact? Less wordy? Clearer to your audience? Revise and resubmit as your instructor directs.
2. Write a paragraph about your own family's history. How did they originally come to this country? You may want to interview a parent or older relative. If you cannot find out information about your early history, you may write about your more recent family history. How long has your family lived in your town? What are some facts you know about the history of your parents and grandparents? Proofread your paragraph for slang, clichés, wordy language, or vague language.

Chapter 38

Sentence Variety

Readers are quickly bored by strings of short, choppy sentences. Creating sentence variety in your writing means writing sentences of different patterns and lengths. To make your sentences more varied and interesting, try to

- combine ideas using appositives;
- combine ideas using adjective clauses;
- combine ideas using an *-ing* or *-ed* verb form.

Combine Ideas Using an Appositive

An **appositive** is a word or phrase that renames a noun that comes before it.

Noun — Appositive

At the movies, we ran into Felicity, my former roommate.

The appositive phrase *my former roommate* renames the noun *Felicity.*

You can use an appositive to combine two simple sentences into a single, more developed sentence. Use commas to set off the appositive from the rest of the sentence.

EXAMPLE Travis sent Dr. Shin [, his business professor,] an e-mail message. ~~Dr. Shin is his business professor.~~

EXAMPLE Antibiotics[,] ~~were~~ the wonder drugs of the 1950s[,] ~~. Antibiotics~~ are becoming less effective against some bacteria.

Combine Ideas Using an Adjective Clause

An **adjective clause** is a group of words that modifies (describes or gives more information about) the noun or pronoun it follows. Adjective clauses are generally introduced by the words *who, whom, which,* and *that* (and, less frequently, *where* and *when*).

Noun — Adjective clause

The Internet, which was originally created for government purposes, is now an essential business tool.

Noun — Adjective clause

All my relatives who live in Indiana came to the wedding.

You can use an adjective clause to combine two simple sentences into a single, more developed sentence. Be sure to punctuate adjective clauses correctly, though. If the adjective clause can be taken out of the sentence without changing the meaning, it is said to be nonessential and requires commas. The first example above includes a nonessential adjective clause. If the adjective clause adds information that is essential to the meaning of the sentence, no commas are needed. The second example above includes an essential adjective clause.

The following are examples of sentences combined using adjective clauses.

EXAMPLE Jody purchased a book from a Web site ~~.~~ *that* ~~The Web site~~ has become famous for its fast service.

EXAMPLE Claire Vizquel *, whom I know from college,* was recently named head nurse at the hospital. ~~I know Claire Vizquel from college.~~

Combine Ideas Using an *-ing* or *-ed* Verb Form

Another way that you can vary your sentences is by using *-ing* and *-ed* verbs as modifiers. As the following sentences demonstrate, these verbs can work by themselves or with other words in a phrase to modify nouns and pronouns.

-ed verb — Noun

Startled, Mrs. Griffin let out a shriek.

-ing verb — Pronoun

Checking the mortgage rates daily, he finally locked in at a low interest rate.

You can vary the structures of your sentences by adding *-ing* and *-ed* verbs as modifiers. Use commas with *-ing* or *-ed* verbs and their accompanying words when they introduce sentences or act as nonessential modifiers (see above for a definition of *nonessential modifier*). If you revise your sentence to include an opening modifier, make sure that the noun or pronoun it modifies comes right after the *-ing* or *-ed* word or phrase.

EXAMPLE *Imagining herself as a single working parent, she*
~~She~~ tried to understand my point of view. ~~She imagined herself as a single working parent.~~

EXAMPLE *Started by Isabel Jones in 1976, the*
~~The~~ Bayside Theater Group recently celebrated its twenty-fifth anniversary. ~~The Bayside Theatre Group was started by Isabel Jones in 1976.~~

Summary

1. Creating **sentence variety** in your writing means writing sentences of different patterns and lengths. Writers can create variety and interest by combining some short sentences to make longer ones. (See p. 433.)
2. Writers can combine ideas using an **appositive,** a word or phrase that renames a noun that comes before it. Use commas to set off the appositive from the rest of the sentence. (See p. 433.)
3. Writers can also combine ideas using an **adjective clause,** a group of words that modifies (describes or gives more information about) the noun or pronoun it follows. Adjective clauses are introduced by words such as *who, whom, which,* and *that.* (See p. 433.)
4. Adjective clauses that are **nonessential**—that is, not necessary—to the meaning of a sentence should be set off from the sentence with commas. **Essential** adjective clauses do not require commas. (See p. 434.)
5. Writers can combine ideas using ***-ing* and *-ed* verbs** as modifiers. These verbs can work by themselves or with other words in a phrase to modify nouns and pronouns. (See p. 434.)

Editing Activities

Practice Creating Sentence Variety

Practice 38-A (Answers appear on p. 487.)

Combine each of the following pairs of sentences into one sentence that uses an appositive or an adjective clause. Be sure to check your use of commas. More than one revision is possible for each pair.

EXAMPLE ~~Many parents are aware of increased social pressure.~~
who are aware of increased social pressure
Many parents wonder if they have passed on a sense of right and wrong to their teenagers.

1. Leslie Lambert wrote an article for the *Ladies' Home Journal* in February 1999.
Leslie Lambert asks the question, "Should you spy on your teen?"
2. The article is written from a parent's point of view.
The article looks at both sides of the question.

3. Lambert begins the article by admitting that she had read part of her daughter's diary.
   The diary had been left open on her daughter's desk.
4. Lambert read only a little of the diary.
   Lambert began to feel ashamed for not respecting her daughter's privacy.
5. The article makes the point that today's teens are exposed to a great deal of sex, drugs, drinking, and smoking.
   Today's teens grow up faster in many ways than teens of earlier generations.
6. David Elkind, Ph.D., is the author of a book about teenagers in crisis.
   David Elkind claims that parents may have to protect their teens.
7. He says that teens have to demonstrate responsibility.
   Teens do not have an absolute right to privacy.
8. Carol Friedland, Ph.D., believes in the need for more communication.
   Carol Friedland says that teenagers normally need time to themselves in a private space.
9. The article provides many examples of caring parents.
   These parents have spied on their teens to find drugs, have confronted the problem, and have helped the teens straighten out their lives.
10. Roger McIntire, Ph.D., warns that parents should not make a habit of spying on their teens or they risk ruining the relationship they have with them.
    Roger McIntire has written a book called *Teenagers and Parents: Ten Steps for a Better Relationship.*

Practice 38-B (Answers appear on p. 487.)

Combine each of the following pairs of sentences into one sentence by using an *-ing* or *-ed* verb as a modifier. More than one revision is possible for each pair.

EXAMPLE

~~Many legendary sports heroes are admired by millions of people.~~
Admired by millions of people, many
^~~Many~~ legendary sports heroes have trouble maintaining their privacy.

1. Joe DiMaggio became an American hero.
   He gained fame as a baseball player for the New York Yankees.
2. DiMaggio appeared at a time when Americans needed role models.
   He was the All-American sports hero who played all aspects of the game well.
3. Joe DiMaggio preferred secrecy and privacy.
   He was a loner who hated crowds.
4. In 1954 he thrust himself into the media limelight.
   He married Marilyn Monroe.
5. They divorced the same year they married.
   DiMaggio and Monroe remained close friends until her death in 1962.
6. Simon and Garfunkel immortalized him in the song "Mrs. Robinson" in 1969.
   They asked, "Where have you gone, Joe DiMaggio?"

7. They sang, "Our nation turns its lonely eyes to you."
   They turned a man into a myth.
8. DiMaggio was voted the "Greatest Living Player" also in 1969.
   "DiMaggio set the standard for the game when the game was the standard for the nation," as one writer has claimed.
9. In the 1970s and 1980s, Joe DiMaggio appeared in TV commercials.
   Joe DiMaggio sold Mr. Coffee coffeemakers.
10. DiMaggio died in February 1999 of lung cancer.
    DiMaggio left behind a legend that will not soon be forgotten.

Practice 38-C

Edit the following paragraph for sentence variety by combining sentences wherever appropriate. (Not all sentences need combining, though.) Use at least one appositive, one adjective clause, one *-ing* verb form, and one *-ed* verb form.

> Women's health has been ignored, some critics claim, for too long. Women's health is an important issue. *Newsweek* magazine devoted an entire issue to women's health in 1999. *Newsweek* believed that many remarkable breakthroughs in medical research made this a timely subject. Many health problems still plague women. The health problems include breast cancer, other cancers, and heart disease. Eating disorders are ten times more likely to affect women than men. Anorexia and bulimia are two examples of eating disorders. Good health for life, therefore, starts when one is young. Good health includes eating right and exercising. Physically active girls are less likely to abuse alcohol, tobacco, or sex, according to research. Peter Nathanielsz is a fetal physiologist. He claims that diseases like diabetes, obesity, and heart disease are programmed before a baby is born. Healthy mothers produce healthy babies. Healthy mothers avoid alcohol, do not smoke, and eat nutritiously. The more women understand their own health issues, the more they can make good decisions for their children.

Edit Your Own Writing for Sentence Variety

1. Choose a paragraph or essay from your portfolio, or use the piece you are currently working on. Look through it carefully to see where you might improve your sentence variety by using appositives, adjective clauses, and *-ing* or *-ed* verbs as modifiers. Your goal is to make your sentences more interesting and enjoyable to your readers.
2. Take a position on the subject of parents spying on teens. Write a detailed paragraph that states and supports your opinion. Pay close attention to your sentence structure by giving your sentences variety as in the exercises above. You may find it easier to write out your thoughts first in a rough draft and then to go back and revise for sentence variety.

Chapter 39

Spelling

A misspelled word in a paragraph or essay can distract a reader from your point and give that reader the impression that you are careless. If you are a poor speller, you can take steps to improve your spelling:

- learn basic spelling rules;
- recognize troublesome words;
- create a personal spelling list;
- recognize the limitations of electronic spellcheckers;
- consult a dictionary regularly.

Learn Basic Spelling Rules

Remembering these four basic spelling rules will help you to correct errors in your writing.

ie and *ei*

Generally, *i* comes before *e* except after *c*, or when the sound is like *a* as in *neighbor* or *weigh.*

i before *e*	bel**ie**ve	rel**ie**f
except after *c*	re**cei**ve	de**cei**ve
sounds like *a*	sl**ei**gh	r**ei**gn

Some exceptions: either, neither, leisure, weird, height, foreign.

Change *y* to *i*

When a word ends in a consonant and *y*, change *y* to *i* before you add an ending.

cry + ed	=	cried
rely + s	=	relies
happy + ness	=	happiness
carry + er	=	carrier

Exception: When adding *-ing* to a word that ends in *y*, do not change *y* to *i*.

When a word ends in a vowel and *y*, do not change the *y* to *i* before you add an ending.

monk**ey** + **s**	=	monkeys
destr**oy** + **er**	=	destroyer

Final Silent *e*

Drop the final silent *e* before adding an ending that begins with a vowel (these letters are vowels: *a*, *e*, *i*, *o*, and *u*).

car**e** + **i**ng	=	caring
fam**e** + **o**us	=	famous
lov**e** + **a**ble	=	lovable
circulat**e** + **i**on	=	circulation

Keep the final silent *e* before adding an ending that begins with a consonant.

us**e** + **f**ul	=	useful
confin**e** + **m**ent	=	confinement

Some exceptions: judgment, truly, argument, awful.

Double the Final Consonant

Double the final consonant of words before adding an ending if *all* of the following are true:

- The word is one syllable or is accented on the final syllable.
- The word ends in a single consonant preceded by a single vowel.
- The ending you are adding begins with a vowel.

stop + ed	=	sto**pp**ed
slip + er	=	sli**pp**er
big + est	=	bi**gg**est
submit + ing	=	submi**tt**ing
refer + al	=	refe**rr**al

Recognize Troublesome Words

You can also improve your spelling if you understand why some words in English are troublesome. The following words are often misspelled because

- the same sounds in English are often spelled differently;
- words are often not spelled the way they sound;
- mispronounced words do not sound the way they are spelled.

Same Sound, Different Spellings

Some words that contain the same sound are spelled differently. Such words may contain suffixes like *-ar* and *-er, -ant* and *-ent, -ance* and *-ence, -able* and *-ible.*

calend**ar**/disast**er**	reluct**ance**/independ**ence**
descend**ant**/perman**ent**	irresist**ible**/indispens**able**

Entire words may also sound alike but be spelled differently. Such words are called **homophones.** Examples of homophones include *capitol/capital, principle/principal, sundae/Sunday.* (Chapter 40 contains a full glossary of these commonly confused words.)

Sounds Are Deceptive

Further, words may not be spelled the way they sound. Such words as *nuisance, marriage,* and *maneuver* may pose problems because of the vowel combinations they contain. When the *-ui, -ia,* and *-eu* combinations are pronounced, one vowel sound is emphasized, and so a writer may think their proper spellings are *nusance, marrige,* and *manuver.*

Also, letter combinations may have different sounds, depending on the words in which they appear. For example, the *-ough* combination has varying pronunciations in the following words: *rough, bough, bought, through, though, cough.*

Mispronunciation Causes Misspelling

Finally, mispronunciation or changes in pronunciation cause misspellings. The dropping of sounds, such as the *c* in words like *acquire* or *acquaint,* can lead writers to spell them wrong. Other sounds that are dropped in words like *mathematics* and *temperature* can lead to faulty spellings such as *mathmatics* and *temperture.*

Finally, pronouncing the *-er* sound when saying words like *monstrous* and *disastrous* can result in versions such as *monsterous* and *disasterous.*

Create a List of Frequently Misspelled Words

A good way to improve your spelling is to keep a list of the words you commonly misspell. Some of the following troublemakers may be on your list.

Frequently Misspelled Words

absence	accustomed	aggravate	argument
accept	achieve	aggressive	ascend
acceptable	acknowledge	a lot	assassination
accessible	acquaint	apparent	assessment
accidentally	acquire	appearance	beginning
accommodate	address	appropriate	belief
accumulate	adolescence	arctic	believe

breath
breathe
business
calendar
carriage
category
cemetery
certain
changeable
column
commitment
committed
competent
conceit
conceive
condemn
conscience
conscious
consistent
convenience
convenient
courteous
criticism
criticize
curiosity
deceive
definite
definitely
dependent
descend
descendant
desirable
desperate
develop
disappear
disappoint
disastrous
discipline
discriminate
dissatisfied
dominant
duel
eighth
eligible
embarrass
environment
exaggerate
exceed
excellent
exercise
exhaust
existence
familiar
favorite
February
fluorescent
fulfill
government
guarantee
guard
harass
humorous
incidentally
incredible
independence
indispensable
inevitably
interference
irrelevant
irresistible
irritable
judgment
knowledge
leisure
length
lenient
license
livelihood
luxury
magnificent
maintenance
manageable
manufacturer
marriage
mischievous
morale
moccasin
necessary
noticeable
nuisance
occasion
occasionally
occur
occurrence
opportunity
optimistic
parallel
perceive
permanent
permissible
persevere
persistence
personnel
persuade
possession
potato
precede
preference
preferred
privilege
procedure
propaganda
publicly
pursue
quantity
questionnaire
recede
receipt
receive
recognize
recommend
referral
referred
relief
relive
repetition
resistance
restaurant
rhythm
ridiculous
seize
separate
similar
stationery
superintendent
supposed (to)
suppress
tomato
transferred
unanimous
unnecessary
used (to)
vacuum
vengeance

Recognize the Limitations of Electronic Spellcheckers

Electronic spellcheckers can help improve your spelling, but be aware that computer software programs and hand-held electronic devices will not highlight misspellings that are actual words. For example, a spellchecker would not catch these mistakes:

> *plain*
> I eat a ~~plane~~ bagel every morning.
>
> *and*
> Jack ~~an~~ Jill went up the hill.
>
> *There*
> ~~Their~~ he is.

The original words are wrong in these sentences, but these words are not misspelled. After you use a spellchecker, proofread your paper to catch usage problems.

Consult a Dictionary

Get into the habit of relying on a current dictionary to help you correct your spelling. *But how can I look up a word if I can't even spell it?* If you find using a regular dictionary difficult when checking for spelling errors, use a spelling dictionary, which will help you to find a word even when you have trouble spelling it. Ask your school's librarian if the library has a spelling dictionary.

Summary

1. Learning four **basic spelling rules** can help you to become a better speller: choosing between *ie* and *ei* (see p. 438), changing the *y* to an *i* before adding an ending (see p. 438), knowing whether to drop or keep the final silent *e* (see p. 439), and doubling the final consonant (see p. 439).
2. Recognizing **troublesome words** can help you to become a better speller. Some people have difficulty when similar sounds are spelled in different ways (see p. 440), when words are not spelled the way they sound (see p. 440), or when they mispronounce words (see p. 440).
3. Creating a **personal list** of words that you misspell can help you to improve your spelling. (See p. 440.)
4. **Electronic spellcheckers** can be useful tools for writers, but spellcheckers look only for words that are misspelled, not misused (see p. 441). When in doubt about spelling, check your **dictionary** (see p. 442.)

Editing Activities

Identify and Correct Spelling Errors

Practice 39-A (Answers appear on p. 488.)

Each of the following sentences contains one frequently misspelled word. Replace the incorrect spelling with the correct spelling in each sentence.

EXAMPLE

> *favorite* *knowledge*
> Lily's ~~favrite~~ pastime is improving her ~~knowlege~~ of useless trivia.

1. The Pentagon spends an incredable four billion dollars a year on the Ballistic Missile Defense, or "star wars," program.
2. Americans have spent 4.5 billion dollars since 1977 on liscenced *Star Wars* products.
3. Two out of every five American teens believe their parents are too lenient about disipline.
4. Eighty-five percent of the coral reefs in the Indian Ocean were killed in 1998 by rising sea tempratures.
5. One American in twenty born today will have the priviledge of spending time in jail sometime in his or her life.
6. One out of every four abortion clinics in the United States suffered a disasterous and violent act from protesters in 1998.
7. Half of all Mexican gray wolves released back from captivity are inevitibly shot.
8. One of every three women who breastfeeds a baby developes mastitis, a breast infection.
9. It has been determaned that two thousand Chinese people die each day of smoking-related illnesses.
10. In an agressive campaign, fourth-graders in Denver raised $35,000 to free slaves in Sudan; as a result of their efforts, six hundred people received their freedom.

Practice 39-B (Answers appear on p. 488.)

Each sentence below contains two misspelled words that break one of the four rules presented in this chapter. Edit each sentence, replacing the incorrect spelling with the correct spelling.

EXAMPLE My ~~neice~~ *niece* Brienna is an excellent ~~swimer~~ *swimmer*.

1. If you want to recieve A's in college, you must truely commit yourself to hard work.
2. More importantly, haveing a strong self-esteem and relying on your abilitys as a learner will help you get the most out of your education.
3. If you possess the readyness and the motiveation to learn, you will succeed.
4. Understanding your own brain's design can be usful in helping you understand how you process information and sieze knowledge.
5. The brain has three parts to it: the hind brain, which performs surviveal functions; the midbrain, which controls emotionnal and sexual activity; and the cortex, which is made up of two sides—left and right.
6. The left brain comes formated for language, and it also is responsible for sequencing and analyzeing information.
7. This left side is logiccal and systematic, capable of describing, defineing, and counting.
8. The right side, however, is more refined in its proceses, takeing in information more holistically and instantly.

9. The right brain has the capacity to percieve ideas and make connections immediatly among ideas that are extremely different.
10. The parts of the brain do not operate in isolateion, but they work together in permiting you to learn and to live.

Practice 39-C

Edit the following paragraphs, correcting all misspelled words. The numbers in parentheses at the end of each sentence indicate how many words are misspelled in that sentence.

On March 29, 1979, the wurst nucleur disastar in United States history occured at Three Mile Island in Harrisburg, Pennsylvania. (4) Early in the mourning of March 28, two water pumps in Unit 2's secundary cooling system failed, and heat began to rise in the reacter coar. (4)

Radioactive steem was released into the atmosfere, allarms sounded, and offishuls declared a "general emergancy," the industry's highest level of warning. (5) The next day, March 29, varius people assesed the damadge to the fasility. (4) That same day, 40,000 gallons of slitely radioactive waistwater was released into the Susquehanna River. (2) Oficials were reluctent to admit the seriousness of the accidant, hesitent to send people into a pannic. (5) Too days later, Governer Thornburgh advized residants within ten miles to stay in there homes, closed twenty-three schools and urged pregnent women and young children within five miles of the plant to leave. (6) Sunday, April 1, President Jimmy Carter and First Lady Rosalyn Carter visited TMI and held a news conferance; some ressidents of the area felt releived by his presents. (4) A shrinking hydrogin bubble signaled the lessoning of the crissis, and on April 9 people were called back and schools were reopened. (3) Unit 2 was closed permenantly, and resadents still claim that cancer rates are higher in the area. (2) However, by mid-April 1979, a very scarey time was over for America. (1)

Edit Your Own Writing for Spelling Errors

1. Look through your own writing in your portfolio to find a paragraph or essay in which you had some problems with spelling. Do your misspellings match any in this chapter? Add any words you have misspelled to your spelling list. (Use the correct spelling in your list.) Make other corrections as your instructor directs.
2. Write a paragraph about whether you think you are more "left brained" (logical, systematic) or "right brained" (creative, abstract). Include specific details as you write. Use at least five of the words on the "Frequently Misspelled Words" list in this chapter.

Chapter 40

Commonly Confused Words

Writers confuse certain words that sound alike or have similar meanings. For example, you might write *affect* when you mean *effect, lose* when you mean *loose,* or *there* when you mean *their.* The following is a glossary of commonly confused words for you to use as a handy reference. The glossary provides a definition and an example for each word. In addition, you may want to keep a personal list of words that you confuse often.

If you write on a computer, do not depend on your spellchecker to highlight any of these words. The spellchecker looks for words that are misspelled, not misused. In the following sentence, for example, the words *there* and *their* are spelled correctly, but each is used incorrectly.

EXAMPLE ~~There~~ *Their* parking stickers are on the table over ~~their~~ *there*.

Commonly Confused Words

Word	Common meaning or usage	Example
accept	to take or receive	I accept the nomination.
except	excluding	Everyone is here except Lianne.
advice	a suggestion	I will always remember his advice.
advise	to suggest or recommend	Maybe a lawyer can advise you.
affect	to influence	Her opinion will affect our decision.
effect	a result of something	The effects of the decision will be widespread.
already	previously or before	I already took Introduction to Marketing.
all ready	completely prepared	I'm all ready to take Marketing II this semester.

among	in the company of or surrounded by (used with more than two people or objects)	Among her five sisters, Maxine is the shortest.
between	used to connect, relate, or separate two people or objects	Let's keep that information between you and me.
assure	to promise	He assured me that the car would be ready tomorrow.
ensure	to make certain	To ensure our 10:00 arrival, we took the 8:00 flight.
insure	to make certain (usually in a legal or financial context)	Urban Life insured the science building for $25 million
complement	to complete; make whole	The videotape presentation complements their proposal.
compliment	give praise	Our boss complimented us for our hard work on the project.
conscious	aware, awake	Even after the accident, she remained conscious.
conscience	a sense of right and wrong	My conscience won't let me tell a lie.
farther	more distant	He lives farther from school than I do.
further	to a greater extent or degree	We will look into the parking issue further.
fewer	used with things that are countable or quantifiable	She had fewer headaches when she avoided caffeine.
less	used with things that are not countable or quantifiable	He has less freedom in this work environment.
here	in this location	Sign here, please.
hear	to perceive sound	Did you hear the fire engines last night?
its	possessive form of *it*	The tornado made its way across the county.
it's	contraction for *it is*	It's my birthday today.
knew	past tense form of *know*	She knew him before they worked together.
new	opposite of *old*	We need some new ideas.

know	to understand	I know why you failed the exam.
no	opposite of *yes*	No, I don't have her e-mail address.
lose	to misplace	Did he lose his book?
loose	not confined, not tight	The cable connection is too loose.
passed	past tense of the verb *to pass*	Jason passed the exam.
past	having happened before	I have visited Mexico twice in the past.
principal	head of a school; most important	"Outdated technology is the principal problem with our library," said the school principal.
principle	a standard of beliefs; a rule	One principle that should guide our choice in this matter is fairness.
quiet	not making noise	The audience was quiet during the play.
quite	to a certain degree	I was quite angry after our conversation.
right	correct	The author is right when he says his childhood was troubled.
write	to compose (or what you do in this class)	She will write about her life in her autobiography.
than	as compared to	She has been here longer than I have.
then	next	The air conditioner failed, and then the room became too hot.
their	possessive form of *they*	The instructors canceled their classes today.
there	indicates a place	Several students are over there.
they're	contraction for *they are*	They're trying to find some information.
threw	past tense form of the verb *to throw*	Joe threw a snowball at me.
through	from side to side or end to end; finished	I ran through the hallway when I was through with my exam.
to	preposition; verb part (as in *to dance, to sing*)	To my surprise, she loves to sing country songs.
too	overly, also	They were too angry to listen, but I'm angry too.
two	the number 2	I work two jobs.

wear	to have on	Will we have to wear uniforms?
where	indicates a location	Where can I buy wide-leg jeans?
weather	atmospheric conditions	If the weather is nice, we'll eat lunch outside.
whether	if; in case	Whether you're going or not, I'm leaving now.
whose	possessive form of *who*	I know whose backpack this is.
who's	contraction of *who is*	Who's meeting us at the train station?
your	pronoun indicating ownership	The tag is sticking out of your shirt.
you're	contraction for *you are*	Oh, you're right. My tag is sticking out.

Summary

1. Writers confuse certain words that **sound alike** or **have similar meanings.** (See p. 445.)
2. Refer to the **glossary** in this chapter as you edit your own writing. (See pp. 445–48.)
3. Keeping a **personal list** of words that you confuse often is a good way to master your own troublemakers. (See p. 445.)
4. If you write on a computer, do not depend on your **spellchecker** to highlight commonly confused words. The spellchecker looks for words that are misspelled, not misused. (See p. 445.)

Editing Activities

Practice Using the Right Word

Practice 40-A (Answers appear on p. 488.)

Pay special attention to the underlined words in each of the following sentences. Some are used correctly, and others are not. Write the correct form of any of the words that are used incorrectly. Write "correct" over any underlined words that are used correctly.

EXAMPLE

Whether *quiet* *correct*
~~Weather~~ I'm in a ~~quite~~ room or a noisy one, I have difficulty memorizing new information.

1. Clark McKowen, whose known for his book *Get Your* A *Out of College*, offers many helpful hints to students.
2. Although students must except their responsibility to work hard, their are also tips they can use to improve skills such as memorizing.

3. McKowen's advise, first, is to relax when you have to memorize information.
4. According to McKowen, these strategies can effect relaxation: playing slow music, taking a walk, or closing your eyes and imagining being in a restful place.
5. Although students are often under stress when they need to memorize, its important for they're success that they be able to relax first to ready the brain.
6. McKowen ensures students that there brains know how to format information if they allow their brains to browse threw the information casually at first.
7. When a person is relaxed and has browsed through the information, then he or she is already to begin memorizing.
8. Some students can go farther in their memorization by using mnemonic devices, or memory tricks.
9. McKowen, however, emphasizes his "Mess-Around Theory": the principal idea behind it's success is to make learning more like play.
10. He says to play around with material until the brain makes its own patterns; than memorize anything that the brain has not learned on it's own.

Practice 40-B (Answers appear on p. 488.)

Each of the following sentences contains two or more words that are misused. Edit the sentences, substituting the correct form for the misused word.

EXAMPLE My Uncle Douglas ~~new~~ *knew* he was doing the ~~write~~ *right* thing when he took the job as director of the KidSmart Day Care Center.

1. Accept for the principle, the only men usually seen in an elementary school are the custodial staff.
2. Today, however, men like Gerald Snyder in Palmyra, Pennsylvania, are effecting students in classrooms as there teachers.
3. Men are making more of a difference in many female-dominated fields then they have in the passed, just as woman are moving into traditionally male occupations.
4. Ten years ago their were less men in jobs like teaching and nursing.
5. Mr. Snyder, however, was adviced to follow his conscious and do what he would enjoy.
6. Tom Peifer, who's previous experiences include college football, now insures the care of patients in intensive care as a nurse.
7. Mr. Peifer coaches high school baseball, and he knows that he looses respect from some of his players because of there stereotypes about male nurses.
8. Jamie Reisinger, who works for the YWCA counseling women about date rape, receives complements from women who realize that he brings a knew perspective to the job.

9. Weather or not a man goes into a "man's" field, he needs too determine what will fit his abilities and goals.
10. Wear a person works should be based on more than society and it's prejudices.

Practice 40-C

Underline the words that are misused in the following paragraph, and then correct each of the words that you have underlined.

> Universal Studios spent 2.7 billion dollars to open the Islands of Adventure theme park in 1999 in order to compete against Disney World, there rival. While Disney World sold 42 million tickets to it's park in 1998, Universal Studios sold only 9 million to its Universal Studios Florida, just ten miles down the road. The knew park, which appeals to older children, has not effected the success of the long-standing favorite, which appeals to younger children. To compliment its park, Universal Studios is also building a deluxe hotel, a City Walk of restaurants, and a huge parking garage too make the park a vacation destination. The new park contains six islands, all different in there theme. Marvel Super Hero Island, who's rides are sure to effect even the strongest of heart, contains a green Incredible Hulk Coaster and Dr. Doom's Fearfall. Another island, Toon Lagoon, has for it's principle attraction Popeye's Barges, which insures that passengers get soaked. One of the most interesting islands is Jurassic Park, whose landscape recreates Michael Crichton and Steven Spielberg's prehistoric feel. T-Rex is already to do battle against Mickey Mouse in the Florida swamps.

Edit Your Own Writing for Commonly Confused Words

1. Look through your portfolio for a paragraph or essay in which you misused one or more of the words listed in this chapter (look especially for *its/it's, there/their,* and *who's/whose,* as well as *effect/affect* and others you might have trouble with). Rewrite any sentences that contain the misused words, or follow your instructor's directions about correcting your errors.
2. Write a detailed paragraph about your own study habits. Are there strategies you follow that you know improve your effectiveness? Do you have any study habits that get in the way of your success? Include at least five words from this chapter, used correctly, in your paragraph.

Chapter 41

Sexist Language

Sexist language is word choice that reflects sex-role stereotypes or refers only to members of either sex. When you write, avoid using

- *-man* and *-men* words when the word could also refer to a woman or women;
- feminized words that unnecessarily call attention to gender;
- generic masculine pronouns—*he, him,* and *his* used to refer to members of both sexes.

Avoid *-man* and *-men* Words

Sexist words and phrases often include the word *man* or *men.* Although these words historically have meant "humankind in general," they reflect stereotypical thinking.

EXAMPLE Susan is a ~~freshman~~ ^*first-year student* at Tarrant County College.

EXAMPLE Delta Express is a popular airline among ~~businessmen.~~ ^*business travelers.*

Avoid Feminized Words

Attempts to feminize a word, title, or role often result in gender stereotyping of women. When you write, ask yourself whether identifying a person's gender is necessary.

EXAMPLE We are hiring a ~~cleaning lady~~ ^*housecleaner*.

Alternatives to Common Examples of Sexist Language

Sexist	Nonsexist
anchorman	anchor
businessman	business executive, businessperson
chairman	chair, chairperson

congressman	lawmaker, legislator, member of Congress
fireman	fire fighter
foreman	supervisor
insurance man	insurance agent
mailman	letter carrier
male nurse	nurse
man, mankind	people, humans, humanity, humankind
to man (verb)	to staff, to operate
man-made	manufactured, synthetic
manpower	personnel or staff
meter maid	meter reader
mothering	parenting
policeman, policewoman	police officer
salesman, saleswoman	salesperson, sales associate
stewardess	flight attendant
weatherman	meteorologist, weather forecaster
waitress	server
woman doctor	doctor

Avoid Generic Use of Masculine Pronouns: *he, him,* and *his*

Though it was acceptable in the past, using masculine pronouns to refer to people who may be female is viewed as sexist today. Here are three ways to revise sexist language.

1. Try using *he or she* instead of *he* and *him or her* instead of *him.* (Be careful not to overuse these pairs.)
2. Try rewriting the sentence using plural forms instead of singular forms. (Keep in mind, however, that if you make the subject plural, the verb must also be plural.)
3. Try rewriting the sentence without pronouns.

Sexist	Nonsexist
An engineer uses his problem-solving skills every day.	An engineer uses his or her problem-solving skills every day. OR Engineers use their problem-solving skills everyday. OR An engineer uses problem-solving skills every day.
Everyone should submit a first draft before he schedules a peer conference.	Everyone should submit a first draft before he or she schedules a peer conference. OR Students should submit a first draft before they schedule a peer conference. OR Everyone should submit a first draft before scheduling a peer conference.

Summary

1. **Sexist language** is language that reflects sex-role stereotypes or refers only to members of either sex. (See p. 451.)
2. Avoid using ***-man*** **and** ***-men*** **words** when the word could also refer to women. (See p. 451.)
3. Avoid using **feminized words** that unnecessarily signal gender. (See p. 451.)
4. Avoid **generic use of masculine pronouns *(he, him, his)*** to refer to members of both sexes. (See p. 452.)
5. Correct generic use of masculine pronouns by

   replacing *he* with *he or she* and by replacing *him* with *him or her* (see p. 452)
   using plural forms instead of singular forms (see p. 452)
   rewriting the sentence without pronouns (see p. 452)

Editing Activities

Identify and Correct Sexist Language

Practice 41-A (Answers appear on p. 488.)

Edit each of the following sentences carefully, eliminating sexist language. Some sentences will need more than one change.

EXAMPLE The average American ~~workingman~~ worker is motivated by the possibility of personal success.

1. Mankind has always seemed to love power and money.
2. When a congressman lobbies to become part of an important committee, he is trying to position himself into a more powerful role.
3. The businessman who "networks" at a convention is trying to make contacts that will advance his career.
4. Wars have been fought over small pieces of land when one leader wants more added to his domain.
5. A doctor may schedule additional tests for his patients in order to get a larger insurance payment.
6. A professional athlete will sometimes hold out of participation in his sport in order to negotiate a little more cash in his contract.
7. A lawyer often bills his clients for more hours than he has actually devoted to the case.
8. Even a minister may preach especially fervently to get his congregation to put more money into the collection plate.
9. Not everyone, however, lives his life for more power and money.
10. One may spend his time doing good for others while also making his own life better.

Practice 41-B (Answers appear on p. 488.)

Edit each of the following sentences, replacing sexist language with nonsexist alternatives.

EXAMPLE Two ~~women~~ doctors just published an article about health-care practices in countries at war.

1. As John boarded the plane for Washington, D.C., he asked the stewardess for a magazine.
2. He wanted to read up on the Kosovo crisis so he would have good questions to ask his congressman.
3. As he sat next to a businessman, he noticed that the man was reading the *New York Times.*
4. A front-page headline referred to the manpower being sent to the Serbian province and the number of bombs falling daily.
5. John began a conversation and found out that his plane companion was an insurance man.
6. "I was a mailman before going into sales," the man explained.
7. John said, "I want to be a news anchorman."
8. "In fact, I'm traveling to Washington to meet with a female professor and a member of the legislature about the Kosovo war," John continued.
9. The man said enthusiastically, "My daughter has a job at the Capitol, and she knows many lawmakers."
10. He continued, "Let me introduce you to her after I call a businessman friend to give us a ride to Capitol Hill."

Practice 41-C

Edit the following paragraph carefully for sexist language. Replace any sexist language with nonsexist language.

In an article called "A Loaded Question: What Is It about Americans and Guns?" the writer and essayist Leonard Kriegel explains that Americans have always been fascinated by guns. He wonders how a person can view owning a gun as his right. A gun owner might even regard her gun a thing of beauty. Kriegel explains how one man's fear and suffering can be another man's freedom and pleasure. While one person might see owning a gun as a symbol of independence, another may view a gun as a sign of his power. Another man may support his opinion by using the cliché, "Guns don't kill. People do!" Kriegel, however, has come to the opinion that fear is at the root of both sides of the gun control argument and that every man really wants the same thing: safety for his family. Perhaps the best thing to do is to leave guns in the hands of policemen and military men.

Edit Your Own Writing for Sexist Language

1. Look through your portfolio for a paragraph or essay in which you have used sexist language or in which you have awkwardly used *he or she, him or her,* or *his or her.* Make revisions and corrections as your instructor directs.
2. Write a detailed paragraph in which you discuss what kinds of people have power in American society. Make sure you define the word "power" as it is used in your discussion. After your paragraph is complete, revise carefully to eliminate sexist language.

Part Eight

Editing Sentences for ESL Challenges

Diagnostic Test for Part Eight: Editing Sentences for ESL Challenges

Use this test to check your skills with nouns, articles, verbs, and prepositions. Answers appear on page 489.

A. Each of the following sentences contains a noun error. Correct each sentence.

1. We sought three informations about the new development.
2. We should buy fruits for the salad.
3. I would like rices as a side dish.
4. Her impatiences made her a tough supervisor.

B. Insert the article—*a, an,* or *the*—that makes the best sense in the following sentences.

5. _____ Y2K bug, although much hyped, caused very few problems.
6. My roommate just got _____ new Toyota 4x4 for graduation.
7. My mother is _____ accountant in our family.
8. My father is _____ accountant in a large firm.
9. She bought _____ bag of Sour Patch Kids candy.

C. Each of the following sentences contains a verb error. Rewrite each sentence using the correct form of the verb.

10. I don't expect seeing him again.
11. He refused waiting for her another minute.
12. My dad dislikes to buy used cars.
13. Marie enjoys to play tennis every afternoon.
14. Sonja is wanting to change her major.

D. Identify the prepositions in the following sentences.

15. We arrived at the hotel for the conference.
16. Many examples of student projects appear in the appendix.

17. She completed her work with the computer during the workshop.
18. Around my town, people from different neighborhoods mix and mingle.

E. Choose a suitable preposition for each sentence.

19. We found the lost kitten _____ the closet door. *(across* or *behind)*
20. Look _____ the refrigerator for the mop. *(at* or *beside)*
21. Walk _____ the path to keep from ruining the new grass. *(on* or *until)*
22. Wait _____ Friday to turn in your journal. *(until* or *by)*

Chapter 42

Nouns and Articles

Some writers who are new to the English language have difficulty determining when to use the words *a, an,* or *the*—called **articles**—before nouns. To understand articles, you first have to understand nouns. This chapter focuses on these three troublespots:

- understanding count and noncount nouns;
- understanding proper and common nouns;
- using articles correctly.

Count and Noncount Nouns

Nouns are words that represent people, places, things, or ideas. English nouns can be sorted into count nouns and noncount nouns. **Count nouns** are nouns that can be counted. They can be singular or plural, as shown in the following examples:

Count Nouns

student	**One student** won the Susan B. Anthony leadership award.
	Twenty students received scholarships.
city	**The city** is home to me.
	I have lived in **three major cities** in the past ten years.
Web site	**My company's Web site** was designed by Mariana Gutierrez.
	She has designed hundreds of **Web sites.**

Noncount nouns—which usually represent general categories, emotions, and abstractions—cannot be broken down into distinct, countable parts and cannot be made plural. They are always singular. They can, however, be preceded by quantifiers (words that express amounts) such as *less, more, much, some,* and *a lot of.* Here are some examples of noncount nouns:

Noncount Nouns

information	I need **some information** about home mortgages. [It would be incorrect to say *She gave me two informations.*]
dissatisfaction	I hope my **dissatisfaction** wasn't too obvious. [It would be incorrect to say *My dissatisfactions were obvious.*]
advice	My uncle has given me a lot of **advice** about car shopping. [It would be incorrect to say *He gave me many advices about it.*]

Many food and beverage words are noncount nouns: *tea, water, wine, rice, bread, chicken, salt, sugar,* and so forth. Sometimes these nouns are used with the plural *-s* ending to mean "different kinds of," as in *That store carries teas from all over the world.* Often, we put food and beverages into the plural form by using units: *two pieces of fruit* rather than *two fruits,* or *several glasses of wine* rather than *several wines.*

Common and Proper Nouns

Another way to sort nouns is to think about whether they are general or specific. **Common nouns** are not capitalized and do not refer to specific people, places, things, or ideas. **Proper nouns,** on the other hand, are capitalized and do refer to specific people, places, things, or ideas. While *country* is a common noun, for example, *Greece,* a specific country, is a proper noun. The common noun *ship* is not capitalized, but the name of a particular ship, the *Titanic,* is capitalized. In general, no article is needed with a singular proper noun.

EXAMPLE The plaintiff cringed when ~~the~~ Judge Judy announced her verdict.

EXAMPLE ~~The~~ Lake Michigan is busy this time of year.

However, *the* is used with most plural proper nouns.

EXAMPLE We went to see ^*the* Baltimore Orioles play.

EXAMPLE We skied ^*the* Alps last March.

Using Articles Correctly

The articles *a, an,* and *the* are used to show that a word is a noun. *A* and *an* are called ***indefinite articles*** because they do not indicate a specific person, place, thing, or abstraction:

A wedding is a festive event.

The article *the,* on the other hand, makes a specific reference and is therefore labeled a ***definite article:***

The Maria Shriver–Arnold Schwarzenegger wedding attracted guests from politics and Hollywood.

Choose the correct article by determining whether the noun is count or noncount, whether the noun is singular or plural, or whether the noun refers to something or someone specific and known to the reader. Here are three basic rules to follow:

1. Use *the* if the reference is specific—regardless of whether the noun is count, noncount, singular, or plural:

   the half-eaten apple — the couple's anxiety
   the course registration forms — the neighbor's dogs

2. Use *a* or *an* for all singular count nouns if they refer to something nonspecific or unknown to the reader:

   a doctor — an accountant
   a tomato — an onion

   Do not use *a* or *an* with noncount or plural nouns.
3. Use *a* before words that begin with a consonant sound (made by all letters in the alphabet except *a, e, i, o, u*):

   a park — a baby — a van — a yak — a historian

   Use *an* before words that begin with a vowel *(a, e, i, o, u)* sound and before words beginning with a silent *h*:

   an island — an umbrella — an all-terrain vehicle — an honor

Summary

1. English **nouns** (words that represent people, places, things, or ideas) can be sorted into **count** nouns and **noncount** nouns. Count nouns are nouns that can be counted *(cat/cats).* They can be singular or plural. Noncount nouns cannot be broken down into distinct, countable parts and cannot be made plural *(imagination).* They are always singular. (See p. 461.)
2. **Common nouns** are not capitalized and do not refer to specific people, places, things, or ideas *(country).* **Proper nouns** are capitalized and do refer to specific people, places, things, or ideas *(Greece).* (See p. 462.)
3. The **articles** *a, an,* and *the* are used to signal nouns. *A* and *an* are referred to as *indefinite* articles because they do not signal a particular person, place, thing, or abstraction. The article *the,* on the other hand, makes a specific reference and is called a *definite* article. (See p. 462.)
4. Use *the* if the reference is specific, whether the noun is count, noncount, singular, or plural.

5. Use *a* or *an* for all singular count nouns if they refer to something nonspecific or unknown to the reader. Do not use *a* or *an* with noncount or plural nouns. (See p. 463.)
6. Use *a* before words that begin with a consonant (all letters in the alphabet except *a, e, i, o,* and *u*) sound. Use *an* before words that begin with a vowel *(a, e, i, o, u)* sound. (See p. 463.)

Editing Activities

Identify and Correct Errors with Articles

Practice 42-A (Answers appear on p. 489.)

Mark each of the underlined nouns in the following sentences as a count noun (C) or a noncount noun (N).

EXAMPLE

C C N
A talented artist has the ability to create beauty from a blank canvas.

1. Leonardo da Vinci's painting the *Mona Lisa* is arguably the most famous work of art in the world.
2. The *Mona Lisa*'s smile has captured the imagination of people for five centuries.
3. Historians have discussed whether the woman was real or just a creation.
4. Almost everyone has some familiarity with the famous painting.
5. Many commercial products have used the name Mona Lisa for advertising.
6. The image has been widely copied, such as when *The New Yorker* magazine put Monica Lewinsky's face as Mona Lisa on its cover in 1998.
7. Elton John wrote a song in the 1970s about people in New York called "Mona Lisas and Madhatters."
8. Bob Dylan sang, "Mona Lisa had the highway blues; you can tell by the way she smiles."
9. More recently, Shawn Colvin sang, "It's nothing, just you and the Mona Lisa" in the lyrics to one of her songs.
10. Whatever it is that fascinates people about her, millions go to the Louvre in Paris every year just to get a glimpse of the real thing.

Practice 42-B (Answers appear on p. 489.)

There are no articles in the following sentences. Fill in each of the blanks with the correct article: *a, an,* or *the.* If no article is needed, place an X in the blank.

EXAMPLE Most couples try to choose __a__ meaningful location for their wedding ceremony.

1. Last weekend, I attended _____ strangest wedding ceremony—completely by accident!
2. Both _____ bride and _____ groom were long-distance runners, so they planned to marry at _____ end of _____ Boston Marathon.
3. _____ groom wore _____ pair of _____ black running shorts and _____ T-shirt that looked like a tuxedo.

4. With her white running outfit, _____ bride wore _____ antique bridal veil.
5. The couple had to get _____ special permission from _____ city to have their videographer ride in front of them in _____ golf cart.
6. All along _____ race route, crowds cheered _____ couple as they ran hand-in-hand.
7. They finished _____ race in three hours and _____ fifty-two minutes.
8. As they crossed _____ finish line, they were joined by _____ minister and their friends and family—all of whom were dressed in _____ athletic clothing.
9. After _____ couple said their vows and exchanged _____ kiss, they were interviewed by _____ local news station.
10. I saw _____ bizarre wedding _____ second time when I turned on my television later in _____ evening.

Practice 43-C

Edit the following paragraph, adding articles *(a, an,* or *the)* before nouns where necessary.

As twenty-first century begins, times have never been better for African-Americans in United States. Employment and home ownership are up for African-Americans, but crime rate is down. More African-Americans are in college than ever before in this country. Because of United States' booming economy—longest boom in peacetime in American history—people of all races have benefited from opportunities provided by more money and more jobs. Many of America's heroes and role models are black (for example, Michael Jordan, Lauryn Hill, Colin Powell), and number of blacks elected to public office has increased tremendously since 1970. *Newsweek* poll indicates that African-Americans are more optimistic about their futures over next ten years than are whites. Other statistics, however—ones that demonstrate negative trend—are not so good. High-school drop-out rate has increased for blacks since 1991, and 25 percent of African-Americans still live below poverty line. While 72 percent of all whites own their own homes, only 46 percent of blacks do. Median weekly earnings, especially for black male, trail those of white man substantially. So, while many gains are being made in African-American community, there is still room for growth, prosperity, and equity.

Edit Your Own Writing for Article Errors

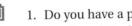

1. Do you have a problem with articles—*a, an,* and *the?* If you are not a native speaker of English, you may find English articles confusing. Look through your portfolio for a paragraph or essay in which you might have left out or misused articles. Revise as your instructor directs you.
2. Write a detailed paragraph describing a ceremony or special event that you have seen. Use the strategies presented in this chapter to edit your writing for article errors.

Chapter 43

Special Problems with Verbs

Native speakers of English face many challenges in mastering English verbs. If English is not your first language, you will encounter similar challenges. This chapter addresses three important areas to review in order to use verbs correctly in your writing:

- deciding between the *to* form and the *-ing* form of a verb;
- using the progressive tense;
- using phrasal verbs.

Deciding between the *to* Form and the *-ing* Form of a Verb

The *to* form of a verb is called an **infinitive.** It includes the word *to* followed by the base form of a verb.

> *To retire* at age forty-five is my goal.
>
> He wants *to sing* at the baseball game.
>
> My instructor advised me *to take* this course.

The *-ing* form of the verb is called a **gerund** when it functions as a noun.

> *Traveling* by bus is no fun.
>
> She quit *singing* to study *dancing.*
>
> I enjoy *taking* college courses.

Sometimes deciding whether to use an infinitive or a gerund in a sentence is difficult. In making this decision, you need to find the main verb in the sentence. Some verbs can be followed by an infinitive; some can be followed by a gerund; and some can be followed by either. Unfortunately, there is no easy rule to learn. With practice and feedback, you will begin to use correct verb structures.

Verbs That Can Be Followed by an Infinitive But Not by a Gerund (partial list)

afford	decide	intend	plan	seem
agree	demand	learn	prepare	tend
ask	expect	manage	pretend	wait
attempt	fail	need	promise	want
consent	hope	offer	refuse	

EXAMPLE George promised ^*to go* ~~going~~ to the bank after work.

EXAMPLE I expect ^*to get* ~~getting~~ a large tax refund this year.

Verbs That Can Be Followed by a Gerund But Not by an Infinitive (partial list)

admit	deny	finish	practice	risk
advise	discuss	imagine	quit	suggest
appreciate	dislike	keep	recall	tolerate
avoid	enjoy	miss	regret	
consider	escape	postpone	resist	

EXAMPLE Sayanh denied ^*knowing* ~~to know~~ who created the computer virus.

EXAMPLE Jin-Cho enjoys ^*doing* ~~to do~~ grammar exercises in the computer lab.

Verbs That Can Be Followed by an Infinitive or a Gerund (partial list)

begin	forget	like	remember	try
continue	hate	love	stop	

Ivana *remembered to bring* her calculator.

Ivana *remembered bringing* me flowers when we were young.

Using the Progressive Tense

Verbs in English often consist of more than one word. For example,

Baotong *is working* for Allied Electronics.

In this sentence, the verb consists of two words. The first is the helping verb *is;* the second is the *-ing* form of the verb *to work.* Together, a form of *be* and an *-ing* verb make the **progressive tense,** which expresses continuous—or ongoing—action.

When you join these *to be* verbs

Present am/are/is

Past was/were

Future will be

with the *-ing* forms of some verbs, you create the present, past, and future progressive tenses:

I am working. (present progressive)

They were working. (past progressive)

He will be working. (future progressive)

Certain English verbs cannot form the progressive tense. In general, these verbs express a state of being or mental activity rather than ongoing action.

Verbs That Cannot Form the Progressive Tense

appear	contain	involve	need	suppose
believe	have	know	see	understand
belong	hear	mean	seem	want

EXAMPLE Sonia ~~is believing~~ *believes* in herself.

EXAMPLE DeShawn will ~~be understanding~~ *understand* the situation after he reads the letter.

Using Phrasal Verbs

Phrasal verbs contain a verb plus one or two particles. Particles are usually prepositions or adverbs that, when attached to the verb, change its meaning. Phrasal verbs are tricky because their meanings often cannot be predicted by knowing the meanings of the individual words. For this reason, phrasal verbs cause problems for some writers learning English as a foreign language.

Please *break down* the costs in this estimate.

In his job as a waiter, John *puts up with* a lot of abuse.

The phrasal verb *break down* (to separate) consists of the verb *break* and the particle *down.* The two words combine to form a new, separate meaning. Similarly, the meaning of the phrasal verb *put up with* (to tolerate) has little relation to the meaning of the verb *put* (to place). Again, with practice and feedback, you will use these idiomatic English verbs correctly in your writing.

Common Phrasal Verbs (partial list)

ask out	(ask for a date)	bring up	(mention; talk about)
blow up	(destroy; act with anger)	brush up on	(familiarize oneself)
break up	(end a partnership)	buy out	(purchase)

call off	(cancel)	hand in	(submit)
catch on	(learn)	hang up	(end a phone call; delay)
check out	(investigate)	help out	(assist)
check up on	(measure progress)	lay off	(release from a job)
come across	(encounter)	let down	(disappoint)
come up with	(invent)	look up	(find information)
count on	(rely on)	make fun of	(ridicule)
do over	(repeat)	pass out	(distribute; faint)
drop off	(deliver)	pick up	(make happy)
eat out	(go to a restaurant)	put up with	(tolerate)
fall back on	(use as an aid)	run into	(meet unexpectedly)
fall through	(fail to happen)	set up	(prepare; establish)
figure out	(discover; solve)	show up	(arrive)
find out	(discover)	take care of	(do)
get away with	(succeed by deception)	turn off	(cause to lose interest; shut off)
get out of	(avoid)	watch out for	(notice; be aware of)
give up	(quit)		
goof off	(act silly)		

Some phrasal verbs can be separated in sentences. Others cannot, as shown in the following examples.

SEPARABLE

My employer *laid off* four managers. (correct)

My employer *laid* four managers *off*. (correct)

INSEPARABLE

My supervisor said she could *count on* me. (correct)

My supervisor said she could *count* me *on*. (incorrect)

Talking with native speakers and getting feedback from them when you write are the best ways to learn how to use phrasal verbs correctly.

Summary

1. Some nonnative speakers of English have trouble deciding whether to use an **infinitive** or a **gerund.** An infinitive includes the base form of a verb preceded by the word *to (to read)*. A gerund is the *-ing* form of the verb when it functions as a noun *(reading)*. (See p. 466.)
2. When deciding between using an infinitive and using a gerund, look for the **main verb** in the sentence. Some verbs can be followed by an infinitive; some can be followed by a gerund; and some can be followed by either. Check the charts in this chapter for guidance. (See p. 467.)

3. The **progressive tense** (which expresses continuous action) is made from a form of *be* + *-ing* verb (I *am reading*). Some English verbs cannot form the progressive tense. (See p. 468.)
4. **Phrasal verbs** are multiword verbs whose meanings are often unpredictable. For example, the meaning of *turn down* (to reject) has little to do with the meanings of *turn* and *down*. (See p. 468.)

Editing Activities

Identify and Correct Verb Errors

Practice 43-A (Answers appear on p. 489.)

Complete each of the following sentences, adding either an infinitive or a gerund of your choice after the underlined word so that the sentence makes sense and is grammatically correct. You may add words if necessary.

EXAMPLE I always seem *to write* better when I do a rough draft of a paper.

1. Many students expect _____ good grades without understanding what academic success involves.
2. They often resist _____ enough hours on homework.
3. Many also do not consider _____ notes or redoing sloppy assignments.
4. To achieve success, students should attempt _____ every assignment well in advance.
5. Unsuccessful students generally postpone _____ projects until the last minute.
6. They often fail _____ enough time to do quality work.
7. Students also should not wait _____ for tests until the night before.
8. Successful students often begin _____ for a test days in advance.
9. This allows them to learn _____ certain skills rather than to cram information into their heads.
10. Being a successful student means that one must avoid _____ time but instead must use time to his or her advantage.

Practice 43-B (Answers appear on p. 490.)

To practice using progressive tenses correctly, revise each of the following sentences to include one of the progressive forms of the underlined verb, if possible. If a sentence includes a verb that cannot form the progressive tense, write "correct" over the verb.

EXAMPLE Scientists ~~discover~~ *are discovering* new evidence that contradicts old theories.

1. New archaeological discoveries change the way anthropologists understand the history of Americans.
2. Until recently, scientists believed that the first Americans walked across a land bridge from Asia.

3. Anthropologists discover artifacts in places from Peru to South Carolina that contradict this theory, however.
4. Evidently, people lived on the American continent over fifteen thousand years ago.
5. These people used stone tools like those previously found in Spain and France.
6. We know now that people painted cave paintings in Brazil long before the Asian ancestors arrived.
7. Scientists identify many skeletons whose origins contradict the Asian land-bridge theory.
8. A skull found in Nevada appears to resemble the Norse, long before Leif Erikson's trip to the continent.
9. The new theory supposes that people traveled by boat from Europe along a frozen shoreline fifteen to twenty thousand years ago.
10. Apparently, the American continent has always been a place to which many different peoples have migrated.

Practice 43-C

Revise the following paragraph by substituting a suitable phrasal verb from the list in this chapter for each underlined verb. You may separate your phrasal verb if you need to.

> Every day, hundreds of couples across America decide to end their marriages. For various reasons they decide not to tolerate their spouses anymore. Certainly in any marriage, couples encounter difficulties. Many couples have learned, however, to discover ways to cope. Clear and honest communication will settle most couples' problems. Couples need to create ways to talk openly about conflicts. They need to establish ground rules for discussions so that each person can talk without being interrupted. Couples need to notice changes in their partner's moods. They should not have to rely on others to understand their spouses' feelings. With better communication so many marriages might not disintegrate.

Edit Your Own Writing for Verb Errors

1. Look over your portfolio to find a paragraph or essay in which verb forms have been a challenge. Have you used infinitives where you should have used gerunds, or vice versa? Have you formed progressive tenses correctly, and have you known when *not* to form the progressive tense? Have you used phrasal verbs correctly? Revise your writing and resubmit as your instructor directs.
2. Why do you think so many marriages do not last? Write a detailed paragraph expressing and supporting your theory. Proofread your writing for correct verb forms.

Chapter 44

Prepositions

Students learning English as a second language often have difficulty using **prepositions**—words that express relationships between nouns, pronouns, and verbs and other words in a sentence. This chapter will help you to understand

- time and place prepositions;
- adjective + preposition combinations.

Time and Place Prepositions

The prepositions that are often most troublesome for nonnative speakers of English are those that show time and place.

After the party, they walked home. (time)

She stood *behind* me in line. (place)

Some languages have no equivalents for English prepositions. Other languages include prepositions that are common in English, but they are used differently. For example, speakers of Spanish say *en* to mean both "in" or "on."

The following list includes frequently used time and place prepositions:

Common Time and Place Prepositions

about	at	by	into	toward
above	before	down	near	under
across	behind	during	of	until
after	below	except	on	up
against	beneath	for	over	upon
along	beside	from	since	with
among	between	in	through	within
around	beyond	inside	to	

Use *at, on, in,* and *by* Correctly

The prepositions *at, on, in,* and *by* are especially tricky because they express both time and place. You can best familiarize yourself with the correct uses of these prepositions by talking with native speakers of English and by reading stories, articles, advertisements, or anything else written in English as often as you can.

The following sentences show time and place prepositions being used correctly:

Jorge's plane will arrive *at* 3:20 P.M. (time)
We will meet Jorge *at* the terminal gate. (place)

Please tell Mariette the essay is due *on* the 21st. (time)
Mariette placed her finished essay *on* the instructor's desk. (place)

My cousins will visit us *in* July. (time)
They will march with us *in* the Independence Day parade. (place)

Please submit your report *by* Monday. (time)
Office supplies are located *by* the fax machine. (place)

Use *of* Correctly

The preposition *of,* besides expressing time and place, also shows relationships between people and things.

Manuel is a friend *of* mine.

Gloria's song was the best *of* all.

Sometimes writers use *of* where other prepositions should be used.

EXAMPLE In this area, there are many opportunities ~~of~~ *for* work.

EXAMPLE Getting an education is the first step ~~of~~ *toward* success.

If you are unsure whether you are using *of* correctly, consult your instructor for guidance.

Adjective + Preposition Combinations

Nonnative speakers of English are sometimes confused about which preposition should follow an adjective (a word that describes a noun or pronoun). These expressions are often idiomatic—that is, they depend upon common use rather than logic or grammatical rules. Knowing how to use them correctly will involve some memorization and practice. Here are some common examples of adjective + preposition combinations:

afraid of	confused by	proud of
angry about	excited about	responsible for
aware of	full of	sorry for
bothered by	interested in	tired of

EXAMPLE

for
Lindy was feeling sorry ~~in~~ herself until she realized that she got the job.

Summary

1. **Prepositions** are words that express relationships between nouns, pronouns, and verbs and other words in a sentence. Writers often have difficulty with prepositions that show time and place. (See p. 472.)
2. *At, in, on,* and *by* are especially tricky because they can be used to express both time and place. (See p. 473.)
3. Some writers use *of* where other prepositions should be used. (See p. 473.)
4. Certain adjective + preposition combinations are determined by common use and not by grammar or logic. (See p. 473.)

Editing Activities

Identify and Correct Preposition Errors

Practice 44-A (Answers appear on p. 490.)

Underline all of the prepositions in the following sentences. Label each preposition "time," "place," or "relationship" to show how it is used in the sentence.

EXAMPLE

relationship *place*
Of all the restaurants in town, China Garden is my favorite.

1. Let's eat at the China Garden after work.
2. Don't worry, the menu has plenty of vegetarian dishes.
3. Can you meet me at seven o'clock?
4. China Garden is located on the west end of Temple Street.
5. To get to Temple Street, take the train from Washington Street to Buckley Square.
6. At Buckley Square, go over the footbridge and down to the street level.
7. You will see a tall brick church. Take a left just before the church.
8. You will then be on Temple Street.
9. Go by the Home Depot and Burger King. China Garden is on the right, just beyond a row of mailboxes.
10. If you leave work at 6:30, you should be there by 7:00.

Practice 44-B (Answers appear on p. 490.)

In each of the following sentences, replace any prepositions that are used incorrectly.

EXAMPLE Two events ~~on~~ *in* 1969 changed Americans' view ~~to~~ *of* their world.

1. On 10:56 P.M. at July 20, 1969, astronaut Neil Armstrong made history.
2. It was then that he stepped by the *Apollo 11* spacecraft to become the first person to walk at the moon.
3. Armstrong spoke the now-famous words: "That's one small step to man, one giant leap of mankind."
4. He was followed immediately of Buzz Aldrin, his crewmate.
5. Through the miracle at technology, millions of people watched the landing in television by their own homes.
6. Later that summer, the Woodstock Music and Arts Fair took place on Bethel, New York.
7. Though only 186,000 tickets to the outdoor concert were sold, over 500,000 people traveled to Bethel to peace, love, and music.
8. The music in artists such as the Grateful Dead, Jimi Hendrix, Janis Joplin, and Joan Baez reflected the political and social themes important to millions on people.
9. In the time the three-day outdoor concert ended, a generation of Americans was defined.
10. Today's music continues to be influenced from the music of the Woodstock artists.

Practice 44-C

Edit the following paragraph, replacing prepositions where necessary.

I moved to the United States from the Dominican Republic one year ago. I was interested on getting a better education for me and my family. I was aware for programs that help immigrants to get jobs, but I did not know about all of the help available for adults learning English as a second language. I was excited in a new opportunity, but afraid for failure. I signed up to some classes and studied hard. I knew I would have to be responsible to doing my homework and practicing my new skills. I still have a lot to learn, but I am proud in myself for taking the first step.

Edit Your Own Writing for Preposition Errors

1. Look through your portfolio to find a paragraph or essay in which you have used prepositions incorrectly. Revise your writing and resubmit it as your instructor directs.
2. Write a detailed paragraph about learning English or another language as a second language. What was the biggest challenge for you? How do you feel about your accomplishment now? Proofread your work for correct use of prepositions.

Answers to Diagnostic Tests and A and B Practice Sets

Part Five. Editing Sentences for Grammar

Diagnostic Test, p. 337
The correct answer to each item is followed by a number in parentheses. This number indicates the chapter you should review if you answered the item incorrectly.

A.
1. S (23) **2.** F (23) **3.** RO (24) **4.** S (23)
5. RO (24) **6.** F (23) **7.** S (23) **8.** S (23)

B.
9. cooks (25) **10.** watch (25) **11.** hate (26)
12. is (25) **13.** come (26)

C.
14. I (27) **15.** he (27) **16.** his or her (27)
17. whom (27) **18.** their (27)

D.
19. A (28) **20.** A (28) **21.** B (28) **22.** B (28)
23. A (28)

E.
24. U (29) **25.** U (29) **26.** U (29) **27.** U (29)
28. C (29)

F.
29. it was well-directed (30)
30. beginning to engage in uncharacteristic activities (30)
31. she is very intelligent (30)
32. they could also symbolize his feelings and emotions (30)

Chapter 23, Fragments

Practice 23-A, p. 343
1. F; The number-one health and safety problem in the American workplace is RSI, which stands for Repetitive Strain Injury.
2. F; According to the U.S. Bureau of Labor Statistics, RSI is now responsible for more than 60 percent of all workplace-related illnesses.
3. F; Repetitive Strain Injuries involve damage caused by misuse or overuse of certain nerves, muscles, and tendons.
4. F; RSI affects workers whose jobs involve performing repetitive tasks. Such workers include computer operators, postal workers, and musicians.
5. S
6. F; Many people who do a lot of keyboard typing and mouse clicking have suffered severe damage in their wrists because of constant, repeated compression of certain nerves.
7. F; You may be familiar with some of the most common forms of RSI, especially carpal tunnel syndrome and tendonitis.
8. F; Since these types of injuries develop over time, American workers had a difficult time proving that RSI was a work-related injury.
9. F; According to the RSI Center at the Massachusetts Institute of Technology, you may be at risk for developing an RSI if your job involves repetition of small, rapid movements.
10. S

Practice 23-B, p. 344, suggested revisions
1. *The Hot Zone*, a terrifying but true story by Richard Preston, presents the account of an outbreak of the Ebola virus in the early 1990s.
2. The author admits that he changed some of the names but insists that the facts are true.
3. For example, he claims that many of the events took place in Reston, Virginia, and Washington, D.C.

4–5. Because of the location of the virus's origin, the Ebola virus, whose formal name is Ebola Zaire, is named for the Ebola River, a tributary of the Congo or Zaire River in Africa.
6–7. It is a "level 4" virus, called a "hot" virus, with an incubation period of less than twenty-four days and symptoms that include bleeding out of body openings and a breakdown of almost all of the body's tissues.
8–9. Since the virus had originated in monkeys being used for research, two Army veterinarians, Major Nancy Jaax, and her husband, Major Gerald Jaax, helped to isolate and control the virus.

10. Preston's book, an interesting and compelling story of the outbreak, introduces readers to one of nature's deadliest mysteries.

Chapter 24, Run-Ons

Practice 24-A, p. 348, suggested revisions

1. The earth as we know it took hundreds of millions of years to evolve, and it balances itself over time.
2. Modern society has harmed this balance by introducing chemicals and radiation into the environment.
3. Between 1945 and 1960 alone, over 200 synthetic chemicals were introduced into the environment.
4. America generates four pounds of solid waste, or garbage, per person per day; much of this waste is recyclable.
5. The Environmental Protection Agency calls for four steps to help with the landfill problem, including reducing waste and recycling.
6. The EPA also recommends burning waste when possible before sending the rest to a landfill.
7. Recycling saves up to 95 percent of the energy and water used to make goods from raw materials, and it creates up to 90 percent less water and air pollution.
8. Many companies are finding that recycling pays off. For example, AT&T recycles twenty-five truckloads of metals and plastics every day.
9. An organization called Planet Ark includes information called "Fifteen Ways to Save the Planet" on their Web site, located at www.planetark.com.
10. One example is to use water wisely, by turning the tap off while brushing your teeth; another involves walking or using public transportation whenever possible.

Practice 24-B, p. 349

1. People are not always successful in college; some experience difficulties during the first year.
   People are not always successful in college because some experience difficulties during the first year.
2. One of the main difficulties is time management; inefficient use of time keeps students from getting everything done.
   One of the main difficulties is time management. Inefficient use of time keeps students from getting everything done.
3. Students also have problems understanding professors' vocabulary because they may not be used to some of the academic language.
   Students also have problems understanding professors' vocabulary, not being used to some of the academic language.
4. Students should try to stay with the course. Often they begin to understand with more exposure to the concepts.
   Students should try to stay with the course since often they begin to understand with more exposure to the concepts.
5. Reading the textbook can also be hard since textbooks are sometimes written in academic language.
   Reading the textbook can also be hard; textbooks are sometimes written in academic language.
6. Students are often not ready for the reading load of a college course. They do not allow enough time in their schedules to get everything done well.
   Students are often not ready for the reading load of a college course, so they do not allow enough time in their schedules to get everything done well.
7. Some students try to work too much because they need the extra money.
   Some students try to work too much; they need the extra money.
8. Students should do their best to limit working hours because trying to do too much adds more stress to their lives.
   Students should do their best to limit working hours. Trying to do too much adds more stress to their lives.
9. Finally, students can become bored when they just cannot relate to a class.
   Finally, students can become bored; they just cannot relate to a class.
10. Finding ways to apply the course content to life can help, and seeing education as a route to a better job also keeps people in college.

Finding ways to apply the course content to life can help. Seeing education as a route to a better job also keeps people in college.

Chapter 25, Subject-Verb Agreement

Practice 25-A, p. 354

1. The Copyright Law of 1976, which was written by lawmakers, **protects** owners of copyrighted material.
2. A number of members of Congress **recognize** that this law needs to be updated.
3. With the rise of technology like the Internet **come** new problems with how to balance creative protection with public interest and access.
4. For example, modifying computer programs and copying compact disks **are** now easy tasks because of new technologies.
5. Many members of the American workforce **wonder** who owns the material that exists on their company's computer network.
6. A committee including members from academia and the publishing world **has** helped to create new guidelines about using copyrighted material.
7. Students and their professor **are** allowed to use copyrighted material for educational purposes.
8. Students in a computer class studying the Internet **are** not allowed to copy copyrighted material onto their own Web sites.
9. Several new laws, like the 1998 Digital Millennium Copyright Act, **update** the 1976 law to include new technologies, like distance education.
10. Though they may copy protected works, a student and her teacher **are** held liable if they use the work for personal gain outside the classroom.

Practice 25-B, p. 355

1. The use of performance-enhancing drugs **is** becoming more and more of a problem every year.
2. Correct
3. Erwan Mentheour, a French cyclist, **admits** that he took several drugs before being caught in 1997.
4. "Doping," as it is called among world-class athletes, **has** become a serious threat to the integrity and appeal of sports.
5. Charles Yesalis of Penn State University, an expert on drug use in the Olympics, **claims** that the International Olympic Committee has known about the problem for forty years.
6. Athletes across the sports spectrum **are** getting caught; however, many others are not.
7. Correct
8. Human growth hormone and erythropoietin (EPO) often **cause** severe heart problems.
9. Unnatural levels of testosterone **are** known to cause liver cancer and impotence.
10. Better drug-detecting methods and technology **are** a beginning to help sports clean up its act.

Chapter 26, Verb Forms and Verb Tenses

Practice 26-A, p. 361

1. was **2.** was **3.** were **4.** was; was **5.** was **6.** have been; were **7.** were; was **8.** was; were **9.** is being **10.** be

Practice 26-B, p. 362

1. In 1999 millions of Americans **drove** to the beach for a family vacation.
2. While many people have **flown** on airplanes, cars remain the choice for cheap transportation.
3. The beach has **taken** the prize for years for the top vacation destination for families and individuals.
4. Many people enjoy **lying** in the sun or romping in the waves.
5. Who hasn't **shaken** sand from shoes and blankets at some time or another?
6. Even the threat of skin cancer has not **shrunk** the numbers of people at beaches.
7. MTV's "Spring Break" has **seen** tremendous increases in attendance over the past couple of years.
8. Beach vacation packages have **broken** records recently in numbers of trips booked.
9. The beaches have **gotten** more crowded, but people still go.
10. The beach has **given** families and individuals of all ages a place to go for nature, relaxation, and fun.

Chapter 27, Pronouns

Practice 27-A, p. 370

1. *TV Guide* magazine frequently publishes **its** lists of favorite TV shows and characters.

2. Recently, **it** published a feature article called "TV's 50 Greatest Characters Ever!"
3. Number one on the list was Louie DePalma, a character on the show *Taxi* known for **his** meanness.
4. Lucy Ricardo is rated number three for **her** zany, crazy antics on the *I Love Lucy* show.
5. A more recent TV character, Roseanne, made the list for **her** "ferocious humor."
6. Editors of the magazine listed Kramer of *Seinfeld* as **their** 35th pick for **his** "vibrating, head-shaking, arm-waggling" entrances.
7. Xena is listed for **her** being a "bodacious battle-ax," and **she** is cited as being a "prehistoric Sipowicz."
8. Of course, Andy Sipowicz of *NYPD Blue,* known for **his** harshness and insensitivity, also made the list at number 23.
9. Even a cartoon character, Homer Simpson, made the list for **his** being a "coarse, oafish, self-involved, oblivious, overgrown child."
10. And would anyone doubt that Steve Urkel would make this kind of list for **his** annoying nerdiness on *Family Matters*?

Practice 27-B, p. 370

1. Everyone seems to have **his or her** own opinion about how to raise children.
2. My husband and **I** have been criticized for letting our son use a pacifier.
3. **The criticism** bothered us for a while, but we realized **a pacifier** was right for us and for our baby.
4. Some parents feel that **it's** okay to let their young children sleep with them.
5. For those parents **who** have trouble sleeping, sharing a bed with an infant may not be the smartest idea.
6. Many parents today favor letting **children** cry themselves to sleep.
7. Letting our baby cry himself to sleep was not a practice that appealed to my husband and **me,** though.
8. Our baby would fall asleep when one of us sang to him or rocked him. **This practice** made us all happy.
9. Whenever my mother and I discuss parenting styles, she always says that she was much more strict than **I.**
10. However, I remember when my mother let my baby sister eat a whole box of cookies because **my mother** was tired.

Chapter 28, Adjectives and Adverbs

Practice 28-A, p. 374, suggested revisions

1. Every Saturday morning, I sit at my **kitchen** table to make a **grocery** list.
2. After writing down **ordinary** things like *milk, butter,* and *eggs* on my list, I look **carefully** through the refrigerator and cabinets for items to add.
3. I then check the **morning** newspaper **thoroughly** to see if there are **free** coupons that will help me to save money.
4. I always go to the **local** farmstand first for **fresh** tomatoes, **sweet** corn, **juicy** apples, and **ripe** bananas.
5. At the supermarket, I travel **slowly** up and down the aisles listening to the **noisy** chatter of other shoppers.
6. A **helpful** woman at the fish counter was **loudly** telling a **curious** man how to make a **lemon** marinade for swordfish.
7. I found myself in the **extremely** awkward position of reaching over the woman for a bottle of **spicy** marinade.
8. In the cereal aisle, a **busy** mother was trying **hopelessly** to stay in control with **four** kids reaching out **greedily** for everything they saw.
9. While in the cleaning products aisle, I **always** try to choose the **most effective** brands.
10. The last thing I do before I check out is recycle my **aluminum** cans and **glass** bottles, and then I congratulate myself on a job **well** done.

Practice 28-B, p. 375

1. new **2.** visually **3.** aggressive **4.** Recently
5. best **6.** certainly **7.** really **8.** least desirable
9. better **10.** extremely

Chapter 29, Misplaced and Dangling Modifiers

Practice 29-A, p. 379

1. Stress affects almost everyone at one time or another.
2. A little stress is helpful in that it actually channels resources of the body.
3. Thinking and memory get better during moments of stress in the body.

4. The sense of pain is also dulled during stressful events.
5. More blood carrying oxygen is sent to the brain and muscles.
6. After a long period of stress, the immune system cannot keep infection from taking a harmful toll on the body.
7. Delayed stress affects nearly all people who work in naturally stressful occupations.
8. Chronic stress results from setting off the stress response on the body too often.
9. Cortisol, a substance created only during stress, can become toxic to brain cells.
10. More and more diseases, like heart disease and digestive disorders, are being linked to chronic stress.

Practice 29-B, p. 380, suggested revisions

1. Before writing a research paper, one should consult the Internet as a source of information.
2. Varying in the quality of information it contains, each Internet source must be evaluated for its reliability.
3. To evaluate an Internet site for reliability, a writer must identify the author of the site.
4. While surfing the site, a writer should follow any clues about the author's expertise.
5. Before using information on a site, a writer must verify the facts.
6. Because of their research expertise, university faculty usually host reliable sites.
7. Though containing advertisements and promotional material, many sites sponsored by organizations are professionally checked.
8. Before quoting or copying information from a commercial Web site, a writer should contact the company.
9. When reprinting a company's Web site logo, a Web author must request permission of the company.
10. Using borrowed information, research writers can use the Internet as a great source if they know how to cite electronic sources properly.

Chapter 30, Parallelism

Practice 30-A, p. 384, suggested revisions

1. Successful students know how to manage their time, how to deal with professors, and **how to read effectively.**
2. They take notes effectively, know when to listen carefully, and **understand the importance of organization.**
3. Three problems students encounter with time are taking too much time on unimportant tasks, **engaging in spontaneous activities,** and not building some flexibility into their schedules.
4. Effective students are organized, efficient with time, and **able to set goals.**
5. Studying for the hard subjects first, knowing your best time of day, and **establishing a good study place** all help one be a better student.
6. A successful student also takes risks, is able to focus attention, and **displays curiosity.**
7. To lessen stress, a successful student laughs, relaxes, or **participates in a physical activity.**
8. No matter what courses you take, it's important to set positive goals, establish study patterns, and **keep track of achievements.**
9. Other pieces of advice from effective students include learning to say "no," getting enough rest, and **doing two things at once.**
10. While being a successful student may seem difficult, being prepared, positive, and **determined** will certainly help.

Practice 30-B, p. 384, suggested revisions

1. Tourist locations like Florida and California are home to both wealthy people and **people who work for minimum wage.**
2. People are either getting rich or **struggling to get by.**
3. Wealthy developments drive up housing costs both for the ones who can afford it and **for the ones who are scraping up enough to buy groceries.**
4. People who need to work in tourist areas find it more difficult to find housing than **to find a job.**
5. Jobs in busy areas are plentiful for people with higher level job skills and **for people with entry-level skills.**
6. The problem is both being able to afford to live in busy areas and **being able to pay for utilities.**
7. According to the National Coalition for the Homeless, it takes either a job paying $8.89 an hour or **free childcare** for the single mother to afford a one-bedroom apartment.

8. Whether they are restaurant employees or **store clerks,** many entry-level workers cannot afford adequate housing today.
9. Since jobs are easy to find in tourist areas, many high-school graduates believe it is better to go straight to work than **to go to college.**
10. College, however, provides not only an education but also **preparation for a career.**

Part Six. Editing Sentences for Punctuation and Mechanics

Diagnostic Test, p. 389
The correct answer to each item is followed by a number in parentheses. This number indicates the chapter you should review if you answered the item incorrectly.

A.

1. Bring the following items to the meeting**:** a notebook, a calendar, and a list of ideas for how to improve the student senate. (35)
2. One of the **first-time** members of the committee recently made the suggestion that we design a student senate Web site. (35)
3. One of President **Wegner's** goals for the campus is to have a stronger student government. (32)
4. Perhaps Lena Mejía**,** our writing lab director**,** can recommend a good designer. (31)
5. The student senate helps to coordinate activities during the year**;** it also advises the administration on school policy. (33)
6. Our group can be an important link among students**,** faculty**,** and administrators. (31)
7. We try especially hard to meet commuter **students'** needs. (32)
8. Though being a student senator takes time**,** it offers a valuable opportunity for building leadership skills. (31)
9. Please come to next **week's** meeting. (32)

B.

10. "Why are we studying these things in writing class**?**" Jess asked.

"Learning to be a better reader will improve your writing**,**" Professor Creager replied.

"But," Jess continued, "what does reading have to do with writing**?**"

"For starters," Professor Creager explained, "if you become a better reader of other people's writing, it's likely that you will be a better reader of your own writing. Being a better reader of your own writing means you will more easily spot problem areas and make revisions."

Jess thought about this idea and then added, "Yeah, then I could put myself in my reader's shoes." (34)

C.

11. Canal Street, French Quarter, New Orleans (36)
12. Rev. Banserick, Our Lady of Mercy Church (36)
13. Music Appreciation, Dixieland, Preservation Hall (36) **14.** Detroit, Michigan (36) **15.** New Orleans (36) **16.** Bourbon Street (36) **17.** Budweisers (36) **18.** Pete Fountain, Johnny Adams (36)

Chapter 31, Commas

Practice 31-A, p. 394

1. One of the most important battles ever fought occurred on the beaches of **Normandy, France.**
2. Referred to as **D-Day, this** battle began the Allied invasion to free Europe from Hitler's Nazis.
3. Dwight D. **Eisenhower, who** later became president of the United **States, was** the Supreme Commander of the Allied troops.
4. Occurring on **June 6, 1944, the** D-Day invasion led to many deaths on the beaches.
5. Thousands of Allied soldiers **died, but** the area was finally won.
6. Once the Allies were securely in **France, they** could move on to Paris and ultimately to Berlin.
7. Steven Spielberg's Oscar-winning movie *Saving Private **Ryan,*** **which** begins with the Normandy **invasion, takes** a harsh look at war.
8. The movie features Tom **Hanks, Matt Damon, and** Ted Danson.
9. The first **half-hour, which** presents some of the most realistic battle scenes ever **filmed, shows** the attack on the Normandy beaches.
10. The movie portrays the **heroism, the struggles, and** the senselessness of war.

Practice 31-B, p. 395

1. The career counselor asked the **class, "How** many of you know what career field you want to enter?"
2. "I would like to be a computer **programmer," replied Joshua, "because** they make a lot of money."

3. "You will have to take math and **science," the** counselor explained.
4. "That's **okay," Joshua replied, "since** I like those subjects."
5. "I just wanted to make sure that you understand the requirements of a job you're interested **in," the** counselor said.
6. Li Xian then **asked, "What** kinds of courses do I need in order to become a nurse?"
7. "You will also need to take lots of science **courses," the** counselor answered.
8. "If I'm not so great at **science," Jerome asked, "what** are my options?"
9. The counselor **replied, "That** depends on your talents and your interests."
10. "You might want to read *What Color Is Your **Parachute?***, **by** Richard Nelson **Bolles, in** order to explore your interests and to find a suitable career **path," she** advised.

Chapter 32, Apostrophes

Practice 32-A, p. 399

1. Many students suffer from a learning disability called dyslexia, and they **can't** distinguish among certain letters or make meaning from words.
2. **They'll** often switch certain letters, like **t's** and **r's.**
3. Dyslexic students might not be able to read a **teacher's** instructions on the board because such students **can't** form images from words.
4. One of dyslexic **students'** major problems is that they read very slowly.
5. **They're** often so used to the problem that they don't realize they have it.
6. **Dyslexia's** other name is Development Reading Disorder, or DRD.
7. One of **DRD's** side effects is that mathematics is often difficult.
8. Students **aren't** able to translate the symbols into thought.
9. A **student's** self-esteem suffers when he or she suffers from DRD.
10. Although learning disorders tend to run in families, early intervention can help **students'** achievement.

Practice 32-B, p. 400

1. Outside Millville, Pennsylvania, Camp **Horizon's** campers arrive ready for a week full of fun.
2. These campers suffer from skin **diseases** like psoriasis and alopecia.
3. Begun in 1995 by Dr. Howard Pride, Camp Horizon gives kids with special **problems** a camp experience.
4. Here these kids do **crafts,** enjoy water activities, and meet new friends.
5. Amy Paller, M.D., who works and teaches at Northwestern **University's** Children's Memorial Hospital in Chicago, says that these kids need to be around other kids who have skin problems.
6. Kids get daily skin treatment at Camp **Horizon's** Med Shed.
7. Campers who admit that they have few friends at home meet **others** who need companionship.
8. Two other diseases common among these **campers** are ichthyosis and ectodermal dysplasia.
9. **It's** hard to imagine having scales or not being able to sweat; these children, however, are used to **people's** stares and comments.
10. Camp Horizon gives them a week to enjoy the **outdoors** and the understanding friendship of other children.

Chapter 33, Semicolons

Practice 33-A, p. 403

1. Howard Gardner's theory of multiple intelligences explains why some people are better than others at learning in certain **ways; moreover, everyone** is successful in a different area.
2. Gardner has described eight types of **intelligence; however, some** people may be good in several areas.
3. Two of the types are *musical* and ***visual*; these** are not normally thought of as intelligences but as talents.
4. Gardner makes a distinction between a talent and an **intelligence; he** claims that an intelligence is natural, not learned.
5. Two other intelligences are *interpersonal* and ***intrapersonal*; these** abilities involve dealing with others and understanding one's self.
6. Another type of intelligence involves physical **activity; however, this** does not necessarily mean athletic ability.
7. *Verbal* and *mathematical* are two easily accepted types of **intelligence; people** who do well on standardized tests like the SAT probably have one of these abilities.

8. The *naturalist* intelligence explains why some people have "green **thumbs"; meanwhile, others** cannot grow plants no matter how hard they try.
9. Understanding that people possess different intelligences is **important; school** and work situations should be changed to suit these differences.
10. We all need to understand ourselves **better; therefore, we** should try to determine our own intelligences or strengths.

Practice 33-B, p. 404

1. Destin, **Florida; South** Padre Island, **Texas; and** Ocean City, Maryland, are all cities with popular tourist beaches.
2. Cities that draw tourists for other attractions are San Antonio, **Texas; Anaheim, California; and** Washington, D.C.
3. Orlando, Florida, is home to Disney World, maybe the world's most popular theme **park; Universal** Studios, a busy theme park devoted to **movies; and** Epcot Center, a combination entertainment and learning park.
4. Many cities, such as Chicago, **Illinois; Atlanta, Georgia; and** San Diego, California, draw large numbers of travelers for conferences.
5. The Art Institute of Chicago, one of the world's most famous **museums; the** United Center, the arena that is home to the **Bulls; and** the Magnificent Mile, a famous shopping area, are three reasons Chicago is a popular place to visit.
6. Three of the largest cities in the United States are New York, New **York; Los** Angeles, **California; and** Houston, Texas.
7. Coastal Maine, famous for **lobster; New** Orleans, Louisiana, location of the French **Quarter; and** Memphis, Tennessee, Elvis Presley's famous birthplace, attract their share of tourists each year.
8. Texas Stadium, home of the Dallas **Cowboys; Fenway** Park, Boston's famous ball **field; and** Three Rivers Stadium, located in the heart of Pittsburgh, bring visitors to their cities regularly.
9. Even smaller towns, such as Sedona, **Arizona; Martha's** Vineyard, **Massachusetts; and** Petoskey, Michigan, enjoy a lively tourist trade.
10. Gettysburg, **Pennsylvania; Tombstone, Arizona; and** Charlottesville, Virginia, draw visitors every year because of their historical significance.

Chapter 34, Quotation Marks and Italics

Practice 34-A, p. 408

1. The professor **asked, "Who** has begun the research project on ***The Great Gatsby*?"**
2. **"You** might begin with the journals ***American Literature*** and ***Studies in the Novel***, found in our **library," she** advised.
3. **"A** good source for the history of the **period," she explained, "would** be the ***New Yorker*** magazine, which began the same year that the novel was **published."**
4. **"What** about looking in the ***Encyclopedia Britannica*?" Ciro** asked.
5. **"You** should not use general encyclopedias for academic research **papers," she explained, "except** for very general **information."**
6. The professor told the students about some other sources they could use for research on the novel and on F. Scott Fitzgerald's short **story "Babylon Revisited."**
7. Kevin said that he had found an informative article **called "Platonism in *The Great Gatsby*" in** the journal ***Midwest Quarterly.***
8. **"Can** we compare ***The Great Gatsby*** to ***Adventures of Huckleberry Finn*?" asked** Keisha.
9. **"You** may do **that," answered** the **professor, "if** you have developed a solid **thesis."**
10. **"Be** sure to document all of your information, using the ***MLA Handbook for Writers of Research Papers*," she** added.

Practice 34-B, p. 409

1. ***Prevention*** magazine **claims, "Sleep** isn't the only way to feel more **rested."**
2. Dr. Kristine Clark **says, "People** should eat their heaviest meal at breakfast for more energy during the **day."**
3. She **says, "Digesting** food late at night takes energy, which should be used for sleeping **well."**
4. The magazine **article "Get More Energy" states, "Iron** is an important element for creating **energy."**
5. In his book ***The Promise of Sleep,*** Dr. William C. Dement **claims, "A** sleep diary is a good way to calculate how much sleep a person really **needs."**
6. Dr. James Maas **says, "People** should add fifteen minutes to their sleep time until they feel totally rested the next **day."**

7. His book ***Power Sleep*** **claims, "Almost** everyone should add at least one more hour to their current sleep time to feel their **best."**
8. **"Drinking** lots of water can also boost **energy," claims** Dr. Clark.
9. Dr. Diane Wetzig **says, "Learning** to deal with daily stresses better can boost our energy **levels."**
10. In the book ***Strength Training*** by Dr. Wayne Westcott, the author **claims, "Physical** exercise stimulates the release of hormones that affect your brain and make you feel more **energized."**

Chapter 35, Other Punctuation

Practice 35-A, p. 414

1. Several college courses are considered difficult by most **students: physics**, calculus, and statistics.
2. Correct
3. Taking language courses challenges many students for one basic **reason: their** listening skills need improvement.
4. Writing gives students difficulty in several **areas: sentence** structure, poor mechanics, and shallow topics.
5. Correct
6. Many majors can require five years to **complete: education**, business, or science.
7. Some students take courses for one **reason: to** get a good job.
8. Correct
9. A college education, however, should mean more than job **training: it** should prepare students for life.
10. Correct

Practice 35-B, p. 414

1. Are kids today**—especially kids of baby-boomer parents**—spoiled by having too many possessions?
2. Do today's children expect to have the best of everything **(and this includes toys, clothes, computers, and cars)** even when their parents cannot afford it?
3. Many blame television for giving kids the **I-want-it-all** attitude.
4. Writer Martha Fay **(her article "Sedated by Stuff" appeared in the magazine *Civilization* in 1999)** says that kids learn early that stuff equals acceptance.
5. Fay claims that it's easier for parents to say yes than to say **no: they** really do not want to disappoint their children.
6. She says that in her case**—and in the case of many others certainly**—"going overboard" has to do with trying to make up for not spending enough time with her kids.
7. Fay claims that our culture has no **agreed-upon** value except money.
8. Psychiatrist Annie Boland says that we are a consumer **society: buying** things is one of our highest priorities.
9. The parents of these baby-boomer parents grew up in the Great Depression **(the time in American history when we were the poorest as a nation).**
10. Many think the current consumerism and spoiling of our children is a natural progression from **hard-fought** battles against poverty.

Chapter 36, Capitalization and Abbreviation

Practice 36-A, p. 421

1. Though many people are aware of the **Holocaust,** few are aware that nearly 1.5 million **Armenians** were slaughtered by the **Turks** in the early part of the twentieth century.
2. Important people, such as **Rev. Martin Luther King Jr., Mahatma Gandhi,** and **Nelson Mandela,** changed the course of history.
3. **World War I** and **World War II,** the **Boer War,** and the **Vietnam War** were all important conflicts that changed world maps.
4. In fact, many new countries were born in the last century: **Zimbabwe,** the **People's Republic of China,** and the **Czech Republic.**
5. Important companies like **Ford Motor Company, Microsoft,** and **Sega** made millions as they changed transportation, technology, and entertainment.
6. Symbols of twentieth-century progress include the **Empire State Building,** the channel tunnel that links **England** and **France,** and the ***Apollo*** moon landings.
7. The **Warsaw Treaty,** the **Suez Canal,** and **China's** cultural revolution all made an impact on the century.
8. Disasters, like the sinking of the ***Titanic,*** the burning of the ***Hindenburg,*** and the **Oklahoma**

City bombing will be well remembered into the twenty-first century.

9. Sports figures like **Jim Thorpe, Nadia Comaneci,** and **Michael Jordan** helped to make the century memorable.
10. The **Wright** brothers' flight at **Kitty Hawk,** the Soviet Union's ***Sputnik,*** and ***Soyuz's*** orbiting of the earth all marked tremendous advancements for flight in the twentieth century.

Practice 36-B, p. 421

1. Gregg Jonas, **Jr.,** spoke at our student-organized conference this past weekend on current issues.
2. He said that the **NAACP** continues to gain strength as a voice for equality and fairness.
3. Another speaker was Dolores Lopez of the **FBI,** formerly of the **IRS.**
4. Her topic was white collar crime in the age of **PCs** and **fax** machines.
5. A man from the audience, Jesse Okampa, **C.P.A.,** agreed with Agent Lopez.
6. The **a.m.** sessions were held in the university auditorium.
7. For the sessions after lunch we met in the distance learning classroom and watched a **VCR** tape of a presentation.
8. **Sgt.** Sherry Bates of the **U.S.** Army addressed us about world matters.
9. She explained that the **E.U.** must work at better cooperation among member states, especially between the **U.K.** and France.
10. As an expert on the former **U.S.S.R.,** she helped us to understand those countries' current economic challenges.

Part Seven. Editing Sentences for Word Use

Diagnostic Test, p. 425

The correct answer to each item is followed by a number in parentheses. This number indicates the chapter you should review if you answered the item incorrectly.

A.

1. one in a million (37) **2.** from the depths of despair; old man (37) **3.** bury the hatchet; to the bitter end (37) **4.** In this day and age; through thick and thin (37) **5.** To make a long story short; bummed (37) **6.** breathe a sigh of relief; what's up (37)

B. Answers may vary.

7. about; on (37) **8.** Because (37) **9.** in; about (37) **10.** for; to retrain (37)

C. Suggested revisions

11. Jane, my roommate, is majoring in criminal justice. (or *My roommate Jane is majoring in criminal justice.*) (38)
12. She wants to work as a prison official after she graduates from college organizing daily activities for the inmates. (38)
13. Her father was a police officer, commended on several occasions for meritorious behavior. (38)
14. She is a very determined person who knows that she can make a difference in the world. (or *A very determined person, she knows that she can make a difference in the world.*) (38)

D.

15. deceive (39) **16.** relies (39) **17.** submitting (39) **18.** lovable (39) **19.** Correct **20.** irresistible (39) **21.** embarrassed (39) **22.** Correct

E.

23. all ready (40) **24.** advice (40) **25.** fewer (40) **26.** than (40) **27.** whose (40)

F.

28. congressman (41) **29.** male nurse (41) **30.** man-made (41)

Chapter 37, Word Choice

Practice 37-A, p. 430, suggested revisions

1. Here at the turn of the century, swing dancing has become **many people's favorite form of dancing.**
2. A club in Manhattan, for example, offers nearly forty different classes on this **popular** trend—dances from the 1930s and the 1940s.
3. A 1998 commercial for khaki pants is partially credited with swing's resurgence, making many people **eager** to learn the "new" dance form.
4. Certain movies and **new rock bands influenced by the old swing bands,** like the Brian Setzer Orchestra, have also introduced people to this **dance phenomenon.**
5. Although some people think swing dancing is **easy to do,** instructors explain that even though **the aerial moves attract people's attention,** learning the **basic steps must come first.**
6. **Because of the popularity of swing dancing,** dance instructors in larger cities like New York and Boston **have lots of business** helping **new dancers** learn **steps** like the East Coast Swing.

7. Another, more challenging, dance is the Lindy Hop, a **lively** dance first practiced by Harlem African Americans.
8. Famous swing artists of the 1930s, such as Jimmie Lunceford, Chick Webb, and Benny Goodman, made audiences want to **get up and dance to the music.**
9. Interestingly, at that point **"experts"** warned against this **popular** new dancing because of its "dangerously hypnotic influence."
10. Modern **swing dancers** are drawn to the same **contagious** rhythms and **honest** fun that this **active** dancing provides.

Practice 37-B, p. 431, suggested revisions

1. **Today** people of just about every nationality live in the United States.
2. From this country's founding throughout its history, immigrants have come here **to** make a new life.
3. **Possibly** your family originated from Asia, Europe, South America, or **Africa.**
4. Unless you are **Native American,** your **ancestors were from another country.**
5. **As a result of widespread immigration,** a large **number** of different ethnicities make up this **country.**
6. Immigrants **tend** to join together in cities **for** jobs and **community.**
7. **Because** many new residents of the United States have difficulty speaking English, good jobs are often unavailable, and they find themselves in **poverty.**
8. Often **immigrants** find themselves doing jobs that others do not want, **such as hard labor and unattractive service occupations.**
9. Other challenges and frustrations, such as finding **acceptance,** also plague new immigrants.
10. Recent immigrants often face intolerance from more established populations because of race or **fear of change.**

Chapter 38, Sentence Variety

Practice 38-A, p. 435, suggested revisions

1. Leslie Lambert, who wrote an article for the *Ladies' Home Journal* in February 1999, asks the question, "Should you spy on your teen?"
2. The article, which is written from a parent's point of view, looks at both sides of the question.
3. Lambert begins the article by admitting that she had read part of her daughter's diary, which had been left open on her daughter's desk.
4. Lambert, who read only a little of the diary, began to feel ashamed for not respecting her daughter's privacy.
5. The article makes the point that today's teens, who grow up faster in many ways than teens of earlier generations, are exposed to a great deal of sex, drugs, drinking, and smoking.
6. David Elkind, Ph.D., author of a book about teenagers in crisis, claims that parents may have to protect their teens.
7. He says that teens, who do not have an absolute right to privacy, have to demonstrate responsibility.
8. Carol Friedland, Ph.D., who believes in the need for more communication, says that teenagers normally need time to themselves in a private space.
9. The article provides many examples of caring parents who have spied on their teens to find drugs, have confronted the problem, and have helped the teens straighten out their lives.
10. Roger McIntire, Ph.D., author of a book called *Teenagers and Parents: Ten Steps for a Better Relationship,* warns that parents should not make a habit of spying on their teens or they risk ruining the relationship they have with them.

Practice 38-B, p. 436, suggested revisions

1. Gaining fame as a baseball player for the New York Yankees, Joe DiMaggio was an American hero.
2. Appearing at a time when Americans needed role models, DiMaggio was the All-American sports hero who played all aspects of the game well.
3. Preferring secrecy and privacy, Joe DiMaggio was a loner who hated crowds.
4. Marrying Marilyn Monroe in 1954, he thrust himself into the media limelight.
5. Divorced the same year they married, they remained close friends until her death in 1962.
6. Simon and Garfunkel, asking, "Where have you gone, Joe DiMaggio?" immortalized him in the song "Mrs. Robinson" in 1969.
7. Singing "Our nation turns its lonely eyes to you," they turned a man into a myth.
8. Voted the "Greatest Living Player" in 1969, "DiMaggio set the standard for the game when

the game was the standard for the nation," one writer has claimed.

9. In the 1970s and 1980s he appeared on TV commercials, selling Mr. Coffee coffeemakers.
10. Leaving behind a legend that will not soon be forgotten, DiMaggio died in February 1999 of lung cancer.

Chapter 39, Spelling

Practice 39-A, p. 442

1. incredible **2.** licensed **3.** discipline **4.** temperatures **5.** privilege **6.** disastrous **7.** inevitably **8.** develops **9.** determined **10.** aggressive

Practice 39-B, p. 443

1. receive, truly **2.** having, abilities **3.** readiness, motivation **4.** useful, seize **5.** survival, emotional **6.** formatted, analyzing **7.** logical, defining **8.** processes, taking **9.** perceive, immediately **10.** isolation, permitting

Chapter 40, Commonly Confused Words

Practice 40-A, p. 448

1. who's, correct **2.** accept, there **3.** advice **4.** affect **5.** it's, their **6.** assures, their, correct, through **7.** correct, correct, all ready **8.** further, correct **9.** correct, its **10.** correct, then, its

Practice 40-B, p. 449

1. **Except** for the **principal,** the only men usually seen in an elementary school are the custodial staff.
2. Today, however, men like Gerald Snyder in Palmyra, Pennsylvania are **affecting** students in classrooms as **their** teachers.
3. Men are making more of a difference in many female-dominated fields **than** they have in the **past,** just as women are moving into traditionally male occupations.
4. Ten years ago **there** were **fewer** men in jobs like teaching and nursing.
5. Mr. Snyder, however, was **advised** to follow his **conscience** and do what he would enjoy.
6. Tom Peifer, **whose** previous experiences include college football, now **ensures** the care of patients in intensive care as a nurse.
7. Mr. Peifer coaches high school baseball, and he knows that he **loses** respect from some of his players because of **their** stereotypes about male nurses.
8. Jamie Reisinger, who works for the YWCA counseling women about date rape, receives **compliments** from women who realize that he brings a **new** perspective to the job.
9. **Whether** or not a man goes into a "man's" field, he needs **to** determine what will fit his abilities and goals.
10. **Where** a person works should be based on more than society and **its** prejudices.

Chapter 41, Sexist Language

Practice 41-A, p. 453, suggested revisions

1. **People have** always seemed to love power and money.
2. When **congressional delegates lobby** to become part of an important committee, **they are** trying to position **themselves** into **more powerful roles.**
3. The **business executive** who "networks" at a convention is trying to make contacts **for career advancement.**
4. Wars have been fought over small pieces of land when **leaders try to expand their domains.**
5. A doctor may schedule additional **patient tests** in order to get a larger insurance payment.
6. A professional athlete will sometimes hold out of participation in **the sport** in order to negotiate a little more cash in **the contract.**
7. A lawyer often **bills clients** for more hours than **the case actually cost.**
8. Even a minister may preach especially fervently to get **the congregation** to put more money into the collection plate.
9. Not everyone, however, **lives life** for more power and money.
10. **People** may spend **their** time doing good for others while also making **their own lives** better.

Practice 41-B, p. 454, suggested revisions

1. As John boarded the plane for Washington, D.C., he asked the **flight attendant** for a magazine.
2. He wanted to read up on the Kosovo crisis so he would have good questions to ask his **legislator.**

3. As he sat next to a **business traveler,** he noticed that the man was reading the *New York Times.*
4. A front-page headline referred to the **number of troops** being sent to the Serbian province and the number of bombs falling daily.
5. John began a conversation and found out that his plane companion was an **insurance salesperson.**
6. "I was a **letter carrier** before going into sales," the man explained.
7. John said, "I want to be a news **anchor.**"
8. "In fact, I'm traveling to Washington to meet with a **professor** and a member of the legislature about the Kosovo war," John continued.
9. The man said, enthusiastically, "My daughter **waits tables** in a café next to the Capitol, and she knows many lawmakers."
10. He continued, "Let me introduce you to her after I call a **friend in business** to give us a ride to Capitol Hill."

Part Eight. Editing Sentences for ESL Challenges

Diagnostic Test, p. 459

The correct answer to each item is followed by a number in parentheses. This number indicates the chapter you should review if you answered the item incorrectly.

A.

1. We sought **information** about the new development. (42)
2. We should buy **fruit** for the salad. (42)
3. I would like **rice** as a side dish. (42)
4. Her **impatience** made her a tough supervisor. (42)

B.

5. The (42) **6.** a (42) **7.** the (42) **8.** an (42) **9.** a (42)

C.

10. I don't expect **to see** him again. (43)
11. He refused **to wait** for her another minute. (43)
12. My dad dislikes **buying** used cars. (43)
13. Marie enjoys **playing** tennis every afternoon. (43)
14. Sonja **wants** to change her major. (43)

D.

15. at, for (44) **16.** of, in (44) **17.** with, during (44) **18.** Around, from (44)

E.

19. behind (44) **20.** beside (44) **21.** on (44) **22.** until (44)

Chapter 42, Nouns and Articles

Practice 42-A, p. 464

1. count, noncount, count **2.** count, noncount, count, count **3.** count, count, count **4.** noncount, count **5.** count, noncount **6.** count, count **7.** count, count **8.** noncount, count **9.** count, count **10.** count, count, count

Practice 42-B, p. 464, suggested answers

1. Last weekend, I attended the strangest wedding ceremony—completely by accident!
2. Both the bride and X groom were long-distance runners, so they planned to marry at the end of the Boston Marathon.
3. The groom wore a pair of X black running shorts and a T-shirt that looked like a tuxedo.
4. With her white running outfit, the bride wore an antique bridal veil.
5. The couple had to get X special permission from the city to have their videographer ride in front of them in a golf cart.
6. All along the race route, crowds cheered the couple as they ran hand-in-hand.
7. They finished the race in three hours and X fifty-two minutes.
8. As they crossed the finish line, they were joined by a minister and their friends and family—all of whom were dressed in X athletic clothing.
9. After the couple said their vows and exchanged a kiss, they were interviewed by a local news station.
10. I saw the bizarre wedding a second time when I turned on my television later in the evening.

Chapter 43, Special Problems with Verbs

Practice 43-A, p. 470, suggested answers

1. Many students expect **to make** good grades without understanding what academic success involves.
2. They often resist **spending** enough hours on homework.
3. Many also do not consider **typing** notes or redoing sloppy assignments.

4. To achieve success, students should attempt **to complete** every assignment well in advance.
5. Unsuccessful students generally postpone **beginning** projects until the last minute.
6. They often fail **to allow** enough time to do quality work.
7. Students also should not wait **to study** for tests until the night before.
8. Successful students often begin **preparing** for a test days in advance.
9. This allows them to learn **to master** certain skills rather than to cram information into their heads.
10. Being a successful student means that one must avoid **wasting** time but must instead use time to his or her advantage.

Practice 43-B, p. 470

1. New archaeological discoveries **are changing** the way anthropologists understand the history of Americans.
2. Correct
3. Anthropologists **are discovering** artifacts in places from Peru to South Carolina that contradict this theory, however.
4. Evidently, people **were living** on the American continent over fifteen thousand years ago. **(Also correct as is)**
5. These people **were using** stone tools like those previously found in Spain and France. **(Also correct as is)**
6. We know now that people **were painting** cave paintings in Brazil long before the Asian ancestors arrived. **(Also correct as is)**
7. Scientists **are identifying** many skeletons whose origins contradict the Asian land-bridge theory.
8. Correct
9. The new theory supposes that people **were traveling** by boat from Europe along a frozen shoreline fifteen to twenty thousand years ago. **(Also correct as is)**
10. Correct

Chapter 44, Prepositions

Practice 44-A, p. 474

1. at (place), after (time) **2.** of (relationship) **3.** at (time) **4.** on (place), of (place) **5.** to (place), from (place), to (place) **6.** at (place), over (place), down (place), to (place) **7.** before (place) **8.** on (place) **9.** by (place), on (place), beyond (place) **10.** at (time), by (time)

Practice 44-B, p. 474

1. **At** 10:56 P.M. **on** July 20, 1969, astronaut Neil Armstrong made history.
2. It was then that he stepped **from** the *Apollo 11* spacecraft to become the first person to walk **on** the moon.
3. Armstrong spoke the now-famous words: "That's one small step **for** man, one giant leap **for** mankind."
4. He was followed immediately **by** Buzz Aldrin, his crewmate.
5. Through the miracle **of** technology, millions of people watched the landing **on** television **in** their own homes.
6. Later that summer, the Woodstock Music and Arts Fair took place **in** Bethel, New York.
7. Though only 186,000 tickets to the outdoor concert were sold, over 500,000 people traveled to Bethel **for** peace, love, and music.
8. The music **of** artists such as the Grateful Dead, Jimi Hendrix, Janis Joplin, and Joan Baez reflected the political and social themes important to millions **of** people.
9. **By** the time the three-day outdoor concert ended, a generation of Americans was defined.
10. Today's music continues to be influenced **by** the music of the Woodstock artists.

(Continued from page iv)

Clark, Kristine. "Get Energy." *Prevention.* September, 1999: 110–119.

Cose, Ellis. "The Good News about Black America." *Newsweek.* June 7, 1999: 28–40.

Cramer, Richard Ben. "The DiMaggio Nobody Knew." *Newsweek.* March 22, 1999: 52–60.

Fay, Martha. "Sedated by Stuff." *Civilization.* August/September 1999: 38–39.

Groopman, Jerome. "Contagion." *The New Yorker.* September 13, 1999: 34–49.

Ingram, Jay. "Welcome to the Tongue-Show" from *The Science of Everyday Life* by Jay Ingram. Copyright © 1989 by Jay Ingram. Reprinted by permission of Penguin Books Canada Limited.

Kaplan, David A., and Corie Brown. "$3 Billion Screams." *Newsweek.* March 15, 1999: 60–62.

Kriegel, Leonard. "A Loaded Question: What Is It about Americans and Guns?" *Harper's.* May 1992: 45–51.

McKowen, Clark. *Get Your* A *Out of College: Mastering the Hidden Rules of the Game.* Menlo Park, CA: Crisp Publications, 1996.

McWhirter, Nickie. "What You Do Is What You Are," February 26, 1982. Reprinted by permission of the Detroit Free Press.

Milspaw, Yvonne, and Mario Cattabiani. "Memories of TMI." *Central PA.* March, 1999: 34–43.

Nash, J. Madeleine. "The Case for Cloning," *Time.* February 9, 1998. © 1998 Time Inc. Reprinted by permission.

Preston, Lydia. "Camp Happiness." *Ladies' Home Journal.* August, 1999: 78.

Rowan, Roy. "Homeless Bound," *People Weekly.* March 5, 1990. Roy Rowan/People Weekly © 1990 Time Inc.

Stewart, Doug. "This Joint is Jumping." *Smithsonian.* March 1999: 60–74.

Tannen, Deborah. "'You Be the Monster and Chase Me': Children At Play." From *The Argument Culture* by Deborah Tannen. Copyright © 1998 by Deborah Tannen. Reprinted by permission of Random House, Inc.

University System of Georgia Distance Education Listings screen shot. Reprinted by permission of the University System of Georgia.

Index

Use the Writer's Checklists on these pages to help you revise your paragraphs and essays. The page numbers listed after each checkpoint refer to places in the text where you can find more help.

☑ Writer's Checklist: Revising a Paragraph

_____ Before revising, did you take a break from your draft or ask for feedback from viewers? (See page 49.)

Focus

_____ Does your paragraph have a clearly stated topic sentence that includes your narrowed topic plus a controlling idea? (See page 44.)

_____ Does your topic sentence state something that you can show, explain, or prove in a paragraph? (See page 44.)

Unity

_____ Did you read your draft carefully, noting places where you detour from your main point? (See page 76.)

_____ Have you revised so that every sentence in your paragraph supports your controlling idea? (See page 76.)

Support

_____ Have you included enough support (details, facts, and evidence) to convince your audience of your main point? (See page 79.)

_____ Is your support organized in the most logical manner for your purpose and audience? (See page 65.)

Coherence

_____ Are ideas linked smoothly and clearly by transitional words and phrases and by key words and phrases? (See page 82.)

_____ Have you combined any short, single-idea sentences into longer sentences that express related ideas clearly and more effectively? (See page 86.)

_____ Did you choose a point of view and primary verb tense and stick with them? (See page 87.)